2014 Annual Competitiveness Ranking and Simulation Study for ASEAN-10 and Development Strategies to Enhance Asia Economic Connectivity

NUS National University of Singapore

Lee Kuan Yew School of Public Policy
ASIA COMPETITIVENESS INSTITUTE

In 2016 ACI was ranked 13th globally, 2nd in Asia and 1st in Singapore amongst 90 think-tanks world-wide under the "Best University Affiliated Think-Tank" category by Think-Tanks & Civil Societies Program at The University of Pennsylvania, USA

About ACI

The Asia Competitiveness Institute (ACI) was established in August 2006 as a research centre at the Lee Kuan Yew School of Public Policy (LKYSPP), National University of Singapore (NUS). It aims to build the intellectual leadership and network for understanding and developing competitiveness in the Asia region. ACI seeks to contribute to the enhancement of inclusive growth, living standards and institutional governance through competitiveness research on sub-national economies in Asia. It identifies mitigating issues and challenges for potential public policy interventions through close collaboration with regional governments, business corporations, policy think-tanks and academics. ACI's three key research pillars include (i) sub-national economies level competitiveness analysis and city-level liveability analysis, (ii) firm-level competitiveness analysis in 16 Asia economies, and (iii) Singapore's long-term growth strategies and public policy analysis.

ACI's value propositions may be encapsulated in its acronym:

Analytical inputs to initiate policies for policy-makers and business leaders in Asia

Capacity building to enable others through improvement in productivity and efficiency

Intellectual leadership to create pragmatic models of competitiveness and inclusive growth

The institute's core research competencies can also be encapsulated in this acronym describing our evidence-based assessments conducted on public policies for **A**SEAN in the context of the rise of **C**hina and **I**ndia.

Vision and Mission

- ACI's over-arching vision is to build up its research credibility with policy impact, contributing as a professional, world-class think-tank.
- ACI's mission is to establish our niche as a leading policy think-tank by identifying competitiveness trends, opportunities and challenges, as well as promoting competition and synergising complementarities amongst Asian economies and business corporations.
- ACI endeavours to articulate sound recommendations, entice discourse, and shape agenda in the arena of public policy amongst Asian governments.
- ACI undertakes evidence-based analysis of public policy issues and decisions, in order to provide assessment of their effectiveness as well as economic and societal impact.
- Our eight key research focuses are
  - I. Identify trends of competitiveness and policy analysis on trade and investment of ASEAN, within the regional context of competition and complementarities with China and India.
  - II. Identify competitive strengths and conduct policy analysis on Singapore within the context of regional economies with international benchmarking.
  - III. We have signed Memoranda of Understanding with The World Bank (2015 and 2016) and European Central Bank (2015).
  - IV. We have signed Memoranda of Understanding with Shanghai Academy of Social Sciences (2016), Shandong Academy of Social Sciences (2015), Chongqing Municipal People's Government (2015), China Institute for Reform and Development, Haikou (2015) and Counsellors' Office of the People's Government of Guangdong Province (2015).
  - V. We have signed Memoranda of Understanding with six Chief Ministers' Offices in Andhra Pradesh (2015), Bihar (2015), Chhattisgarh (2015), Madhya Pradesh (2015), Odisha (2015) and Punjab (2015).
  - VI. We have signed Memoranda of Understanding with Indonesia Investment Coordinating Board (2014), Indonesian Agency for Agricultural Research and Development at Ministry of Agriculture (2014), Indonesian President's Delivery Unit for Developing Monitoring and Oversight (2013) and Employer's Association of Indonesia (2013).
  - VII. We are regularly releasing three indices on liveability ranking including 64 Global Cities, 100 Greater China Cities and 17 Shandong Cities.
  - VIII. We have established an Ease of Doing Business Index on Attractiveness to Investors, Business Friendliness and Competitive Policies for 21 states and federal territories of India and 33 provinces of Indonesia.

Founding Patron and International Advisory Panel

Founding Patron: Mr George Yeo
Visiting Scholar, Lee Kuan Yew School of Public Policy, National University of Singapore
& Former Minister of Foreign Affairs, Singapore

International Advisory Panel

Co-Chairs:

Professor Michael Porter (2006-2010)
Bishop William Lawrence University Professor

Ms Marjorie Yang (2006-2012)
Chairman, Esquel Group

Members:

Professor Kishore Mahbubani
Dean, Lee Kuan Yew School of Public Policy, National University of Singapore

Dr Kuntoro Mangkusubroto
Head, President's Delivery Unit for Developing Monitoring and Oversight (UKP4), Indonesia

Mr Narayana Murthy
Chairman, Infosys Technologies Limited

Mr Philip Yeo
Chairman, SPRING Singapore

Mrs Ow Foong Pheng
Permanent Secretary, Ministry of Trade and Industry

Ms Yong Ying-I
Permanent Secretary, Public Service Division

Professor Chan Kam Leung Alan
Dean, College of Humanities, Arts and Social Sciences, Nanyang Technological University

Asia Competitiveness Institute

Co-Directors: Associate Professor Tan Khee Giap (2011 till now) Professor Tan Kong Yam (2011 till now)

2014 Annual Competitiveness Ranking and Simulation Study for ASEAN-10 and Development Strategies to Enhance Asia Economic Connectivity

Tan Khee Giap
Co-Director, Asia Competitiveness Institute
Lee Kuan Yew School of Public Policy, National University of Singapore

Sangiita Yoong Wei Cher
Research Assistant, Asia Competitiveness Institute
Lee Kuan Yew School of Public Policy, National University of Singapore

Sasidaran Gopalan
Research Fellow, Asia Competitiveness Institute
Lee Kuan Yew School of Public Policy, National University of Singapore

Nguyen Le Phuong Anh
Research Associate, Asia Competitiveness Institute
Lee Kuan Yew School of Public Policy, National University of Singapore

Reviewers

Bustanul Arifin
Professor, University of Lampung and
Board of Founder/Senior Economist, Institute for Development of Economics and Finance, Indonesia

Roehlano Briones
Senior Research Fellow, Philippine Institute for Development Studies, Philippines

Basant Kumar Kapur
Professor, Department of Economics, National University of Singapore, Singapore

Sothea Oum
Economist, Economic Research Institute for ASEAN and East Asia (ERIA)

Vo Tri Thanh
Vice President, Central Institute for Economic Management, Vietnam

Steven Wong
Deputy Chief Executive, Institute of Strategic and International Studies, Malaysia

NUS National University of Singapore

World Scientific

Published by

World Scientific Publishing Co. Pte. Ltd.
5 Toh Tuck Link, Singapore 596224
USA office: 27 Warren Street, Suite 401-402, Hackensack, NJ 07601
UK office: 57 Shelton Street, Covent Garden, London WC2H 9HE

British Library Cataloguing-in-Publication Data
A catalogue record for this book is available from the British Library.

2014 ANNUAL COMPETITIVENESS RANKING AND SIMULATION STUDY FOR ASEAN-10 AND DEVELOPMENT STRATEGIES TO ENHANCE ASIA ECONOMIC CONNECTIVITY

ISBN 978-981-3108-58-5
ISBN 978-981-3108-59-2 (pbk)

Typeset by Stallion Press
Email: enquiries@stallionpress.com

Printed in Singapore

CONTENTS

FOREWORD

Competitiveness is at the heart of every economic development strategy. The East Asian miracle and the more recent stellar rise of China are stories of countries building up and strengthening their competitive edge. As ASEAN and the East Asian nations are expected to sustain their strategic positions in the global value chains, its large, young and higher-income population will create the much needed domestic and intra-regional market in the continuously weak global demand environment. Nonetheless, maintaining national competitiveness is always a pertinent challenge.

In this context, the Asia Competitiveness Institute (ACI)'s competitiveness analysis for ASEAN-10 is extremely timely. What I find most impressive about this research is that it not only presents the ranking of countries but also pinpoints areas for improvement and provides concrete policy recommendations for each country. In this regard, the ACI's effort is among the most insightful today. Additionally, the Asia Economic Connectivity Vision 2030 proposed by the ACI provides a great starting point for reflections on the potential partnership between ASEAN and China, India as well as the rest of Asia. The ACI's study also shows how regional and multilateral agreements and institutions, which are often viewed as political instruments of major nations in their competition for influence, are actually needed for ASEAN to accelerate infrastructure projects and revitalise trade and investment. Tapping into the enormous potential of Asian intra-regional cooperation could prove to be an effective strategy for ASEAN not only to balance their dependence on the West but also to achieve economic sustainability. This is the vision for ASEAN that the ACI and I both share.

Given the heterogeneity in terms of economic development and competitiveness within ASEAN, each member country is facing its own distinct challenges. At the same time, this diversity offers unique opportunities for further regional integration. I believe the day is no longer far off when ASEAN becomes a prosperous, harmonious and collaborative community. I thus value this research as a useful roadmap for this pursuit. While this study is necessary for all policymakers in the region, it also provides valuable insights for captains of industries and business leaders to renew their views about the region and its future. It is critical that multinational corporations as well as local companies understand the factors behind the changes and transitions happening in many parts of the region so that they will be well-positioned in welcoming them.

I hope the ACI will continue its excellent work as well as look into exploring various themes. I extend wholehearted support for the ACI's research projects and look forward to collaborating with the ACI in the future.

Mr Mahendra Siregar
Vice Minister of Trade, Indonesia, 2009–2011
Vice Minister of Finance, Indonesia, 2011–2013
Chairman, Indonesia Investment Coordinating Board (BKPM), 2013–2014

PREFACE

The aftermath of the 2008–2009 Global Financial Crisis has seen ASEAN-10 not only rebounding strongly, but also rising consistently as one of the world's fastest-growing regions. The pertinent question now is how ASEAN can maintain this growth momentum and leverage on its increasing integration, with the launch of the ASEAN Economic Community in December 2015, to propel itself as a key node for global investment flows. The bloc's diversity in terms of development stages can prove to be a source of synergy that, if harnessed well, will strengthen its collective competitiveness. The region's proximity to large emerging economies, such as China and India, generates significant potential benefits, but only if the 10 ASEAN economies earnestly address their weaknesses while enhancing their strengths. This potential is the focus of this seminal research, now in its second edition, undertaken by the Asia Competitiveness Institute (ACI) at the Lee Kuan Yew School of Public Policy (LKYSPP), National University of Singapore (NUS).

This book presents the latest empirical findings on the relative competitiveness of the ASEAN-10 economies. The framework described in this book is one of a kind, going beyond ranking to incorporate a *what-if* policy simulation on how each economy can improve its competitiveness. A customised approach such as this, rather than a one-size-fits-all approach, is vital for a region as diverse as ASEAN. The competitiveness analysis is placed within the overarching strategic thrust of the ASEAN-centric Asia Economic Connectivity Vision 2030, which aims to facilitate wider physical and information connectivities across Asia. Finally, the Geweke causality analysis provides greater insights into the causal drivers of competitiveness and growth, with a focus on the region's top-performing economies (namely, Singapore and Malaysia) and the transitional economies of Cambodia, Laos and Vietnam. Extensive sets of data, compiled from reputable sources and on-the-ground surveys and supported by rigorous evidence-based quantitative methodologies, serve as the basis for this ambitious blueprint for ASEAN leaders, policymakers, managers, thinkers and others who are interested in the region.

With this publication on ASEAN, as well as similar companion volumes on Greater China, India and Indonesia, the ACI has taken the lead in understanding and developing competitiveness in Asia. We hope this study augments the ongoing policy discourse in ASEAN and helps the region to fulfil its potential and to transform the lives of its people.

Professor Kishore Mahbubani
Dean
Lee Kuan Yew School of Public Policy
National University of Singapore

ACKNOWLEDGEMENTS

We, from the Asia Competitiveness Institute (ACI) at Lee Kuan Yew School of Public Policy (LKYSPP), National University of Singapore (NUS), have combined leading-edge research methodologies with extensive data collection efforts to evaluate and track economic competitiveness since 2000 at both national and sub-national levels for over 100 Asian economies, including Greater China, India, Indonesia and ASEAN-10. Building upon our previous works, in 2014 we extended our study to include various published volumes on *2014 Annual Provincial and Regional Competitiveness Analysis for Greater China Economies: Development Strategies under the New Normal, 2014 Regional Competitiveness Analysis and a Master Plan on Regional Development Strategies for India, 2014 Provincial and Inaugural Regional Competitiveness Analysis: Safeguarding Indonesia's Growth Momentum, 2014 Annual Competitiveness Analysis and Development Strategies for Indonesian Provinces*, as well as for ASEAN-10 as in this volume.

In this book, the *2014 Annual Competitiveness Ranking and Simulation Study for ASEAN-10 and Development Strategies to Enhance Asia Economic Connectivity*, we lay out the concept and five broad proposals of the ASEAN-centric Asia Economic Connectivity Vision 2030 (AECV2030). The competitiveness analysis for ASEAN-10 economies is also improved and updated. Holistically, the ACI offers evidence-based assessment of economic, institutional and social indicators at the macro level, and sectoral indicators at the micro level for competitiveness evaluation. Furthermore, Geweke analysis was undertaken to offer a deeper understanding of the transitional economies, namely Cambodia, Laos and Vietnam, as well as top performers in the region, namely Singapore and Malaysia. Singapore's economic development since its independence is also reviewed in this volume as the country celebrates its golden jubilee year in 2015.

When ASEAN was established in 1967, the entity faced a monumental challenge of harmonising its diverse backgrounds, cultures and working systems to achieve greater regional integration. Almost 50 years later, having braved through various political and economic pressures such as the Asian Financial Crisis and the global financial tsunami, there is now an apparent resurgence of growth momentum within the bloc. Modern-day ASEAN, with the participation of 10 countries, is now more closely integrated in terms of trade and investment flows as well as capital and labour input, as seen in the many levels of economic partnerships involving multiple combinations of countries. As such, it is pivotal that friendly rivalry, as in marrying competition with cooperation, remains the cornerstone of the vision for a seamlessly connected and highly competitive ASEAN. In this spirit, the ACI seeks to contribute to, as well as to promote, rigorous and dynamic policy analysis and formulation in the region in years to come.

The publication of this book would not have been possible without the tremendous support from various country experts, from the public and private sector, who attended the ASEAN Review Seminar organised by the ACI at LKYSPP, NUS on 26th August 2014. We wish to record our heartfelt gratitude for the time and effort invested by the following reviewers who evaluated and gave their constructive comments on the respective chapters as incorporated in this book:

Dr Bustanul Arifin
Professor, University of Lampung and Board of Founder/Senior Economist, Institute for Development of Economics and Finance, Indonesia

Dr Roehlano Briones
Senior Research Fellow, Philippine Institute for Development Studies, Philippines

Dr Basant Kumar Kapur
Professor, Department of Economics, National University of Singapore, Singapore

Dr Sothea Oum
Economist, Economic Research Institute for ASEAN and East Asia (ERIA)

Dr Vo Tri Thanh
Vice President, Central Institute for Economic Management, Vietnam

Mr Steven Wong
Deputy Chief Executive, Institute of Strategic and International Studies, Malaysia

We would also like to place on record our appreciation for the support and encouragement from Dean Kishore Mahbubani; Associate Professor Eduardo Araral, Vice Dean (Research); Mr Donald Low, Associate Dean (Research and Executive Education); and other colleagues at LKYSPP. Finally, this book would not have been possible without the dedicated effort of all research and administrative staff at the ACI. Thus we note with tremendous appreciation the high team spirit of all ACI staff including Dr Linda Low, Evan Tan Beng Kai, Vincent Kwan Wen Seng, Yap Xin Yi, Tracy Cai Jiao and Nurliyana Binte Yusoff.

Tan Khee Giap
Sangiita Yoong Wei Cher
Sasidaran Gopalan
Nguyen Le Phuong Anh
Asia Competitiveness Institute
Lee Kuan Yew School of Public Policy
National University of Singapore

ABOUT THE AUTHORS

Tan Khee Giap is Co-Director of the Asia Competitiveness Institute (ACI) and Associate Professor at the Lee Kuan Yew School of Public Policy (LKYSPP), National University of Singapore (NUS). He is also the Chairman of the Singapore National Committee for Pacific Economic Cooperation. Upon graduating with a PhD from University of East Anglia, England, in 1987 under the Overseas Research Scheme awarded by the Committee of Vice-Chancellors and Principals of the Universities of the United Kingdom, he joined the banking sector as a treasury manager and served as secretary to the Assets and Liabilities Committee for three years. Thereafter, he taught at the Department of Economics and Statistics, National University of Singapore, 1990–1993. Dr Tan joined Nanyang Technological University in 1993 and was Associate Dean, Graduate Studies Office, 2007–2009. Dr Tan has consulted extensively with the various government ministries, statutory boards and government-linked companies of the Singapore government. He has also served as a consultant to international agencies such as the Asian Development Bank, Asian Development Bank Institute, United Nations Industrial Development Group, World Gold Council, ASEAN Secretariat, Central Policy Unit of Hong Kong, Kerzner International, Las Vegas Sands and Marina Bay Sands. Dr Tan is the lead author of eight books and has published widely in international refereed journals. His current research interests include econometric forecasting, Cost of Living Index, Global Liveable Cities Index and competitiveness analysis on 31 provinces in China, 35 states in India and ASEAN-10 economies. Dr Tan was Deputy President of the Singapore Economic Society, 2004. He served in the 2002 Economic

Review Committee (ERC), served as Chairman of the Task Force on Portable Medical Benefits (PMB), served as the Deputy Chairman of the IPS Forum for Economic Restructuring (IFER) in 2003 and served as a member of the Resource Panel of the Government Parliamentary Committee for Transport and Government Parliamentary Committee for Finance and Trade since 2007. Dr Tan has extensively advised and guided multinational corporations leading to public listings, especially those companies from Mainland China and Taiwan. He is also currently an Independent Director of the publicly listed Artivision, BreadTalk Group, Boustead Projects and TEE Land.

Sangiita Yoong Wei Cher is Research Assistant at the Asia Competitiveness Institute (ACI) at the Lee Kuan Yew School of Public Policy (LKYSPP), National University of Singapore (NUS). Sangiita graduated with a second upper joint honours bachelor's degree from NUS and Australian National University (ANU) in both economics and actuarial studies in 2012. Sangiita was an ASEAN scholar and was on the Dean's list during her studies. At ACI, her work focuses on data analysis and competitiveness studies of the Greater China economies. She is also the coordinator for the project on growth slowdown analysis by income thresholds. She has co-authored a review article on public policy in Singapore, a journal paper in the International Journal of Chinese Culture and Management, and two books on *Annual Analysis of Competitiveness, Simulation Studies and Development Perspective for 34 Greater China Economies* and *2014 Annual Provincial and Regional Competitiveness Analysis for Greater China Economies: Development Strategies under the New Normal*. Sangiita's research interests include competitiveness analysis of Greater China economies, quantitative data analysis and econometric modelling.

Sasidaran Gopalan is Research Fellow at the Asia Competitiveness Institute (ACI) at the Lee Kuan Yew School of Public Policy (LKYSPP),

National University of Singapore (NUS). Prior to joining the ACI, he was based in Hong Kong as a Post-Doctoral Fellow at the HKUST Institute for Emerging Market Studies and HKUST Jockey Club Institute for Advanced Study at the Hong Kong University of Science and Technology (HKUST). Dr Gopalan completed his PhD in Public Policy, specialising in International Finance and Policy at the School of Policy, Government and International Affairs (SPGIA), George Mason University, USA. He has published two co-authored books with leading publishing houses, several academic articles in refereed international journals, book chapters in edited volumes, a number of policy briefs as well as op-eds for leading global financial dailies. Dr Gopalan's research interests span the broad fields of financing for development and international macroeconomic and financial policies with respect to emerging and developing economies in Asia. At the ACI, he is the lead coordinator for research projects specific to India. He also supervises and contributes to the formulation as well as implementation of all the empirical research projects, targeted towards journal publications and broader policy outreach.

Nguyen Le Phuong Anh is Research Associate at the Asia Competitiveness Institute (ACI) at the Lee Kuan Yew School of Public Policy (LKYSPP), National University of Singapore (NUS). Phuong Anh received her Bachelor (Honours) degree in Economics from Nanyang Technological University (NTU), Singapore, and a Master of Science degree in Development Studies from London School of Economics and Political Science (LSE), United Kingdom. Prior to joining the ACI, she gained extensive experience working in the financial sector with OCBC, DBS and Bloomberg L.P. in Singapore, and additionally held a research internship position at the Mekong Institute in Khon Kaen, Thailand. At the ACI, she co-authored a book titled *2014 Annual Indices for Expatriates and Ordinary Residents on Cost of Living, Wages and Purchasing*

Power for World's Major Cities. She is currently coordinating the competitiveness ranking and simulation studies for the ASEAN-10 economies. Phuong Anh's research interests include economic development policy, international political economy, ASEAN economies and applied econometrics.

LIST OF ABBREVIATIONS

A*STAR	Agency for Science, Technology and Applied Research
ABMI	Asian Bond Market Initiative
ACCC	ASEAN Connectivity Coordinating Committee
ACI	Asia Competitiveness Institute
ADB	Asian Development Bank
ADBI	Asian Development Bank Institute
AEC	ASEAN Economic Community
AECV2030	Asia Economic Connectivity Vision 2030
AFC	Asian Financial Crisis
AFTA	ASEAN Free Trade Area
AIF	ASEAN Infrastructure Fund
AIIB	Asian Infrastructure Investment Bank
AMF	Asian Monetary Fund
AMRO	ASEAN+3 Macroeconomic Research Office
APEC	Asia-Pacific Economic Cooperation
ASEAN	Association of Southeast Asian Nations
ATIGA	ASEAN Trade in Goods Agreement
AVA	Agri-food and Veterinary Authority
B&R	Belt & Road
BCMP	Break-Even Cost-Recovery Market Pricing
BOOT	Build-Operate-Own-and-Transfer
BOT	Build-Operate-Transfer
BRN	Brunei
CBA	Cost-Benefit Analysis
CEPA	Closer Economic Partnership Arrangement

CET	Continuous Education and Training
CI	Confidence Interval
CIS	Commonwealth of Independent States
CHN	China
CLM	Cambodia, Laos and Myanmar
CLMV	Cambodia, Laos, Myanmar and Vietnam
CLV	Cambodia, Laos and Vietnam
CMI	Chiang Mai Initiative
CMIM	Chiang Mai Initiative Multilateralisation
COT	Competitiveness Over Time
CPF	Central Provident Fund
CSEC	China-Singapore Economic Corridor
DBFO	Design-Build-Finance-Operate
DWT	Deadweight Tonnage
EAED	East Asian Economic Development
ECOWAS	Economic Community of West African States
EDB	Economic Development Board
EIU	Economist Intelligence Unit
EPI	Environment Performance Index
ERIA	Economic Research Institute for ASEAN and East Asia
EU	European Union
FAO	Food and Agriculture Organisation
FBMC	Financial, Businesses and Manpower Conditions
FDI	Foreign Direct Investment
FG	Flying Geese
FTAs	Free Trade Agreements
FTAAP	Free Trade Area of Asia Pacific
G2G	Government to Government
GCC	Gulf Cooperation Council
GCR	Global Competitiveness Report
GDP	Gross Domestic Product

GE	General Election
GEP	Globalisation and Economic Policy
GFC	Global Financial Crisis
GFT	Global Financial Tsunami
GIC	Government Investment Corporation
GIS	Government and Institutional Setting
GLCs	Government-Linked Companies
GMID	Global Market Information Database
GMS	Greater Mekong Sub-region
GNI	Gross National Income
HDB	Housing & Development Board
HRD	Human Resource Development
ICT	Information and Communication Technology
IDN	Indonesia
IE	International Enterprise
IFAD	International Fund for Agricultural Development
IMCB	Institute of Molecular and Cell Biology
IMD	International Management Development
IMF	International Monetary Fund
IMTGT	Indonesia-Malaysia-Thailand Growth Triangle
IND	India
IPCC	Intergovernmental Panel on Climate Change
IPRs	Intellectual Property Rights
IT	Information Technology
JVs	Joint Ventures
KBE	Knowledge-Based Economy
KHM	Cambodia
KPIs	Key Performance Indicators
LKYSPP	Lee Kuan Yew School of Public Policy
LNG	Liquefied Natural Gas
LOI	Letters of Intent
MNCs	Multinational Corporations

MOU	Memorandum of Understanding
MP3EI	Masterplan for Acceleration and Expansion of Indonesia's Economic Development
MPAC	Master Plan on ASEAN Connectivity
MRT	Mass Rapid Transit
MS	Macroeconomic Stability
MSR	Maritime Silk Road
MYS	Malaysia
MWP	Minimum Wage Policy
NACT	Network of ASEAN-China Think-Tanks
NAFTA	North American Free Trade Agreement
NDB	New Development Bank
NDP	National Solidarity Party
NEAT	Network of East Asian Think-Tanks
NGOs	Non-Government Organisations
NIEs	Newly Industrialised Economies
NSWs	National Single Windows
NTBs	Non-Tariff Barriers
NUS	National University of Singapore
OECD	Organisation for Economic Co-operation and Development
OPs	Opposition Parties
PAP	People's Action Party
PECC	Pacific Economic Cooperation Council
PHL	Philippines
PLA	People's Liberation Army
PMETs	Professional, Managers, Executives and Technicians
PORIM	Palm Oil Research Institute of Malaysia
PPPs	Public-Private Partnerships
PPP	People's Power Party
QLID	Quality of Life and Infrastructure Development
R&D	Research and Development

RCEP	Regional Comprehensive Economic Partnership
ROI	Returns on Investment
ROOs	Rules of Origin
RP	Reform Party
RULC	Relative Unit Labour Cost
S&T	Science and Technology
SARS	Severe Acute Respiratory Syndrome
SDA	Singapore Democratic Alliance
SDP	Singapore Democratic Party
SEZs	Special Economic Zones
SFP	Singaporeans First Party
SGP	Singapore
SMEs	Small and Medium-sized Enterprises
SOEs	State-Owned Enterprises
SPP	Singapore People's Party
SVAR	Structural Vector Autoregressive
SWFs	Sovereign Wealth Funds
TAIs	Transparent Affordability Indices
TEU	Twenty-foot Equivalent Unit
TFP	Total Factor Productivity
THA	Thailand
TPP	Trans-Pacific Partnership
UAE	United Arab Emirates
UN	United Nations
UNCTAD	United Nations Conference on Trade and Development
UNDP	United Nations Development Programme
UNESCO	United Nations Organisation for Education, Science and Culture
UNFCCC	United Nations Framework Convention on Climate Change
US	United States

VTN	Vietnam
WCY	World Competitiveness Yearbook
WEF	World Economic Forum
WFP	World Food Programme
WIS	Workfare Income Supplement
WP	Workers' Party
WTO	World Trade Organisation

LIST OF TABLES AND FIGURES

Chapter 3

Chapter 5

Chapter 1

ACI PROPOSED MASTER PLAN FOR ASIA ECONOMIC CONNECTIVITY VISION 2030 (AECV2030)

1.1 Introductory Notes

Both the Association of Southeast Asian Nations (ASEAN) and China, as well documented within the general story of Asia, are heralded as successful models of economic growth and development in their own right.[1] India is emerging and potentially progressing as a new regional engine of growth. Lessons can be learned from its history and globalisation as facilitated by the increasingly ubiquitous information communication technology (ICT) and evolving geo-economics and geopolitics. While levels of economic competitiveness as well as national idiosyncrasies differ in ASEAN, China and India, their outward-looking approach to international trade, foreign direct investment (FDI) and migration of multinational corporations (MNCs) is key to such adaptation with alacrity. The leaps they made have lifted millions out of poverty, contributed to the increase in the global middle-income class and created new economic dynamics with far-reaching ramifications. With populous Asia regions, including Northeast Asia,

[1] Economic growth is quantitative in terms of national output, while economic development is qualitative in terms of the rising standards of living including environmental sustainability, which may take place in sequence; however, after take-off, they may occur in parallel with competitiveness as the overarching strategy. Development status, as developed or developing, is based on a per capita basis, with development as emphasis.

South Asia and Southeast Asia, hosting some two-thirds of global humanity, there is a pressing need for a more balanced and sustainable economic growth and development, commensurate with environmental sustainability.

With rising China and emerging India rendering their strong presence in global economics and finance, Asia is at a crossroads again. All Asian countries have both national goals and ambitions to fulfil, coupled with amicable competition with each other, based upon the principles of collaboration, cultivation of trust and stability, and a pro-active form of trade diplomacy. The Asia Competitiveness Institute (ACI) at the Lee Kuan Yew School of Public Policy (LKYSPP), National University of Singapore (NUS), resonates with this evolving trend through many pioneering studies on competitiveness of ASEAN, Greater China, India and Indonesia,[2] including a process in envisioning a master plan for Asia, the Asia Economic Connectivity Vision 2030 (AECV2030) with Asian aspirations. This ACI study aims to offer astute workable policies and strategies for regional economic cooperation through five broad proposals, facilitated by the 21st century globalisation under a collective mindset. The Asian story via the AECV2030, with ASEAN and China initiating the journey, can go from strength to strength to enact a defining sequel for Asia as a whole in the new millennium.

A key priority of the ACI is evidence-based research using quantitative methodologies for policy-evaluation and formulation. For ASEAN, China and India in the AECV2030, the ACI has a database drilled down to the granularity of sub-national statistics, supplemented and complemented by surveys and consultative meetings with all stakeholders from government, private sector to non-governmental organisations (NGOs). Moreover, all literature and information, including formal

[2] See Tan *et al.* (2013a), Tan *et al.* (2013b), Tan *et al.* (2013c) and Tan *et al.* (2013d) for books on competitiveness of Indonesia, ASEAN, India and Greater China, respectively.

academic publications and informal information such as media reports, are built up into an ACI Catalogue as a continuing research into regional integration.[3] The case for the AECV2030 in this chapter focuses on aligning national positioning for best interests to seek sectoral engines for growth in response to global and local trends through more in-depth studies, as the array of opportunities offered for selection is infinite.

Various combinations and permutations for national as well as subregional involvement across ASEAN and China in the first instance will involve India. Be it the ASEAN way[4] with its ASEAN-X principle,[5] maritime ASEAN and/or mainland ASEAN, having ASEAN-10 at the centre of the Asia Pacific provides sufficient options and flexibility, which can be replicated in the AECV2030 with an equally diverse China.[6] It is paramount to accommodate different stages of economic growth and development to match national and regional aspirations. New modalities including numerous forms of public-private partnerships (PPPs), growth clusters in economic corridors and NGOs will enhance the menu of options, with emphasis on sustainable development based on competiveness. It is a sea change, literally and figuratively.

---

[3] See the ACI's Catalogue of AECV2030 for academic materials and media materials, both covering ASEAN and related development.

[4] Economic integration in ASEAN works on the principle of sovereign states cooperating without domestic interference, unlike the European Union (EU) which pools sovereignty in supranational institutions as the deepest stage of an economic union, with one single currency.

[5] ASEAN-X is a formulaic principle which allows ASEAN projects to proceed without immediate full participation of all member states; an established consensual agreement giving ASEAN projects the spirit, support and endorsement, while other ASEAN members may join at a later time when able or desired.

[6] On the changing balance of power in the Asia Pacific, refer to The Economist (2014) special report, The Pacific Age, containing the following articles – Galleons and gunships; The flying factory; America's big bet; Your rules or mine?; Oil and water; Pacific pumas; ¡Salud!; Merchants or missionaries?

President Xi proposed the 21st Century Maritime Silk Road initiative in his speech to the Indonesian Parliament on 2nd October 2013, which Premier Li Keqiang reiterated at the 16th ASEAN + China Summit in Brunei on 9th October 2013.[7] China's version of the 21st Century Maritime Silk Road, with its emphasis on connectivity with Southeast Asia, South Asia and Africa, is a system of multi-modal and multi-track connections.[8] With a diverse spectrum of stakeholders and owners in projects to galvanise the ACI's five broad proposals, the AECV2030 is deemed best driven by ASEAN leadership, with ASEAN track record for open, consultative and consensual decision-making. A pragmatic collaborative model, used to articulate each party's competitiveness and interests comprehensively and feasibly, could then tap into other ACI studies' rich in-house database and extensive network of research think tanks, government departments and private sector partners, which include civil societies.

China's proposed Maritime Silk Road, followed by its elaborated Belt & Road (B&R) that is to be facilitated by the Asian Infrastructure Investment Bank (AIIB), remains part of the ACI's on-going research. More research studies are in the pipeline to analyse all perspectives from ASEAN to Greater China, South Asia, continuing on to Central Asia and the Middle East. Each region has its nuances to grasp. For South Asia, the emphasis is the way India on looks at the B&R. For the Middle East, the importance of Iran and its collaboration with the Gulf Cooperation Council (GCC) is clear. With the choke point in the Strait of Hormuz, the alternative Fujairah Port in the United Arab Emirates (UAE), utilised for direct access into Indian Ocean, is already operational; unsurprisingly, there is also another proposal to build a tunnel below the Strait of Hormuz. A further extension of the Chinese rail

[7] See Szczudlik-Tatar (2013) and ACI AECV2030 Catalogue for all speeches.

[8] Another is China's overland Silk Road Economic Belt plans, concentrated on the Commonwealth of Independent States (CIS, former Soviet Union), the Middle East and Europe. See Page (2014a) and Page (2014b).

system in Tibet to be linked to that of India through the Nathu La pass can also greatly improve access to the sea from Qinghai and Tibet via Calcutta. It is all a matter of how cross-border checks and documentation of various authorities along the route for security, immigration and customs among others can flow smoothly.

1.2 An Overview on Related Background

As an overview related to history, economic, trade and investment background, Section 1.2 begins by outlining the macroeconomic framework leading on to the development of the AECV2030, firstly with a brief historical overview of trade patterns as a useful preamble. Subsequently, the section elaborates on the tracing of the historical flying geese model of phased economic development. The contextual experiences of the East Asian development model have established a new paradigm of Asian trade. Given the thesis of this chapter is grounded on an ASEAN-centric approach to the AECV2030, we reported on the empirical findings of the structural vector autoregressive (SVAR) model for eight ASEAN economies. The SVAR model provides some insights from another ACI study on trade flows for the World Bank. Finally, we worked through the on-going economic restructuring of China under the era of New Normal, which then led to window of opportunities and challenges for the AECV2030.

Section 1.3 discusses the AECV2030 with Asian aspirations in greater detail. Section 1.4 is on the ACI's mission and commitment to the AECV2030, with tentative proposed routes for the vision discussed in Section 1.5. These proposed routes, together with the new initiatives, set the agenda for five broad ACI proposals with strategic thrusts in Section 1.6. These five ACI proposals are, logically and sequentially, based on different stages of economic growth and development in synchrony with varying appetites in competitiveness. They remain a work-in-progress as the ACI plans additional field trips and events via an open consultative approach, especially to identify projects as already announced. These include those related to the new visions under President Joko Widodo and Prime Minister Narendra Modi tutelage. A consensual approach is imperative while the ACI aims to make the AECV2030 with the rising China a defining point of discussion and dialogues, living up to its name of connectivity.

Section 1.7 shows the tangible results from the projection of selected target performance indicators for 2030, which serve to monitor and track the progress in materialising the AECV2030 according to the projected outcomes. All are sensitive to socio-economic-environmental considerations of the various constituents and the region as a whole. The Asian way is to be respected,[9] as emphasised in Section 1.8 as concluding remarks. The most important policy implication is for the AECV2030 to be ASEAN-centric. Apart from the political economy aspects of initiatives from China, involving Asia and even beyond as in the B&R, the role of ASEAN at least for such connectivity as complementing and supplementing ASEAN's own plans makes ASEAN a natural partner in general. In particular, the AECV2030 twins well with its Master Plan on ASEAN Connectivity (MPAC) in 2010.[10]

1.2.1 Patterns of Asian Trade

Trade as an engine of growth in economic literature is well-documented and proven, from ancient times via traditional conduits by land, to technological advances of sea-borne and air-borne trade, to ICT-facilitated electronic-trade and variants as e-commerce. Both geographical masses and space allow tradable to expand as non-tradeable to move across borders. Patterns of trade involve both composition and direction of trade, which are well researched in the literature. How

[9] See Studwell (2013) on how Asia works.

[10] MPAC was formulated as a blueprint for achieving the three pillars of the ASEAN community — ASEAN Political-Security Community, ASEAN Economic Community (AEC) and ASEAN Socio-Cultural Community. See ASEAN Secretariat (2010).

trade patterns follow from theories and models described in the flying geese model and its corollary of the East Asian economic development model, as described in this section, serve as preludes to the AECV2030. In all instances, both China and ASEAN's focus on export-oriented trade and development is underscored, recently such a "made-in-India" strategy is also being advocated by Prime Minister Narendra Modi.

For ASEAN in particular, President Joko Widodo's vision of Indonesia as the world's maritime axis is befitting of Indonesia's archipelagic formation of some 14,000 islands. During his presidential campaign in 2014, President Widodo proposed an ambitious plan of maritime toll roads and a sea-lane to be regularly served by cargo ships between western and eastern parts of the country.[11] This initiative can tackle the high transportation costs of logistics and wide price difference between the west and east to even up their respective competitiveness. Equally, it is deemed as complementary to China's ambition for its proposed 21st Century Maritime Silk Road, or at least, one segment of that.[12]

From ASEAN perspectives, it is as important that the maritime ASEAN, Indonesia and the Philippines, be brought up to speed to parallel the mainland ASEAN. Likewise, catching China's attention in both maritime and land-based connectivity forms a two-pronged ASEAN strategy to prove its worth as an ASEAN-centric approach. Confidence-building as an early harvest with the ASEAN segment of China's more overarching multi-lane 21st Century Maritime Silk Road is catalytic in more ways than just financially. Multiplier effects include tangible business opportunities for all stakeholders and the intangible forging of values and mindsets for collaboration and cooperation.

[11] See Shekhar and Liow (2014) for their analysis of President Widodo's presidential campaign to transform Indonesia into a global maritime axis.

[12] See Tan *et al.* (2013a) for analyses of Indonesia, especially as a maritime axis and Hussain (2014) on Indonesia's key role in China's Maritime Silk Road plans.

Already, China became ASEAN's largest trading partner in 2009, which is attributable to "the integration of ASEAN economies into China-centric regional production networks" formed in late 1990s; ASEAN countries positioned themselves as exporters of commodities and intermediate goods to China and benefited from the Chinese developing into an exporting behemoth of finished goods as a key manufacturing and assembly hub.[13] With the China-induced commodity boom in hiatus, if not over, both ASEAN and China need trade and investment growth and expansion beyond commodities.

Putting geopolitics and security issues aside to focus on economics and competitiveness, patterns of trade and exchange are part and parcel of tapping the FDI and MNCs for economic growth and development. Standard economic literature has argued for the efficacy of such agents for transfers of technology, management, skills as human resource development (HRD), as well as world-class brands of MNCs, with market access back to the countries of FDI donors. A package deal of Asia's attractiveness to the FDI and MNCs is a source of new trade patterns. In turn, the many bilateral free trade agreements (FTAs)[14] complement, supplement and even rival both regional and multilateral trade liberalisation by ASEAN and the World Trade Organisation (WTO), respectively.

It is no different from the historical Roman Empire to the British Empire or Marco Polo's adventures eastward into China in the 13th century, that the old Silk Road as overland and maritime (see Figure 1.1) is contrasted with the progression to the B&R. Geographically beyond overland Asia, the 21st Century Maritime Silk Road completes the circuit into the Middle East and Southern Europe,

---

[13] In 2013, ASEAN-China trade grew to US$350 billion, forming 14% of ASEAN total trade, and is expected to further increase to US$500 billion by the end of 2015. See Basu Das (2015, 7).

[14] Refer to www.bilaterals.org for extensive listings of FTAs, both country-by-country and by grouping like ASEAN-wide FTAs.

Figure 1.1. Old Overland and Maritime Silk Road

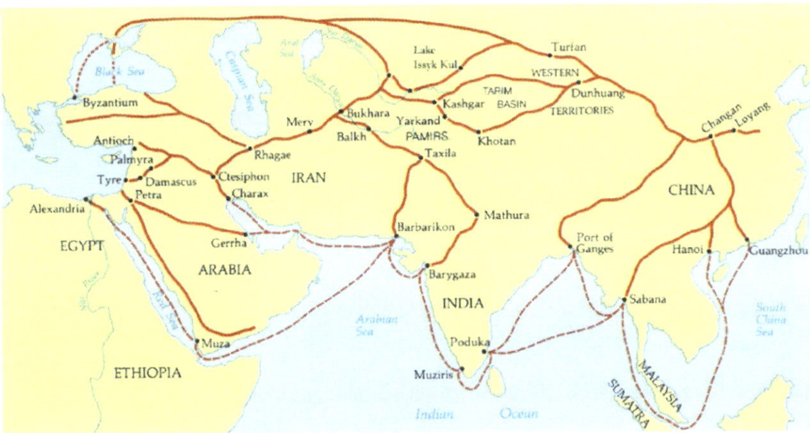

Source: National Geographic.[15]

as well as East Africa in the first instance. Expedited by modern modalities of transportation including ICT, the potential of what is feasible is up to the imagination.

Thus, Chinese President Xi Jinping's initiative is not merely reviving the Maritime Silk Road, but a New 21st Century Silk Road and Economic Belt connecting China with Central Asia, the Middle East and Europe. All of the initiatives are for economic and environmental cooperation, physical connectivity, infrastructure investment and socio-cultural linkages across Asia. Together, these form China's complete B&R with the AIIB financing infrastructure. The allusion to traditional silk roads are historical and inspiring, with new modalities in transportation promising to revitalise a core circuit of ancient exchange. Quintessentially, it marks the point where China has arrived on the basis of it being the second largest economy in the world according to the nominal gross domestic product (GDP) in 2010,

[15] See Hiebert (2012).

overtaking Japan.[16] Its population of 1.36 billion is the largest globally;[17] no less in magnitude is its US$3.73 trillion[18] of official foreign currency reserves in early 2015. China is deploying all resources at its command to restructure its economic architecture and trade patterns as evidenced in its largesse relative to more financially strapped countries, notably the United States (US) and the European Union (EU). It is another sea change, literally and figuratively, for China and ASEAN in proximity.

In economic parlance, trade as a growth engine facilitates more efficient allocation of natural resources based on comparative advantage, with both costs and benefits to be weighed as mutually beneficial. Strategic trade policy *de facto* tweaked as policy-induced competitive advantage is another facet of political economy to be reckoned with. The latter, rather than the former, has enabled resource-deficit city-states of Hong Kong and Singapore, and other newly industrialised economies (NIEs) such as South Korea and Taiwan to make their great leaps since the 1960s by export-oriented trade despite their different governance structures, cultural heritage or geographical endowment.

The NIEs shared a significant common feature in their initial labour-intensive and export-oriented focus, which accounted for "more than 50% of total manufactured exports from all developing countries" by the end of the 1980s despite their aggregate share of population of developing countries being less than 3%.[19] This was a conscientious endeavour to assimilate their respective economies into the global trade regime via competitive export strategies.

---

[16] According to Japanese officials, on a seasonally unadjusted, nominal dollar basis, Japan's GDP in 2010 was $5.47 trillion compared to China's GDP of $5.88 trillion. See Kajimoto and Kihara (2011) and Dickie (2011).

[17] See The World Bank (2015).

[18] See Yao (2015).

[19] See Chow and Kellman (1993, 6).

The global financial tsunami (GFT) since 2008, with the reality of an on-going global economic slump that is sharper in some countries more than others, even halts seemingly unstoppable China in GDP targets and trade surplus. As demand falls off in recessionary advanced economies, including the US and EU, a return to the decoupling thesis[20] for significant growth is taking place across Asia to lead global trade development. More of this follows in Section 1.2.3 on the East Asian economic development model. Clearly, China makes no apologies for all these ideas as they also provide alternative growth engines and strategies as its growth stage reaches a New Normal era with the GFT slowdown hitting China.[21] Its state-owned enterprises (SOEs) have also come of age to be globally seeking opportunities. It may be as timely to rebalance structurally, as China has turned from a food exporter to a food importer by being the factory of the world. Agriculture is not necessarily inferior, with the requisite science and technology (S&T) and research and development (R&D).

Realistically, intra regional trade policies aimed to maximise gains in GDP, trade and jobs derived from static gains need to be differentiated by relatively superior dynamic trade gains with trading partners in developed countries. This further fuels the debate between North-South trade and South-South trade. The dynamic aspects are from the technology transfers of both technical and human skills via the FDI and MNCs. Simultaneously, trade policies with an eye towards the opening of regional borders must minimise the costs, from exploitative colonial patterns of trade to environmental degradation and other unwanted practices.

---

[20] An example of economic decoupling is if emerging markets, as in Asia especially China, can take over the American lead as the importer-of-last resort as an alternative, especially since the GFT, which in turn fuelling Asia economic cooperation or integration as the developing world is learning to spread its wings. See The Economist (2008).

[21] See Tan *et al.* (2015b) on Greater China.

1.2.2 The Flying Geese Model

As a historical background, which also demonstrates the empirical evidence of economic growth in Asia in general and ASEAN in particular, a review of the flying geese model and its corollary as the East Asian economic development model is germane.

The flying geese (FG) model was first developed by Japanese economists, including the pioneering efforts by Kaname Akamatsu who wrote about industrial development in the 1930s[22] before his 1962 English article on a historical pattern of economic growth in developing countries.[23] The wild flying geese concept was further developed by others including Kojima Kiyoshi.[24] With statistical analysis, Akamatsu, Kojima and others noticed a pattern of Japanese industrial development whereby the sequence resembled the triangular formation of wild flying geese. The model was used to explain the iterative process of industrialisation adopted by developing economies, where capital investment and development, as well as the rationalisation of production processes, evolved in a cascading fashion from a 'lead goose'. This was Japan as the leading model in Asia with successive 'follower geese', as shown in Figure 1.2.

More broadly, the FG model in Figure 1.2 depicts the changing of the leading goose through the transfer of capabilities from developed to developing countries on a global basis since the Industrial Revolution in the West. It is based on more than natural resources as comparative advantage, to further incorporate the notion of Porter's policy-induced

---

[22] See the ACI Catalogue for a listing of Akamatsu's articles in both Japanese and English, and other Japanese economists in expanding the wild flying geese model.

[23] See Akamatsu (1962) for his economic theory on the 'wild-geese-flying pattern' in English.

[24] See Kojima (2000), which has a bibliography of numerous papers by other Japanese economists on the theory.

Figure 1.2. International Flying Geese Model, 1940-2010 and Beyond

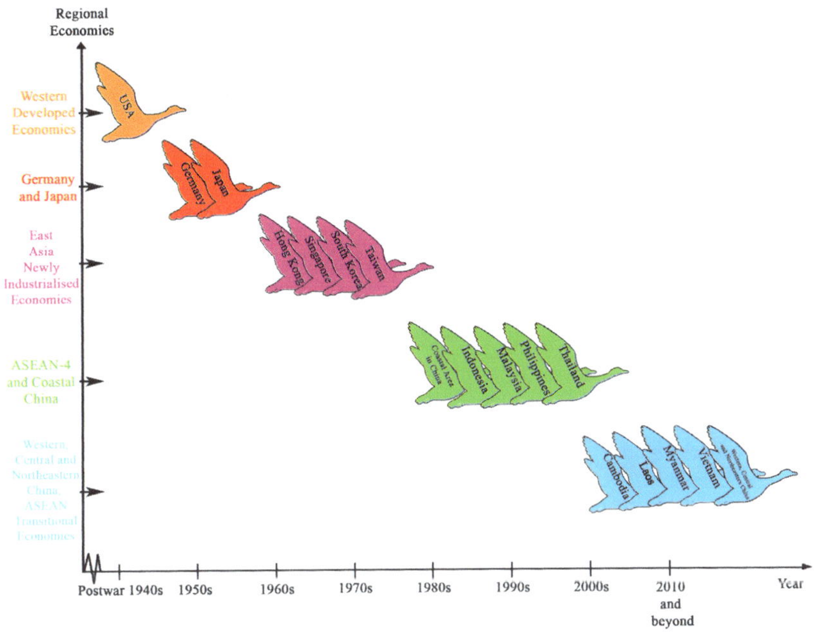

Source: Asia Competitiveness Institute.

competitive advantages.[25] Policies aimed at overall competitiveness in terms of a conducive business and policy environment add to factor-based comparative advantages, to streamline allocation of available resources to industries in a country to be most productive and competitive.

---

[25] Factor-based comparative advantage argues for the intensive use of factors that a country possesses in abundance, namely land, labour, natural resources and capital, whereas the competitive advantage of nations looks at ways to shape the operating environment, as in strategies for innovation and competitiveness as well as the institutional and legal governance structures, within which firms function, in order to cultivate national advantages. See Porter (1990).

The flying geese pattern (Figure 1.2) observed in the post-war development of countries has a change in holders of the industrial baton, which was passed on over several time intervals:

- 1950s: the US relocated steel, textile and other traditional industries to Germany and Japan, as the US focused on developing semiconductors, telecommunications, computers and other emerging technology-intensive industries.
- 1960s to 1980s: Japan and Germany shifted their labour-intensive and resource-intensive industries to East Asia's NIEs, allowing them to catch up on developing integrated circuits, precision machinery, fine chemicals, household appliances, automobiles and other high value-added technology-intensive industries.
- 1990s: Europe, Japan together with the four Asian dragons of Hong Kong, Singapore, South Korea and Taiwan gradually began to relocate their industries, which were becoming less competitive in their own countries or regions, to China's coastal regions of the special economic zones (SEZs) introduced by Deng Xiao Ping's opening up of China, and the ASEAN-4, namely Indonesia, Malaysia, Philippines and Thailand.
- Post-2000: Due to rising wages and higher land costs in China's SEZs, the Chinese government encouraged and incentivised MNCs to shift their high cost, high energy consuming, labour-intensive and environmentally taxing industries and production processes to the relatively undeveloped inland regions. This domestication of the flying geese model is for China to maintain or regain international competitiveness and to ensure a more balanced regional development.

The use of SEZs is not new in the literature of ASEAN growth triangles,[26] but it was new, only to Deng Xiaoping's socialism with

[26] See Toh and Low (1993).

Chinese characteristics. A dual flying geese approach for China also involves migration of some industries to resource-abundant Indonesia and others, such as the newer ASEAN states of Cambodia, Laos, Myanmar and Vietnam (CLMV).

Generally, as seen in Figure 1.2, developed countries or regions move up the production value chain or industrial ladder towards high value-added activities. This is as per Adam Smith's theory for international division of labour and specialisation, refined by David Ricardo in the theory of comparative advantage based on the concept of opportunity cost. Along with FDI and MNC activities, there is a constant and dynamic discarding and relocating of labour-intensive and low value-added manufacturing industries in exchange for more sophistication and upgrading. Such industrial restructuring and diversification by both hosts and recipients of FDI need two sets of hands to clap in unison. National and regional competitiveness mean a constant rationalisation of changing capacities and capabilities with external trends as equally dynamic as a challenge and response.

Specifically within ASEAN region, there is scope for interchanging of the lead 'prime goose', the role historically played by Japan and increasingly by China. Chinese and Japanese industries relocate their production facilities to take advantage of cost efficiencies in the developing ASEAN countries or to better capture expansion opportunities with tax advantage given the various prevailing regional free trade agreements. This is in line with the "Made in China 2025" plan, which aims to shift China's manufacturing sector toward higher value-added, sophisticated industrial activities, and "away from simple, labour-intensive production" by the year 2025.[27] In particular, the CLMV will be able to use their abundant low-cost labour and natural resources to attract FDI and MNCs to move up the FG model.

[27] See Abe (2015) for details on manufacturing transformation in the "Made in China 2025" plan.

To be clear, such migration of industries by developed economies up the industrial ladder is obviously motivated by profit maximisation that finesses the S&T as well as R&D. Accompanying technological expertise provides HRD together with continuous education and training (CET) to ensure employability more than mere employment creation. As the developed economies or leading goose advance to proceed into more S&T and R&D pursuits, they combine globalisation with localisation to help recipients of FDI to establish ASEAN and Asian products and brands.

While the rest of the advanced world disseminates advanced techniques via the FG model, it is as imperative and challenging for ASEAN and Asian R&D to emerge and be specific to their respective local contexts. A word of caution pertains to how much and how long any export of 'dirty' (pollution-prone) industries should be tolerated, as they tend to be the ones relocated as well as labour-intensive industries. This is where the right policies of safeguarding finite resources, protecting both human skills with CET and the environment must be heeded from the outset.

1.2.3 East Asian Economic Development Model

Evolving from the FG model is the East Asian economic development (EAED) model. Following from the CLMV as the latest ASEAN entrants in joining the FG model, they simultaneously latch on to the EAED pattern of growing export-oriented economies by engaging in international trade. The CLMV quad then attempted to leapfrog to catch up on industrialisation and supply chains but with lesser degree of success. EAED model is equally enabled by globalisation and its attendant trends.[28]

[28] The lines become increasingly blur, in what divides physical goods and intangible services as well as their being tradeable and non-tradeable, respectively morphed over time. Thus, FDI and MNCs are in both manufacturing and services; witness Apple and Google launching watches or self-driving cars.

Globalisation's intensification since the 1990s was made possible by the information revolution. Information technology (IT) then ICT, creating a global "information superhighway",[29] coupled by the lowering of tariff and non-tariff barriers (NTBs) facilitated by the WTO multilateral trade liberalisation and regional and bilateral FTAs, intensified the globalisation process. The resulting growth in global trade also spurs more intense competition among global economies based on both comparative advantage from natural endowment and competitive advantage as induced by policies. Emerging economies, especially those in Asia with an abundant highly skilled labour supply that commands lower wages than their Western counterparts, sparked a reshuffling of production networks due to shifts in locations and sectors in terms of employment creation and changes in human capital formation.

Building and embellishing on the FG model coupled with the EAED model with Japan as the leading goose, decanting industries has spawned more ASEAN "miracle economies".[30] More than the FG model, the EAED model has an extra message in that the Asian state capitalism, as demonstrated in Japan Inc., Singapore Inc. and many government-led cases across Asia as government-driven modernisation and industrialisation, has shown itself to be a viable alternative.[31] It is in contrast to the Western *laissez-faire* market development paths taken by historic first-mover countries of industrialisation.

---

[29] See Fukuyama (1995, 23) for the impact of information technology on economic development.

[30] See The World Bank (1993). *The East Asian Miracle* was a landmark World Bank report, which rationalised East Asian economic development via an international panel of contributors and editors, through the financial assistance of the Government of Japan. While Asian success may have been more by perspiration (labour-intensive industries) than inspiration (S&T and R&D), it takes time, as experienced by Singapore and Malaysia, to ratchet up into high-technology pursuits, even as technology cycles get shorter and faster.

[31] See Low (1998) and Low (2004).

The nature of sustainable rapid economic development in the Asian region has, by and large, been indicative of the necessity of a strategically targeted "consistent set of government policy interventions" in determining the genuine competitiveness of an economy, something the crisis events of 1997 made starkly evident among the developing Asian countries.[32] In other words, while economic efficiency is the universal rule of the 'what', it also matters 'how' it is to be attained. In this sense, purely local business practices, not pure ideology, justifies the AECV2030 for economies that share much cultural affinities, bearing many resemblances alongside similarities in their profile of needs.

Nonetheless, the basic economic strategy is explicit in the EAED model, namely strategic infrastructure investment to unlock production bottlenecks as a prerequisite for economic take-off. Thus, a forward-looking and prudent government must first overcome constraints for infrastructure investment, in order to facilitate greater "industrial learning" within society, through growing export capabilities across firms.[33] Due to the relatively massive capital requirements, the long gestation period and the long-term nature of returns on investment (ROI) for infrastructure projects, its cost of financing tends to be expensive and sources of funding are strained through keen competition by other fund commitments. This results in existing financial bottlenecks.[34]

---

[32] See Studwell (2013, xv).

[33] Industrial learning expresses the idea that knowledge obtained for the development of industrial technology and capacity build-up often occurs through corporate activity on an intra-firm level in a competitive environment, rather than within the setting of formal education, noted in Studwell (2013, xxii–xxiii).

[34] In addressing financial bottlenecks adequately, this calls for financial development and financial deepening as another priority for government policymaking. Financial development refers to institutional financial structures: firm access to credit, individuals' ability to raise funds and the growth of a bond-issuance market etc., whereas financial deepening specifically refers to the growth of financial assets, as can be illustrated by the measure of M2 (time plus demand deposits) to GDP or more broadly, M3 (financial liabilities) to GDP ratios. See The World Bank (1993).

To address these challenges, given the culturally observed thriftiness of Asians (at least, of the post-war generations), the mobilisation of large pools of Asian saving deposits and pension funds coupled with strategic reinvestment programmes will advance financial development and deepening. Different approaches to tap such household savings, to be invested towards resolving infrastructure deadlocks, have been proven in the experience and successes of the EAED model. Be it through perspiration or inspiration (as per later stages in innovation, with progressive S&T and R&D derived from advanced industrial players), the AECV2030 is the right conduit. It serves to release production bottlenecks through strategically investing in comprehensively planned regional infrastructure, followed by the rest of upgrading. Undoubtedly, infrastructure, from transportation to energy, is a prerequisite condition for economic acceleration.

Be it large or small, a population is a destiny with its respective challenges to respond to. None, however, will escape the less desirable middle-income trap without proper preparation.[35] Investment in HRD and CET in response to and for innovation *per se* requires entrepreneurship for creativity and inventiveness, which are crucial. Together, they are also obvious social equalisers as ingredients for total factor productivity (TFP) and an inclusive society. Importantly, a prolonged period of social stability is a significant priority, without which social mobility, preferably based upon meritocracy, cannot prevail in a sustainable manner. Again, these are stages to be processed and responded to accordingly.

Stronger economies, which have comparative advantages in terms of capital, technology and competitive skills, should play an active role in meeting pressing infrastructure bottlenecks. Private sector involvement in PPPs saw it joining hands with governments to significantly reduce any growth inertia and imbalanced regional development. For

[35] See Zhuang, Vandenberg and Huang (2012, 7–10, 24), and Aiyar *et al.* (2013, 18–19, 28–37).

a balanced, sustainable and inclusive regional economic and social integration, both physical and soft infrastructure provisions for greater connectivity are increasing. While traditionally and predominantly viewed as indispensable, international and regional public goods requiring cross-border coordination, new PPP modalities, including NGOs, are emerging to finesse the rest in synchrony. Indeed, the 'Asianisation' of the new global economic architecture is fast arriving.[36]

All parties are responsibly aware of how effective leadership and good governance at the helm play a paramount role in harnessing and promoting especially infrastructure investment, as well as identifying the opportune timing for projects to kick-start. The ACI has the conviction that a longer-term roadmap for Asia connectivity should be planned ahead as visionary. The ACI is determined on the basis of comparative, competitive advantages and productivity, with cumulative efforts and experiential learning, to harness the timeliness of the AECV2030.

1.2.4 Structural Vector Autoregressive Model on Trade Flows of Eight ASEAN Economies

The decoupling phenomenon, noted in Section 1.2.1, and signs of this shift in the economic centre of gravity towards Asia are increasingly apparent since the GFT. This is further confirmed in the ACI study on trade flows performed for the World Bank. The study is to evaluate the

[36] See Kawai, Morgan and Rana (2014) for a discussion on how the post-war global economic architecture is no longer adequate to address the needs of the international economy, and how a new regional economic framework, particularly in Asia, can contribute towards both regional and global public goods to support development. President Widodo declared at the Asian-African Conference 2015 that "there is a shifting world reality... those who say the global economic problems shall only be solved through the World Bank, the IMF and the ADB, these are obsolete ideas," and reiterated the need for change. See Danubrata and Greenfield (2015).

economic interdependence among countries in ASEAN since the implementation of its MPAC in 2010.

Adopting the Structural Vector Autoregressive (SVAR) model for eight ASEAN economies and three control economies,[37] several noteworthy results are drawn from the analysis of 110 bilateral export-share series from 2001 to 2013. By examining the 5-year multiplier effects for the periods before and after the introduction of MPAC in 2010, it is found that although the OECD is still the dominant engine of growth for the eight ASEAN economies, China's growth effect on ASEAN has increased considerably, particularly for Cambodia, Malaysia, the Philippines, Singapore and Thailand, and is drawing near to the OECD levels (see Tables 1.1, 1.2 and 1.3).[38]

The multiplier effects of the eight ASEAN economies on each other however, remain rather limited in comparison to OECD and China. While neither ASEAN nor East Asian intra-regional trade has been better than their extra-regional trade,[39] both the decoupling premise and upkeep of Asian trade momentum operate in tandem to provide an alternative source of regional growth, which "needs to be enhanced through increased intra-regional trade, to compensate for the fall in export demand in advanced economies."[40] It is as contentious, as it may be a sign of a promise for the proposed AECV2030 with the greater intra-regional demand.

---

[37] The eight ASEAN economics in the SVAR model are Brunei (BRN), Cambodia (KHM), Indonesia (IDN), Malaysia (MYS), Philippines (PHL), Singapore (SGP), Thailand (THA) and Vietnam (VTN), and the three control economies are China (CHN), India (IND) and the Organisation for Economic Co-operation and Development (OECD), which includes trading partners Australia, South Korea, Japan, EU and US.

[38] Notable values greater than 0.20 are in bold on the result tables.

[39] Simply put, ASEAN imports more capital goods and even high-technology consumer products from the developed industrial countries, in contrast to ASEAN's exports of low value-added resource-based products to advanced manufacturing hubs; effectively a form of neocolonialism however defined.

[40] See Bhattacharyay (2009, 8).

Table 1.1. Five-Year Multiplier Effects of a One Percent Point Positive Growth Shock on Each of the Eleven Economies (Pre-2010)

	Engine of Growth										
	Eight ASEAN Economies								**Control Economies**		
	BRN	**KHM**	**IDN**	**MYS**	**PHL**	**SGP**	**THA**	**VTN**	**CHN**	**IND**	**OECD**
BRN	0.751	0.003	0.186	0.128	0.042	0.137	0.073	0.100	**0.409**	0.090	**2.703**
KHM	0.002	1.162	0.114	**0.206**	0.060	**0.241**	0.111	0.193	**0.670**	0.112	**4.406**
IDN	0.001	0.001	0.762	0.042	0.012	0.047	0.021	0.024	0.116	0.022	**0.631**
MYS	0.007	0.013	**0.221**	1.271	0.101	**0.455**	0.207	**0.233**	**0.989**	0.183	**5.376**
PHL	0.003	0.006	0.118	**0.232**	0.836	**0.238**	0.119	0.135	**0.661**	0.101	**3.611**
SGP	0.011	0.019	**0.426**	**0.709**	0.158	1.266	0.294	**0.380**	**1.443**	**0.265**	**7.531**
THA	0.005	0.033	**0.234**	**0.421**	0.122	**0.418**	0.894	**0.304**	**1.135**	0.192	**6.195**
VTN	0.000	0.005	0.021	0.038	0.012	0.041	0.019	1.952	0.117	0.018	**0.686**
CHN	0.002	0.004	0.065	0.114	0.032	0.123	0.063	0.080	1.207	0.066	**2.338**
IND	0.001	0.002	0.039	0.068	0.020	0.080	0.037	0.049	0.214	0.632	**1.209**
OECD	0.001	0.005	0.096	0.175	0.053	0.185	0.096	0.114	0.612	0.100	4.162

Note: Highlighted are the values greater than 0.20.
Source: Asia Competitiveness Institute and The World Bank.

Table 1.2. Five-Year Multiplier Effects of a One Percent Point Positive Growth Shock on Each of the Eleven Economies (Post-2010)

	Engine of Growth										
	Eight ASEAN Economies								**Control Economies**		
	BRN	**KHM**	**IDN**	**MYS**	**PHL**	**SGP**	**THA**	**VTN**	**CHN**	**IND**	**OECD**
BRN	0.753	0.009	0.163	**0.203**	0.048	0.180	0.122	**0.266**	**0.745**	0.131	**3.266**
KHM	0.006	1.169	0.184	**0.263**	0.070	**0.318**	0.166	**0.282**	**1.078**	0.151	**4.533**
IDN	0.001	0.003	0.770	0.048	0.013	0.053	0.027	0.040	0.177	0.031	**0.665**
MYS	0.012	0.023	**0.281**	1.278	0.104	**0.451**	**0.238**	**0.358**	**1.426**	**0.221**	**5.243**
PHL	0.006	0.013	0.177	**0.244**	0.844	**0.288**	0.162	**0.241**	**1.035**	0.141	**3.971**
SGP	0.019	0.036	**0.511**	**0.711**	0.154	1.277	**0.328**	**0.552**	**2.014**	**0.309**	**7.333**
THA	0.010	0.057	**0.319**	**0.438**	0.128	**0.425**	**0.929**	**0.448**	**1.636**	**0.239**	**6.131**
VTN	0.000	0.007	0.030	0.042	0.012	0.041	0.025	1.970	0.178	0.024	**0.706**
CHN	0.003	0.009	0.092	0.127	0.038	0.135	0.083	0.136	1.397	0.088	**2.398**
IND	0.003	0.004	0.056	0.072	0.019	0.083	0.041	0.076	**0.297**	**0.642**	**1.188**
OECD	0.005	0.013	0.157	**0.215**	0.065	**0.232**	0.139	**0.224**	**1.048**	0.147	4.747

Note: Highlighted are the values greater than 0.20.
Source: Asia Competitiveness Institute and The World Bank.

Table 1.3. Differences in Multiplier Effects for Pre-2010 and Post-2010 Tables

	Engine of Growth										
	Eight ASEAN Economies								Control Economies		
	BRN	KHM	IDN	MYS	PHL	SGP	THA	VTN	CHN	IND	OECD
BRN	0.002	0.006	–0.023	0.075	0.006	0.043	0.049	0.166	0.336	0.041	0.563
KHM	0.004	0.007	0.070	0.057	0.010	0.077	0.055	0.089	0.408	0.039	0.127
IDN	0.000	0.002	0.008	0.006	0.001	0.006	0.006	0.016	0.061	0.009	0.034
MYS	0.005	0.010	0.060	0.007	0.003	–0.004	0.031	0.125	0.437	0.038	–0.133
PHL	0.003	0.007	0.059	0.012	0.008	0.050	0.043	0.106	0.374	0.040	0.360
SGP	0.008	0.017	0.085	0.002	–0.004	0.011	0.034	0.172	0.571	0.044	–0.198
THA	0.005	0.024	0.085	0.017	0.006	0.007	0.035	0.144	0.501	0.047	–0.064
VTN	0.000	0.002	0.009	0.004	0.000	0.000	0.006	0.018	0.061	0.006	0.020
CHN	0.001	0.005	0.027	0.013	0.006	0.012	0.020	0.056	0.190	0.022	0.060
IND	0.002	0.002	0.017	0.004	–0.001	0.003	0.004	0.027	0.083	0.010	–0.021
OECD	0.004	0.008	0.061	0.040	0.012	0.047	0.043	0.110	0.436	0.047	0.585

Source: Asia Competitiveness Institute and The World Bank.

1.2.5 Rising China and Economic Restructuring in the Era of New Normal

As pivotal to China rising, first sufficiently by 2010 to overtake Japan in GDP terms to emerge as second only to the US then to assume the same mantle of leadership in Asia, a multi-pronged approach is clearly discernible. China has arrived in more ways than one, with President Xi at the helm in announcing a series of initiatives in 2014 as counter-recessionary measures, which are part of the drive towards confronting and coping with the New Normal while still achieving the China dream.[41]

[41] Gracie (2014) describes the anti-corruption measures and the plans for economic reforms put in place under President Xi, as part of the China dream and New Normal slogans to confront and cope with economic restructuring and rebalancing. President Xi first highlighted the need for a New Normal in Henan Province in May 2014, with further elaboration at the November 2014 Asia-Pacific Economic Cooperation meeting in Beijing; see Xinhuanet (2014). The China dream, first announced by President Xi Jinping in November 2012 while at an exhibition at the National Museum of China in

Using the historical Silk Road as a focal point to brand China's international aspirations, additional evocative by-products have emerged under this aegis to carry this movement forward.[42] Beside the B&R initiative,[43] other simultaneous strategic moves include the China-initiated AIIB and China's US$50 million donation to the Food and Agriculture Organisation (FAO) of the United Nations (UN) to support South-South cooperation among others.[44]

This reinforcing of China's economic *raison d'être* is geared as an assurance of China's peaceful rise by engaging ASEAN as strategic partners. As shown in Figure 1.3, China clearly has ambitions beyond ASEAN or Asia in terms of its serial assembly of trade routes.[45] The timing and sequential unveiling is interesting. With the 21st Century Maritime Silk Road announced in 2013, followed with more clarity and thought on the AIIB, China responds to the GFT and the New Normal in 2014, while at the same time not conceding the China dream re-emphasised for good measure, albeit problematically.

In substance, the AIIB is most logical as a compelling line of economic reasoning, first to reflect that China has the financial means to

---

Beijing, was reiterated at the Boao Forum conference in March 2015; see Yang (2012), Xi (2015) and Tan *et al.* (2015) for more.

[42] See the ACI Catalogue of the AECV2030 for media materials including the "19th Investment & Trade Forum for Cooperation between East and West China & the Silk Road International Exposition" in 22–26 May 2015 in Xi'an, aimed to promote communication and cooperation along the Silk Road Economic Belt.

[43] The B&R initiative include both the overland Silk Road Economic Belt and the 21st Century Maritime Silk Road, for which President Xi announced a US$40 billion Silk Road Fund in November 2014; see Kennedy and Parker (2015) and Tian (2015).

[44] See the ACI Catalogue of media materials for details of these announcements, notably views, controversies and debate from the rest of the world on such path-breaking strategies in general, and the AIIB as rival to the World Bank and Asian Development Bank (ADB), in particular.

[45] See Page (2014a) and Page (2014b).

Figure 1.3. New Silk Roads

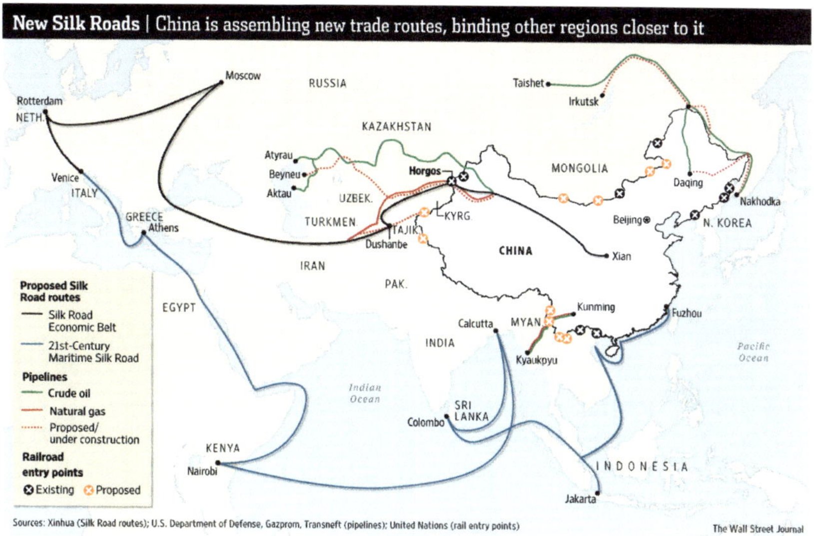

Source: The Wall Street Journal.[46]

plug the gap to invest in infrastructure in Asia and mimic the Asian Development Bank (ADB) as an adjunct of the World Bank. The McKinsey Global Institute has indicated that ASEAN requires US$7 trillion in 2013 real dollar terms for infrastructure, housing and commercial space from 2014 to 2030.[47] The Asian Development Bank Institute (ADBI) also noted infrastructure investment needs for connectivity of the 32 developing member countries in Asia and the Pacific to be at US$8.22 trillion between 2010 and 2020, and specifically, US$5.47 trillion for East and Southeast Asia, or 67% of the total (see Table 1.4). Many scholars, policymakers, representatives of the

[46] From Page (2014a).

[47] See McKinsey Global Institute (2014, 85–88).

Table 1.4. National Infrastructure Investment Needs in Asia, 2010–2020: Sub-region and Sector (2008 US$ billion)

Sector/Subsector	East and Southeast Asia	South Asia	Central Asia	The Pacific	Total
Electricity	3,182.46	653.67	167.16	—	4,003.29
Transportation	1,593.87	1,196.12	104.48	4.41	2,898.87
Airports	57.73	5.07	1.41	0.10	64.31
Ports	215.20	36.08	5.38	—	256.65
Rails	16.14	12.78	6.03	0.00	34.95
Roads	1,304.80	1,142.20	91.65	4.31	2,542.97
Telecommunications	524.75	435.62	78.62	1.11	1040.10
Telephones	142.91	6.46	4.45	0.05	153.87
Mobiles	339.05	415.87	71.97	0.95	827.84
Broadband	42.78	13.29	2.21	0.11	58.39
Water and Sanitation	171.25	85.09	23.40	0.51	280.24
Water	58.37	46.12	8.60	0.14	113.22
Sanitation	112.88	38.97	14.80	0.36	167.02
Total	5,472.33	2,370.50	373.66	6.02	8,222.50

Source: Bhattacharyay (2010).[48]

World Bank Group and members of the intelligentsia from across the Asian region have reiterated the critical nature of infrastructure investments and the timeliness for said developments at this stage of Asian economic growth.[49] As equally reasonable is China's own capability in infrastructure with the SOEs in the lead, having showcased itself in the

[48] See Bhattacharyay (2010, 11–13, Table 5).

[49] At the 2014 ACI Annual Conference, speakers presented their findings on the infrastructure needs of Asia, the AIIB and infrastructure cooperation between emerging powers; see Gopalan (2014), Mandri-Perrott (2014) and Wuryanto (2014).

Beijing Olympics in 2008[50] and bullet trains linking Beijing and Shanghai,[51] in the first instance.

It is unsurprising, in terms of geo-economics (not least, geopolitics too), that when the finalised list of prospective founding members of the AIIB was announced in April 2015, some 57 countries had applied and received approval.[52] They include the European nations of Britain, France, Germany, Italy, and Norway, as well as Russia, Australia and South Korea, which submitted their applications just prior to the closing date.[53] This further demonstrates the far-reaching prospective benefits that can be gained from a joint cooperative arrangement for development in Asia. It is equally of no surprise that the US, Canada and Japan have not chosen to become founding members, but Taiwan's wish to participate has run into the usual difficulties.[54]

Undoubtedly, the AIIB epitomises the tussle between the traditional American lead in Asia and a rising China, to contain or accommodate, in economic terms as well. Against this new development in global economic architecture along with many new ASEAN financial institutional arrangements and FTAs,[55] the AIIB rising to the occasion is in

---

[50] See Thomas (2008) on the assessment of the International Olympic Committee on the Beijing Olympics.

[51] See Tian (2011) for details on the opening of the Beijing-Shanghai bullet train.

[52] Of the applicant countries, 34 are from Asia, 18 from Europe, two from Africa, two from Oceania and one from Latin America; see Zheng (2015).

[53] See Kajimoto *et al.* (2015) and Kuo (2015) for more on the countries that applied to join the AIIB in early 2015.

[54] See Sender (2015) for more on the debate within Japan for joining the AIIB, as well as Cole (2015) and Zheng (2015) on Taiwan's application for the AIIB membership.

[55] The updating of the post-Asian Financial Crisis (AFC) Chiang Mai Initiative (CMI) currency swap arrangements into the more substantial US$240 billion Chiang Mai Initiative Multilateralisation (CMIM) agreement in 2009, along with the ASEAN+3 Macroeconomic Research Office (AMRO) surveillance unit for the monitoring and ongoing assessment of financial situations in CMIM member countries to detect emerging vulnerabilities and evaluate repayment capacity of borrowers, are two such

reality healthy for both China in particular and Asia in general, *sans* Japan.

Japan's exceptionalism is also in more ways than one, going from the leader in the Asian miracle to a much-subdued Japan, which Prime Minister Shinzo Abe tries to revive through the three arrows of Abenomics.[56] Simultaneously, Japan is also awakening to its nationalism and sovereignty, as after generations of compliance to its American alliance, a new Japan faced with a rising China is as needful. This calls for as much strategic economic creativity as innovation in products by its superior S&T as well as R&D.[57] This movement towards taking the high technology path is also evident in China, which is realigning from being the factory of the world towards Premier Li's "Made in China 2025" outline announced in March 2015.[58] A rising China meeting the US in a post-GFT era with its allies in the EU and Japan is timely for China to seize its opportunity.

In view of the shifting response by the US, from the initial rejection of the AIIB,[59] the US probably did rethink of the AIIB as it became increasingly global by its array of founding members, more so with the 'Asianisation' of existing Western-led international economic architecture

---

institutions calibrated and designed in response to the GFT, to strengthen regional financial safety nets. See Kawai, Morgan and Rana (2014, 83–92).

[56] The three arrows of Abenomics are: an aggressive monetary policy, fiscal consolidation and the hardest, socio-economic reforms as a growth strategy. See Yoshino and Taghizadeh-Hesary (2014).

[57] In 2010, Japan promulgated its Cool-Japan Initiative coupled with Cool Japan Fund Inc. in 2013 to position its creative industry as a new driver, as one of its 21 strategic projects for a rebirth of Japan, akin to what the UK did successfully in 1997. See Ministry of Economy, Trade and Industry (2010 and 2013).

[58] To this end, the Chinese government has set aside a fund of 40 billion yuan to support small- and medium-sized enterprises, as well as emerging industries as part of the "Made in China 2025" plan. For more, see Abe (2015).

[59] Parallels may be drawn to the US response post-AFC in rejecting the creation of an Asian Monetary Fund (AMF).

in finance and trade. The US cannot afford to miss the opportunity to influence the AIIB in conforming to corporate governance standards and best practices. It has since relented, as "the United States stands ready to welcome new institutions into the international development architecture," declaring that "co-financing projects with one or more of the existing institutions…" like the ADB and the Global Infrastructure Fund under the World Bank Group would mean "the lessons of the past 70 years are respected and the high quality standards developed over time are maintained".[60]

Indeed, the AIIB promises to offer a new approach towards multilateral decision-making, as it is more consensual. On veto powers, a further iteration by the Chinese Foreign Ministry declared that "no such powers even exist within the new bank's shareholder system,"[61] hence "the notion of China seeking for or giving up the veto power in the AIIB does not make sense."[62] Thus, while China may be the largest subscriber to the AIIB, paying half of the initial subscribed capital of US$50 billion,[63] in place of powers of veto, China's SOEs with good ROIs stand to profit as the developers in infrastructure. China will also gain goodwill across Asia.

The prospect of increased competition between the multilateral development banks, including the BRICS New Development Bank (NDB)[64], as well as the diversity encompassed by the broad

[60] See Sheets (2015) for the full commentary on multilateral development banks by Nathan Sheets, Under Secretary for International Affairs at the US Treasury of the Obama administration.

[61] See China Central Television (2015).

[62] Foreign Ministry Spokesperson Hua Chunying confirmed this when responding to a question on the power of veto in the AIIB at a press conference on March 25, 2015. For more, see Ministry of Foreign Affairs of the People's Republic of China (2015).

[63] The authorised capital is set as US$100 billion. See Reisen (2015).

[64] Conceived at the 5th BRICS Summit in Durban, South Africa, the NDB, which is to be operational by end of 2015, starts with US$50 billion, increasing to $100 billion over

representation of countries among the AIIB's founding members, may well lead to improvements in how global institutions are managed, and also upward pressures to increase support for Asian infrastructure, to contribute to the reform and raising of international standards for project selection and project monitoring.[65]

Two cases stand out prominently as an infrastructure war seems to be in the making. First, on 21st May 2015, Japan upped its *ante* on the AIIB as Prime Minister Shinzo Abe announced a big increase for infrastructure investment in Asia, together with its affiliation in the ADB.[66] While China-initiated AIIB has a planned capital of US$100 billion, Japan and the ADB will jointly add US$110 billion to finance innovative infrastructure in the next 5 years from 2015, which is a hefty increase of 30% over past funding. Furthermore, a Japan-Mekong summit took place in July 2015, where Japan pledged US$6.1 billion in aid to support the Mekong Five of Cambodia, Thailand, Vietnam, Myanmar and Laos, in a bid to increase Japanese influence in the region to balance the rise of China.[67] Japan has been involved indirectly through the ADB in the Greater Mekong Basin for the six economies, namely

---

time, contributed equally by Brazil, Russia, India, China and South Africa; each cannot increase its share of capital without all other four members agreeing. See Rajendran (2014).

[65] On April 2015, Singapore's Deputy Prime Minister Tharman Shanmugaratnam commented on the benefits of competition between the AIIB and Western-led institutions of the World Bank and the International Monetary Fund (IMF), as well as the possibility of having a candidate from Singapore represented within the management of the AIIB, which would enhance the multinational standing of the bank's management. See Yong (2015) and Mayeda and Chen (2015).

[66] Prime Minister Abe announced a "Partnership for Quality Infrastructure" plan by the Japanese government in May 2015, to support Asian infrastructure through significantly increasing financing, empowering Japanese multilateral institutions and improving cooperation on the ground between countries. See Fensom (2015).

[67] Specifically, the Dawei special economic zone, which Myanmar and Thailand jointly invested in, was singled out as a project of interest to the Japanese. See Harding (2015).

Cambodia, China (specifically Yunnan Province and Guangxi Zhuang Autonomous Region), Laos, Myanmar, Thailand and Vietnam since 1992. This Greater Mekong Sub-region (GMS) programme celebrated two decades of cooperation in 2012.[68]

The other case is of the US, which may require some rethinking although it is not a founding AIIB member. An official from the US State Department revealed on 16 June 2015 that a new Asia infrastructure facility to "coordinate and market US infrastructure to the region" was being considered.[69] Whether this is "a race to the top in corporate governance, and not a race to the bottom,"[70] in making developing Asia better off, Asia is definitely best off with both funding and creative ways the powers-to-be are competing for to finesse hard and soft infrastructure.

Both the AIIB and the AECV2030 encompassing the 21st Century Maritime Silk Road and China dream are both still works-in-progress, and after-thoughts and new initiatives such as B&R are following up at their heels. The new team at the political helm under President Xi Jinping is testing the wind for reactions from the region and world at large, as ideas and pronouncements are floated. Some ideas such as the AIIB came to crystallisation of sorts, but others are awaiting further assessment of B&R; nonetheless, all ideas merge together as China's ambition at home and abroad. Incessantly in the media around the world,[71] and discussed by many think tanks and consultancy companies,

---

[68] See ADB (2012).

[69] A director of Maritime Southeast Asia Affairs at the US State Department shared that the in-the-works facility would operate as a "one-stop shop", aimed at providing comprehensive infrastructure solutions by coordinating between individual US actors to offer ready-made packages for projects, similar to those competitors from Japan and China. See Parameswaran (2015a).

[70] See Mahbubani (2015a).

[71] See for instance "ASEAN's Connectivity Challenge" in *The Diplomat*, 27 June 2015 by Teodoro (2015); "Will the AIIB one day matter?" by Pettis (2015) as reported in

China remains in the limelight, with a couple of reports by Moody's[72] exemplifying the sentiments, both responses and challenges.

Amidst the geopolitics of disputes over the Spratly Islands concerning many in ASEAN and with Japan taking a harsher military and naval stance over Diaoyu / Senkaku Islands, while on the other hand pursuing the AIIB and B&R, the geo-economics has to be more realistic. As Professor Wang Gungwu noted, Chinese civilisation has historically focused on accumulating "economic wealth and technological brilliance", this remains true, be it in the guise of the AIIB or B&R.[73] It is more so with rapidly growing China, given sufficient financial wherewithal at its disposal. The core of his argument is that in the last decade or so, the rise of China and India has changed the power balance and some pushback can be discerned from the Eurasian core.[74] Notably, the naval power rivalry between the US and China is worrisome given the territorial disputes in the South China Sea and the East China Sea.

In the era of New Normal, China is faced with challenging circumstances of excess capacity as the export machinery slows down, and surplus of capital as local investment opportunities narrow, which fundamentally resulted from the policy-induced economic rebalancing strategy. China is to encourage domestic demand through services

---

Foreign Policy, 11 April 2015; "Beijing's Master Plan for the South China Sea" by Zhang (2015) reported in *Foreign Policy*, 23 June 2015; and "In Indonesia, Caution Urged With China's New 'Silk Road' Plans" in *Jakarta Globe*, 31 May 2015.

[72] Two releases in July 2015 by Moody's Investor Services provided analysis covering about two-thirds of the sovereigns across the Belt and Road, with more than half rated as sub-investment grade. See Moody's (2015a, 2015b).

[73] Wang's essay in *The Straits Times,* 1 June 2015, was part of the SG+50: Future Trends 2065 Essay Series and came a day after the Shangri-La Dialogue, a high-level security summit that brought together top defence officials from around the world; see Wang (2015a). This is followed by his essay by invitation entitled "China's Eurasia strategy to counter US naval power" in *The Straits Times,* 1 August 2015; Wang (2015b).

[74] See Ooi (2014).

sectors such as e-commerce, financial services and lifestyle-driven demand, which have seen some good employment creation in 2015. As dependency on external demand for China is reduced, the slowing export markets in the US and EU had led to significant job losses and redundancies in the manufacturing sector. The ongoing economic restructuring thus calls for industrial revamping, to reform SOEs further and greater investment diversification. Capacity utilisation rates are measured by dividing output by capacity; the capacity utilisation of China's steel industry as of 2015 has slipped below 70% while rates of other steel producing countries are at around 90%. Excess capacity and finding outlet are perhaps amongst the most serious problems China is confronting.

In the transition of economic rebalancing, the push for urbanisation is yet to produce the level of domestic demand needed to sustain the much needed employment creation with the GDP growth at 7%. The B&R strategy thus would help to re-direct excess capacity and surplus capital out from China, but how to attract them and accommodate those much-in-need economies of Asia requires both coordination and synergy under the AECV2030 strategy. Social stability is as crucial an ingredient to macroeconomic stabilisation as full employment, price stability and a sustainable rate of economic growth. Having achieved quantitative economic growth, qualitative economic development is timely. Environmental sustainability goes together with economic sustainability. Switching from export-led focus to domestic-driven demand is easier said than done. However, in all politics, it is domestic politics that prevails, as always.

1.2.6 The Window of Opportunities and Challenges for AECV2030

A further justification for the AECV2030 stems from Maddison's ground-breaking work as an economic historian who documented

Table 1.5. Relative Shares of Global Gross Domestic Product by Percentage for Major Economies: 1–2030 A.D. (%)

% / year	1	1000	1500	1600	1700	1820	1870	1913	1950	1973	2003	2030
China	25.4	22.1	24.9	29.0	22.3	32.9	17.1	8.8	4.6	4.6	15.1	25.0
India	32.0	28.1	24.4	22.4	24.4	16.0	12.1	7.5	4.2	3.1	5.5	12.0
Japan	1.1	2.7	3.1	2.9	4.1	3.0	2.3	2.6	3.0	7.8	6.6	8.0
A Total	58.6	52.9	52.3	54.2	50.9	51.9	31.5	18.9	11.8	15.5	27.3	45.0
Western Europe	13.7	9.1	17.8	19.8	21.9	23.0	33.1	33.0	26.2	25.6	19.2	17.0
US	0.3	0.4	0.3	0.2	0.1	1.8	8.9	18.9	27.3	22.1	20.6	21.0
Russia	1.5	2.4	3.4	3.4	4.4	5.4	7.5	8.5	9.6	9.4	3.8	5.0
B Total	15.4	11.9	21.5	23.4	26.4	30.2	49.5	60.4	63.1	57.1	43.6	43.0
A + B Total	74.0	64.7	73.8	77.7	77.3	82.2	81.0	79.4	74.8	72.5	70.9	**88.0**

Source: Maddison (2007) and Asia Competitiveness Institute.[75]

global GDP estimates for respective countries and regions beginning from 1 A.D. Maddison demonstrated that from year 1 A.D. to 1820, the bulk of global GDP resided with China, India and Japan; a total of 51.9% *vis-à-vis* 30.2% for Europe, US and Russia.[76] In particular, the tilt of GDP from Asia to the West only occurred in 1870, when the total GDP for Europe, US and Russia surpassed the total GDP of China, India and Japan for the first time.

This state of affairs is reversing with continuous global rebalancing of GDP. Table 1.5 shows both Maddison's results up to 2003, together with the ACI updates of global GDP shares to 2030. Indeed, 2030 is poised as the year when total GDP of Asia surpasses the West again

[75]Adapted from Maddison (2007, 381, Table A.6) with estimations for 2030 done by the ACI.

[76]See Maddison (2007, 381).

after a hiatus of 160 years. This reinforces the changing global state of play in growth and competitiveness with a difference. The transferring of industrial technology from developed countries to developing countries through the FG Model and the EAED model has enabled Asia, particularly China, to rise as a challenger to the West and Japan. East Asia with rising China is aggressive in opening up to globalisation and the lessons of history are a force to be reckoned with. By coupling globalisation with soft connectivity via ICT, much more expedient progress is made. Asia makes no apology for the role of government. The private sector as a mingling of foreign MNCs and local small- and medium-sized enterprises (SMEs) requires time to grow. SOEs need to do their share of privatisation as and when they are ready since state capitalism does create opportunities and space as the private sector matures.

Inevitably, as the AECV2030 presages Asia rising as a whole, a revisit to relative shares of global GDP by Maddison (2007) is germane. The world has come a long way since the traditional land and sea trade routes were first used. Given the evolution and development of modern intermodal land, air and sea linkages for transportation of people and cargo, not least, the overlaying of ICT over these dynamics for logistical processing purposes, Table 1.5 suggests an immense opportunity for the AECV2030; but first, a convergence of mindsets is imperative.

After all, Asia boasts of hosting some two-thirds of global humanity, with an estimated population of 4.43 billion people as of 2014.[77] An Asian dream envisioned in the AECV2030 is distinctly different in power structure and dynamics as Asia regains its share in global GDP. Yet, the Western powers may still lead in S&T and R&D in another provocative balancing game for all. Asia working together, as per the AECV2030, needs more thinking-through by all to achieve a balanced and sustainable economic growth and development, commensurate with environmental sustainability.

[77] See World Population Statistics (2014).

China's meteoric economic rise through its own unique variation of the traditional EAED model managed to achieve an average of 9.9% growth "for more than three decades spanning from 1979 to 2011,"[78] as well as great economies of scale and potential for expansion and profitability. This catapulted China to become the largest economy in the world after the US. The inevitable New Normal is as much induced by the economic restructuring, which switched emphasis from quantitative to qualitative GDP growth as it is also time for China to attend to its socio-cultural competitiveness in terms of more equitable income distribution and environmental sustainability. China has as much to learn from Japan's success descending to stagnation with deflation and demographic ageing.

India, as the other large emerging economy with billion-plus population, exhibits great promise as "the second fastest growing major economy in the world" with an average GDP growth rate of 7.5% from 2000 to 2010 and US$4.7 trillion nominal GDP in 2012, ranking India as the third in the world for adjusted GDP by purchasing power parity.[79] How India, with infrastructure as its biggest obstacle, will gain from the AIIB remains to be seen.

Certainly, a vision for regional Asian integration cannot neglect the emergence of Indonesia, which is expected to be one of the six countries that will contribute to approximately 50% of global economic growth from 2011 to 2025.[80] Indonesia is a nation "abundant in natural resources, [with] strategic access to the global mobility network" and is the fourth most populous nation in the world, possessing a significant population dividend with more than 60% of the population aged under 69.[81]

---

[78] See Tan *et al.* (2013d, 4).

[79] See Tan *et al.* (2013c, 1).

[80] The six countries are Brazil, China, India, Indonesia, Russia and South Korea, as per the World Bank's report "Global Development Horizons" released in May 2011. See The World Bank (2011).

[81] See Tan *et al.* (2013a, 35).

Given the development in emerging Asia and the readiness of China to realise its regional ambitions through the B&R and the founding of the AIIB, the time is right for ASEAN, China and India to mobilise as stakeholders to achieve mutual interests. With the formulation of the post-2015 agenda for the ASEAN Economic Community 2015, realising objectives of the B&R through exporting overcapacity of Chinese industries through infrastructure construction and exporting surplus capital through internationalisation of Renminbi should benefit its Asian neighbours;[82] the ASEAN-China partnership has acquired a new strategic and economic dimension.

The ASEAN way to achieve commercially viable development with the shared principle of non-interference in internal affairs remains paramount as guiding tenets in the B&R and AIIB, and their related financial, economic and trade integration, with synergistic infrastructure investment. This window of opportunity provides both parties with valuable leverage for a win-win situation, and the AECV2030 is positioned to solicit the views of stakeholder countries as a professional third-party institute, to canvas and present the views in an objective manner through independent study. The economic trade-offs involved in balancing the debt burden assumed by the AECV2030 countries for connectivity projects and the output gains via exports requires a regional planning perspective, which the ACI seeks to facilitate and provide.

This line of thinking was reflected in a special feature on the B&R published in a *Lianhe Zaobao* article, translated as "The opportunities and challenges brought to our region", where it highlighted that ASEAN, India and China think tanks could form a network that would become a foundational pillar or guide-post for the development of the B&R.[83] To this end, it was further revealed in the article that the ACI would be

---

[82] For an analysis of the objectives of the B&R plan and its credit implications for countries along the routes, see Moody's (2015a, 2015b).

[83] See Chia (2015) for a Special Interview Report on the OBOR by *Lianhe Zaobao* in honour of China's October 1st National Day celebrations, originally entitled 《给本区域带来商机与挑战》.

signing Memorandums of Understanding (MOUs) with national think tanks from each of the ASEAN-10 by 2015. This would position the ACI as the platform to analyse and study respective national think tanks' policy research outputs, to understand each country's respective national interests and investment needs for the AECV2030. For all interested parties of the AECV2030 and B&R, the analogy would be that think tanks are able to open a window of opportunities, but the onus for jumping through remains with the various parties themselves.

National think tanks in particular can help interested parties to understand what each country's development priorities are and know where to focus, that is, to best accommodate and match efforts or processes across countries. It was argued that the gains for ASEAN from the B&R are conditional upon ASEAN refraining from choosing sides or breaking apart. ASEAN countries need to be careful to not be seen as the spokesperson of any of the big powers, as the ASEAN philosophy of neutrality remains paramount. However, if parties remain suspicious of the B&R, they risk getting sidelined or marginalised if they do not closely follow this momentous trend.

The AECV2030, with maritime ASEAN and mainland ASEAN in synchrony, hence seeks to rationalise Asia's growing economic wealth with the compelling forces coming from rising China and potentially rising India. Indonesia, with its historic leadership in ASEAN as an economic locomotive plus a soft power, may forge the friendly rivalry and competitiveness underpinning the AECV2030. Leadership on the Chinese side by President Xi twins the AECV2030. Simply put, the time is opportune for the ACI to dig deeper into a more comprehensive feasibility study for the AECV2030 with all stakeholders aboard.

1.3 Asia Economic Connectivity Vision 2030 (AECV2030) with Asian Aspirations

The AECV2030 aims to facilitate wider physical and information connectivity across Asia in as many multi-modal ways. In contrast to the old Silk Road, the AECV2030 will be thoroughly researched and canvassed in consultative exchanges with all stakeholders by the ACI; it is in essence policy-guided to forge recommendations as actionable and evidence-based. In the process, a dedicated AECV2030 database is designed and updated, drilled down to the sub-national statistical level. This allows commitment to the AECV2030 by each respective country to position its best interests from enhanced trade as an engine for growth with an infinite array of opportunities offered. There are various combinations and permutations for national as well as sub-regional involvement across ASEAN, China and India with greater confidence building. As the drive of globalisation intensifies, the leading Western and East Asian MNCs will provide FDI and expertise, including many forms of PPPs, from build-operate-transfer (BOT) to build-operate-own-and-transfer (BOOT) to design-build-finance-operate (DBFO), and other variations to suit.

With such a diverse spectrum of stakeholders and owners in projects to galvanise five broad ACI proposals, the AECV2030 is best driven by an ASEAN leadership with a track record of an open, consultative and consensual decision-making approach. This leadership role of ASEAN has been recognised by the Chinese government in making ASEAN a main priority in its diplomatic endeavours.[84] In other words, China realises that ASEAN is its best partner, to win over with trust and to bring to fruition its aspirations in Asia and beyond.

In turn, ASEAN is sufficiently pragmatic and realistic about rising China and its global ambitions. Armed with the ACI's consultative approach and ASEAN *spirit de corps* built over four decades since 1967, the ACI can help to articulate each party's competitiveness and

---

[84] In a speech by Vice Premier Zhang Gaoli on 16 September 2014 at the China-ASEAN Expo, Business and Investment Summit, he declared China's intention "on treating ASEAN as a priority direction for the peripheral diplomacy", and their commitment to "support the development and growth of ASEAN, support the community building of ASEAN, and support ASEAN's leading role in regional cooperation". See Zhang (2014).

interests comprehensively and feasibly, building bridges to link when differences in terrain arise. All can tap upon other ACI studies by national, sub-national and regional dimensions, each with rich in-house database plus extensive network with national policy think tanks, private sector actors, civil society and NGOs. What ACI does not know, it knows where to find, which is most crucial.

The importance of an ASEAN-driven vision rests upon the simple fact that it is only when the relevant stakeholders take full ownership of their concerns and issues, can their needs be most fully accounted for in the final outcome. Regional challenges need regional responses and solutions.[85] This is the basis upon which the consultative approach of the ACI operates upon, which leads to the vision of an ASEAN-centric AECV2030. The ACI functions as the facilitator to coordinate varied viewpoints of all parties involved and to collate and identify the common overlaps and respective needs in a cohesive manner. At all times, the ACI aims at providing a common frame of reference based upon its quantitative work and databases with provincial and macro level data for truly informed decision-making.

In the ACI, an opportunity for cohesive development in the region exists, as laid out in the aspirations for the AECV2030, waiting to be tapped comprehensively. In summary, the ACI aims to:

a. To work towards harmonious multilateral relations from the ASEAN core outwards towards China in its proposed AECV2030, facilitating cross-border trade and investment alongside existing

[85] In line with the consultative spirit of the AECV2030, there has been recognition of the need for ongoing dialogue between China and ASEAN for deeper mutual understanding and confidence building. To this end, a China-ASEAN NGO network was put forward at a high level people-to-people dialogue held in Nusa Dua, Bali on May 2015 led by Chinese Vice-premier Liu Yandong, bringing together over 200 members from the private sector, public sector, academia and representatives of NGOs to "address the role of civil society groups in promoting China and ASEAN cooperation". See Atmanta (2015).

pacts, FTAs and others, enhancing governance of institutions, promoting sustainable development along with poverty reduction and social inclusivity in Asia.

b. To promote the realisation of Asian aspirations of providing affordable education, improved healthcare and better housing for all, living in peaceful co-existence in good neighbourly spirit, with mutual respect, trust and dignity.

The ACI believes that these aspirations are attainable as basic human goals deserving of a wider Asian community. It needs economic commitment and political will to realise in partnership with leaders and communities through a coordinated action. A planned ACI road show will therefore present to, and engage private and public stakeholders to identify common business interests, encourage public policy formulations and stimulate catalytic changes. For confidence-building and to draw in more players, the AECV2030 that is based on actionable projects, even pilot projects if need be, is the best practical way once all are convinced of the broad vision.

1.4 ACI Mission and Commitments

As a professional policy think tank specialising in quantitative methodologies and analysis, the ACI has its clear mission and commitments towards the AECV2030, including:

a. Constructively engage all parties on the basis of Chinese initiative and ASEAN-centric consultative approach, with closer economic cooperation amongst emerging South Asian and African countries.
b. Extend the AECV2030 to capitalise on differences in economic comparative advantages, greater market accessibility to the large sub-national economies of China, Indian and Indonesia, including

ASEAN-9, through an "aid-for-trade" approach, and strengthen export competitiveness for weaker economies across continents.[86]

c. Facilitate resource flows to support Asian growth by promoting infrastructure investment, human resources capacity-building, strengthening economic resiliency and transfers of technology to economies in need across continents.
d. Overcome financing, infrastructure and production bottlenecks via various modalities of PPPs further synergised through a consultative approach among economies that are concerned with ownership, and the creation of regional production value chains that will incorporate dimensions from environmental sustainability to an economic ecosystem beneficial to all.

In particular, the ACI will measure progress and improvement through projections for ASEAN and all partners involved, up to 2030. Its methodology broadly captures the effects of changes via the development of key performance indicators (KPIs) pertaining to macroeconomics, infrastructure and human capital. The emphasis of the ACI's proposal lies in the regional build-up and accumulation of physical and human capital, through the stimulation of growth in institutional investments and the sharing of the fruits of growth via declining inequality and improved quality of life, which are captured through improvements in human capital, to achieve economies of scale,[87] and economies of scope.[88]

---

[86] Aid-for-trade are the WTO and World Bank initiatives, as discussed in the paper "Aid for Trade: Harnessing Globalisation for Economic Development" released August 2007; see The World Bank and IMF (2007, 14–26).

[87] Economies of scale refers to cost per unit of production dropping at an accelerated rate relative to increases in the volume of raw materials being processed, producing cost advantages through the scaling up of operations in magnitude. See Chandler (1990, 17–24).

[88] Economies of scope refers to variations of the number of products, which can be produced by the same unit of production using much of the same materials and processes already existent in the unit, bringing about further cost reductions. See Chandler (1990, 17–24).

Furthermore, economies of agglomeration allow for cluster specialisation, a stronger proponent for growth than sheer division of labour.[89] Combined with the resources across Asia yet to be tapped, the compelling logic and plain arithmetic of population and geo-economics by market size, purchasing power and other dynamics are a driving rationale for ASEAN to link up with China in the first instance. China also has much in mutual interests, while awaiting deeper cooperation with India led by Prime Minister Narendra Modi who has a proven track record with his Gujarat model.[90]

1.5 Proposed Physical Infrastructural Connectivity by Air, Rail, Road and Sea

The rise of advances in transportation, containerisation and shipping in revolutionising maritime trade among other land, air and ICT modalities cannot be overstated. All makes trade as absolutely rising in both traditional goods, as well as for services and other non-tradeable. Movement of people, whether permanently or temporarily, adds more dynamism to build the AECV2030 with a human touch, as the Asian way of conducting business emphasises face-to-face communication. Prefigured by Adam Smith over 200 years earlier as division of labour and specialisation, and his disciple David Ricardo in bringing in international trade, the AECV2030 moves one step further in the crucial importance of the cost of transportation for global trade. Even with ICT and over-the-wire trade, physical goods movement by containerisation

---

[89] See seminal paper by Hotelling (1929) who first broached the subject in his model, with many more edited by Glaeser (2010) and Fujita and Thisse (2002).

[90] In theory, capacity-wise, India has the size of China to be the second factory to the world, but India needs time to get itself together to harness the dynamics, be it the flying geese or East Asian economic development as models. Paradoxically, China has discipline, for its model of socialism with Chinese characteristics, while India has democracy.

may be matched in time by cargo air-borne in similar air-ships, more than imaginative science fiction.[91] All creative innovations will drastically reduce freight transportation costs as more reliable too, transforming "global transportation, commerce and manufacturing."[92]

Though the ACI can propose various modes of transportation across continents as part of the grand connectivity nexus for Asia in support of regional growth and development, the focus of the AECV2030 is maritime connectivity as a key priority. This is partly in recognition of the nature of international trade, as approximately "90% of world trade is carried by the international shipping industry."[93] The benefits are enormous as reflected by the growth in trade volumes, from ocean-liners for passengers to ships for dry bulk cargo to oil tankers for crudes and liquefied natural gas (LNG).

Such development can be illustrated by the exponential increase in global shipping since 1986 to 2006, with the widespread adoption of modern methods of international trade, as indicated in Figure 1.4 by the growth path of deadweight tonnage (DWT) in millions per unit increasing by more than 500% globally,[94] and an increase in global capacity of millions of twenty-foot equivalent units (TEUs)[95] increasing by more than threefold and the fleet of ships utilised for international trade expanding by over eight times to stand at 3,514 ships as of 1 January

---

[91] Even with airborne shipping, boundaries are still being pushed with innovative methods for delivering cargo. See Witz (2014).

[92] See Donovan (2004, 10).

[93] As reported in a position paper by the International Chamber of Shipping for the United Nations Commission on International Trade Law; see International Chamber of Shipping (2009, 1).

[94] DWT measures how much weight a ship can safely carry, or phrased differently, the maximum allowed weight when fully loaded.

[95] TEU measures the cargo capacity of container ships and terminals, though it bears mentioning that empty containers are still counted as TEU rather than tonnage, as oftentimes, they are full one-way rather than both.

Figure 1.4. World Container Fleet Development, 1986–2006

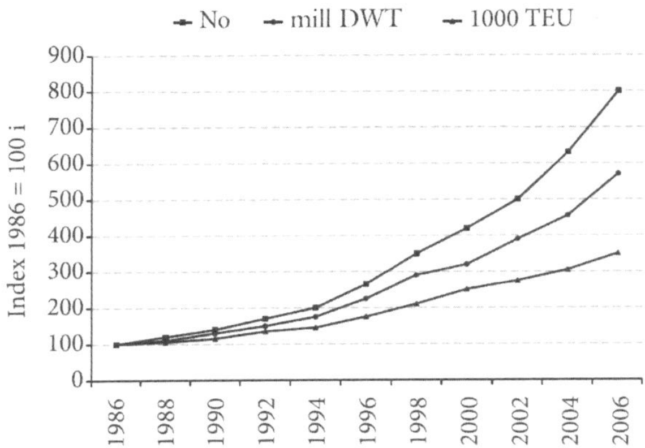

Source: Vasiliauskas and Barysiene (2008).[96]

2006.[97] One needs to look no further for examples of the international nature of shipping than this illustration of how "in today's maritime world, a Korean-built vessel might, for example, be owned by Greeks, registered in Panama, insured and classified in London and chartered by a Danish operator for a voyage under the command of an Indian master, with a Ghanaian first engineer and a Philippine crew provided by a German manning agency."[98]

With respect to the ACI's proposed routes for the AECV2030, Figure 1.5 provides one summary overview to illustrate the proposed connectivity routes for air, maritime, rail and road respectively. If implemented, the proposed multimodal routes for the AECV2030 can greatly enhance competitiveness and economic integration of the region, leading to a more efficient movement of goods, linkages of

[96] See Palmer (2011, 6).

[97] See Vasiliauskas and Barysiene (2008, 311).

[98] From Vasiliauskas and Barysiene (2008, 312, Figure 1).

Figure 1.5. Proposed Asia Economic Connectivity Vision 2030 Transportation Routes

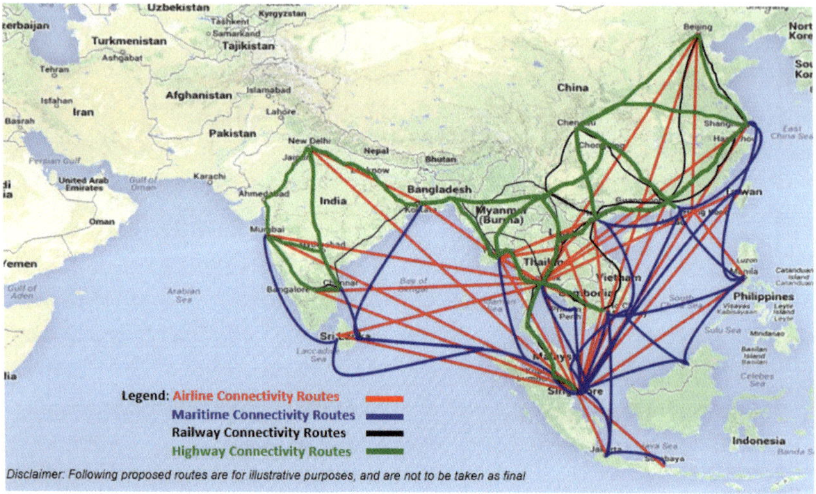

Source: Asia Competitiveness Institute.

services and people to people connections.[99] Such tentative routes of the various proposed modes of transportation need to be further refined to take into account emerging economic activities, financial viability and logistics involved for cross-border connectivity.

Again, it bears repeating that consultation with all private and public stakeholders is a long, arduous process, especially with finance and legalities such as in the case of land acquisition and resettlement, and security issues. Thus, all proposed routes remain a work-in-progress, with studies by the ACI continue to be refined and used for consultation and negotiation among all concerned parties for inputs on the suggested mapping and connectivity of aviation, maritime, railway and

[99] Multimodal transport refers to the carriage of goods by at least two differing modes of transportation.

highway routes. Insofar as infrastructural connectivity is concerned, Asia remains in need. Thus, for ASEAN in joining the dots to ensure complementary and supplementary efforts within its MPAC match China's B&R aspirations and other existing infrastructural funding, is how ASEAN-centric also works.

Under an MOU signed with the World Bank, the ACI is to support the World Bank on the Asian PPP pipeline assessment work at sub-national economy level by adopting three tools related to the PPP developed by the World Bank, which include:

(i) Infrastructure prioritisation tool, which is a methodological approach for countries to assess and determine the most appropriate interventions for infrastructure development;
(ii) PPP state of readiness, which looks at the upstream policy, regulatory and institutional issues needed as precursors for PPP;
(iii) PPP fiscal assessment tool, which is an Excel-based tool developed together with the IMF to determine the impact of PPP projects with respect to the direct and contingent liabilities that are generated as a result of governments embarking on PPPs.

1.6 Five Broad ACI Proposals with Strategic Thrusts

An active consultation process with the stakeholders as owners is paramount to the success of the AECV2030. The five broad proposals as they stand should be understood as a collage of interconnected measures, distilled from the FG model and the EAED model. The ACI's competitiveness analysis at the sub-national economy and city level would illustrate the terrain of requirements we shall need to navigate in order to cultivate the economic environment for a self-reinforcing dynamic of regional growth and development. Recognising that the various members of the AECV2030 are at differing stages of development, this approach allows the ACI to chart out the needs and interest profiles of each party, in order to provide a shared frame of reference to account for pressing regional needs. It recognises domestic constraints, so as to mark out the path of least economic resistance, to release development bottlenecks on the basis of understanding and trust in the direction towards which Asia will be moving.

The five proposals are based on market-oriented potential economic activities, financial feasibility as well as sustainable and inclusive growth under the ASEAN-centric leadership of the vision. Private and public participation would be an important guiding and operational principle, by way of detailed interests identified and clarified with the parties throughout the consultative process. These proposals will hence evolve along with the regional consultation the ACI is undertaking, while holding to the core principles that guide AECV2030. Strategic thrusts as proposed are preliminary, more for grist for the mill of policy-thinking and actionable projects.

1.6.1 Proposal One: Labour-Intensive Manufacturing Migration from Greater China, Korea, Japan and European Union to ASEAN

The whole of ASEAN is well positioned to be a leading manufacturing base, driven largely by Indonesia, Malaysia, and Thailand, supported by the CLMV, to become another factory of the world. In this first proposal, it integrates further with the development, such as the Pan-Beibu Gulf Economic Cooperation, which aims to become a "manufacturing and processing base,"[100] among other things. Proposal One will allow early adopting investors to capitalise on the availability of low-wage labour in ASEAN to increase the region's attractiveness to wider foreign investors based on the FG model of transmitted comparative

[100] See Gu and Li (2009, 18).

advantages. This will require sovereign states to consider strategic thrusts including:

i. Identifying labour-intensive manufacturing migration within China as the domestication of its flying geese paradigm and what spills over to ASEAN, especially Indonesia as resource-rich country and the CLMV as part of the AECV2030.
ii. Strengthening laws and enforcement of intellectual property rights (IPRs), including credible patent systems in order to protect foreign investors' interests and to establish trust in the local business environment, in order to generate stability for a stronger investment climate.
iii. Protecting worker rights by supporting fair labour laws and ensuring occupational health and safety standards.

With the increased investment, a streamlined production and well-networked production supply chain across the Asian continent can be established with designated manufacturing clusters. By coordinating connectivity, overlaps and redundancies can be reduced through improved communication and transmission of information, thus maximising synergistic benefits in further strategic thrusts that can be refined and condensed into workable projects through consultation such as the following:

i. Developing low-cost manufacturing clusters through partnerships with industrial partners, such as Chinese firms, to benefit from technical knowledge transfer.
ii. Streamlining and shortening supply chains to reduce complexity of transactions and increase the value-added per firm.
iii. Providing strong cross-border institutional supports to encourage innovation and growth opportunities.
iv. Promoting information sharing and facilitation of communication across firms within clusters to facilitate knowledge transfers, tapping into dynamic economies of scale via institutional linkages.

v. Early adopters in coordinated industrial investments will increase the region's attractiveness to foreign investors and facilitate greater production relocations by MNCs from Greater China, Korea, EU, Japan and US due to increased ASEAN connectivity and stability, compounding the net benefits of regional economic integration in a cascading fashion.
vi. Designating special industrial and economic zones with preferential tax treatment for MNCs as a springboard for regulatory, corporate and institutional development.
vii. Deriving valuable lessons from the Malaysia-China Kuantan Industrial Park and other joint ventures (JVs) through an open knowledge sharing process, which can be used as a blueprint for future ASEAN-China, ASEAN-Japan and other joint projects.
viii. Increasing bilateral and multilateral cooperation through initiatives such as the proposed China-Malaysia Zheng He Friendship Association for Economy, Trade and Culture to address soft connectivity.

Through the ACI proposed outline, a virtuous cycle of increased technology transfers, greater productivity spillovers and wider employment in Asia as exemplified by the FG model is to be expanded upon and sustained for the region with new technology-driven globalisation. Many other strategic thrusts include:

i. Exploiting synergy and network effects across different countries within the region for mutually beneficial relationships.
ii. Encouraging inter-industry linkages to stimulate technology and knowledge transfers.
iii. Feasibility studies and blueprints for projects exemplifying such cooperation, including the China-Malaysia Qinzhou Industrial Park, China-Singapore Suzhou Industrial Park, China-Singapore Tianjin Eco-city, China-Singapore Guangzhou Knowledge City, China-Singapore Jilin Food Safety Zone and China-Singapore Chongqing Strategic Investment Plan.

1.6.2 Proposal Two: Infrastructure Investment in Connectivity to Enhance Export-Oriented Growth, Inclusive Development and Capital Inflows

Mindful of the different stages of growth and development, in line with the EAED model of export-oriented growth strategy to jumpstart economic vibrancy, it requires both effective institutions and appropriate sequential reforms in a targeted manner to promote inclusive development and sustainable capital inflows across continents. Market viability of projects and bankability are key factors in deciding which initial investments deserve greater priority in order to increase the participation of the private sector. These structural transitions often result in labour displacement. To mitigate the effects of sectoral shifts, workers' skill upgrading for enhanced employability and job-matching programmes will be simultaneously developed to reduce frictional unemployment and to improve the labour pool. Accordingly, strategic thrusts include:

i. Investment participation, involving sovereign wealth funds (SWFs) of economies from ASEAN, China to even the Middle East and East Asia if deemed workable, with the choice of investment projects to be heavily influenced by market forces.
ii. Consolidation of existing financial resources and tapping into resources from the newly established AIIB and other multilateral development banks to jointly finance major infrastructure projects alongside crowding in of the private sector over time.
iii. With existing proven cooperation within ASEAN and ASEAN with its dialogue partners, there is much synergistic logic for the AECV2030 to be in collaboration with the MPAC.

With market players revealing their preferences within an ASEAN framework for economic contest, the development gap between more and less developed economies can then be addressed and bridged through strengthened connectivity and integration along sea, road, rail, air and ICT linkages. Investment in public utilities, power stations, dams, oil and gas transport corridors, allowing for efficient allocation of necessary resources according to a market forces and logic can link up the region according to their developmental needs. More strategic thrusts to propose include:

i. Increasing connectivity across countries by collaborating on cross-border projects as defined in the MPAC involving land, sea, air and ICT as multimodal physical transportation and communication services, which can be further extended, refined or drilled down to suit specific needs by regions, countries, states, provinces or cities, is all a matter of joining the dots in connectivity.
ii. Improving existing transportation networks and increase accessibility to inland production centres through expansion and maintenance of strategic roads and highways must be in parallel with trade facilitation, including customs and immigration procedures.
iii. Modernising and upgrading ICT as well as increasing mainstream accessibility for the wider benefit of SMEs.
iv. With improving trade efficiency, energised economic vitality and enhanced Asia competitiveness, bottlenecks in financing, infrastructure and production will be gradually unblocked, with greater movement of goods and people facilitating opportunities for partnerships.
v. Further building upon the ASEAN-China Free Trade Agreement to include more categories of goods as well as the reduction of NTBs.
vi. Supporting existing ASEAN trade facilitation mechanisms of National Single Windows (NSWs) and business friendly Rules of Origin (ROOs) as measures for a streamlined trade flow.
vii. Increased economic vitality and Asia competitiveness through job creation and entrepreneurial activity can enhance short-term employment opportunities and long-term employability of the labour force.

viii. Promoting capacity-building and capability-building in HRD through upgrading of production infrastructure in areas of comparative advantage, which will increase output and quality of exports to approach international best practice standards across the region.

1.6.3 Proposal Three: Asia as a Food Basket with Enhanced Agricultural Productivity

According to the 2009 Report by the FAO, the current world population stands at 7 billion and will reach 9 billion by 2050, and food production needs to increase by 70% to meet the proposed population growth.[101] As daunting a task as this may seem, the many advances made by China in progressing from food aid receiver to food aid donor, feeding nearly 20% of world population with 9% of the world's arable land, have shown this to be an attainable goal.[102]

In a 2014 report by the FAO, the International Fund for Agricultural Development (IFAD) and the World Food Programme (WFP), it was recognised that to address pressing food insecurity, "sustained political commitment at the highest level is a prerequisite for hunger eradication,"[103] and at the regional level, constructive action is already taking place. China's US$50 million pledge to the FAO on 15 October 2014[104] in support of South-South cooperation, with the goal of having the global south collaborate to exchange key information on development solutions to enhance food security and the propagation of sustainable agricultural development practices, is indicative of the growing

---

[101] See FAO (2009, 2).

[102] To illustrate, annual food production in China increased from 430.67 million tons in 2003 to 601.93 million tons in 2013. See Wang (2014).

[103] See FAO, IFAD and WFP (2014, 55).

[104] See FAO (2014a).

importance agricultural productivity among developed and emerging nations.[105]

Given the rapidly ageing Chinese population, growing urbanisation and the reluctance of younger farmers to stay as rural farmers, it is crucial to promote regional cooperation in agriculture, for plantation crops, fisheries, food processing and other downstream industries, as food security will be a regional concern rather than domestic.

In order to tackle this regional challenge, the emphasis needs to be on each nation's comparative advantage to maximise total regional agricultural produces and food outputs, capitalising on economies of scale to reduce input costs of food production. Strategic thrusts proposed may include:

i. Establishing modern agriculture cooperatives through PPPs to pool and share common resources.
ii. Identifying opportunities for vertical fragmentation of the food processing industry by outsourcing labour-intensive and skill-intensive processes where appropriate.
iii. Encouraging sharing of technology between countries as well as common adoption of best practices such as micro-irrigation and fertigation.[106]
iv. Focusing on production of specific food products based on each country's core competencies, climate and natural endowment of resources.
v. Reducing economic hardship for farmers by easing the transition from one food crop to another through targeted subsidies.

Agriculture remains the largest employer of labour in developing ASEAN, and the emphasis on structural transformation of agricultural

[105] See FAO (2014b).

[106] Fertigation is the agricultural practice of distributing fertilisers, nutrients and other water-soluble products through an irrigation system.

industries played a significant role in unlocking periods of high growth in the success of economies in Greater China today and poverty alleviation for rural inclusion. The role of agricultural development in emerging economies is evolving rapidly in prominence with growing integration and industrialisation of agriculture.[107] Investing in agricultural infrastructure and facilities to increase economies of scale on land and labour productivity, as well as the development and implementation of new technologies and practices to increase crop yield, grows a significant export base for ASEAN, ensuring continued relevance while concurrently pursuing sustainable urbanisation. Strategic thrusts needed may include:

i. Promoting the use of tractors, combine-harvesters and other modernised farming equipment and methods in farms and plantations to reduce the labour intensity of agriculture, increase total factor productivity and raise living standards.
ii. Land reform, which is a critical, albeit difficult, priority to garner economies of scale rather than land fragmentation by hereditary practices.
iii. Educating farmers about sustainable land management practices such as crop rotation.
iv. Improving existing infrastructure through systematic maintenance of irrigation systems and reinforcing mountain terraces to prevent soil erosion.
v. Incentivising S&T and R&D in agriculture as it is not necessarily inferior to manufacturing, to develop productivity-enhancing technologies and practices such as improved usage of fertilisers.[108]

---

[107] See Briones and Felipe (2013).

[108] Singapore has science parks and Biopolis for S&T, R&D facilities relating to agriculture, veterinary sciences, and biology beyond biological stem cell research as well as Malaysia's Palm Oil Research Institute; both measures have been successful.

vi. Developing new varieties of crops (as in green revolution *redux*) with increased resistance to common pests, bacterial infections and viruses, thus reducing the need for harmful pesticides and herbicides.
vii. Rural credit institutions, which are needed to provide farmers with loans and subsidies to increase accessibility to such new technologies and enhanced crop varieties.

To illustrate S&T and R&D initiatives for agricultural productivity, while Singapore is without any agriculture in the traditional form, it has the Agri-Food and Veterinary Authority of Singapore, which is not just for the protection of food. Together with many agro-based and biomedical-based institutes under Singapore's Agency for Science, Technology and Applied Research (A*STAR) with collaboration in universities, including a huge Biomedical Research Institutes & Consortia cluster, it has facilities for research into food baskets. Spinoffs can involve other services such as consultancy, primary services, education and training. Most crucially, its core strength is in logistics, transportation, storage and warehousing, especially of perishable products.

1.6.4 Proposal Four: Regional Cooperation on Sustainable Green and Liveable Ecosystems to Promote Urban Liveability and Environmentally-Sustainable Urbanisation

In one fell swoop, the AECV2030 going green would enable the Asian region to be more constructive and effective within the ongoing United Nations Framework Convention on Climate Change (UNFCCC) and UN Intergovernmental Panel on Climate Change (IPCC). With increased connectivity, come common challenges in maintaining and improving environmental conditions across member states, as domestic concerns gradually develop over time to become regional issues. Learning from the examples of recently industrialised Asian economies, it is important to establish, from the outset, the environmental standards to adhere to in order to devise a sustainable path of development that would not jeopardise shared regional commons, such as the preservation of the Mekong delta.

To achieve this, outlines for forestry, marine conservation, water resource management, waste management and sustainable urbanisation have been formulated. Practicing eco-friendly living habits through energy, water and resource conservation as well as promoting the use of green transportation and renewable energy can help protect the longevity of our shared ecosystems, which can benefit from sharing the experiences of more developed partners in the region, such as Singapore, to guide urban planning in other major cities. First, in relation to forestry, tentative strategic thrusts to establish a green environment through re-forestation include:

i. Encouraging rehabilitation and reforestation of abandoned plantations to establish secondary forests.
ii. Addressing the problem of haze control by regulating slash-and-burn agriculture.
iii. Supporting efforts to curb illegal logging activities in protected forests and habitats.
iv. Preventing further degradation of marginal lands through national action plans, which limit intensive agriculture to the most suitable arable lands.[109]

[109] National action plans coordinated on a regional level are already underway in West Africa. A regional partnership compact for the sustainable and competitive development of agriculture in West Africa was signed in November 2009 by key stakeholders of the Economic Community of West African States (ECOWAS). See OECD (2009).

Engaging further regional cooperation to resolve the problem of over-fishing and support for marine sanctuary and ocean resource conservation involves strategic thrusts such as:

i. Strengthening and enforcing regulations to prohibit over-fishing, especially in the case of threatened or endangered species.
ii. Adhering to seasonal limits on fishing during critical periods such as the fish-spawning season, so as to ensure that population numbers are maintained.
iii. Promoting sustainable fishing while prohibiting the use of bottom trawling and other destructive practices.
iv. Establishing a regional organisation dedicated to monitoring commercial fishing activities and ensuring compliance with limits.
v. Reaffirming each country's commitment to the United Nations Convention on the Law of the Sea, which establishes rights and responsibilities with regard to conservation of living resources in the high seas.
vi. Implementing strong laws to ensure coral reef preservation, in order to preserve marine diversity and ecological stability.
vii. Ensuring that eco-tourism activities in marine sanctuaries adhere to regulatory standards, and are only carried out by licensed tour operators.

Water resource planning and treatment are crucial to an effective functioning of an urban community. For reducing water pollution through proper waste disposal practices and water resource management, tentative strategic thrusts include:

i. Strengthening existing legal standards to prohibit the unlawful disposal of untreated hazardous waste.
ii. Conducting regular inspections and increasing monitoring of factories and heavy industries to ensure compliance with environmental waste laws.

iii. Developing waste processing technologies through PPPs such as the Mitsubishi-PUB project.
iv. Sharing of technology and knowledge from countries such as Singapore regarding water treatment techniques to provide other countries with a valuable learning model.

All these measures contribute to the promotion of the liveability of cities and environmentally sustainable urbanisation, in response to regional urbanisation growth trends across emerging Asia. Increasingly, as developing regional cities become the focal points for economic activity, their capacity to support a burgeoning community of inhabitants in an ecologically responsible way will be a key consideration. Strategic thrusts for this involve:

v. Adopting green technologies such as automated recycling of condensed water from air handling units, the use of heat pipes to reduce humidity without consuming energy and intelligent grid management systems.
vi. Investing in green spaces such as roof gardens to improve the urban environment through improved air quality, reduced heat build-up and rainfall retention, which is essential as Asia enters a period of rapid and unprecedented urbanisation.
vii. Sharing of Singapore's urban development experience to guide urban planning in other major cities.
viii. Practicing eco friendly living habits through energy, water and resource conservation, as well as promoting the use of green transportation and renewable energy.

Specifically, the ACI has built up rapport with its many flagship projects covering Asia and ASEAN as in this book, most of all at the sub-national level with provinces of Indonesia and China, as well as states and federal territories in India, including specific signing of MOUs and Letters of Intent (LOIs). Prime Minister Narendra Modi's vision to build 100 smart cities in India rhymes with the ACI's projects on liveable and smart cities. Indeed, drilling down to projects at the ground level is the only way to go to win support all round. Successful projects beget more projects and confidence-building.

1.6.5 Proposal Five: ASEAN as a Regional Trade, Business and Services Hub for Asia

With the increase in production and distribution activities regionally, services for trade and business play an ever more important role, not only for GDP, income, employment and foreign exchange earnings, but also for contributions to regional integration and the formation of an active economic community.[110] Making some ASEAN cities the prime destination for regional headquarters of business corporations with a competitive and pro-business tax regime is a logical progression given the increased production capabilities and infrastructure improvements that the region will attract through investments in physical and soft connectivity.

Existing ASEAN global telecommunication and financial services clusters are further poised to play a pivotal role in business facilitation with the greater internationalisation of the yuan or RMB taking place. While certain ASEAN and Chinese cities and localities are already deemed world-class in their own rights, there is sufficient room for more facilities, which is also keeping others on their toes in being competitive. Possible strategic thrusts may include:

i. Promoting ASEAN's strengths based on its geographic centrality as well as high degree of regional inter-connectedness.
ii. Building a pro-business environment with competitive tax regimes and governance through political stability and policy continuity to entice business corporations.

[110] See Tullao and Lim (2012, 56).

iii. Enhancing human capital resources through development of an adaptable workforce and increasing availability of key opinion leaders by enhancing liveability of ASEAN cities.
iv. Enabling ASEAN via market forces with various offshore RMB centres, by leveraging on ASEAN strengths as a wholesale funding centre in the region.
v. Increasing liquidity and circulation of the RMB denominated financial instruments in Asia through coordination with the People's Bank of China.
vi. Promoting further growth in ASEAN's non-bank and interbank RMB deposits.

Several cities in ASEAN serve as possible candidates for global trade and services hubs. As a case in point, Prime Minister Lee Hsien Loong of Singapore aims to have Changi Airport Terminal 5 operational by mid-2020 to position Singapore as one aviation hub. Another example involves plans by airport operator Angkasa Pura II to revitalise the first terminal at Soekarno-Hatta by expanding it to 204,445 square metres by 2017 from the current 144,635 square metres to accommodate 18 million passengers annually.[111] Additionally, there is Bangkok's US$1.9 billion project to expand Suvarnabhumi Airport.[112] These plans serve to facilitate ASEAN as a regional aviation, logistics and global trading hub, synergising internationalisation of the SMEs by cooperating with MNCs. Strategic thrusts include:

i. Increasing domestic port capacity and processing speed so as to facilitate cargo loading and unloading as well as reduce vessel stopover time.

[111] See Osman (2014).
[112] See Sriring (2014).

ii. Promoting ASEAN as a hub for SMEs internationalisation, given its combined population of over 600 million,[113] enabling access to a large and diverse market with significant growth potential.
iii. Establishing ASEAN as various hubs, each specialising in varying degrees as a continuum for educational, healthcare and creative services that will also bear dividends in developing the vibrancy of the region as both a tourism hub and an attractive place for highly-skilled foreign labour; leveraging upon the cultural capital of the diverse historical and ethnographical heritage of the various ASEAN members and the improvements to liveability over time.
iv. Enhancing quality of educational, healthcare and creative services by upgrading schools, hospitals and related facilities while at the same time maintaining reasonable costs for foreign students and patients.
v. Increasing the frequency of flights to and from airports located in target tourist destinations through partnerships with regional airlines, with practical and pragmatic air rights.
vi. Reducing the inconveniences and bureaucracies associated with visa procurement and customs processing for international tourists.
vii. Ensuring public order and safety as well as upgrading accommodation and public sanitation facilities in order to boost tourism receipts and ensure a reliable source of income for the local hospitality industry.

1.7 Target Performance Indicators 2030

With the ACI's in-house projections, which factor in existing patterns of regional development and growth coupled with conservative premises for realisation of the goals in the ACI's aforementioned proposal, the

[113] See McKinsey Global Institute (2014, 1–6).

Table 1.6. ASEAN Performance Indicators for 2030

ASEAN Performance Indicators for 2030	
Macroeconomic Indicators	• Gross Domestic Product (GDP) • Export of Goods and Services • Government Revenue (including grants) • Foreign Direct Investment Inflows
Infrastructure Development Indicators	• Length of Railways • Length of Roads • Electric Power Consumption
Human Capital Indicators	• Employed Population • Adult Literacy Rate • Life Expectancy at Birth • Percentage of Population Below Poverty Line

Source: Asia Competitiveness Institute.

following indicators and forecasts in improvement (see Table 1.6) serve two purposes. One is to give tangible and real outcomes for policymakers to communicate effectively with all stakeholders. Two, such KPIs enable tracking and monitoring of progress in implementation of projects to deliver the results. Further cost-benefit analysis (CBA) may emanate to aid in visualising the gains the region stands to benefit from, as well as to prioritise KPIs if needed. All serve to verify that the execution of the phases of economic connectivity development is on time for 2030.

1.7.1 Methodological Approach

Based on the different characteristics of the indicators, there are three different methods used in the projection:

- GDP is projected through comparisons with the potential output estimation.
- Projection modelling, using an autoregressive model with GDP as an independent variable.

- Indicators, which have the potential to be affected by significant policy changes or possess a lack of data points, were handled on a case-by-case basis. The target values for 2030 will be set either from existing academic studies and literature or by benchmarking.
    a. The autoregressive model with GDP as an independent variable was constructed as follows, where t denotes different time periods:

    $$Y_t = \alpha + \beta_1 * Y_{t-1} + \beta_2 * GDP_t + \varepsilon_t$$

    The model coefficients will be estimated separately for each indicator based on actual data from year 2000 to 2013 in the ACI database, or as per the latest data points when available.

    b. The estimated coefficients, together with the GDP projection from part a will be used in the following projection model:

    $$Y_t = \alpha + \beta_1 * Y_{t-1} + \beta_2 * GDP_t$$

    The projection result from the model will be "better than the past trend", as the GDP forecast for ASEAN is at an annual growth rate of 5%, which is slightly better than the potential output growth rate.[114]

    c. The regression model above is mainly based on the observed relationships, which exist between variables during the period 2000 to 2013. However, if there are major policy changes or a lack of sufficient data points for estimating the coefficients, the model will not be able to produce satisfactory projections. In these situations, the indicators were handled on a case-by-case basis. The target values for 2030 would then be estimated using information from existing academic literature or through benchmarking.

---

[114]This figure was based off the growth figure results for the ASEAN-5 (Indonesia, Malaysia, Philippines, Thailand and Vietnam) as provided by the IMF working paper *Potential Growth in Emerging Asia*. See Anand *et al.* (2014, 4–8).

1.7.2 Macroeconomic Indicators

GDP projections of 5% are based on the IMF estimated growth projections for the ASEAN-5 (Indonesia, Malaysia, Philippines, Thailand and Vietnam) (see Figure 1.6). By 2030, GDP is estimated to reach US$2.82 trillion. The adoption of the ACI's recommended proposals as per the AECV2030 plan can enable the region to capitalise on its strengths to realise this figure.

By 2030, export of goods and services by the ASEAN-10 is estimated to reach US$2.42 trillion (Figure 1.7). In line with the proposed model for export-oriented growth through the migration of manufacturing capabilities and an increase in agricultural products, the enhanced synergistic efficiencies and connected markets with lowered barriers will facilitate the continued export-driven growth of Asia through to 2030.

By 2030, FDI is estimated at US$207.42 billion (see Figure 1.8), with funds invested in building up ASEAN connectivity as a business and services hub, as well as infrastructure for competitive production capabilities within the identified clusters. FDI operates as a package

Figure 1.6. GDP Projection to 2030 for ASEAN-10

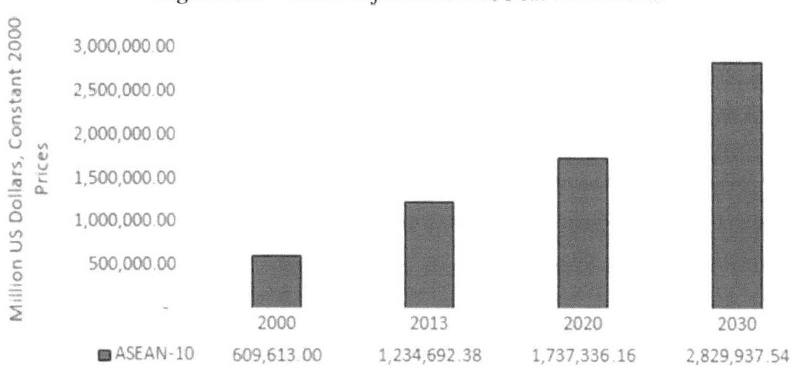

Source: Asia Competitiveness Institute.

Figure 1.7. Export of Goods and Services Projection to 2030 for ASEAN-10

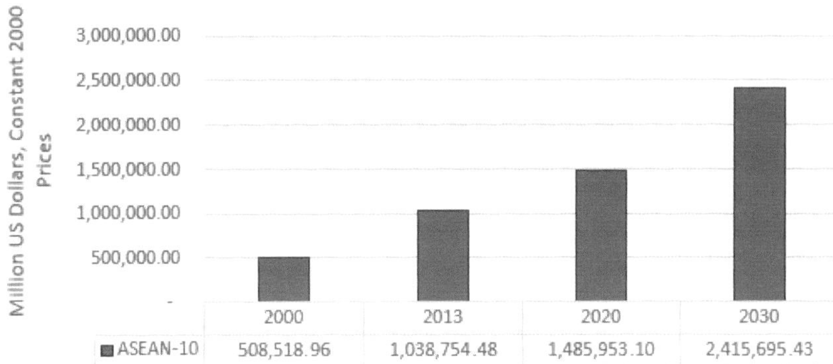

Source: Asia Competitiveness Institute.

Figure 1.8. FDI Inflows Projection to 2030 for ASEAN-10

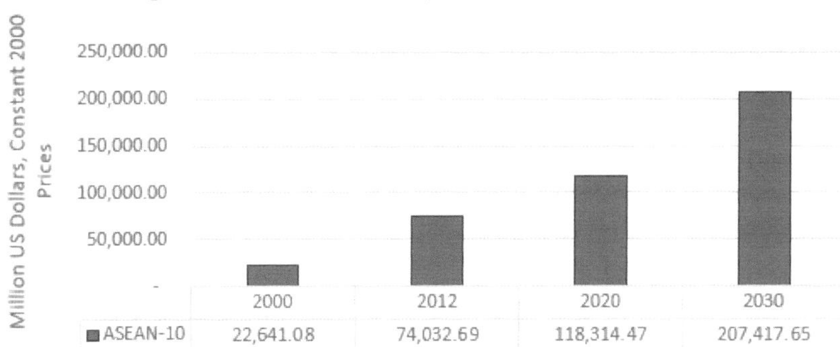

Source: Asia Competitiveness Institute.

deal, and the spillover effects of such investments extend beyond pure financial benefits when coupled with the development of stronger institutions to manage FDI.

Government revenue, as projected from recorded data and forecasted growth rates, will reach US$555.02 billion (see Figure 1.9). An

Figure 1.9. Government Revenue (including Grants) Projection to 2030 for ASEAN-10

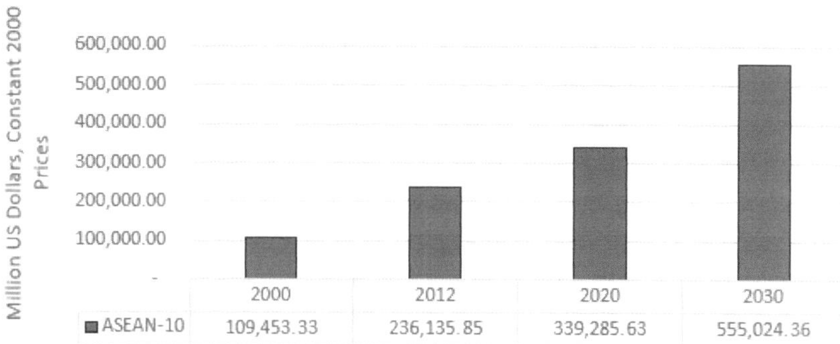

Source: Asia Competitiveness Institute.

environment for generating sustainably increasing government revenue flows requires a focus on applying funds from cross-border investments, aid-for-trade initiatives and multilateral institutions towards increasing competitiveness and growing national income. ASEAN governments, through partnership with public and private sector players across the region in developing public goods for enhancing competitiveness, will be able to improve their fiscal positions and allow for greater policy flexibility and mutually beneficial regional integration.[115]

The GDP, FDI and government revenue indicators are interconnected projected figures, and the benefits from focusing on increasing competitiveness and developing efficiencies could result in further improvements to these projections.

---

[115] For a study of growth and development strategies for ASEAN-10 economies, see Tan *et al.* (2013b).

1.7.3 Infrastructure Development Indicators

Power consumption, the other side of the coin of industrialisation, is estimated to approach 1.82 trillion kilowatts per hour by 2030 (see Figure 1.10), in line with energy needs and a potential GDP growth rate of 5%. This is a significant opportunity for energy producers and exporters, who will stand to benefit from the regions' increased economic connectivity.

By 2030, length of roads may well reach 2.61 million kilometres (see Figure 1.11). This level of road expansion requires infrastructure bottlenecks to be resolved through bilateral and multilateral cooperation, via a public-private cross-border partnership model. Relatedly, structural and regulatory alignment to achieve reduced barriers for ease of movement of goods and people will ensure a steady flow of traffic within an expanded Asian market.

Length of railways was calculated based on the requirements of an expanding ASEAN-10 economy. By 2030, length of railways may approach 28,522 kilometres (see Figure 1.12). Physical connectivity improvements need to be supplemented by shared standards for compatible physical transport infrastructure and ICT linkages across transportation institutions.

Figure 1.10. Electric Power Consumption Projection to 2030 for ASEAN-10

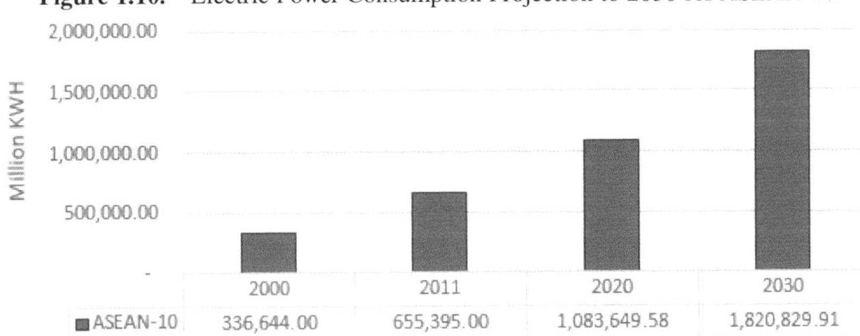

Source: Asia Competitiveness Institute.

Figure 1.11. Length of Roads Projection to 2030 for ASEAN-10

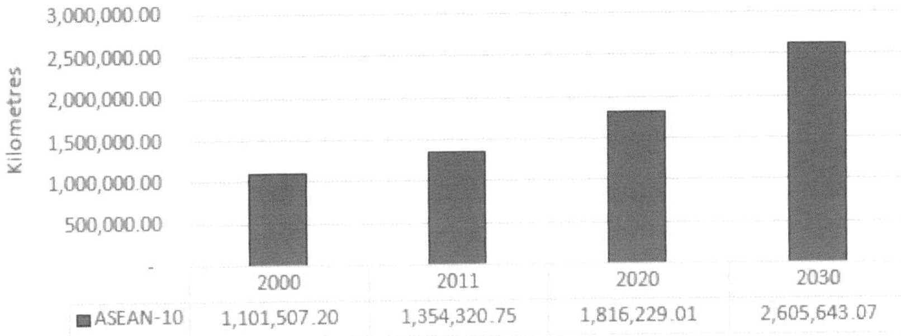

Source: Asia Competitiveness Institute.

Figure 1.12. Length of Railways Projection to 2030 for ASEAN-10

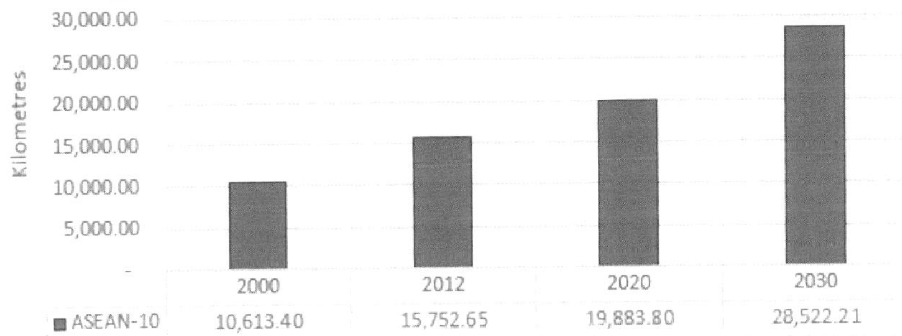

Source: Asia Competitiveness Institute.

1.7.4 Human Capital Indicators

By this measure, adult literacy rates in ASEAN would rise to 99.7% in 2030 (see Figure 1.13). Advancing literacy is a key concern of the AECV2030 in empowering the region to unleash the innovative potential within each respective culture and to move up the industrial ladder with a growing pool of skilled labour, sharing the gains of closer economic integration.

Figure 1.13. Adult Literacy Rate Projection to 2030 for ASEAN-10

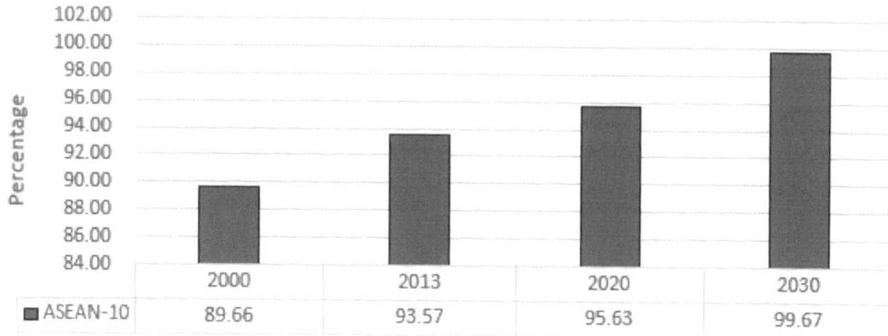

Source: Asia Competitiveness Institute.

The target set for reduction of global poverty to 3% was based on the World Bank's estimate,[116] with a decrease at an average of approximately 0.6% per year up to 2030 (see Figure 1.14). As ASEAN-10 develops over the next decade or so, the wealth gains will erode poverty on absolute terms, with an equitable distribution depending upon effectively coordinated policy and actions across institutions. As economic development in emerging countries has demonstrated real effects upon poverty alleviation, the AECV2030 sees poverty reduction as a direct offshoot of a well-managed regional integration.

By 2030, life expectancy at birth is targeted at approximately 72 years (see Figure 1.15). Technological improvements in healthcare, healthcare delivery and information dissemination among healthcare professionals and the public via ICT are taken to be mutually reinforcing. As institutional linkages and services become more deeply connected, best practices for healthcare will be shared across partnering countries with greater efficiency, providing a network to combat potential health epidemics, which can decimate developing competitiveness.

[116] See The World Bank (2014, 1–7).

Figure 1.14. Percentage of Population Living Below Poverty Line Projection to 2030 for ASEAN-10

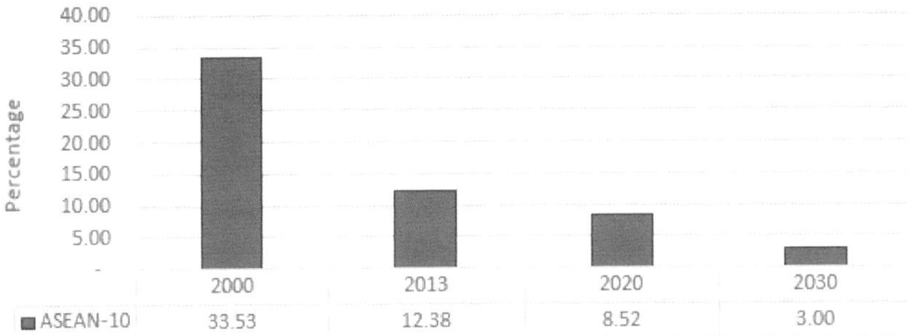

Source: Asia Competitiveness Institute.

Figure 1.15. Life Expectancy at Birth Projection to 2030 for ASEAN-10

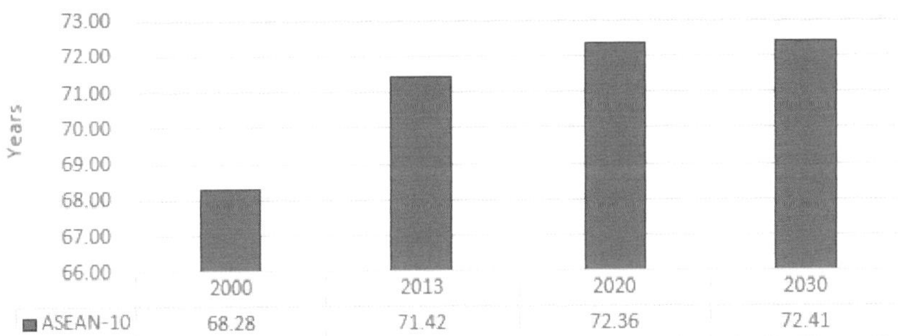

Source: Asia Competitiveness Institute.

The total population employed, with an average of 6.77 million people joining the workforce each year between 2013 and 2030, will reach 397.21 million by 2030 (see Figure 1.16). These projected figures support the push for labour-intensive manufacturing to continue its shift towards ASEAN. This projection reflects the magnitude of the latent potential for growth and development in the region with the ACI's proposed vision, along with regional collaboration allowing for

Figure 1.16. Employed Population Projection to 2030 for ASEAN-10

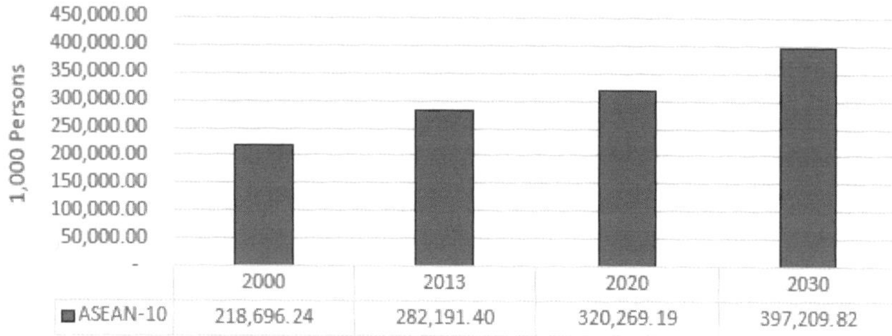

Source: Asia Competitiveness Institute.

technological transfers, greater mobility and well-paced urbanisation to facilitate accelerated growth for all.

1.8 Concluding Remarks

Any proposed AECV2030 remains a work-in-progress, with more feasibility studies as project-based and specialised institutions to delve deeper into many aspects, from finance to sustainable growth. The ACI makes a robust presentation in advocating such bold ideas and plans because the economic fundamentals are present, and aligning those with human touch needs, at least, for the AECV2030 to be communicated to all, including its consultative decision-making approach. In making the five proposals and strategic thrusts, which need continuous reevaluation and adjustment based on emerging events and trends, the following caveats are summarised for attention.

Firstly, it is clear that while both the FG model (see Figure 1.3) and the EAED model remain valid in theory, their application in contemporary times with ICT-induced globalisation and shifting geo-economics (no less geopolitics) has to be reckoned with. Thus, in asking if the CLMV can similarly follow both models as done by the ASEAN-6, it is thought provoking as to whether rising China is the same as rising Japan as the leading goose.

Secondly, China is not Japan in more ways than what the models and the AECV2030 portray (see Figure 1.5). Further studies are needed to answer the remaining questions of how differently Japan developed Southeast Asia into its regional manufacturing base for Japanese FDI and MNCs with mutual gains and how China's industrial relocation may be different, not least with changing times. China has its own inland to prosper, as China itself is one flying geese model, for it to be domesticated and grown to attain the China dream. More questions arise on China's level of S&T and R&D and in what fields it will serve as the next leading goose to host FDI and MNCs.

Thirdly, while the FG model and the EAED model, premised on state capitalism, have both become more acceptable to Western thinking and policymakers, China-initiated AIIB is one aspect of 'Asianisation' of the global economic architecture, which is traditionally Western-led. It is not a new development as the Asian Monetary Fund (AMF) was mooted post-Asian Financial Crisis but was stillborn. Questions on a united ASEAN or some consensus of a pragmatic ASEAN-X way lie in the final state of implementation. Undoubtedly, much remains to be seen with other Asian and non-Asian parties queuing up to participate in a mini-UN-styled international gathering in the AIIB larger than the G20 now as founding members.

Although it is evolving and is an ongoing long-term project, putting the AECV2030 as the leading chapter in this ASEAN volume is precisely for the purpose of rendering the AECV2030 ASEAN-centric. With its MPAC mooted since 2009, ASEAN is most naturally and realistically the right partner for the rest of Asia and China in particular. The emphasis of connectivity within and outside of ASEAN means we need to emphasise on the linking up and synchronising of the MPAC with the AECV2030 potentials.

One projection in 2009 by the ADBI estimated the total infrastructure funding required for ASEAN between 2006 and 2015 to be US$596.1

billion.[117] Specifically, ASEAN has to complete its ASEAN Highway, Singapore-Kunming Railway Link, ASEAN Integrated Inland Waterway Network, and ASEAN Maritime Transport System; all of which are building up into an integrated seamless multimodal ASEAN transport system. Additionally, the ICT infrastructure and services for an e-highway are a given if it is to achieve the 21st century connectivity. Above all, electricity is the main crux, thus resolving all institutional issues in ASEAN energy infrastructure projects may be the first priority.

Both the China-initiated AIIB and China's generous capital contribution as a rich source of funding to finance MPAC projects are as much a part of any China inspired connectivity.[118] With some 50 interested parties at the founding stage, Asian infrastructure is well profiled and balanced on paper, following international rules on governance for accountability and transparency, as well as best practices in both construction and management of projects of such massive scale. Better still, the AIIB has drawn more competition for Japan, the ADB and perhaps even the US to add both financial and technical assistance in creative and innovative multi-modal connectivity.

Both the AFC and GFT have had differential impacts on the political economy of all Asia Pacific economies, from the US to China and the rest of ASEAN. In the end, domestic politics matter in national elections more than international economics and relations, which is entirely true in reality. No matter what is professed for the greater good, the political economy of each economy has to be respected. How each copes and manages with the AFC, the GFT and domestic crises is another

---

[117] See Bhattacharyay (2009, 15–16).

[118] Though it has been observed that the AIIB operates as a pan-Asian bank which throws into question the bank's priorities for the ASEAN grouping, compatibility between ASEAN-China interests, such as the ASEAN economies' contribution to "Chinese-oriented production networks" and the MPAC overlaps with the B&R initiative as a projection of Chinese soft power, provide a compelling basis for complementary action. Rather, the matter becomes one of timing and will. See Basu Das (2015, 2–8).

consideration, in and of itself. Perhaps, odd as it may be, crises draw cooperation and collaboration, as regional or global crises require a regional or international solution. The ACI will continue to monitor the AECV2030 as another of its flagship projects with implications all round in the 'Asianisation' of economic and financial architecture in general and the role of ASEAN-centric strategies in East Asia, in particular.

The ASEAN Secretariat is well established with decades of cooperation and working progressively in the typical ASEAN way. With the MPAC in the works, more project-based proposals for funding, cooperation and collaboration in any ASEAN-X formulation will be precisely what the ACI needs to tease out for the AECV2030. Rendering the AECV2030 ASEAN-centric rides on such historical understanding and bonds. China and many of the interested parties in the AIIB are dialogue partners of ASEAN to begin with. A smooth expansion for the AECV2030 plus the MPAC will ensure ASEAN-centric actions, acting as the right intermediary however defined.[119] The ASEAN Secretariat, for one, is indeed a key player as well as a stakeholder in joining hands with the rest of the AIIB and all other evolving institutions, in changing the paradigm of global economic and financial infrastructure.[120]

All these caveats suggest that for the AECV2030 to be effective and successful, ASEAN must itself remain united, cohesive and strong. Yet, many side issues are as troubling, not causing a break-up of ASEAN *per se*, but they are potential threats and worries. Dubbed as the most successful regional grouping for integration, especially with the

---

[119] The case for ASEAN to support the AIIB as central to the region's architecture can be premised upon the ASEAN-led role that the bank affords the grouping to adopt, rather than as a Chinese or Japanese led endeavour. The recognition that "united advocacy" from ASEAN for AIIB funds would improve the chances of participation of the bank in regional MPAC projects lends weight to the approach of consensual and consultative decision-making as put forward in this chapter. See Basu Das (2015, 7–10).

[120] See Kawai, Morgan and Rana (2014).

ASEAN Economic Community to be completed by 2015, however defined, ASEAN cannot just implode. To play its role with greater relevance with changing geo-economics and geopolitics, a few observations are to be noted with the future of the AECV2030 in mind.

China is involved in territorial disputes from the South China Sea, involving some ASEAN states in the Spratly Islands to the East China Sea over Diaoyu / Senkaku Islands contested by Japan. Whichever is settled first and how each is resolved involve China as the common denominator in preferring bilateral discussions rather than any multilateral framework like the United Nations or the United Nations Convention on the Law of the Sea. Muddying the water, literally and figuratively, of the South China Sea is the bigger divide between China and the US. Indeed, the question of ASEAN unity as an opportunity and challenge becomes even more pressing in light of the "Sino-American rivalry for influence" in the region, with a real possibility of ASEAN "devolving into a house divided against itself" if member states begin to choose sides between the two powers.[121]

Players from China and Thailand also seem to be reviving the possibility of constructing the Kra Canal, which Japan once had interest in, as the oil transport from the Middle East needs to bypass the Strait of Malacca chokepoint to reach the Singapore port. Whether Thailand remains as concerned on potential secession of its southern Muslim parts with the Kra Canal, physically isolating them from the rest of Buddhist-dominant Thailand, remains to be seen. Even if politically feasible, putting in the most modern physical infrastructure, financed by China, Japan, the World Bank or the ADB, the efficiency in managing the various processes, from customs clearance to security is an important point of consideration. So long as Singapore remains competitive in management at its best, both its port and airport remain

[121] See Mahbubani (2015b, 140).

respectable in their own rights. Even if ships and oil tankers bypass Singapore with the Kra Canal, there is ample business to serve the rest of ASEAN, Australasia and beyond.

Thus, while these potential break-up trends in ASEAN are neither new nor immediate as fissures, they bear upon ASEAN in general and Singapore in particular to rethink and strategise accordingly. The ASEAN glue has to remain if the thesis of this chapter is for the AECV2030 to be ASEAN-centric. It takes more than money and capital to make connectivity effective, efficient and lasting. Trade facilitation as in necessary checks by immigration and customs authorities need to be synchronous to the AECV2030 as a whole.

The AECV2030 has set its sights on no less than a new regional master plan that takes stock of the current prevailing willingness to explore closer Asian inter-sovereign cooperation. This has recently come about through the efforts of a pioneering generation of country planners and intelligentsia from what began as a regional project for better stability and national security. The people-centric market integration the ACI envisaged is predicated upon an Asian mode of globalisation, with the confidence of the most dynamic region of growth coming out of the 2008 economic slump. Asians have the capabilities, foresight and wisdom to build upon a foundation that holds great promise to forge new relations and innovative institutions for a collective good.

To this end, the ACI has proposed a bold AECV2030, which understandably needs more work, including field trips and road shows for effective communication and gaining support from all partners willing to join a shared 2030 blueprint forged from diversity, to continue with an ascendant Asian story. The time for action is not luxurious as 2030 beckons and needs to be fleshed out by realistic projects. In the final analysis, ASEAN leadership is imperative. While President Joko Widodo has his agenda on Indonesia as a global maritime axis, it may spur the rest of maritime ASEAN including the other archipelagic spread in the Phillipines to bring some ASEAN glue to seize this opportunity. Realistically, as geo-economics change for a wealthier East Asia and ASEAN all round, geopolitics rising in commensurate is to be expected.

References

Abe, Tetsuya. 2015. "Plan laid out to become manufacturing powerhouse by 2025". *Nikkei Asian Review,* March 6. http://asia.nikkei.com/print/article/79569 (accessed March 25, 2015).

Asian Development Bank. 2012. *Greater Mekong Sub region: Twenty Years of Partnership.* Philippines: Asian Development Bank. http://adb.org/sites/default/files/pub/2012/gms-20-yrs-partnership.pdf (accessed August 3, 2015).

Aiyar, Shekhar, Romain Duval, Damien Puy, Yiqun Wu and Longmei Zhang. 2013. "Growth Slowdowns and the Middle-Income Trap". IMF Working Paper WP/13/71, International Monetary Fund, Washington DC.

Akamatsu, Kaname. 1962. "A historical pattern of economic growth in developing countries". *The Developing Economies* 1 (s1): 3–25.

Anand, Rahul, Kevin C. Cheng, Sidra Rehman and Longmei Zhang. 2014. "Potential Growth in Emerging Asia". IMF Working Paper WP/14/2, International Monetary Fund, Washington DC.

ASEAN Secretariat. 2010. *Master Plan on ASEAN Connectivity.* Jakarta: ASEAN Secretariat. http://www.asean.org/resources/publications/asean-publications/item/master-plan-on-asean-connectivity-2 (accessed September 3, 2014).

Atmanta, Dwi. 2015. "China, ASEAN to set up NGO network". *The Jakarta Post,* May 27. https://shar.es/12gYAh (accessed June 3, 2015).

Basu Das, Sanchita. 2015. "Can the China-led AIIB Support the ASEAN Connectivity Master Plan?" *ISEAS Perspective* 30, June 24. http://www.iseas.edu.sg/documents/publication/iseas_perspective_2015_30.pdf (accessed June 25, 2015).

Bhattacharyay, Biswa Nath. 2009. "Infrastructure Development for ASEAN Economic Integration". ADBI Working Paper 138, Asian Development Bank Institute, Tokyo.

Bhattacharyay, Biswa Nath. 2010. "Estimating Demand for Infrastructure in Energy, Transport, Telecommunications, Water and Sanitation in Asia and the Pacific: 2010–2020". ADBI Working Paper 248, Asian Development Bank Institute, Tokyo.

Briones, Roehlano and Jesus Felipe. 2013. "Agriculture and Structural Transformation in Developing Asia: Review and Outlook". ADB Economics Working Paper 363, Asian Development Bank, Manila.

Chandler Jr., Alfred D. 1990. *Scale and Scope: The Dynamics of Industrial Capitalism.* Cambridge, Massachusetts: Belknap Press.

Chia, Jun-kai 谢俊凯. 2015. "Gei benquyu dailai shangji yu tiaozhan" 给本区域带来商机与挑战" [The opportunities and challenges brought to our region]. *Lianhe Zaobao* 联合早报, October 1. http://lkyspp.nus.edu.sg/aci/wp- content/uploads/sites/4/2015/10/ LHZB_1Oct2015a_.pdf (accessed October 5, 2015).

China Central Television. 2015. "Foreign Ministry dismisses rumoured veto power in the AIIB". Online video, March 25. http://english.cntv.cn/2015/03/25/VIDE1427282882317997.shtml (accessed March 27, 2015).

Chow, Peter C.Y. and Mitchell H. Kellman. 1993. *Trade — The Engine of Growth in East Asia.* New York: Oxford University Press.

Cole, J. Michael. 2015. "Applies to Join AIIB Under 'One China,' Sparking Protests". *The Diplomat,* April 1. http://thediplomat.com/2015/04/taiwan-applies-to-join-aiib-under-one-china-sparking-protests/ (accessed April 6, 2015).

Danubrata, Eveline and Charlotte Greenfield. 2015. "Indonesia calls for new financial global architecture". *Reuters,* April 22. http://reut.rs/1IFFkC5 (accessed April 23, 2015).

Dickie, Mure. 2011. "China economy overtakes Japan". *Financial Times,* February 14. http://on.ft.com/1CrONYA (accessed April 6, 2015).

Donovan, Arthur. 2004. "The Impact of Containerization: From Adam Smith to the 21st Century". *Review of Business* 25 (3): 10–15.

FAO. 2009. *How to Feed the World in 2050/ High Level Expert Forum — How to Feed the World in 2050.* Rome: Food and Agriculture Organisation.

http://www.fao.org/fileadmin/templates/wsfs/docs/expert_paper/ How_to_Feed_the_World_in_2050.pdf (accessed November 20, 2014).

FAO. 2014a. "China pledges $50 million to FAO in support of South-South cooperation". October 15. http://www.fao.org/news/story/en/item/260439/icode/ (accessed November 12, 2014).

FAO. 2014b. *South-South Cooperation.* http://www.fao.org /fileadmin/user_upload/themes/img /south-south cooperation /SCC_brochure2014_EN.pdf (accessed November 12, 2014).

FAO, IFAD and WFP. 2014. *The State of Food Insecurity in the World: Strengthening the enabling environment for food security and nutrition.* Rome: Food and Agriculture Organisation. http://www.fao.org/3/a-i4030e.pdf (accessed November 20, 2014).

Fensom, Anthony. 2015. "Japan Ups Ante on AIIB". *The Diplomat*, May 23. http://thediplomat.com/2015/05/japan-ups-ante-on-aiib/ (accessed June 3, 2015).

Fujita, Masahisa and Jacques-Francois Thisse. 2002. *Economics of Agglomeration: Cities, Industrial Location, and Globalization.* New York: Cambridge University Press.

Fukuyama, Francis. 1995. *Trust: The Social Virtues and the Creation of Prosperity*. New York: Free Press.

Glaeser, Edward L., ed. 2010. *Agglomeration Economics*. Chicago: The University of Chicago Press.

Gopalan, Sasidaran. 2014. "A Win-Win China-India Infrastructure Cooperation: Opportunities and Challenges". Presentation at the 2014 Annual Asia Competitiveness Institute Conference on "Competitiveness Analysis of 112 Asian Economies, Asia Economic Connectivity, Liveable Cities Index for 100 Greater China Cities and Cost of Living Index for Expatriates and Ordinary Residents", Singapore, November 26–27.

Gracie, Carrie. 2014. "Has President Xi Jinping achieved his China Dream?" *BBC News,* December 19. http://www.bbc.com/news/world-asia-china-30544572 (accessed March 27, 2015).

Gu, Xiaosong and Mingjiang Li. 2009. "Beibu Gulf: Emerging Sub-regional Integration between China and ASEAN". RSIS Working Paper 168, S. Rajaratnam School of International Studies, Singapore.

Harding, Robin. 2015. "Japan boosts aid to 'Mekong five' nations". *Financial Times,* July 5. http://on.ft.com/1G11lb4 (accessed July 6, 2015).

Hiebert, Fred. 2012. "2012 Issyk Kul Expedition: Search for a Sunken Palace". *National Geographic,* September 6. http://on.natgeo.com/1VAoYzQ (accessed October 5, 2015).

Hotelling, Harold. 1929. "Stability in Competition". *The Economic Journal* 39 (153): 41–57.

Hussain, Zakir. 2014. "Indonesia 'key in China's vision of Maritime Silk Road'". *The Straits Times*, November 4.

International Chamber of Shipping. 2009. *The Convention on Contracts for the International Carriage of Goods Wholly or Partly by Sea (The "Rotterdam Rules").* http://www.uncitral.org /pdf/english/texts/transport/rotterdam_rules/ICS_PositionPaper.pdf (accessed October 7, 2014).

Jakarta Globe. 2015. "In Indonesia, Caution Urged with China's New 'Silk Road' Plans". May 31. http://jakartaglobe.beritasatu.com/news/indonesia-caution-urged-chinas-new-silk-road-plans/ (accessed June 23, 2015).

Kajimoto, Tetsushi and Leika Kihara. 2011. "Japan economy shrinks in final quarter of 2010". *Reuters,* February 14. http://uk.reuters.com/article/2011/02/14/uk-japan-economy-idUKTRE71D07R20110214 (accessed April 9, 2015).

Kajimoto, Tetsushi, Jeanny Kao, Michael Gold, Ben Blanchard and Sui-Lee Wee. 2015. "Taiwan, Norway seek to join China-backed AIIB, Japan still cautious". *Reuters,* March 31. http://reut.rs/1xREfa2 (accessed March 31, 2015).

Kawai, Masahiro, Peter J. Morgan and Pradumna B. Rana, eds. 2014. *New Global Economic Architecture: The Asian Perspective.* Cheltenham: Edward Elgar.

Kennedy, Scott and David A. Parker. 2015. "Building China's "One Belt, One Road"". *Centre for Strategic & International Studies,* April 3. http://csis.

org/publication/building-chinas-one-belt-one-road (accessed April 9, 2015).

Kojima, Kiyoshi. 2000. "The "flying geese" model of Asian economic development: origin, theoretical extensions, and regional policy implications". *Journal of Asian Economics* 11 (4): 375–401.

Kuo, Lily. 2015. "All of the countries joining China's alternative to the World Bank". *Quartz,* March 30. http://qz.com/372326 (accessed March 31, 2015).

Low, Linda. 1998. *Political Economy in a City-state: Government-made Singapore.* Singapore: Oxford University Press.

Low, Linda, ed. 2004. *Developmental States: Relevancy, Redundancy or Reconfiguration?* New York: Nova Science.

Maddison, Angus. 2007. *Contours of the World Economy, 1–2030 AD: Essays in Macroeconomic History.* Oxford: Oxford University Press.

Mahbubani, Kishore. 2015a. "Why Britain Joining China-Led Bank Is a Sign of American Decline". *The Huffington Post,* March 16. http://huff.to/1Lk5mQG (accessed March 30, 2015).

Mahbubani, Kishore. 2015b. "ASEAN as a Living, Breathing Modern Miracle". *CIRSD Horizons* (2): 136–148.

Mandri-Perrott, Cledan. 2014. "Public-Private Partnerships (PPP) and Infrastructure Financing". Presentation at the 2014 Annual Asia Competitiveness Institute Conference on "Competitiveness Analysis of 112 Asian Economies, Asia Economic Connectivity, Liveable Cities Index for 100 Greater China Cities and Cost of Living Index for Expatriates and Ordinary Residents", Singapore, November 26–27.

Mayeda, Andrew and Sharon Chen. 2015. "Singapore Mulls Need for Nation's Presence in Management of AIIB". *Bloomberg,* April 19. http://bloom.bg/1yEI825 (accessed April 21, 2015).

McKinsey Global Institute. 2014. *Southeast Asia at the crossroads: Three paths to prosperity.* http://www.mckinsey.com/insights/energy_resources_materials/three_paths_to_sustained_economic_growth_in_southeast_asia (accessed January 5, 2015).

Ministry of Economy, Trade and Industry. 2010. The New Growth Strategy: Blueprint for Revitalizing Japan. http://www.meti.go.jp/english/policy/economy/growth/report20100618.pdf (accessed December 8, 2014).

Ministry of Economy, Trade and Industry. 2013. Act on Establishment of the Japan Brand Fund was passed by the Diet and Promulgated. http://www.meti.go.jp/english/press/2013/ 0708_01.html (accessed December 8, 2014).

Ministry of Foreign Affairs of the People's Republic of China. 2015. Foreign Ministry Spokesperson Hua Chunying's Regular Press Conference on March 25, 2015. http:// www.fmprc.gov.cn/mfa_eng/xwfw_665399/s2510_665401/t1248592.shtml (accessed March 27, 2015).

Moody's. 2015a. "One Belt, One Road initiative is credit positive for Chinese debt issuers." *Moody's Investor Service,* July 20. https://www.moodys.com/research/Moodys-One-Belt-One-Road-initiative-is-credit-positive-for--PR_329767 (accessed July 30, 2015).

Moody's. 2015b. "China's Belt and Road Strategy — Credit Positive for Emerging Market Sovereigns." *Moody's Investor Service,* July 28. https://www.moodys.com/research/Moodys-Chinas-Belt-and-Road-Strategy-Credit-Positive-for-Emerging--PR_331106 (accessed July 30, 2015).

OECD. 2009. Regional Partnership Compact for Agricultural Development in West Africa. November 12. http://www.oecd.org/swac/events/regional-partnershipcompactforagriculturaldevelopmentinwestafrica.htm (accessed April 24, 2015).

Ooi, Kee Beng, 2014. *Eurasian Core and Its Edges: Dialogues with Wang Gungwu on the History of the World.* Singapore: Institute of Southeast Asian Studies.

Osman, Nurfika. 2014. "AP II secures Rp 1.5t loan to develop Soekarno-Hatta". *The Jakarta Post*, August 12. https://shar.es/1p7H8W (accessed April 24, 2015).

Page, Jeremy. 2014a. "China Sees Itself at Centre of New Asian Order". *The Wall Street Journal*, November 9. http://on.wsj.com/1ANJ6JL (accessed November 10, 2014).

Page, Jeremy. 2014b. "5 Things to Know about Horgos and China's New Silk Roads". *The Wall Street Journal*, November 9. http://blogs.wsj.com/briefly/2014/11/09/5-things-to-know-about-horgos-and-chinas-new-silk-roads/ (accessed November 10, 2014).

Palmer, Sarah. 2011. "The Maritime World in Historical Perspective". *International Journal of Maritime History* 23 (1): 1–12.

Parameswaran, Prashanth. 2015a. "US Mulls New Asia Infrastructure Facility to Rival Regional Players". *The Diplomat*, June 17. http://thediplomat.com/2015/06/us-mulls-new-asia-infrastructure-facility-to-rival-regional-players/ (accessed June 23, 2015).

Pettis, Michael. 2015. "Will the AIIB one day matter?" *Michael Pettis' China Financial Markets* (blog), April 11. http://blog.mpettis.com/2015/04/will-the-aiib-one-day-matter/ (accessed August 3, 2015).

Porter, Michael E. 1990. *The Competitive Advantage of Nations*. New York: Free Press.

Rajendran, Unmesh. 2014. "BRICS Bank: The New Kid on the Block". *The Diplomat*, July 28. http://thediplomat.com/2014/07/brics-bank-the-new-kid-on-the-block/ (retrieved June 4, 2015).

Reisen, Helmut. 2015. "How the New AIIB Dwarfs the Asian Development Bank". *The Globalist,* April 8. http://www.theglobalist.com/aiib-to-dwarf-adb-loan-portfolio/ (accessed April 9, 2015).

Sender, Henny. 2015. "Japan expected to join Asian Infrastructure Investment Bank". *Financial Times,* March 30. http://on.ft.com/1CoROfs (accessed March 31, 2015).

Sheets, Nathan. 2015. "Building a global infrastructure for growth". *CNBC*, January 7. http://www.cnbc.com/id/102318050 (accessed March 31, 2015).

Shekhar, Vibhanshu and Joseph Chinyong Liow. 2014. "Indonesia as a Maritime Power: Jokowi's Vision, Strategies, and Obstacles Ahead". *Brookings Institution.* http://www.brookings.edu/research/articles/2014/11/indonesia-maritime-liow-shekhar (accessed November 13, 2014).

Sriring, Orathai. 2014. "Thailand to go ahead with $1.9 billion airport expansion: minister". *Reuters*, October 4. http://reut.rs/1Ed73tg (accessed 24 April, 2015).

Studwell, Joe. 2013. *How Asia Works: Success and Failure in the World's Most Dynamic Region.* London: Profile.

Szczudlik-Tatar, Justyna. 2013. "China's New Silk Road Diplomacy". Policy Paper No. 34 (82), The Polish Institute of International Affairs, Warsaw.

Tan, Khee Giap, Mulya Amri, Linda Low and Kong Yam Tan. 2013a. *Competitiveness Analysis and Development Strategies for 33 Indonesian Provinces.* Singapore: World Scientific.

Tan, Khee Giap, Linda Low, Kong Yam Tan and Amanda Lijuan Lim. 2013b. *Annual Analysis of Competitiveness, Development Strategies and Public Policies on ASEAN-10: 2000-2010.* Singapore: World Scientific.

Tan, Khee Giap, Linda Low, Kong Yam Tan and Kartik Rao. 2013c. *Annual Analysis of Competitiveness, Simulation Studies and Development Perspective for 35 States and Federal Territories of India: 2000–2010.* Singapore: World Scientific.

Tan, Khee Giap, Randong Yuan, Sangiita Wei Cher Yoong, and Mu Yang. 2013d. *Annual Analysis of Competitiveness, Simulation Studies and Development Perspective for 34 Greater China Economies.* Singapore: World Scientific.

Tan, Khee Giap, Sangiita Wei Cher Yoong and Randong Yuan. 2015. *2014 Annual Provincial and Regional Competitiveness Analysis for Greater China Economies: Development Strategies under the New Normal.* Singapore: World Scientific.

Teodoro, Joycee A. 2015. "ASEAN's Connectivity Challenge". *The Diplomat,* June 27. http://thediplomat.com/2015/06/aseans-connectivity-challenge/ (accessed August 3, 2015).

The Economist. 2008. "The decoupling debate". March 6. http://www.economist.com/node/ 10809267 (accessed November 9, 2014).

The Economist. 2014. "Special Report: The Pacific Age". November 13. http://www.economist.com/printedition/specialreports?year[value][year]=2014&category=76983 (accessed November 18, 2014).

The World Bank. 1993. *The East Asian Miracle: Economic Growth and Public Policy.* New York: Oxford University Press.

The World Bank. 2011. *Global Development Horizons 2011 — Multipolarity: The New Global Economy.* Washington DC: The World Bank. http://siteresources.worldbank.org /INTGDH/Resources/GDH_CompleteReport2011.pdf (accessed November 19, 2014).

The World Bank. 2014. *Prosperity for All — Ending Extreme Poverty: A Note for the World Bank Group Spring Meetings 2014.* Washington, DC: The World Bank. http://siteresources.worldbank.org /INTPROSPECTS/Resources/334934-1327948020811/8401693-1397074077765/Prosperity_for_All_Final_2014.pdf (accessed April 24, 2015).

The World Bank. 2015. "Population, total". http://tinyurl.com/2ede6ny (accessed April 22, 2015).

The World Bank and IMF. 2007. *Aid for Trade: Harnessing Globalization for Economic Development*. https://www.imf.org/external/np/pp/2007/eng/080107.pdf (accessed November 20, 2014).

Thomas, Katie. 2008. "I.O.C. Issues Glowing Review of Beijing Games". *The New York Times*, November 26. http://nyti.ms/1yRnRqu (accessed April 22, 2015).

Tian, Shaohui. 2015. "Chronology of China's Belt and Road Initiative". *Xinhuanet,* March 28. http://news.xinhuanet.com/english/2015-03/28/c_134105435.htm (accessed April 8, 2015).

Tian, Ying. 2011. "Beijing-Shanghai Bullet Train Tickets to Cost from 555 Yuan". *Bloomberg*, June 13. http://www.bloomberg.com/news/articles/2011-06-13/beijing-shanghai-bullet-train-tickets-to-cost-from-555-yuan-1- (accessed April 22, 2015).

Toh, Mun Heng and Linda Low, eds. 1993. *Regional Cooperation and Growth Triangles in ASEAN.* Singapore: Times Academic Press.

Tullao, Tereso S., Jr. and Hong Hin Lim, eds. 2012. "Developing ASEAN Economic Community (AEC) into a Global Services Hub". ERIA Research Project Report 2011 No. 1, Economic Research Institute for ASEAN and East Asia, Jakarta.

Vasiliauskas, Aidas Vasilis and Jurgita Barysiene. 2008. "An economic evaluation model of the logistic system based on container transportation". *Transport* 23(4): 311–315.

Wang, Qian. 2014. "China goes from hungry nation to farm giant that feeds the world". *China Daily,* October 16.

Wang, Gungwu. 2015a. "SG+50: Future Trends 2065; Singapore's Chinese dilemma' as China rises". *The Straits Times,* June 1.

Wang, Gungwu. 2015b. "China's Eurasia strategy to counter US naval power". *The Straits Times,* August 1.

Witz, Billy. 2014. "Pursuing a Shipping Revolution as Big as His Airship". *The New York Times*, November 10. http://nyti.ms/10SxiFO (accessed November 18, 2014).

World Population Statistics. 2014. "Population of Asia 2014". March 14. http:// www. worldpopulationstatistics.com/population-of-asia-2014/ (accessed September 29, 2014).

Wuryanto, Luky Eko. 2014. "Accelerating Infrastructure Development Programs and Expected Roles of AIIB". Presentation at the 2014 Annual Asia Competitiveness Institute Conference on "Competitiveness Analysis of 112 Asian Economies, Asia Economic Connectivity, Liveable Cities Index for 100 Greater China Cities and Cost of Living Index for Expatriates and Ordinary Residents", Singapore, November 26–27.

Xi, Jinping. 2015. "Towards a Community of Common Destiny and a New Future for Asia". Keynote speech at the Boao Forum for Asia Annual Conference 2015, Hainan, March 28.

Xinhuanet. 2014. "Xi's "new normal" theory". November 9. http://news.xinhuanet.com/english/ china/2014-11/09/c_133776839.htm (accessed March 31, 2015).

Yang, Lina. 2012. "Xi Jinping advocates reform, China Dream". *Xinhuanet*, December 23. http:// news.xinhuanet.com/english/china/2012-12/23/c_132058740.htm (accessed March 31, 2015).

Yao, Kevin. 2015. "China to inject FX reserves into policy banks: Caixin". *Reuters*, April 20. http://reut.rs/1Ej4LeU (accessed April 22, 2015).

Yong, Jeremy Au. 2015. "IMF lauds Tharman's panel leadership in tough times". *The Straits Times*, April 20. http://shar.es/1pfgOQ (accessed April 21, 2015).

Yoshino, Naoyuki and Farhad Taghizadeh-Hesary. 2014. "Three Arrows of "Abenomics" and the Structural Reform of Japan: Inflation Targeting Policy of the Central Bank, Fiscal Consolidation, and Growth Strategy". ADBI Working Paper 492, Asian Development Bank Institute, Tokyo.

Zhang, Gaoli. 2014. "Join Hands to Build the 21st Century Maritime Silk Road and Work for an Even Brighter Future for China-ASEAN Friendship and

Cooperation". Speech at the 11th China-ASEAN Expo and China-ASEAN Business and Investment Summit, Nanning, September 16.

Zhang, Feng. 2015. "Beijing's Master Plan for the South China Sea". *Foreign Policy*, June 23. http://foreignpolicy.com/2015/06/23/south_china_sea_beijing_retreat_new_strategy/ (accessed August 3, 2015).

Zheng, Yangpeng. 2015. "AIIB prospective founders' list increases to 57 nations". *The Washington Post,* April 16. http://chinawatch.washingtonpost.com/2015/04/aiib-prospective-founders-list-increases-to-57-nations/ (accessed April 21, 2015).

Zhuang, Juzhong, Paul Vanderberg and Yiping Huang. 2012. *Growing Beyond the Low-Cost Advantage: How the People's Republic of China can avoid the Middle-Income Trap*. Manila: Asian Development Bank.

Discussant Notes 1.1

Mr Steven Wong
Deputy Chief Executive, Institute of Strategic and International Studies, Malaysia

I would like to focus on just Proposal Two, infrastructure development, as I have given this matter the most thought. This is one of the main supply-side keys to connectivity while the other three proposals are also important because economic activities are needed to justify and finance infrastructure.

We can start by asking why there is a state of under-investment in Asian infrastructure. In the case of Indonesia, the world's largest archipelagic nation, the answer is quite clear, because of the distances involved. The same is true for the Philippines. But this still begs the question. Second, so why are markets for infrastructure not more cross-border and integrated than they are? Our thinking seems to go from national to regional seamlessly but perhaps interests and institutional framework are two entirely different dimensions. A third question is why public-private-partnerships are not proving to be the answer we thought it would be? Is the private sector just not responsive or are there other factors faced that are not taken into account?

I would suggest that the answers to these questions are not a case of ignorance or necessarily even a lack of market incentives. Instead, the work that has gone on shows the real importance of risks and institutional framework. We have long known the characteristics of infrastructure such as indivisibility, long gestation and payback periods, externalities and so forth. Some of these characteristics, thanks largely to technology, have changed and markets are now more contestable and competitive than before, even though elements of monopoly still remain.

The work done by the Asian Development Bank Institute on infrastructure for Asian connectivity is important in this regard and I would recommend that this be read inside out. One of the things pointed out is that many of the essential challenges that we face are at the national level, in particular the lack of legal and regulatory governance and institutional framework.

The risks of infrastructure, however, are a lot more diverse and I have identified four generic blocks that are important to look at: fiscal, financial, market and policy institutions. These four blocks affect all infrastructure development projects and cannot be wished away. For example, demand, duration, currency, construction, supplier, and counterparty risks — these are present whether the projects are in Europe or Asia.

As infrastructure development has to be planned forward, sometimes 20 to 30 years, and there are demand risks, there is a need to over-invest in the initial years in order to get the right amount to meet the rising demand. Sometimes though, the demand does not eventuate and 'white elephants' result. These, in turn, have fiscal and policy consequences. Thus, projects have to be identified, planned and implemented very objectively, critically and carefully.

In the case of national projects, it is usual for there to be concept formulation, feasibility studies, requests for proposals, negotiations, selection, planning and implementation. At each stage, efforts are made to ensure successful performance and to manage, even if not entirely lay off, the risks present. These mainly safeguard against agent-principle, moral hazard and asymmetric information problems rather than risks.

When we move from the national to the regional level, these processes are either missing or watered down. The best examples I can think of are with regard to the ASEAN Infrastructure Fund (AIF) and the Indonesia-Malaysia-Thailand Growth Triangle (IMTGT). National governments are unable to objectively conceive and evaluate cross-border projects and so the responsibility has been given to the Asian

Development Bank. Even then, what countries basically do is to put up national-level projects with limited regional spillovers; in effect, national projects 'masquerade' as regional projects. If you look at how the AIF has performed to date you will see few truly regional projects. In the case of the IMTGT, there are none. There is also a great deal of intra-regional rivalry to be the connectivity hub; every country, from Myanmar to Thailand to Singapore, wants to be the hub.

In short, governments must actively promote infrastructure development with connectivity in mind and therefore not just within their borders but beyond them. Beyond what has already been mentioned, there has to be more competition and unbundling of infrastructure services. Services liberalisation has to be deeper and wider and investment policies must be harmonised. Unfortunately, in some countries, we seem to be going the other way. Non-tariff barriers and other behind-the-border impediments must be lowered. For some countries, especially Cambodia, Laos and Myanmar, liberalising the capital account and/or currency regime is difficult but imperative. Countries cannot finance infrastructure in their own currencies ('original sin') and therefore must do so through an intermediary currency such as the US dollar.

Infrastructure development has been talked about for many years and there have been a number of initiatives, such as the AIF, President Xi Jinping's idea of an Asian Infrastructure Investment Bank and now the Maritime Silk Road. Yet, we keep coming back to the same issues again and again. The devil, as they say, is in the details and until countries can align their interests and come up with comprehensive risk solutions, the infrastructure that is needed may remain on the drawing board.

Discussant Notes 1.2

Dr Vo Tri Thanh
Vice President, Central Institute for Economic Management, Vietnam

I have five brief comments. First, I think the Asia Economic Connectivity Vision 2030 (AECV2030) is a continuation of many things we already have. We already have the Master Plan on ASEAN Connectivity (MPAC) so far. This was a foundation made for the Asia-Pacific Economic Cooperation (APEC) connectivity last year in Indonesia. I believe the Maritime Silk Road (MSR) and AECV2030 need to be looked at in the broader context of liberalisation in the region. Right now, ASEAN is preparing the vision for the ASEAN Economic Community (AEC) beyond 2015, so an announcement by ASEAN leaders can be made by the end of 2014. And just earlier, the Economic Research Institute for ASEAN and East Asia (ERIA) published a book on ASEAN beyond 2015 (*ASEAN Rising — ASEAN and AEC Beyond 2015*). Others include the Regional Comprehensive Economic Partnership (RCEP), which is on liberalisation, connectivity and cooperation, and last but not least, the Trans-Pacific Partnership (TPP). The RCEP and TPP are two kinds of tracks for optimisation of foreign direct investment in the region. So given that, it is not easy to estimate the impacts of the MSR and AECV2030, but at least together with GDP, we need to look at the possibility of narrowing the development gap under these connectivity visions.

Second, traditional security issues can be seen as another side of the coin of liberalisation and connectivity. We accept the free movement of skilled labour, but as for unskilled labour, that could be a problem when we try to strengthen connectivity. We also need to pay more attention to the issue of sustainability. Up till now, as I know, only about 70% of the on-projects under the MPAC already have feasibility studies for social, environment, economic impacts. So you can talk about a vision, but when you pick up the projects, you need to be very careful with the estimation of their various impacts.

My third point on why we need connectivity is a very simple one, which is also why the AEC and RCEP could be so different from the TPP. The idea is that with liberalisation we can have new opportunities to do business and to make money, but we need access to these new opportunities. So connectivity is about access to opportunities created by liberalisation. But that is not enough. We also need to reduce the transaction costs of doing business. Hard and soft connectivity should go together with trade and investment facilitation. And last but not least, we ask for cooperation, especially for capacity building, to exploit effectively the new opportunities. That is why we need the four key elements for effective regional integration, namely liberalisation, connectivity, facilitation and cooperation. That is the paradigm of the AEC and possibly RCEP.

Given that connectivity is very important right now, ASEAN has the ASEAN Connectivity Coordinating Committee (ACCC) for the implementation of the MPAC. Some have suggested that for each country's commission, they need to have public-private-partnership (PPP) units that are closely linked with the ACCC, otherwise PPPs can hardly be realised. Institutions for implementation are very important for ASEAN. But ASEAN coordination is not enough. Right now we have the ASEAN institution, China-ASEAN and Japan-ASEAN cooperation. Is it good to realise the idea of establishing the East Asian Cooperation and Development Fund to facilitate regional cooperation programmes? China has suggested a bank for infrastructure development, but together with that we already have the Asian Development Bank and many other donors. What is the interaction? Are there any political games being played here or is it purely economic?

For my last comment, we do have enough resources, so what is required for infrastructure development and what we can mobilise in reality are huge. But another way is, together with cooperation with the types of institutions I mentioned, would be a regional bond market. We have talked about this for more than 10 years and the progress has been very slow. Therefore we need to regain the momentum for regional bond market development.

Discussant Notes 1.3

Dr Roehlano Briones
Senior Research Fellow, Philippine Institute for Development Studies, Philippines

Let me limit my remarks to Proposal Three — Asia as food basket. I am happy to see that agricultural productivity is so prominent in the Asia Economic Connectivity Vision 2030 (AECV2030). As pointed out in the Asian Development Bank Economics working paper number 363 titled "Agriculture and Structural Transformation in Developing Asia: Review and Outlook" by Roehlano Briones and Jesus Felipe published in 2013, agriculture continues to be the largest employer in Asia. Despite massive structural transformation of output, such transformation appears to have bypassed millions of agricultural households in Asia, many of whom account for the majority of Asia's poor. Given this problem, let me just make a few points:

Urbanisation and rural-urban migration, as highlighted in the AECV2030, are seen on the supply side with a strong recommendation of mechanisation. Urbanisation also has demand side effects, which have had and will continue to have dramatic transformational impacts on domestic markets — think of the supermarket revolution in China, India and Southeast Asia — and will therefore drive the food chain transformation in Asia.

On mechanisation, I favour this where market failure constrains the adoption of cost-minimising technology. However, I caution against wrong ways of promoting mechanisation, as well as addressing social implications, given the large employment role of agriculture.

Lastly, on comparative advantage, I agree this is essential for Asia to realise its potential as a food basket. However, the trade plus specialisation thrust is antithetical to Asian countries' domestic food security policy, which favours self-sufficiency. We should not underestimate the resistance to trade cooperation due to domestic politics, though the suggestion of "targeted subsidies" to farmers affected by trade is worth exploring further.

Discussant Notes 1.4

Dr Bustanul Arifin
Professor, University of Lampung and Board of Founder/Senior Economist, Institute for Development of Economics and Finance, Indonesia

Thank you ACI for inviting me to contribute a little bit here. I would like to first congratulate you on the draft, I appreciate it. My comment complements Dr Briones on the food basket proposal, which is focusing mostly on, maybe we are all aware, the Integrated Food Security Framework of ASEAN. The talk has been conducted many times. The idea is to respond to the global economic crisis in 2009 during which many countries were hit — Philippines, some of Indonesia and so on — but we cannot implement it because, according to Mr Wong, the devil is in the details. Who will be responsible? Which country should the ASEAN food stock be kept in, Malaysia or Thailand? This is not really progressing even though the idea is very good, because we try to really make economic connectivity a reality. Basically when global climate change affects production process, we have to respond. With regard to the proposals, we should provide clear suggestions to individual countries as to how to implement and to translate big visions into details in each country.

Second, on sustainable ecosystem, this approach is actually new in the field of resource economics — we call it payment for ecosystem services. It could be within countries, it could be transnational or transboundary, such as the recent law that is being passed in Singapore about pollution, which is based on the concept of sustainable ecosystem where one or two countries function as the providers and other countries are beneficiaries. The central idea is how the beneficiaries could contribute to the providers of environment services. These include, especially in the upstream and downstream of the Mekong Delta, biodiversity, ecotourism and so on. We would in fact contribute both to the literature and to the policy if we could detail what payment mechanism or compensation mechanism, as a mini-example of the global carbon trading stock, could be implemented here.

For Indonesia, we have developed the Masterplan for Acceleration and Expansion of Indonesia's Economic Development (MP3EI). In terms of connectivity, there are six economic corridors. The idea of this is, because we are an archipelagic country, all parts have to be connected. The main proposal is to build a bridge between Java and Sumatra as part of Trans-Asia connectivity. But there are concerns at home because the share of Java and Sumatra itself is already 85% of GDP. If we connect further, it could be 90%, and politically it is not stable for Eastern Indonesia which is left behind. My suggestion would be focusing not only on roads and bridges but also on ports to avoid congestion. That could make it clear how we try to avoid the devil in the details.

Finally, on institutional strengthening, I support Mr Wong and Dr Briones' ideas of contributing to individual countries' homework as well as capacity building in terms of institutional arrangements and human resource development. With regard to agricultural research and development, I would put it as 'research for development', as in not research for the sake of research but applied research. In addition, I would like to expand the public-private partnership concept to the ABGC, which is the Academics-Business-Government-Civil Society partnership, because we have to invite broader stakeholders to join us in our connectivity vision.

Discussant Notes 1.5

Dr Sothea Oum
Economist, Economic Research Institute for ASEAN and East Asia (ERIA)

First of all, thank you for inviting me to this important gathering. Like the previous speakers, I think this undertaking is commendable, ambitious, and timely for the region. The Asia Economic Connectivity Vision 2030 (AECV2030) discusses important pathways towards the realisation of 'the Asian century', with the re-emergence of China, India and still, the prominent role of Japan as well as robust growth of ASEAN. China is expected to play a more prominent role of leadership in driving this whole process.

My specific concern is, I would like to see the general framework as normally when we talk about connectivity, economic integration, we think about Balassa's stages of economic integration, starting from a basic free trade area to complete regional integration. As Dr Thanh mentioned, because there are a lot of visions and master plans going on in the region, it is worth reviewing existing frameworks on the ASEAN Economic Community (AEC) post-2015, the Master Plan on ASEAN Connectivity (MPAC), the Regional Comprehensive Economic Partnership (RCEP), and Asia Development Bank Institute's ASEAN Vision 2030 for example, to see whether there is commonality between these initiatives so we can leverage on them to push the regional integration efforts forward. But having seen the proliferation of master plans and blueprints, it is better that we can put things in a more operationalised and concrete way so that progress can be made and kept track of.

As for leadership, I think it is encouraging that China should play an important role. I hope that in the final version, specific suggestions should be made to ensure such a qualified leadership role. As it is important to note that China's aggressive expansion in trade and investment in some parts of the world have raised concerns, for example, in my country Cambodia, even though we are very close to China, due to the poor track record of Chinese corporations in their corporate social responsibility. I hope these can be discussed.

As this is a regional undertaking, specific regional policy instruments and institutions need to be emphasised. In addition, all the routes suggested in the vision should be prioritised. Probably in the details, we can take stock of what is happening in terms of the current flows of good, services, people in these selected routes so that concerned countries can buy-in in such an ambitious regional infrastructure project. If the benefits from building such regional connectivity can be assessed, it is natural for these countries to mobilise both external assistance and their own resources to realise this joint undertaking.

I am happy that you also emphasised, in Proposal Five, development of small- and medium-sized enterprises (SMEs) through internationalisation and linkages with multinationals. However, building capacity for SMEs is very difficult because most measures have to be undertaken by individual countries, so a specific way for cross-border assistance to help countries with an underdeveloped SME sector is necessary.

Chapter 2

2014 UPDATE ON ANNUAL COMPETITIVENESS ANALYSIS FOR ASEAN-10

2.1 Introductory Notes

In the tradition of the Asia Competitiveness Institute (ACI) at the Lee Kuan Yew School of Public Policy (LKYSPP), National University of Singapore (NUS), our publications make a distinctive contribution to the literature by focusing on competitiveness analysis at both national and sub-national levels for Greater China, India, Indonesia and the Association of Southeast Asian Nations (ASEAN) countries.[1] Particularly for ASEAN, the ACI has crafted an overarching and systematic methodology (the details of which are covered in the next section of this chapter), employed in this book to assess annually competitiveness at the national level. Since the inaugural volume titled *Annual Analysis of Competitiveness, Development Strategies and Public Policies on ASEAN-10: 2000-2010* (Tan *et al.*, 2013b), the comprehensive competitiveness index developed by the ACI has been used to rank the ASEAN economies in various dimensions. As the ACI aims to provide an update by extending all studies, this updated book thus includes data from 2000 to 2011.

Equally importantly, as the ACI works on evidence-based analysis, this volume is supported by quantitative methodologies, scientifically

[1] See Tan *et al.* (2013a), Tan *et al.* (2013b), Tan *et al.* (2013c) and Tan *et al.* (2013d).

and artfully presented to inform policymakers in each ASEAN member country and thus, enable them to assess their own competitiveness status as well as to identify the gaps that they need to address to benefit from regional and global integration. The ACI's competitiveness framework is thus substantially more nuanced and comprehensive than that of the more traditional and popular competitiveness indices in the literature.[2]

ASEAN was established in 1967[3] in Thailand, with the signing of the ASEAN Declaration (Bangkok Declaration) by Indonesia, Malaysia, Philippines, Singapore and Thailand — the 'founding fathers' of ASEAN. The group was expanded subsequently with the inclusion of five new members — Brunei Darussalam (1984), Vietnam (1995), Laos and Myanmar (1997) and finally Cambodia (1999), commonly referred to as ASEAN-10. A vibrant ASEAN, hosting over 600 million people, translates roughly into one half of China's or India's, or around 9% of the world's total population. With a combined GDP measured in purchasing power parity dollars of US$3.1 trillion in 2010 (see Table 2.1), ASEAN accounts for 4.1% of the world's total output, which is equivalent to about 30% of the economic size of China and 25% less than that of India.

In assessing competitiveness of ASEAN-10 economies, other features are as distinctive, notably geographic advantages. Mainland and maritime ASEAN-10 at the centre of an economically dynamic region is surrounded by India on the west; China, Japan and South Korea on the northeast; and Australia and New Zealand on the south. Enhanced

---

[2] Some examples include Geneva-based World Economic Forum (WEF)'s Global Competitiveness Report, International Management Development (IMD)'s World Competitiveness Yearbook, European Competitiveness Index, Atlas of Regional Competitiveness (Eurochambres, 2007) and EU regional competitiveness index.

[3] ASEAN started in 1967 as a security grouping in the midst of the Vietnam War, uniting Indonesia, Malaysia, the Philippines, Singapore, and Thailand against the 'potential threat' of communist-led insurgency. It was intended as a security community, promoting social and political stability during a turbulent time, which later changed gears to focus more on economic issues after the First Gulf War. In hindsight, visionary leadership then added to ASEAN's resilience and competitiveness (Low, 2004a).

Table 2.1. ASEAN-10 in a Snapshot, 2010

	Population		GDP (PPP$)		
Group	**(Million)**	**Share in World**	**(Billion)**	**Share in World**	**Income Level (World = 1.0)**
ASEAN-10					
Brunei	0.4	0.01%	20.1	0.03%	4.6
Cambodia	14.1	0.2%	30.8	0.04%	0.2
Indonesia	239.9	3.5%	1,032.3	1.4%	0.4
Lao PDR	6.2	0.1%	15.9	0.02%	0.2
Malaysia	28.4	0.4%	431.2	0.6%	1.4
Myanmar	48.0	0.7%	76.8	0.1%	0.1
Philippines	93.3	1.4%	367.8	0.5%	0.4
Singapore	5.1	0.1%	293.4	0.4%	5.2
Thailand	69.1	1.0%	587.5	0.8%	0.8
Vietnam	86.9	1.3%	276.8	0.4%	0.3
ASEAN-10	591.4	8.6%	3,132.7	4.1%	0.5
China	1,337.8	19.4%	10,105.0	13.2%	0.7
India	1,224.6	17.8%	4,122.3	5.4%	0.3
World	6,894.4	100%	76,296.5	100%	1.0

Source: Tan and Tan (2014).

connectivity among East Asian countries deemed as an alternative growth engine to the West (the United States (US) and European Union (EU)), as proposed in Chapter 1, can go a long way in promoting growth and development in the region.

It was with this objective in mind that the ASEAN Economic Community (AEC) was conceptualised in 1997 in the aftermath of the Asian Financial Crisis (AFC).[4] The prime objective of the AEC was to

[4]See ASEAN Secretariat (2008), Basu Das (2012), Basu Das *et al.* (2013) and Hansakul (2013) for assessment of the AEC.

promote the ASEAN-10 bloc as a vehicle to facilitate greater regional connectivity through constructing a competitive and sustainable 'single market and production base' that would not only include higher mobility of labour and capital, but also create a stable, prosperous and highly competitive economic region on the whole.[5] The launch of the AEC, which is scheduled for the end of 2015, can well prove to be a shot in the arm for ASEAN's economic potential. The bloc's diversity comprising both advanced economies, such as Singapore, and developing economies, such as Myanmar, can be a source of synergy, bringing together the various factor endowments such as capital and technological know-how of the advanced economies, as well as the competitive labour pool from the relatively less developed member countries.

While there are likely to be intense pressures on smaller economies to cope with this integration process, it is generally believed that the AEC could bring about a net positive contribution to the ASEAN-10 economies.[6] A significant component of the AEC concerns the notion of competitiveness. In fact, the marked heterogeneity among its members appears to be driven by the differences in their competitiveness as measured by various indicators. Therefore, to narrow the development gap within the bloc, solutions must also come from within individual economies. The ACI's annual competitiveness analysis of the ASEAN-10 thus offers a useful roadmap for policymakers in the respective member states.

Following this Introduction, Section 2.2 details the methodology and data used to derive the rankings as well as the simulation analysis showing how ASEAN-10 economies can improve their competitiveness in various dimensions. This makes the ACI's contribution more instructive than other competitiveness indices that merely report the rankings. Section 2.3 discusses the results of the competitiveness rankings and competitiveness progress over time. The top 20% strengths

[5] See Pushpanathan (2010).

[6] See Verbiest (2011).

and weaknesses of individual ASEAN economies are also presented. This is followed by '*what-if*' policy simulation that shows changes in the standardised scores as well as the rankings for individual economies following the improvement of their top 20% weaknesses. Section 2.4 concludes the chapter with policy implications.

2.2 ACI Competitiveness Framework and Methodology

2.2.1 Literature Review on Competitiveness

The notion of regional or *in situ* competitiveness has been explored in various ways. Initially, in the 1980's, 'competitiveness' was considered as part of the private sector domain, especially in relation to firm performance.[7] Over time, the discourse has expanded onto the domain of macroeconomics, as shown by the establishment of "Council on Competitiveness" or similar institutions in various advanced industrialised countries. Some scholars acknowledge that it is primarily firms that compete, not nations, regions, or places.[8] However, the performance of those firms depends on various factors that are embedded in the firm's location. These include quality of labour and infrastructure, governance, costs of doing business, as well as the performance of competing and complementary firms around the area.[9]

Two of the most highly cited cross-country competitiveness studies at the moment are the World Competitiveness Yearbook (WCY) by the IMD World Competitiveness Centre and the World Economic Forum (WEF)'s Global Competitiveness Report (GCR). The WCY defines competitiveness as composed of four factors: (i) economic performance, (ii) government efficiency, (iii) business efficiency, and

[7] See Porter (1980).

[8] See Krugman (1994).

[9] See Camagni (2002), Kitson, Martin and Tyler (2004) and Bristow (2010).

(iv) infrastructure. Each factor is further made up of five criteria, so that there are 20 criteria in total. The WCY uses equal weights such that each criterion contributes 5% weight, and each factor contributes 25% weight to the overall competitiveness index.[10] Most of the data used are statistical indicators sourced from international, regional and national organisations. However, substantial perception data sourced from executive surveys also supplement the statistical data.

The GCR breaks down its Global Competitiveness Index into three sub-indices: (i) basic requirements, (ii) efficiency enhancers, and (iii) innovation and sophistication factors.[11] Each of the three sub-indices has a different number of pillars. The basic requirements sub-index has four pillars: institutions, infrastructure, macroeconomic environment, and health and primary education. The efficiency enhancers sub-index is composed of six pillars: higher education and training, goods market efficiency, labour market efficiency, financial market development, technological readiness, and market size. Lastly, the innovation and sophistication factors sub-index consists of two pillars: business sophistication and innovation. Most of the data that make up these pillars and sub-indices come from executive opinion surveys.

2.2.2 ACI Competitiveness Framework

While the notion of competitiveness has been defined in various ways, the ACI's approach to competitiveness is eclectic and comprehensive as it takes into account different factors that collectively shape the ability of a nation or region to achieve substantial and inclusive economic development over a sustained period of time.

In line with this overarching thrust, the ACI defines competitiveness through four environments: (i) Macroeconomic Stability, (ii) Government and Institutional Setting, (iii) Financial, Businesses and

---

[10] See IMD World Competitiveness Center (2014).

[11] See World Economic Forum (2014).

Manpower Conditions, and (iv) Quality of Life and Infrastructure Development. These four environments carry equal weightage (25%) in the computation of the Overall Competitiveness score. Following a nested approach, each environment comprises three sub-environments of the same weightage (33.3%) (see Figure 2.1). While giving different weights to different environments and sub-environments based on their importance seems more appropriate, the method is nonetheless arbitrary and contentious. Thus, equal distribution of weight reflects a

Figure 2.1. ACI Competitiveness Framework

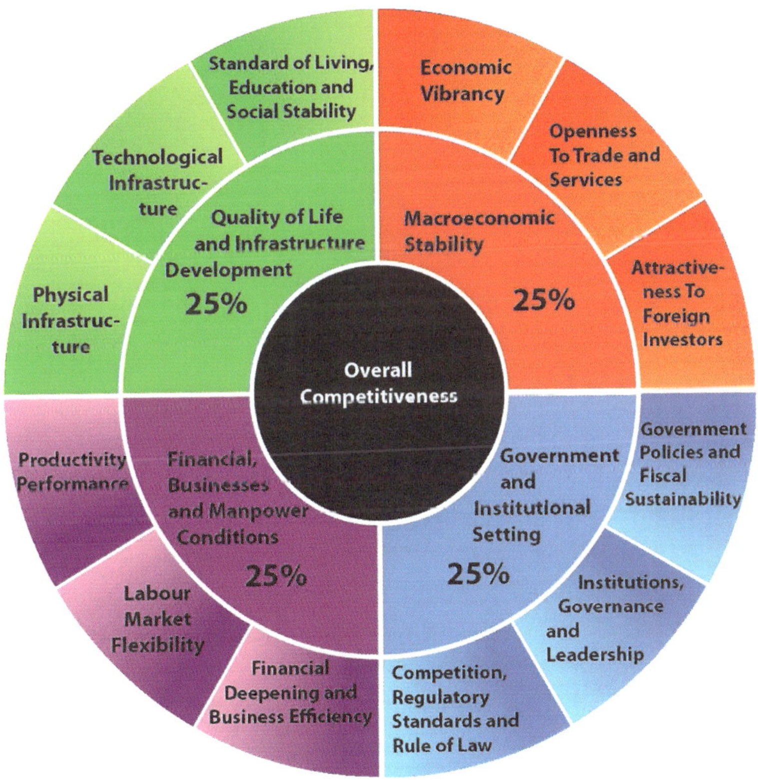

Source: Asia Competitiveness Institute.

balanced view toward the different factors that make up an overall notion of competitiveness.

The ACI's framework provides a holistic, integrated and systematic way of examining national competitiveness. Two environments are specifically related to economic performance, namely Macroeconomic Stability (MS) and Financial, Businesses and Manpower Conditions (FBMC). MS encompasses aggregated macroeconomic conditions which include: (i) Economic Vibrancy, (ii) Openness to Trade and Services, and (iii) Attractiveness to Foreign Investors. FBMC, on the other hand, represents the microeconomy, particularly firms and factors that impact their performances. FBMC thus comprises: (i) Financial Deepening and Business Efficiency, (ii) Labour Market Flexibility, and (iii) Productivity Performance. The remaining two environments are institutional and social in character. Government and Institutional Setting (GIS) covers the efficacy of government institutions and rule of law. This environment consists of: (i) Government Policies and Fiscal Sustainability, (ii) Institutions, Governance and Leadership, and (iii) Competition, Regulatory Standards and Rule of Law. Lastly, Quality of Life and Infrastructure Development (QLID) combines infrastructure, health and education services, environmental standards and social security. The three sub-environments are: (i) Physical Infrastructure, (ii) Technological Infrastructure, and (iii) Standard of Living, Education and Social Stability.

There are a total of 121 indicators used in the ACI's competitiveness rankings and simulations for ASEAN-10 economies in the period 2000–2011 (see Appendix 1). The extensive number of indicators ensures robust interpretation of each environment and sub-environment in the Overall Competitiveness score. Depending on data availability, some environments and sub-environments may have more indicators than others. Nonetheless, this is not an issue as they simply average out. This also allows a certain amount of flexibility in adding or removing indicators when updating the rankings in the future, so long as the overall structure of the four environments and 12 sub-environments remains unchanged.

2.2.3 Data Sources

The data for the 121 indicators used in this study were collected from various sources, of which the bulk of it comes from official data sources such as the World Bank World Development Indicators, Asian Development Bank (ADB) and WEF's Global Competitiveness Index. Other sources include Economist Intelligence Unit (EIU), Global Market Information Database (GMID), UNESCO Institute for Statistics, International Monetary Fund (IMF) World Economic Outlook Database, United Nations Conference on Trade and Development (UNCTAD), IMD World Competitiveness Yearbook, Environment Performance Index (EPI), International Telecommunication Union ICT Indicators Database, United Nations Development Programme (UNDP), Reporters Without Border and the Cingranelli-Richards Human Rights Dataset.

2.2.4 Computation of Standardised Scores

The next important question in terms of methodology is how to aggregate the different types of data into one coherent way of analysis. Given that there are 121 different indicators in this research with different values or quantity terms, such as GDP in millions of US dollars and population in number, how do we resolve these different units of measurement?

The ACI uses the statistical methodology of 'standardised score'. The standardised score is a relative comparison to see how well the performance of a certain economy is in comparison to the average economy. Therefore, the unit of measurement is no longer relevant. The standardised score has no unit of measurement because it simply measures relative performances among economies, whatever the indicator is.

In statistical terms, it measures how many standard deviations away each economy is from the average economy (see Appendix 2 for technical explanation). If an economy has a standardised score of zero, it is basically an average performer in terms of that particular indicator. Having a negative score means that the economy performs below average. Having a positive score, on the other hand, means an above-average performance.

The further away the score is from zero, the further away the performance of said economy is from the ASEAN-10 average. If an economy has a high positive score, it means it is far above the average score. The standardised scores for each indicator are then aggregated at the sub-environment level, then re-aggregated at the environment level, and finally aggregated again at the overall level. This allows comparison of performance of the 10 ASEAN economies at different levels, from the Overall Competitiveness to specific indicators in the four environments.

2.2.5 *What-if* Competitiveness Simulation Analysis

A competitiveness ranking in itself is like a beauty contest; it merely identifies who are doing well and who are facing challenges, but stops short of giving more constructive advice on improving the rankings. The ACI index goes one step further by tackling the 'so what' question. What is the policy implication of a competitiveness ranking result for a particular economy? The data used in the ACI index allows us to do an in-depth analysis of the performance of each economy according to the different indicators, sub-environments and environments. By analysing the said data, we are able to identify not just the Overall Competitiveness ranking, but also specific indicators in which the economy is doing well or struggling. This allows us to come up with policy recommendations for each economy.

The ACI thus conduct the '*what-if*' competitiveness simulation that is based on an improvement of each economy's top 20% weakest indicators, and a re-calculation of the standardised score based on such improvement. To do this, we first look at each economy and sort the different indicators for each economy from the highest to the lowest score. This allows us to identify the 24 weakest indicators (the bottom 20% of the 121 indicators) for each economy.

Next, we raise the scores of these 24 weakest indicators to match the average score. This means their average score is raised to zero if it was negative previously. For other economies, which are already competitive, their scores are not discounted and thus remain unchanged. Once these scores are raised, we re-calculate the ranking, assuming that other economies stay constant. We carry out this simulation one-by-one for each economy. Each economy would then have a new, improved standardised score. This allows us to answer the question: if a particular economy improves on its set of weakest indicators, assuming other economies remain constant, how would that economy's competitiveness ranking improve?

2.3 Competitiveness Analysis of ASEAN-10 Economies, 2000–2011

In this section, we present the Overall Competitiveness rankings as well as the rankings for the four environments as derived from the standardised scores for each economy over the period 2000–2011. The scores for individual sub-environments are visualised in the median and maximum web analysis. The findings on the '*what-if*' competitiveness simulation are also discussed.

2.3.1 Overall Competitiveness

Table 2.2 and Figure 2.2 show the Overall Competitiveness ranking along with each economy's scores for the period 2000–2011. As presented in Table 2.2, only five ASEAN economies, namely Singapore (first), Malaysia (second), Thailand (third), Brunei (fourth) and Cambodia (eighth), maintained the same rankings throughout the study period. While Malaysia improved its positive scores in 2011, it is still

Table 2.2. Overall Competitiveness Rankings and Scores, 2000–2011

	OVERALL									
	1		2		3		4		5	
Rank	**Economy**	**Score**	**Economy**	**Score**	**Economy**	**Score**	**Economy**	**Score**	**Economy**	**Score**
2000	Singapore	2.1239	Malaysia	0.9908	Thailand	0.5458	Brunei	0.3689	Philippines	–0.1195
2001	Singapore	2.1000	Malaysia	0.9536	Thailand	0.6112	Brunei	0.3851	Philippines	–0.0875
2002	Singapore	1.9583	Malaysia	1.0812	Thailand	0.7688	Brunei	0.3517	Philippines	–0.1576
2003	Singapore	1.9688	Malaysia	1.1016	Thailand	0.7234	Brunei	0.3638	Indonesia	–0.1557
2004	Singapore	1.9523	Malaysia	1.1292	Thailand	0.7011	Brunei	0.4030	Indonesia	–0.1152
2005	Singapore	2.0054	Malaysia	1.1140	Thailand	0.6922	Brunei	0.3512	Philippines	–0.1869
2006	Singapore	1.9707	Malaysia	1.1402	Thailand	0.6548	Brunei	0.3579	Indonesia	–0.0792
2007	Singapore	2.0348	Malaysia	1.1206	Thailand	0.5445	Brunei	0.2986	Indonesia	–0.0012
2008	Singapore	2.1125	Malaysia	1.0198	Thailand	0.5143	Brunei	0.3318	Indonesia	0.0342
2009	Singapore	2.1774	Malaysia	0.9289	Thailand	0.4893	Brunei	0.3507	Indonesia	0.0415
2010	Singapore	2.1097	Malaysia	1.0029	Thailand	0.4872	Brunei	0.3896	Indonesia	0.0842
2011	Singapore	2.0944	Malaysia	1.1388	Thailand	0.4710	Brunei	0.3683	Indonesia	0.0013

(Continued)

Table 2.2. *(Continued)*

	OVERALL									
	6		7		8		9		10	
Rank	**Economy**	**Score**	**Economy**	**Score**	**Economy**	**Score**	**Economy**	**Score**	**Economy**	**Score**
2000	Indonesia	–0.1641	Vietnam	–0.3582	Cambodia	–0.9110	Myanmar	–1.1786	Laos	–1.2981
2001	Indonesia	–0.1994	Vietnam	–0.3341	Cambodia	–0.9157	Laos	–1.2175	Myanmar	–1.2957
2002	Indonesia	–0.2266	Vietnam	–0.2931	Cambodia	–0.9383	Laos	–1.2438	Myanmar	–1.3006
2003	Philippines	–0.2447	Vietnam	–0.2738	Cambodia	–0.9813	Myanmar	–1.2111	Laos	–1.2908
2004	Philippines	–0.2419	Vietnam	–0.3663	Cambodia	–0.9640	Laos	–1.2053	Myanmar	–1.2930
2005	Indonesia	–0.2245	Vietnam	–0.3420	Cambodia	–0.9627	Laos	–1.1435	Myanmar	–1.3033
2006	Philippines	–0.2224	Vietnam	–0.3548	Cambodia	–0.9667	Laos	–1.1568	Myanmar	–1.3437
2007	Philippines	–0.2155	Vietnam	–0.3108	Cambodia	–0.9851	Laos	–1.1571	Myanmar	–1.3288
2008	Vietnam	–0.2904	Philippines	–0.2994	Cambodia	–0.9996	Laos	–1.1324	Myanmar	–1.2908
2009	Vietnam	–0.1959	Philippines	–0.4250	Cambodia	–1.0402	Laos	–1.0526	Myanmar	–1.2741
2010	Vietnam	–0.2230	Philippines	–0.4467	Cambodia	–1.0013	Laos	–1.1364	Myanmar	–1.2663
2011	Philippines	–0.3593	Vietnam	–0.4492	Cambodia	–0.8869	Laos	–1.1085	Myanmar	–1.2699

Source: Asia Competitiveness Institute.

Figure 2.2. Overall Competitiveness — 2000, 2010 and 2011

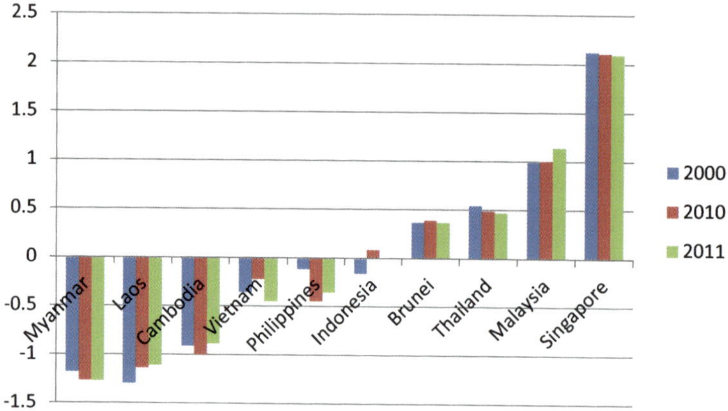

Source: Asia Competitiveness Institute.

scoring a distant second to Singapore, which also seems to be recovering from the 2008 Global Financial Crisis (GFC). Indonesia's scores turned slightly positive since 2008. The scores matter more than improvement in rankings as Indonesia overtook the Philippines on a couple of occasions, for instance in 2003 and 2006.

For those with negative scores, as seen in Table 2.2, Myanmar seemed worse off in 2011 as compared to 2000 while Vietnam and the Philippines, in particular, plunged more negatively in 2011 compared to 2000.[12]

[12] This pattern is consistent with the widely cited Global Economic Forum's competitiveness index, which reveals that Singapore ranked second overall among the 144 economies included in the report and Cambodia turned out to be a relative under-achiever in the ASEAN-10 at the 85th place. Marked differences were also observed in the Global Competitiveness Report 2012–2013 as countries like Malaysia and Brunei Darussalam at the 25th and 28th place, respectively, did relatively well compared to the rest. They were followed by Thailand at 38th and Indonesia at 50th. The Philippines (65th) and Vietnam (75th) ranked better than Cambodia though still lagging behind the other economies in the region (Geiger, 2013).

2.3.2 Macroeconomic Stability

In Table 2.3, the top two positions for Macroeconomic Stability remained the same as for Overall Competitiveness with Indonesia at third place and Thailand at fourth place, all with positive scores for 2000–2011. Singapore remained fairly consistent in scores, which were still more than double those of Malaysia. Thailand's scores did fall since 2008, due to the GFC and internal events. Indonesia doubled its scores between 2000 and 2011. Brunei was challenged by the Philippines only in 2007, with its negative score turning positive by 2010 and increasing quite impressively by 2011. Myanmar 10th has to heed Laos among the CLMV grouping.

For the three sub-environments under Macroeconomic Stability, Figure 2.4 for Economic Vibrancy shows Indonesia as the top performer in 2011, followed by Singapore, Malaysia and Thailand. Indonesia is rising as a middle-income country and its emerging soft power is clear.

In Figure 2.5 for Openness to Trade and Services and Figure 2.6 for Attractiveness to Foreign Investors, Singapore was at the top, followed by Thailand at the second position for Openness to Trade and Services, and Malaysia at the second position for Attractiveness to Foreign Investors. Myanmar at the ninth place was ahead of Laos but remained at the 10th position, as seen in Figure 2.6, for Attractiveness to Foreign Investors throughout the years, with the Philippines joining the CLMV with negative scores.

Table 2.3. Macroeconomic Stability Rankings and Scores, 2000–2011

MACROECONOMIC STABILITY										
Rank	**1**		**2**		**3**		**4**		**5**	
	Economy	**Score**	**Economy**	**Score**	**Economy**	**Score**	**Economy**	**Score**	**Economy**	**Score**
2000	Singapore	2.1562	Malaysia	0.9077	Thailand	0.6735	Indonesia	0.2341	Brunei	–0.1823
2001	Singapore	2.0598	Malaysia	0.8756	Thailand	0.7058	Indonesia	0.1872	Brunei	0.0519
2002	Singapore	1.9859	Malaysia	0.9133	Thailand	0.7521	Indonesia	0.2821	Brunei	0.0130
2003	Singapore	2.1198	Malaysia	0.8732	Thailand	0.6850	Indonesia	0.3986	Brunei	–0.0977
2004	Singapore	2.1520	Malaysia	0.8813	Thailand	0.7722	Indonesia	0.3135	Brunei	–0.1465
2005	Singapore	2.1533	Malaysia	0.9081	Thailand	0.7493	Indonesia	0.2526	Brunei	–0.1120
2006	Singapore	2.0974	Malaysia	0.8844	Thailand	0.7543	Indonesia	0.4073	Brunei	–0.1111
2007	Singapore	2.0896	Malaysia	0.9295	Thailand	0.7381	Indonesia	0.4565	Philippines	–0.2148
2008	Singapore	2.1087	Malaysia	0.8279	Thailand	0.7582	Indonesia	0.6014	Brunei	–0.1712
2009	Singapore	2.2261	Thailand	0.7064	Malaysia	0.6693	Indonesia	0.6105	Brunei	–0.1573
2010	Singapore	2.2035	Malaysia	0.7255	Thailand	0.5937	Indonesia	0.5660	Brunei	0.0178
2011	Singapore	2.2375	Malaysia	0.7825	Indonesia	0.5680	Thailand	0.4867	Brunei	0.0409

(Continued)

Table 2.3. *(Continued)*

Rank	**MACROECONOMIC STABILITY**									
	6		**7**		**8**		**9**		**10**	
	Economy	**Score**	**Economy**	**Score**	**Economy**	**Score**	**Economy**	**Score**	**Economy**	**Score**
2000	Philippines	−0.2725	Vietnam	−0.3460	Cambodia	−0.5335	Myanmar	−1.1980	Laos	−1.4393
2001	Vietnam	−0.2157	Philippines	−0.3299	Cambodia	−0.5333	Laos	−1.1871	Myanmar	−1.6142
2002	Vietnam	−0.2474	Philippines	−0.2482	Cambodia	−0.6372	Laos	−1.1955	Myanmar	−1.6182
2003	Vietnam	−0.3144	Philippines	−0.3716	Cambodia	−0.6918	Myanmar	−1.2389	Laos	−1.3623
2004	Philippines	−0.3833	Vietnam	−0.5008	Cambodia	−0.5935	Laos	−1.1639	Myanmar	−1.3310
2005	Philippines	−0.3865	Vietnam	−0.4697	Cambodia	−0.6246	Laos	−1.0249	Myanmar	−1.4458
2006	Philippines	−0.3337	Vietnam	−0.5096	Cambodia	−0.7202	Laos	−0.9756	Myanmar	−1.4933
2007	Brunei	−0.2931	Vietnam	−0.4951	Cambodia	−0.8055	Laos	−0.9818	Myanmar	−1.4235
2008	Vietnam	−0.4876	Philippines	−0.5150	Cambodia	−0.7689	Laos	−1.0369	Myanmar	−1.3165
2009	Vietnam	−0.4063	Philippines	−0.6331	Cambodia	−0.8452	Laos	−0.9051	Myanmar	−1.2651
2010	Vietnam	−0.4257	Philippines	−0.4841	Cambodia	−0.7914	Laos	−1.1302	Myanmar	−1.2751
2011	Philippines	−0.4335	Vietnam	−0.6299	Cambodia	−0.7457	Laos	−1.0551	Myanmar	−1.2514

Source: Asia Competitiveness Institute.

Figure 2.3. Macroeconomic Stability — 2000, 2010 and 2011

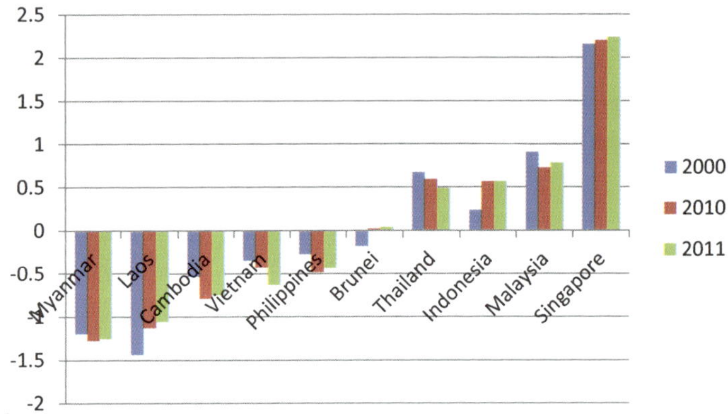

Source: Asia Competitiveness Institute.

Figure 2.4. Macroeconomic Stability (Economic Vibrancy) — 2000, 2010 and 2011

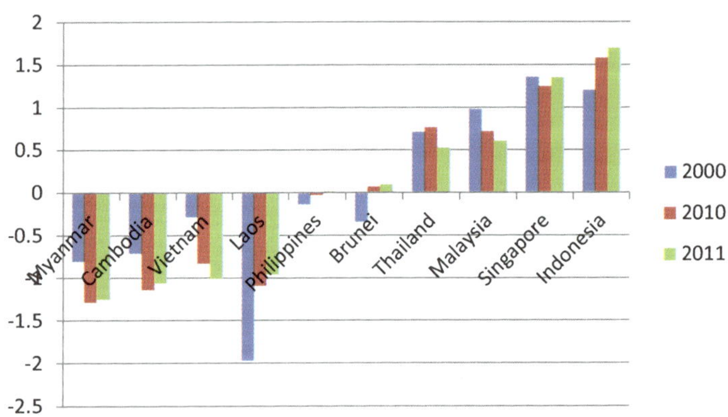

Source: Asia Competitiveness Institute.

Figure 2.5. Macroeconomic Stability (Openness to Trade and Services) — 2000, 2010 and 2011

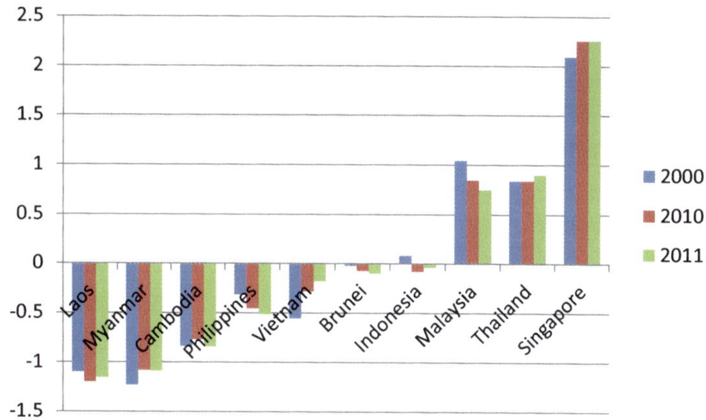

Source: Asia Competitiveness Institute.

Figure 2.6. Macroeconomic Stability (Attractiveness to Foreign Investors) — 2000, 2010 and 2011

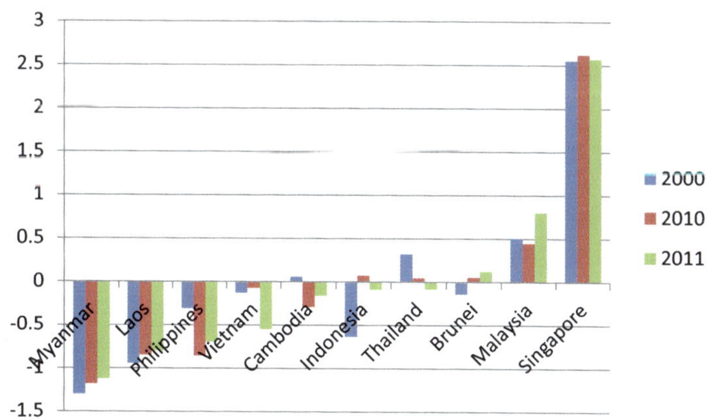

Source: Asia Competitiveness Institute.

2.3.3 Government and Institutional Setting

The same duo, Singapore and Malaysia, occupied the top two places in the Government and Institutional Setting ranking over the period of 2000–2011, but only Malaysia improved its score in 2011 (see Table 2.4). Brunei overtook Thailand by 2009, but both registered positive scores compared to the rest of ASEAN.

For the three selected years in Figure 2.7, Singapore remained ahead as a developmental state with a strong role of government that is not captured by special interests,[13] which attracts foreign direct investment (FDI) and multinational corporations (MNCs) alike, given the incentives by the government to site their headquarters in the city-state in order to capitalise on surging trends in ASEAN and East Asia, as well as connectivity to South Asia. Laos stayed at the 10th position with the rest of the CLMV at the bottom. That said, older ASEAN economies with negative scores, such as Indonesia and the Philippines, need to mind the law and order for political stability as a prime source of economic competitiveness. It is necessary and is a priority even if democracy as a luxury good naturally follows with maturity in economic growth and development, and resultant prosperity to spur social and political development as a whole.

Singapore was at the top rank for three sub-environments, namely Government Policies and Fiscal Sustainability (Figure 2.8), Institutions, Governance and Leadership (Figure 2.9) and Competition, Regulatory Standards and Rule of Law (Figure 2.10) for the selected years. The Philippines recovered only a tad in 2011, as seen in Figure 2.9. From the same figure, it can be seen that Thailand's score plunged more

[13] A developmental state in theory is defined as one that promotes long-term entrepreneurial activities among the industrial elites comprising key business groups, and resists growth-compromising demands from special interest groups, that is, not be captured to lose sight of its mission. Alternatively, a developmental state is defined as embedded in local social groups through close associational ties between state bureaucrats or technocrats and domestic social classes, but the state avoids being captured by the latter to retain its autonomy — see Low (2001), Low (2004b) and Low (2008).

Table 2.4. Government and Institutional Setting Rankings and Scores, 2000–2011

GOVERNMENT AND INSTITUTIONAL SETTING										
Rank	**1**		**2**		**3**		**4**		**5**	
	Economy	**Score**	**Economy**	**Score**	**Economy**	**Score**	**Economy**	**Score**	**Economy**	**Score**
2000	Singapore	2.2693	Malaysia	0.7820	Thailand	0.5544	Brunei	0.4529	Philippines	–0.0825
2001	Singapore	2.2597	Malaysia	0.7858	Thailand	0.5783	Brunei	0.3796	Philippines	–0.0315
2002	Singapore	2.1408	Malaysia	0.9519	Thailand	0.7242	Brunei	0.2528	Philippines	–0.1287
2003	Singapore	2.0910	Malaysia	0.9197	Thailand	0.8536	Brunei	0.2530	Vietnam	–0.1458
2004	Singapore	2.0482	Malaysia	1.0397	Thailand	0.7397	Brunei	0.4226	Philippines	–0.2537
2005	Singapore	2.0332	Malaysia	1.1002	Thailand	0.7199	Brunei	0.4004	Philippines	–0.1866
2006	Singapore	2.1020	Malaysia	0.9913	Thailand	0.6583	Brunei	0.4256	Philippines	–0.2348
2007	Singapore	2.1706	Malaysia	0.9937	Thailand	0.5547	Brunei	0.4324	Philippines	–0.2147
2008	Singapore	2.3313	Malaysia	0.8253	Thailand	0.4646	Brunei	0.4439	Vietnam	–0.2743
2009	Singapore	2.3899	Malaysia	0.6473	Brunei	0.5178	Thailand	0.4600	Indonesia	–0.2614
2010	Singapore	2.3214	Malaysia	0.7887	Brunei	0.4853	Thailand	0.4054	Indonesia	–0.1357
2011	Singapore	2.2404	Malaysia	1.0061	Brunei	0.5430	Thailand	0.3730	Indonesia	–0.3216

(*Continued*)

Table 2.4. *(Continued)*

Rank	6		7		8		9		10	
	GOVERNMENT AND INSTITUTIONAL SETTING									
	Economy	Score	Economy	Score	Economy	Score	Economy	Score	Economy	Score
2000	Vietnam	−0.3243	Indonesia	−0.5557	Cambodia	−0.7959	Myanmar	−1.0355	Laos	−1.2647
2001	Vietnam	−0.2665	Indonesia	−0.5096	Cambodia	−0.8640	Myanmar	−1.1387	Laos	−1.1930
2002	Vietnam	−0.1978	Indonesia	−0.4630	Cambodia	−0.8837	Myanmar	−1.1935	Laos	−1.2030
2003	Philippines	−0.2891	Indonesia	−0.3601	Myanmar	−0.9579	Cambodia	−1.0387	Laos	−1.3259
2004	Vietnam	−0.2650	Indonesia	−0.4214	Cambodia	−0.9789	Laos	−1.0923	Myanmar	−1.2388
2005	Vietnam	−0.2802	Indonesia	−0.5244	Cambodia	−0.9321	Laos	−1.1148	Myanmar	−1.2155
2006	Indonesia	−0.2431	Vietnam	−0.3787	Cambodia	−0.9419	Laos	−1.1174	Myanmar	−1.2614
2007	Indonesia	−0.3442	Vietnam	−0.3722	Cambodia	−0.9003	Laos	−1.1335	Myanmar	−1.1865
2008	Philippines	−0.3074	Indonesia	−0.4274	Cambodia	−0.9678	Myanmar	−1.0213	Laos	−1.0670
2009	Vietnam	−0.2710	Philippines	−0.4816	Cambodia	−0.9052	Laos	−1.0353	Myanmar	−1.0606
2010	Vietnam	−0.3307	Philippines	−0.4000	Cambodia	−0.9332	Myanmar	−1.0384	Laos	−1.1629
2011	Philippines	−0.3356	Vietnam	−0.5225	Cambodia	−0.7659	Myanmar	−1.0832	Laos	−1.1339

Source: Asia Competitiveness Institute.

Figure 2.7. Government and Institutional Setting — 2000, 2010 and 2011

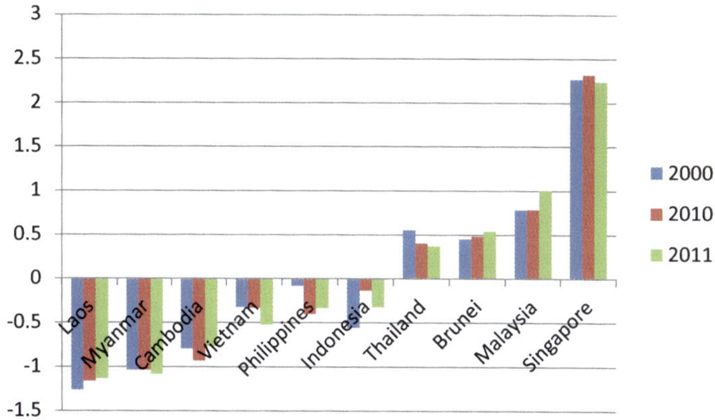

Source: Asia Competitiveness Institute.

Figure 2.8. Government and Institutional Setting (Government Policies and Fiscal Sustainability) — 2000, 2010 and 2011

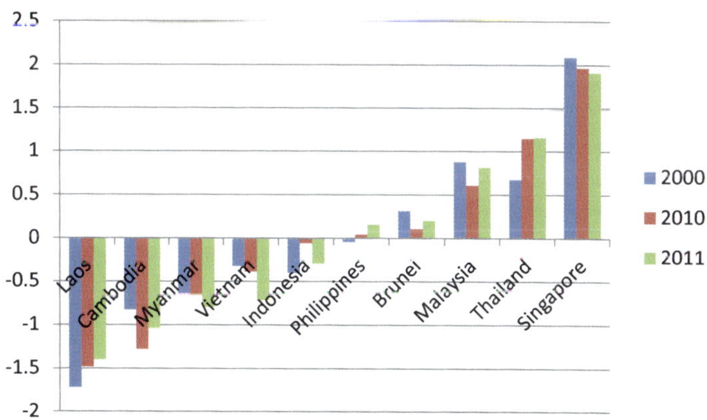

Source: Asia Competitiveness Institute.

negatively in 2011, reflecting the struggle for governance and leadership. Myanmar ranked eighth according to Figure 2.8, and 10th in Figure 2.9 and 2.10.

Figure 2.9. Government and Institutional Setting (Institutions, Governance and Leadership) — 2000, 2010 and 2011

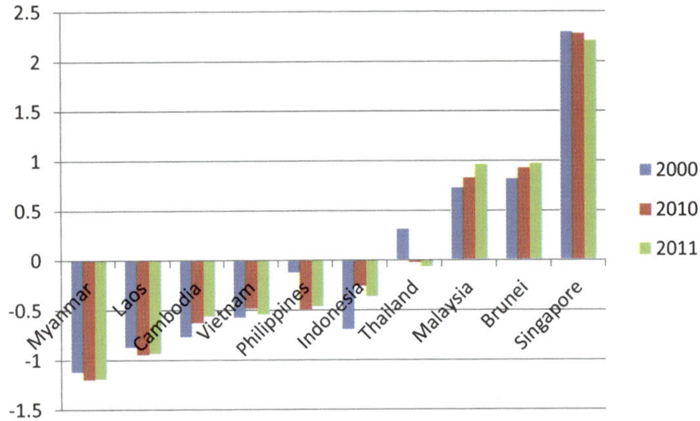

Source: Asia Competitiveness Institute.

Figure 2.10. Government and Institutional Setting (Competition, Regulatory Standards and Rule of Law) — 2000, 2010 and 2011

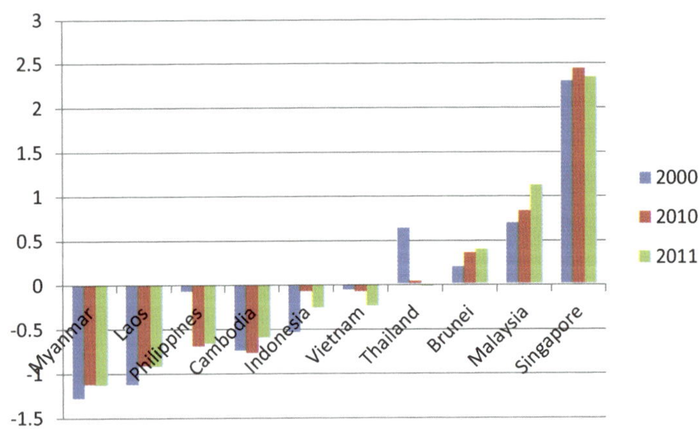

Source: Asia Competitiveness Institute.

2.3.4 Financial, Businesses and Manpower Conditions

The trio of Singapore, Malaysia and Thailand remained at the top in Table 2.5, with Brunei as the only other country with positive scores for Financial, Businesses and Manpower Conditions Ranking over the period of 2000–2011, all mirrored in Figure 2.11 for the three selected years (2000, 2010 and 2011). By 2007, Myanmar 10th was losing its position to Cambodia and Laos as shown in Table 2.5.

In Figure 2.11, among the older ASEAN economies, Indonesia and the Philippines deserve some attention, but Indonesia recovered to small positive scores in 2010 and 2011. Malaysia was catching up with Singapore by 2011. Even Singapore succumbed somewhat in the sub-environments shown in Figure 2.12 to 2.14, and was definitely doing worse in 2011 compared to 2010.

For Financial Deepening and Business Efficiency (Figure 2.12), the same trio, Singapore, Malaysia and Thailand, were at the top positions. However, Malaysia took the top place for Labour Market Flexibility (Figure 2.13) and Brunei was also at the top for Productivity Performance (Figure 2.14). Singapore fared less well in 2011 in all three sub-environments, notably Labour Market Flexibility.

Table 2.5. Financial, Businesses and Manpower Conditions Rankings and Scores, 2000–2011

FINANCIAL, BUSINESSES AND MANPOWER CONDITIONS										
Rank	**1**		**2**		**3**		**4**		**5**	
	Economy	**Score**	**Economy**	**Score**	**Economy**	**Score**	**Economy**	**Score**	**Economy**	**Score**
2000	Singapore	1.8869	Malaysia	1.2310	Thailand	0.5368	Brunei	0.3147	Indonesia	–0.0369
2001	Singapore	1.9363	Malaysia	1.0842	Thailand	0.7104	Brunei	0.2913	Philippines	–0.0349
2002	Singapore	1.6130	Malaysia	1.3420	Thailand	0.9718	Brunei	0.3104	Vietnam	–0.1548
2003	Singapore	1.5874	Malaysia	1.4110	Thailand	0.8429	Brunei	0.4400	Vietnam	–0.0425
2004	Singapore	1.5480	Malaysia	1.4322	Thailand	0.8202	Brunei	0.4044	Indonesia	–0.0859
2005	Singapore	1.7594	Malaysia	1.2542	Thailand	0.8434	Brunei	0.2397	Vietnam	–0.0425
2006	Singapore	1.6762	Malaysia	1.4368	Thailand	0.7728	Brunei	0.3098	Vietnam	–0.1293
2007	Singapore	1.6784	Malaysia	1.4990	Thailand	0.5284	Brunei	0.3076	Indonesia	0.0258
2008	Singapore	1.7821	Malaysia	1.3812	Thailand	0.5387	Brunei	0.1980	Indonesia	0.1038
2009	Singapore	1.8066	Malaysia	1.3836	Thailand	0.5433	Brunei	0.1705	Vietnam	0.0838
2010	Singapore	1.6513	Malaysia	1.4975	Thailand	0.6865	Brunei	0.2125	Indonesia	0.0470
2011	Malaysia	1.6294	Singapore	1.6175	Thailand	0.7782	Brunei	0.0608	Indonesia	0.0347

(*Continued*)

Table 2.5. *(Continued)*

FINANCIAL, BUSINESSES AND MANPOWER CONDITIONS										
Rank	**6**		**7**		**8**		**9**		**10**	
	Economy	**Score**	**Economy**	**Score**	**Economy**	**Score**	**Economy**	**Score**	**Economy**	**Score**
2000	Vietnam	–0.1058	Philippines	–0.1546	Laos	–1.1772	Myanmar	–1.2098	Cambodia	–1.2851
2001	Indonesia	–0.1551	Vietnam	–0.1942	Myanmar	–1.1363	Laos	–1.2167	Cambodia	–1.2850
2002	Philippines	–0.1730	Indonesia	–0.2728	Myanmar	–1.1025	Cambodia	–1.2353	Laos	–1.2988
2003	Philippines	–0.3015	Indonesia	–0.3105	Cambodia	–1.1277	Laos	–1.2223	Myanmar	–1.2768
2004	Vietnam	–0.0973	Philippines	–0.3100	Cambodia	–1.1730	Myanmar	–1.2214	Laos	–1.3174
2005	Philippines	–0.0745	Indonesia	–0.3262	Myanmar	–1.2151	Cambodia	–1.2159	Laos	–1.2224
2006	Philippines	–0.2417	Indonesia	–0.2446	Cambodia	–1.0677	Myanmar	–1.2262	Laos	–1.2862
2007	Vietnam	–0.0496	Philippines	–0.3526	Cambodia	–1.0834	Laos	–1.2674	Myanmar	–1.2863
2008	Vietnam	–0.0771	Philippines	–0.2737	Cambodia	–1.0748	Laos	–1.1988	Myanmar	–1.3794
2009	Indonesia	0.0279	Philippines	–0.4368	Laos	–1.0628	Cambodia	–1.2148	Myanmar	–1.3013
2010	Vietnam	0.0404	Philippines	–0.6348	Laos	–1.0776	Cambodia	–1.1366	Myanmar	–1.2862
2011	Vietnam	–0.3231	Philippines	–0.4007	Cambodia	–1.0941	Laos	–1.1028	Myanmar	–1.2002

Source: Asia Competitiveness Institute.

Figure 2.11. Financial, Businesses and Manpower Conditions — 2000, 2010 and 2011

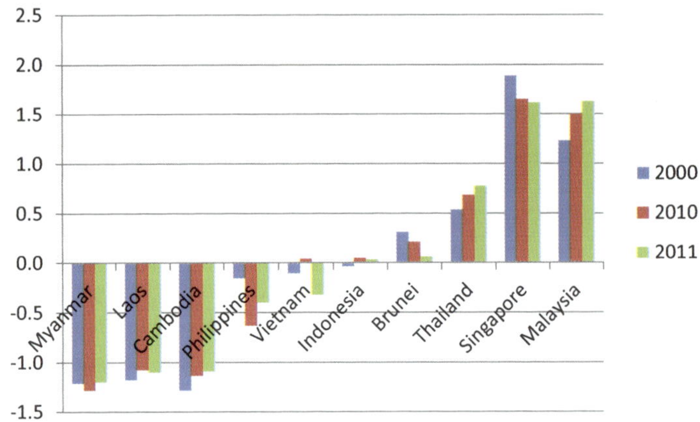

Source: Asia Competitiveness Institute.

Figure 2.12. Financial, Businesses and Manpower Conditions (Financial Deepening and Business Efficiency) — 2000, 2010 and 2011

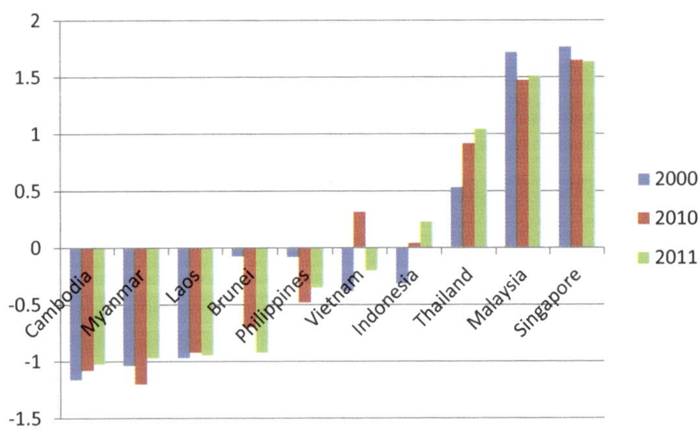

Source: Asia Competitiveness Institute.

Figure 2.13. Financial, Businesses and Manpower Conditions (Labour Market Flexibility) — 2000, 2010 and 2011

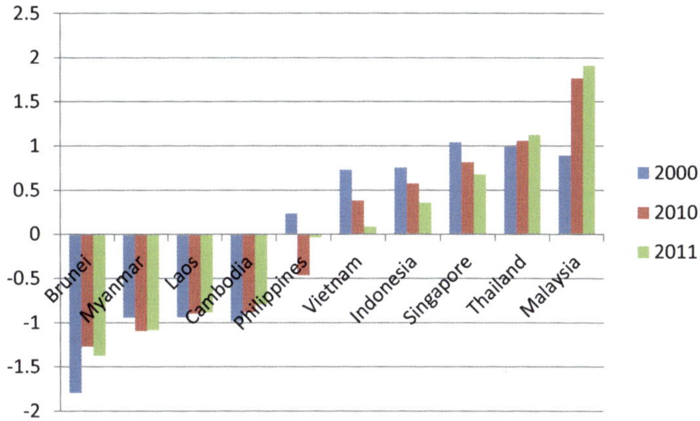

Source: Asia Competitiveness Institute.

Figure 2.14. Financial, Businesses and Manpower Conditions (Productivity Performance) — 2000, 2010 and 2011

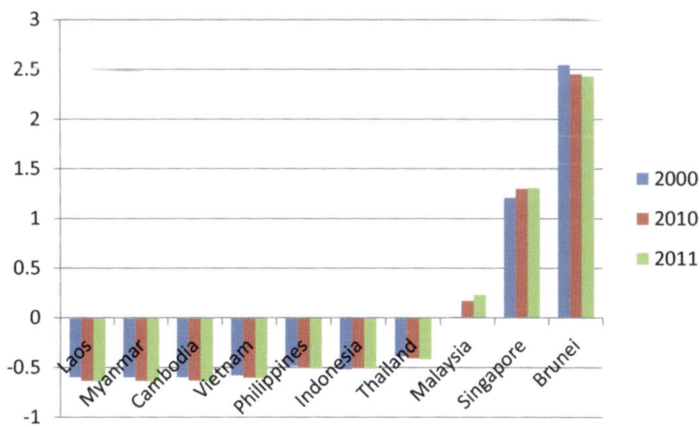

Source: Asia Competitiveness Institute.

2.3.5 Quality of Life and Infrastructure Development

Singapore, Malaysia and Brunei were at the top three places for Quality of Life and Infrastructure Development (see Table 2.6). The trio and Thailand were the only four countries with positive scores throughout the period as the Philippines turned negative in 2002 and since 2005. These rankings are reflected in Figure 2.15 for three selected years (2000, 2010 and 2011).

For the three sub-environments, Singapore and Malaysia held their top two positions for Physical Infrastructure (Figure 2.16), but Brunei overtook Malaysia at second place for Technological Infrastructure (Figure 2.17) and Standard of Living, Education and Social Stability (Figure 2.18). Laos ranked 10th in Physical Infrastructure (Figure 2.16) and Myanmar ranked 10th in the remaining two sub-environments (Figure 2.17 and 2.18).

Table 2.6. Quality of Life and Infrastructure Development Rankings and Scores, 2000–2011

QUALITY OF LIFE AND INFRASTRUCTURE DEVELOPMENT										
Rank	**1**		**2**		**3**		**4**		**5**	
	Economy	**Score**	**Economy**	**Score**	**Economy**	**Score**	**Economy**	**Score**	**Economy**	**Score**
2000	Singapore	2.0026	Malaysia	0.9585	Brunei	0.8591	Thailand	0.3722	Philippines	0.0417
2001	Singapore	1.9991	Malaysia	1.0029	Brunei	0.7909	Thailand	0.4080	Philippines	0.0522
2002	Singapore	1.9456	Malaysia	1.0357	Brunei	0.8039	Thailand	0.5690	Philippines	–0.0687
2003	Singapore	1.9009	Malaysia	1.1041	Brunei	0.8271	Thailand	0.4472	Philippines	0.0051
2004	Singapore	1.8869	Malaysia	1.0627	Brunei	0.8956	Thailand	0.4097	Philippines	0.0012
2005	Singapore	1.9222	Malaysia	1.1083	Brunei	0.8498	Thailand	0.4033	Philippines	–0.0857
2006	Singapore	1.8676	Malaysia	1.1674	Brunei	0.7818	Thailand	0.3875	Philippines	–0.0636
2007	Singapore	2.0343	Malaysia	0.9684	Brunei	0.7231	Thailand	0.3124	Philippines	–0.0624
2008	Singapore	2.0208	Malaysia	0.9446	Brunei	0.8241	Thailand	0.2453	Philippines	–0.0721
2009	Singapore	2.0509	Malaysia	0.9147	Brunei	0.8336	Thailand	0.1942	Philippines	–0.1023
2010	Singapore	2.0717	Malaysia	0.9092	Brunei	0.8075	Thailand	0.2192	Indonesia	–0.1483
2011	Singapore	2.0707	Malaysia	1.0225	Brunei	0.7913	Thailand	0.1986	Philippines	–0.2313

(*Continued*)

Table 2.6. *(Continued)*

QUALITY OF LIFE AND INFRASTRUCTURE DEVELOPMENT										
Rank	**6**		**7**		**8**		**9**		**10**	
	Economy	**Score**	**Economy**	**Score**	**Economy**	**Score**	**Economy**	**Score**	**Economy**	**Score**
2000	Indonesia	–0.2839	Vietnam	–0.6262	Cambodia	–0.9520	Myanmar	–1.1708	Laos	–1.2011
2001	Indonesia	–0.3062	Vietnam	–0.6370	Cambodia	–0.9173	Laos	–1.1888	Myanmar	–1.2037
2002	Indonesia	–0.4356	Vietnam	–0.5501	Cambodia	–0.9260	Laos	–1.1838	Myanmar	–1.1900
2003	Indonesia	–0.3369	Vietnam	–0.5683	Cambodia	–0.9793	Laos	–1.1374	Myanmar	–1.2626
2004	Indonesia	–0.2568	Vietnam	–0.5694	Cambodia	–1.0245	Laos	–1.1400	Myanmar	–1.2653
2005	Indonesia	–0.2828	Vietnam	–0.5495	Cambodia	–1.0045	Laos	–1.1243	Myanmar	–1.2369
2006	Indonesia	–0.2308	Vietnam	–0.3763	Cambodia	–1.0685	Laos	–1.1661	Myanmar	–1.2990
2007	Indonesia	–0.1429	Vietnam	–0.3009	Cambodia	–1.0706	Laos	–1.1510	Myanmar	–1.3104
2008	Indonesia	–0.1443	Vietnam	–0.2942	Cambodia	–1.0888	Laos	–1.1160	Myanmar	–1.3195
2009	Vietnam	–0.1688	Indonesia	–0.2155	Cambodia	–1.0826	Laos	–1.0931	Myanmar	–1.3312
2010	Vietnam	–0.1558	Philippines	–0.2273	Cambodia	–1.0535	Laos	–1.0719	Myanmar	–1.3508
2011	Vietnam	–0.2762	Indonesia	–0.2763	Cambodia	–0.8524	Laos	–1.0304	Myanmar	–1.4165

Source: Asia Competitiveness Institute.

Figure 2.15. Quality of Life and Infrastructure Development — 2000, 2010 and 2011

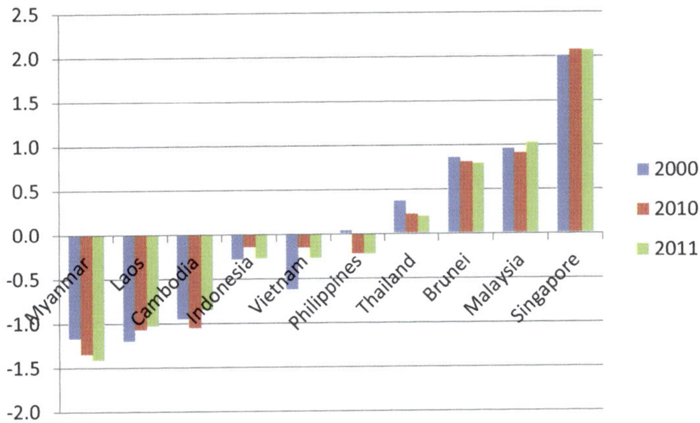

Source: Asia Competitiveness Institute.

Figure 2.16. Quality of Life and Infrastructure Development (Physical Infrastructure) — 2000, 2010 and 2011

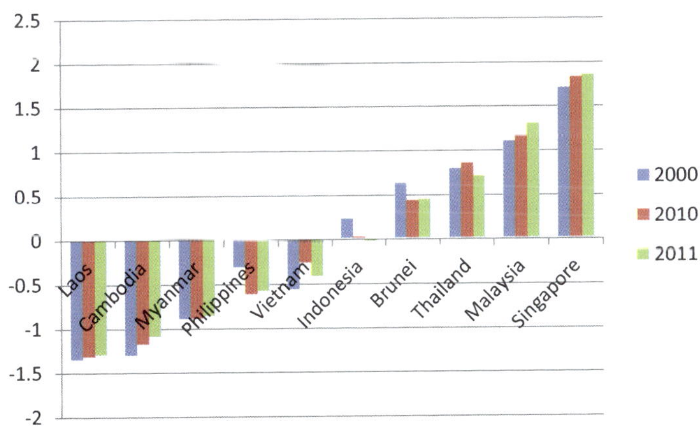

Source: Asia Competitiveness Institute.

Figure 2.17. Quality of Life and Infrastructure Development (Technological Infrastructure) — 2000, 2010 and 2011

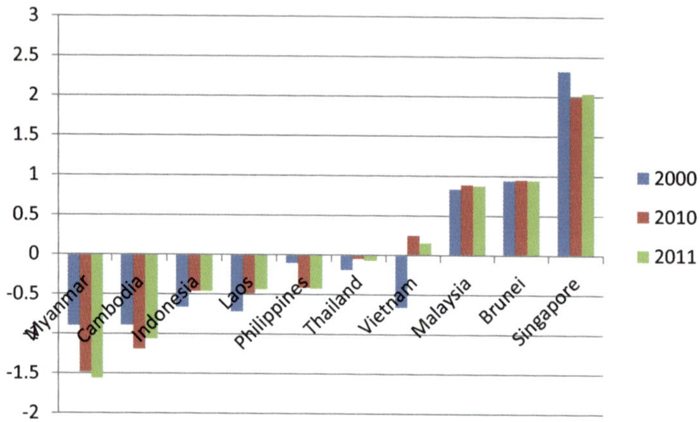

Source: Asia Competitiveness Institute.

Figure 2.18. Quality of Life and Infrastructure Development (Standard of Living, Education and Social Stability) — 2000, 2010 and 2011

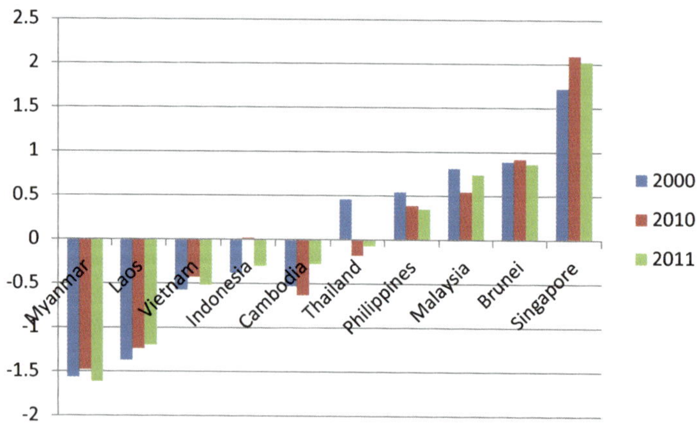

Source: Asia Competitiveness Institute.

2.3.6 Competitiveness Over Time Analysis

To offer a better comparison of Competitiveness Over Time (COT), the study period of 2000–2011 was split into two periods, namely 2000–2005 (Period A) and 2006–2011 (Period B). For all the 13 figures (Figure 2.19 to 2.31) charted for the COT analysis, countries above the 45-degree line improved their competitiveness in the second period relative to the first period; a position below the line means they did better in the earlier period (Period A); a position on the line means no change for both periods. Singapore being at the top of most of the 45-degree lines of the COT analysis is consistent with the rankings in Section 2.3.1 to 2.3.5.

Figure 2.19. Competitiveness Over Time Analysis for Overall Competitiveness, Period B (2006–2011) Against Period A (2000–2005)

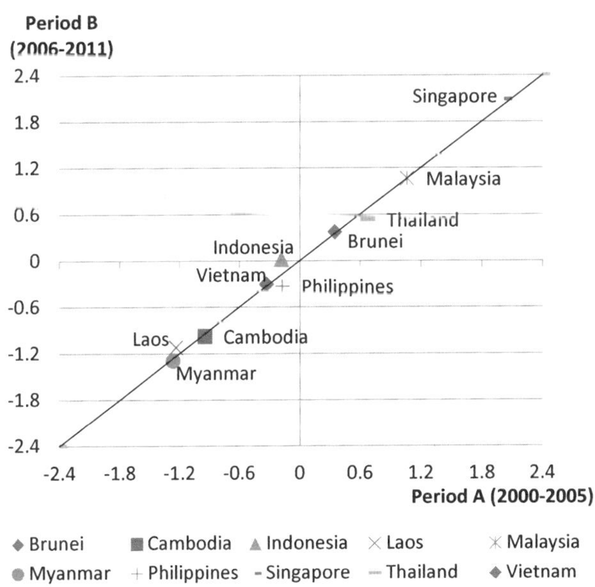

Source: Asia Competitiveness Institute.

Figure 2.20. Competitiveness Over Time Analysis for Economic Vibrancy, Period B (2006–2011) Against Period A (2000–2005)

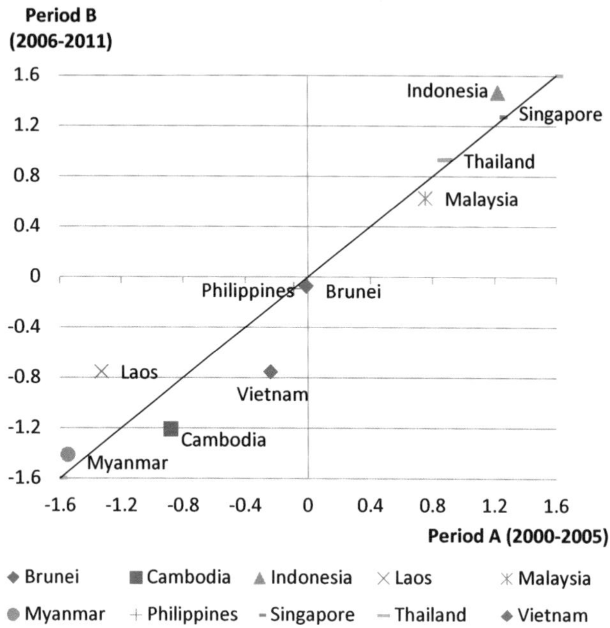

Source: Asia Competitiveness Institute.

Such COT analysis is useful as it signals how ASEAN-10 individually and as a group learnt and drew lessons in competitiveness from both domestic and external factors and situations. The AFC was the main event in ASEAN in Period A, apart from other global swings. The GFC, on the other hand, is the feature in Period B. Realistically, ASEAN-10 has enjoyed as much riding on regional and global surges as part of the boom-and-bust cycle of globalisation in general, and financial globalisation, in particular.

In Figure 2.19 for Overall Competitiveness, Singapore, Malaysia, Brunei, Vietnam, Cambodia and Myanmar remained on the 45-degree

Figure 2.21. Competitiveness Over Time Analysis for Openness to Trade and Services, Period B (2006–2011) Against Period A (2000–2005)

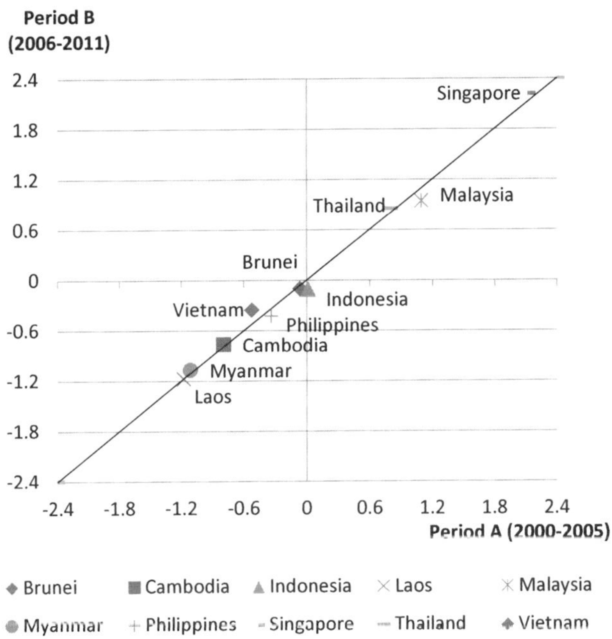

Source: Asia Competitiveness Institute.

line. The Philippines and Thailand were below the line, implying that their Overall Competitiveness was better in Period A than Period B. On the other hand, Indonesia and Laos improved over time as they fared better in Period B.

In Figure 2.20 for Economic Vibrancy as one of the sub-environment under Macroeconomic Stability, Indonesia led at the top and also improved over time, as did Laos and Myanmar. Singapore, Thailand and the Philippines were on the 45-degree line. Well below the line, indicating a better performance in Period A and not improving over time, were Vietnam and Cambodia; it was similar

Figure 2.22. Competitiveness Over Time Analysis for Attractiveness to Foreign Investors, Period B (2006–2011) Against Period A (2000–2005)

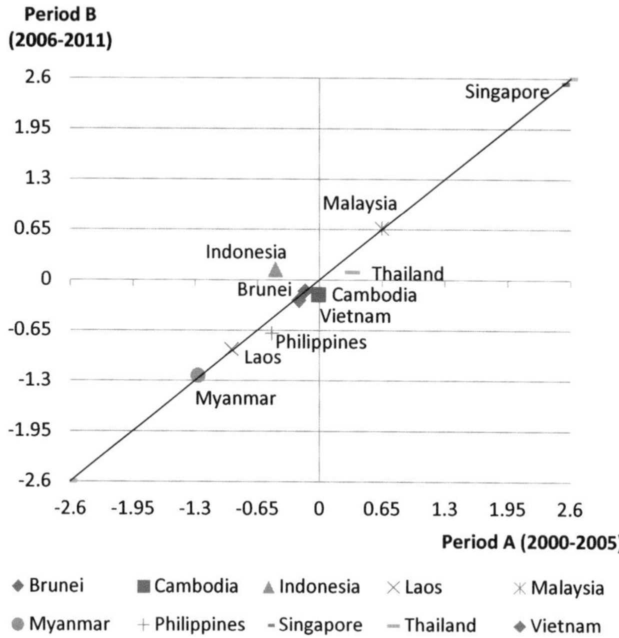

Source: Asia Competitiveness Institute.

for Brunei and Malaysia, but their positions were closer to the 45-degree line.

In the other two sub-environments, Openness to Trade and Services (Figure 2.21) and Attractiveness to Foreign Investors (Figure 2.22), all of ASEAN-10 clustered along the 45-degree line with the exception of Indonesia in Figure 2.22, where it did slightly better in improving competitiveness in Period B. Thailand, Cambodia and the Philippines, however, fared better in Period A in terms of Attractiveness to Foreign Investors. Coping with the AFC and GFC with domestic regime changes do give cause for pause for FDI and MNCs.

Figure 2.23. Competitiveness Over Time Analysis for Government Policies and Fiscal Sustainability, Period B (2006–2011) Against Period A (2000–2005)

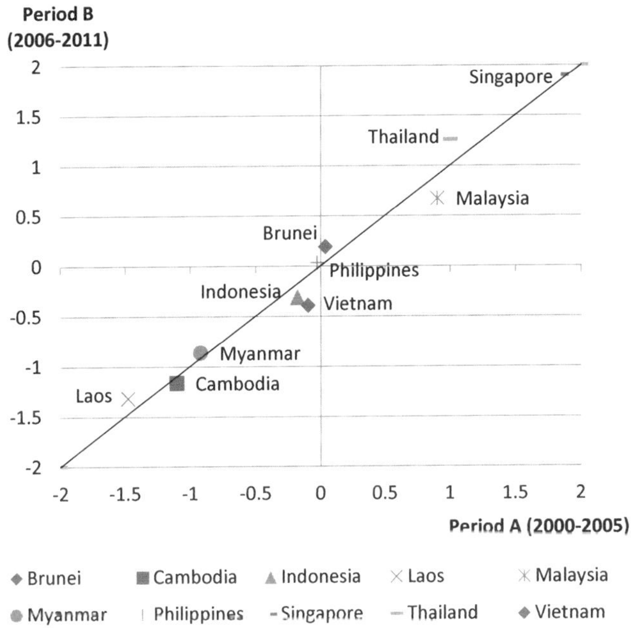

Source: Asia Competitiveness Institute.

For the first of the three sub-environments of Government Institutional Setting, Government Policies and Fiscal Sustainability, Figure 2.23 shows that Singapore, the Philippines, Myanmar and Cambodia were on the 45-degree line; Thailand, Brunei and Laos were above the line as they improved their competitiveness over time, while the rest of the countries were below the line. Again, all coincided with how respective economies coped with financial crises and events which followed.

In Figure 2.24 for Institutions, Governance and Leadership, it is heartening to see improvement over time, as the majority of the

Figure 2.24. Competitiveness Over Time Analysis for Institutions, Governance and Leadership, Period B (2006–2011) Against Period A (2000–2005)

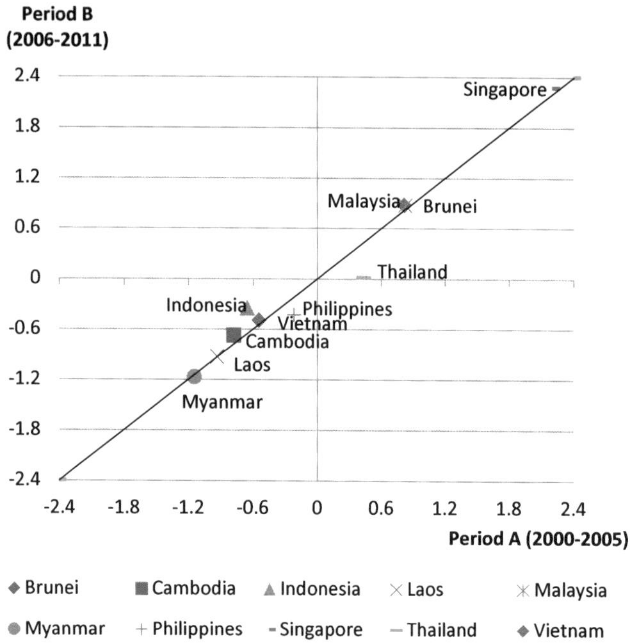

Source: Asia Competitiveness Institute.

ASEAN-10 were returning to be on the line, with the exception of Thailand and the Philippines. Indonesia even improved and fared better in Period B. Unsurprisingly, the performance for Competition, Regulatory Standards and Rule of Law (Figure 2.25) seems to generally be consistent with that seen in Figure 2.24.

In Figure 2.26 for Financial Deepening and Business Efficiency as a sub-environment of Financial, Businesses and Manpower Conditions, both Indonesia and Vietnam were clearly more competitive in Period B. For Labour Market Flexibility (Figure 2.27), Malaysia most

Figure 2.25. Competitiveness Over Time Analysis for Competition, Regulatory Standards and Rule of Law, Period B (2006–2011) Against Period A (2000–2005)

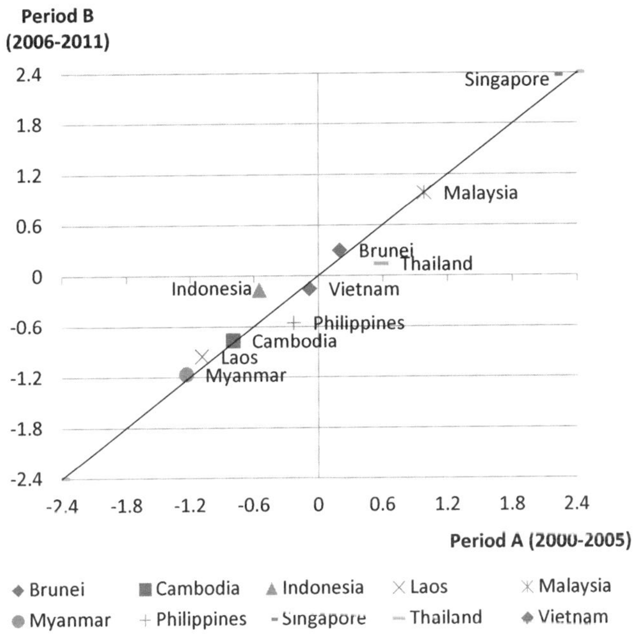

Source: Asia Competitiveness Institute.

decidedly improved over time. Brunei was the lead for Productivity Performance (Figure 2.28), with the rest of ASEAN clustering on the 45-degree line.

For the three sub-environments under Quality of Life and Infrastructure Development, Figure 2.29 for Physical Infrastructure shows that all of ASEAN-10 was lying close to the 45-degree line, with Indonesia and the Philippines having not improved as much over time and thus were a little below the line. In Figure 2.30, Vietnam has definitely improved in Period B for Technological

Figure 2.26. Competitiveness Over Time Analysis for Financial Deepening and Business Efficiency, Period B (2006–2011) Against Period A (2000–2005)

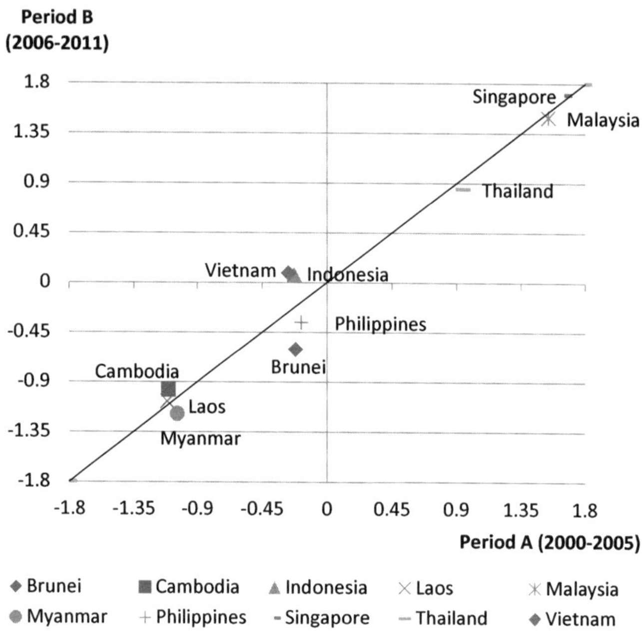

Source: Asia Competitiveness Institute.

Infrastructure, but not the Philippines, Myanmar, Cambodia and Singapore as they were below the line. For Standard of Living, Education and Social Stability (Figure 2.31), Singapore and Indonesia improved most markedly over time, followed by Vietnam. In contrast, Thailand being well below the line fared worse in Period B as compared to Period A.

In all Figures 2.19 to 2.31, although any deviations from the 45-degree line were not large, it is the relative distances that matter. ASEAN-10 engaged as a whole in continuing efforts to stay on course, be resilient, each in their own respective way, is vital for

Figure 2.27. Competitiveness Over Time Analysis for Labour Market Flexibility, Period B (2006–2011) Against Period A (2000–2005)

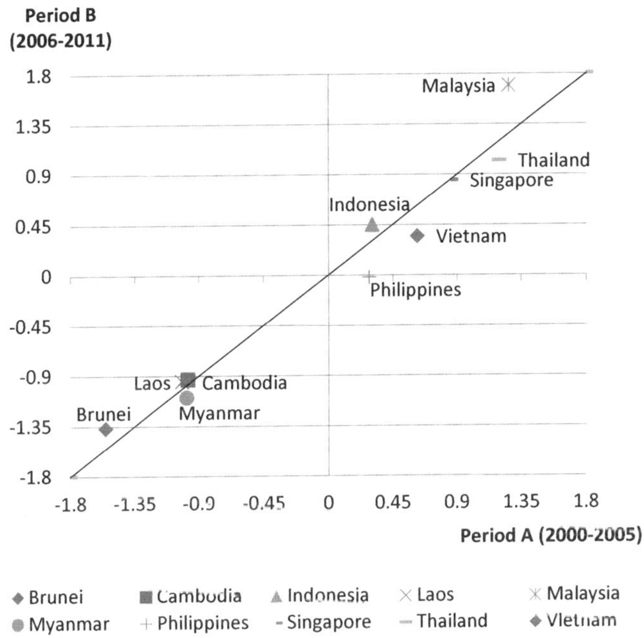

Source: Asia Competitiveness Institute.

long-term economic growth and development in general, and competitiveness in particular. Neither overly stated improvement nor understated deterioration over time engenders confidence and credibility for longer staying FDI and MNCs, which need the gestation time for projects to take off into sustainable profitability. Change is inevitable, but smooth incremental changes as digested, absorbed and turned into opportunities are clearly more strategically pragmatic and welcoming for the FDI and MNCs as well as domestic investors.

Figure 2.28. Competitiveness Over Time Analysis for Productivity Performance, Period B (2006–2011) Against Period A (2000–2005)

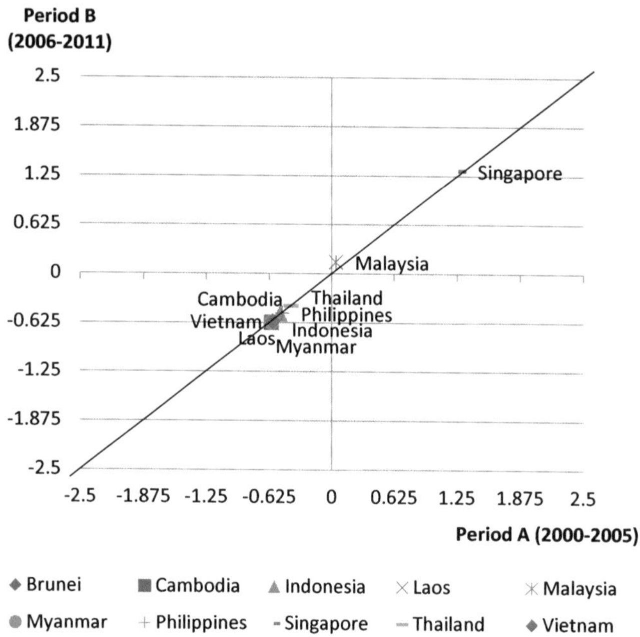

Source: Asia Competitiveness Institute.

It is clear from the COT analysis over the last decade or so that there is a notable heterogeneity within ASEAN-10. On balance, more countries have shown drastic improvement while Thailand has experienced domestic political turmoil and the Philippines with fits of exuberant growth and checkmates. The latter is blessed with a large quality workforce abroad, which expands to the Middle East Gulf states, a true competitive fillip to return home if jobs are created.

The appetite for competitiveness obviously varies, from Singapore as absolutely resolute in watching every ranking from the WEF to

Figure 2.29. Competitiveness Over Time Analysis for Physical Infrastructure, Period B (2006–2011) Against Period A (2000–2005)

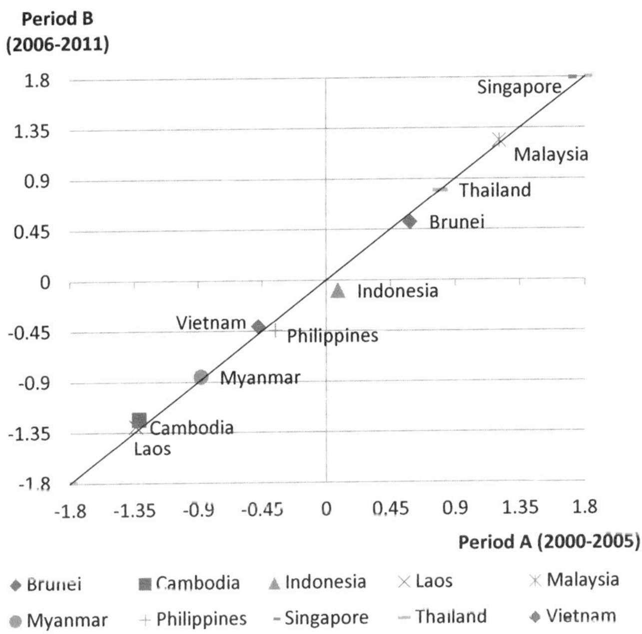

Source: Asia Competitiveness Institute.

World Bank's survey on doing business, in which it is at the top rank. Brunei may be more complacent, but not tantamount to a resource curse.[14] Indonesia is another clear outlier in terms of its exponential

[14] The resource curse depicts countries with finite, natural resources may fail to develop in other sectors or squander wealth bringing financial problems to future generations. A related concept is the Dutch disease, which describes a problem of economic dislocations due to large fluctuations in the real price of oil, mineral or agricultural export resulting in labour and capital wastefully shifting production back and forth from sector to sector.

Figure 2.30. Competitiveness Over Time Analysis for Technological Infrastructure, Period B (2006–2011) Against Period A (2000–2005)

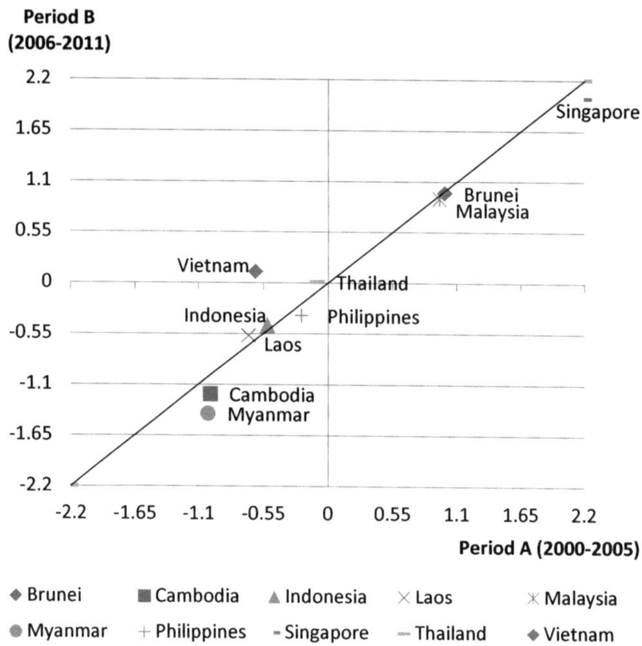

Source: Asia Competitiveness Institute.

improvement since the AFC and regime change to another general election and presidential new order in 2014. Overall, any 'competitiveness divide' within the ASEAN-10 is underscored with a renewed momentum to be elaborated in Section 2.4.

Of the CLMV, Myanmar stands as a last opportunistic frontier to be seized by its own national and foreign investors, be it private

Figure 2.31. Competitiveness Over Time Analysis for Standard of Living, Education and Social Stability, Period B (2006–2011) Against Period A (2000–2005)

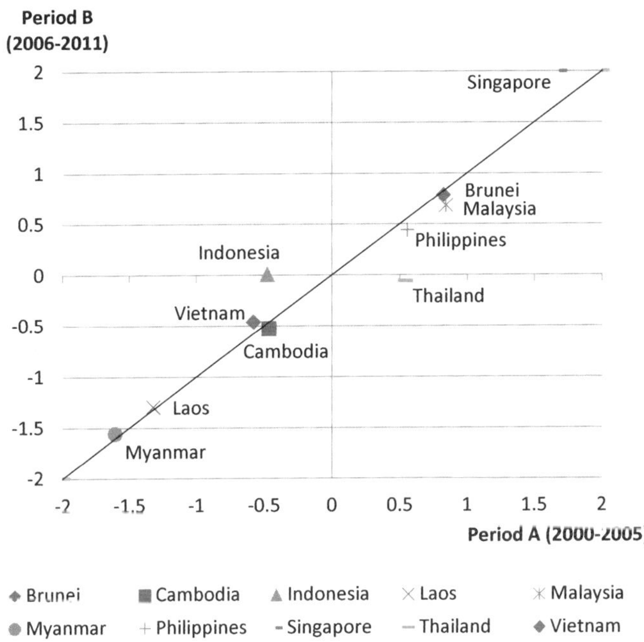

Source: Asia Competitiveness Institute.

business, government to government (G2G) or public-private partnerships to reinforce its liberalisation. Another pleasant surprise comes from the performance of others such as Laos, which even surpassed the rankings of Cambodia. In other words, forewarned is forearmed; instead of complacency, competitiveness, not head-on rivalry, is the ASEAN way.

2.3.7 Maximising Strengths and Minimising Weaknesses

In this section, the top 20% strongest indicators list and top 20% weakest indicators lists for each ASEAN economy will be first discussed. The analysis will be mindful of the contexts of high-income (Singapore and Brunei), middle-income (Indonesia, Malaysia, the Philippines and Thailand) and lower-middle-income and low-income transitional economies (CLMV). This is followed by analyses of web charts depicting each ASEAN economy's competitiveness *vis-à-vis* the ASEAN median (average ASEAN-10) and maximum competitiveness (set by the top ASEAN economy).

2.3.7.1 *Top 20% Strongest and Weakest Indicators Lists*

Starting with Brunei, its top 20% strongest and top 20% weakest indicators are shown in Tables 2.7 and 2.8, respectively. The diminutive oil-rich state has no fiscal constraint with budget balance (#2) and gross domestic savings (#6), yet among its weakest indicators in Table 2.8 are tax burden (#116) and tax/government revenue (#117). While prudence at the helm may not be as needy as compared to resource-deficit Singapore, government expenditure with long-lasting sustainable outcomes is wise. Perhaps, more heed can also be paid to health expenditure (#112).

For Cambodia (Tables 2.9 and 2.10), it seems to have neither outstanding strengths nor weaknesses in terms of attracting FDI and MNCs, with labour being both a strength (#15) and a weakness (#112). Balancing its strongest indicators in Table 2.9 such as corporate income tax (#4) and bureaucracy/red tape (#19) with weakness in ease of starting business (#99) will align its relative latecomer status for FDI and MNCs better, more than supporting infrastructure, manpower, costs or market demand. Lack of cronyism in (#24) is good, although availability of high quality management staff needs to be improved. Table 2.10

Table 2.7. Top 20% Strongest Indicators List for Brunei, 2011

Rank	20% Strongest Indicator	Score	Environment
1	Agriculture, Value Added Per Worker	2.8559	FBMC
2	Budget Balance	2.7557	GIS
3	Industry, Value Added Per Worker	2.7237	FBMC
4	Current Account Balance	2.3365	MS
5	Religious Unrest	2.2931	QLID
6	Gross Domestic Savings	2.1263	MS
7	Government Environmental Protection Policies	1.9913	GIS
8	Government Consumption Expenditure	1.9656	GIS
9	Access to Print Media	1.9141	QLID
10	Personal Computers	1.8994	QLID
11	Corporate Income Tax	1.6836	MS
12	Political Change	1.5511	GIS
13	Information and Communication Technology (ICT) Expenditure	1.4888	QLID
14	Human Development Index	1.4654	QLID
15	Sovereign Debt Risk	1.4302	FBMC
16	Secondary Schooling	1.4268	QLID
17	Government Stability	1.4042	GIS
18	Public Security and Safety	1.3024	QLID
19	Government Responsiveness	1.2408	GIS
20	High Quality Management Staff	1.2258	FBMC
21	Quality of Regulatory Environment	1.2090	GIS
22	Quality of Government Policies	1.1558	GIS
23	Lack of Corruption	1.1351	GIS
24	Access to Sanitation	1.1299	QLID

Source: Asia Competitiveness Institute.

Table 2.8. Top 20% Weakest Indicators List for Brunei, 2011

Rank	20% Weakest Indicator	Score	Environment
98	Population	–0.8587	QLID
99	Daily Organic Water Pollutant Emissions	–0.8613	QLID
100	International Tourism Receipts	–0.8787	MS
101	Availability of Scientists and Engineers	–0.8918	FBMC
102	Imports of Goods and Services	–0.8956	MS
103	International Reserves	–0.9033	GIS
104	Labour Force	–0.9044	FBMC
105	Output Agriculture (Value Added)	–0.9162	MS
106	Deposit Interest Rate	–0.9238	GIS
107	Market Capitalisation	–0.9508	FBMC
108	Tax Revenue	–0.9528	GIS
109	Gross Domestic Product	–0.9904	MS
110	Listed Domestic Companies	–0.9982	FBMC
111	Output Services (Value Added)	–1.0173	MS
112	Health Expenditure	–1.1294	QLID
113	Domestic Credit Provided by the Financial Sector	–1.1956	FBMC
114	Regional Competitiveness	–1.1969	GIS
115	Gross Fixed Capital Formation	–1.3542	MS
116	Tax Burden	–1.4082	GIS
117	Tax Revenue/Government Revenue	–1.5291	GIS
118	Ease of Starting Business	–1.5705	GIS
119	Cost of Management Staff	–1.8974	FBMC
120	Cost of Production Labour	–1.9687	FBMC
121	Claims on Private Sector	–2.5805	FBMC

Source: Asia Competitiveness Institute.

Table 2.9. Top 20% Strongest Indicators List for Cambodia, 2011

Rank	20% Strongest Indicator	Score	Environment
1	Freedom of Religion	2.2361	QLID
2	Freedom of Speech	1.5275	QLID
3	Government Environmental Protection Policies	1.2987	GIS
4	Corporate Income Tax	1.2267	MS
5	Health Expenditure	1.1718	QLID
6	Daily Organic Water Pollutant Emissions	1.1232	QLID
7	Unemployment Rate	0.8903	FBMC
8	Freedom of Press	0.8566	QLID
9	International Monetary Fund Credit	0.7779	GIS
10	External Debt	0.7560	GIS
11	Cost of Management Staff	0.7136	FBMC
12	Primary Schooling	0.7046	QLID
13	Tax Burden	0.6637	GIS
14	Traffic Congestion	0.6259	QLID
15	Cost of Production Labour	0.6146	FBMC
16	Real GDP Growth	0.3865	MS
17	Legislature/Parliament (Functioning of Government System)	0.2521	GIS
18	Business Impact of Rules on FDI	0.2205	MS
19	Bureaucracy/Red Tape	0.1715	GIS
20	Inflation	0.1413	MS
21	Monopolies and Cartel	0.0635	GIS
22	Tax Revenue/Government Revenue	0.0589	GIS
23	Exchange Rate Appreciation	–0.0140	GIS
24	Lack of Cronyism	–0.0388	GIS

Source: Asia Competitiveness Institute.

Table 2.10. Top 20% Weakest Indicators List for Cambodia, 2011

Rank	20% Weakest Indicator	Score	Environment
98	Output Industry (Value Added)	–0.9246	MS
99	Ease of Starting Business	–0.9257	GIS
100	High Quality Management Staff	–0.9440	FBMC
101	Market Capitalisation	–0.9508	FBMC
102	University and Post-Graduate Education	–0.9623	QLID
103	Networked Readiness Index	–0.9953	QLID
104	Human Development Index	–0.9964	QLID
105	Listed Domestic Companies	–0.9982	FBMC
106	Availability of Scientists and Engineers	–1.0021	FBMC
107	Gross Domestic Product	–1.0059	MS
108	Output Services (Value Added)	–1.0149	MS
109	Tax Revenue	–1.0270	GIS
110	Government Revenue (Including Grants)	–1.0270	GIS
111	Information and Communication Technology (ICT) Expenditure	–1.0328	QLID
112	Labour Activism	–1.0558	QLID
113	Sovereign Debt Risk	–1.1043	FBMC
114	Regional Competitiveness	–1.1155	GIS
115	Internet Subscribers	–1.1217	QLID
116	Gross Domestic Savings	–1.1769	MS
117	Urban Population	–1.2517	QLID
118	Interest Rate Spread	–1.3699	GIS
119	Access to Water	–1.8661	QLID
120	Literacy Rate	–1.9723	QLID
121	Access to Sanitation	–2.1378	QLID

Source: Asia Competitiveness Institute.

can thus be a checklist of what to prioritise as a more constructive approach to competitiveness.

For Indonesia, its top 20% strongest indicators (Table 2.11) include population (#1) and labour force (#3), implying that labour-intensive agriculture in a dualistic economic structure is logical. This is backed by output (value-added) of agriculture, industry and services (#2, #4 and #5, respectively). Downstream agro-processing industrial activities can support job creation and gainful employment for Indonesia as a potential food basket while it also seeks industrialisation via a natural resource-based approach. What it needs is the right government direction and awareness of competitiveness with market discipline.

Equally supportive as strength for the corporate sector and entrepreneurial growth is domestic companies (#23) as listed in Table 2.11. It can further optimise strengths in cost of management staff (#14) and labour cost (#18), even if lack of cronyism (#21) means no hidden business cost. It does need to heed weaknesses perceived as nationalism (#108) and high quality management staff (#116) as shown in Table 2.12.

Laos seems to be quietly rising to the occasion to join its ASEAN partners, even with some rivalry, albeit on a smaller scale. For instance, as seen from Table 2.13, among its top strongest indicators are manpower costs (#8 and #9) and ease of starting business (#23). Literacy rate (#120 in Table 2.14) as one of its top weakest indicators is a stark reminder for human resource development (HRD). All are complementary and supplementary features across ASEAN to attract FDI and MNCs. Telecommunications system (#1) will play up Laos's strengths and ameliorate some of its weaknesses.

Malaysia is a credible challenger to Singapore in Overall Competitiveness and even surpassed Singapore as the top in 2011 for Financial, Businesses and Manpower Conditions. Its top 20% strongest indicators are presented in Table 2.15 while its top weaknesses can be seen in Table 2.16. Table 2.15 seems to be taken from Singapore as a

Table 2.11. Top 20% Strongest Indicators List for Indonesia, 2011

Rank	20% Strongest Indicator	Score	Environment
1	Population	2.6420	QLID
2	Output Agriculture (Value Added)	2.5634	MS
3	Labour Force	2.5594	FBMC
4	Output Industry (Value Added)	2.4039	MS
5	Output Services (Value Added)	2.0353	MS
6	Gross Fixed Capital Formation	1.5707	MS
7	Freedom of Speech	1.5275	QLID
8	Gross Domestic Product	1.5113	MS
9	Market Capitalisation	1.4518	FBMC
10	Claims on Private Sector	1.1941	FBMC
11	Government Revenue (Including Grants)	1.0748	GIS
12	Tax Revenue	1.0692	GIS
13	Political System Risk	1.0350	GIS
14	Cost of Management Staff	0.7136	FBMC
15	Regional Competitiveness	0.6847	GIS
16	Availability of Scientists and Engineers	0.6275	FBMC
17	Deposit Interest Rate	0.5354	GIS
18	Cost of Production Labour	0.5280	FBMC
19	Secondary Schooling	0.5246	QLID
20	Foreign Direct Investment Inflows	0.5189	MS
21	Lack of Cronyism	0.5174	GIS
22	Imports of Goods and Services	0.5095	MS
23	Listed Domestic Companies	0.4871	FBMC
24	Tax Burden	0.4804	GIS

Source: Asia Competitiveness Institute.

Table 2.12. Top 20% Weakest Indicators List for Indonesia, 2011

Rank	20% Weakest Indicator	Score	Environment
98	Health Expenditure	–0.6944	QLID
99	Institutional Sophistication	–0.7087	GIS
100	Domestic Credit to Private Sector	–0.7204	FBMC
101	Labour Unrest	–0.7307	QLID
102	Personal Computers	–0.7356	QLID
103	Openness to Trade	–0.7439	MS
104	Freedom of Religion	–0.7454	QLID
105	Public Security and Safety	–0.7529	QLID
106	Social Unrest	–0.7778	QLID
107	Internet Subscribers	–0.7876	QLID
108	Lack of Discrimination Against Investors	–0.8730	MS
109	Access to Sanitation	–0.8876	QLID
110	Labour Market Rating	–0.8974	FBMC
111	Lack of Market Distortion due to State Ownership	–0.9045	GIS
112	Policy Towards Private Enterprise Rating	–0.9159	GIS
113	Quality of Central Bank/Monetary Authority	–0.9177	GIS
114	Government Stability	–0.9212	GIS
115	Money Supply (M2)	–0.9279	GIS
116	High Quality Management Staff	–0.9440	FBMC
117	Information and Communication Technology (ICT) Expenditure	–1.0328	QLID
118	Air Quality	–1.1595	QLID
119	Unemployment Rate	–1.6321	FBMC
120	International Monetary Fund Credit	–2.1700	GIS
121	External Debt	–2.4789	GIS

Source: Asia Competitiveness Institute.

Table 2.13. Top 20% Strongest Indicators List for Laos, 2011

Rank	20% Strongest Indicator	Score	Environment
1	Telecommunications System	2.7500	QLID
2	Urban Population Growth	2.6298	QLID
3	Daily Organic Water Pollutant Emissions	1.1232	QLID
4	Unemployment Rate	0.9397	FBMC
5	International Monetary Fund Credit	0.8246	GIS
6	External Debt	0.7306	GIS
7	Gross Fixed Capital Formation	0.7186	MS
8	Cost of Management Staff	0.7136	FBMC
9	Cost of Production Labour	0.6146	FBMC
10	Traffic Congestion	0.6118	QLID
11	Real GDP Growth	0.4829	MS
12	Government Environmental Protection Policies	0.4566	GIS
13	Claims on Private Sector	0.2255	FBMC
14	Political Change	0.1945	GIS
15	Corporate Income Tax	0.1838	MS
16	Tax Burden	0.0268	GIS
17	Tax Revenue/Government Revenue	0.0037	GIS
18	Government Consumption Expenditure	–0.0316	GIS
19	Primary Schooling	–0.1307	QLID
20	Exchange Rate Appreciation	–0.1337	GIS
21	Inflation	–0.3331	MS
22	Budget Balance	–0.3477	GIS
23	Ease of Starting Business	–0.3844	GIS
24	Air Quality	–0.4096	QLID

Source: Asia Competitiveness Institute.

Table 2.14. Top 20% Weakest Indicators List for Laos, 2011

Rank	20% Weakest Indicator	Score	Environment
98	Religious Unrest	–1.0029	QLID
99	Bureaucracy/Red Tape	–1.0071	GIS
100	Information and Communication Technology (ICT) Expenditure	–1.0328	QLID
101	Foreign Owned Companies	–1.0335	MS
102	Monopolies and Cartel	–1.0456	GIS
103	Strength of Auditing and Reporting Standards	–1.0478	GIS
104	Gross Domestic Product	–1.0483	MS
105	Output Services (Value Added)	–1.0501	MS
106	Tax Revenue	–1.0527	GIS
107	Government Revenue (Including Grants)	–1.0544	GIS
108	Labour Activism	–1.0558	QLID
109	Effectiveness of Legal System	–1.0583	GIS
110	Lack of Cronyism	–1.0668	GIS
111	Local Road System	–1.1000	QLID
112	Sovereign Debt Risk	–1.1043	FBMC
113	Regional Competitiveness	–1.1969	GIS
114	Legislature/Parliament (Functioning of Government System)	–1.2066	GIS
115	Secondary Schooling	–1.3058	QLID
116	Current Account Balance	–1.3388	MS
117	Money Supply Growth (M2)	–1.6015	MS
118	Access to Water	–1.6535	QLID
119	Lending Rate	–1.8401	GIS
120	Literacy Rate	–1.9723	QLID
121	Interest Rate Spread	–2.4247	GIS

Source: Asia Competitiveness Institute.

Table 2.15. Top 20% Strongest Indicators List for Malaysia, 2011

Rank	20% Strongest Indicator	Score	Environment
1	Listed Domestic Companies	2.1783	FBMC
2	Monopolies and Cartel	1.7773	GIS
3	Quality of Banking and Financial System	1.7296	FBMC
4	Rail Facilities	1.6076	QLID
5	Extent of Staff Training	1.5790	FBMC
6	Ease of Starting Business	1.5435	GIS
7	Air Quality	1.5158	QLID
8	Market Capitalisation	1.4817	FBMC
9	Levelness of Playing Field	1.4635	MS
10	Money Supply (M2)	1.4356	GIS
11	Corporate Governance	1.4272	GIS
12	Government Stability	1.4042	GIS
13	Legislature/Parliament (Functioning of Government System)	1.3928	GIS
14	Quality of Stock Market Regulatory Authority	1.3847	FBMC
15	Availability of Scientists and Engineers	1.3306	FBMC
16	Domestic Credit to Private Sector	1.3165	FBMC
17	Port Facilities	1.3004	QLID
18	Internet Subscribers	1.2933	QLID
19	Intellectual Property Rights Protection	1.2727	GIS
20	Domestic Credit Provided by the Financial Sector	1.2607	FBMC
21	Strength of Auditing and Reporting Standards	1.2515	GIS
22	Government Responsiveness	1.2408	GIS
23	Airport Facilities	1.2368	QLID
24	High Quality Management Staff	1.2258	FBMC

Source: Asia Competitiveness Institute.

Table 2.16. Top 20% Weakest Indicators List for Malaysia, 2011

Rank	20% Weakest Indicator	Score	Environment
98	Government Environmental Protection Policies	0.1290	GIS
99	Unemployment Rate	0.0989	FBMC
100	Secondary Schooling	0.0942	QLID
101	Foreign Direct Investment Inflows	0.0807	MS
102	Gross Fixed Capital Formation	0.0729	MS
103	Access to Print Media	0.0715	QLID
104	Cost of Production Labour	–0.0005	FBMC
105	Health Expenditure	–0.0202	QLID
106	Corporate Income Tax	–0.0248	MS
107	Urban Population Growth	–0.0269	QLID
108	GDP Per Capita	–0.1278	MS
109	Claims on Private Sector	–0.1424	FBMC
110	Industry, Value Added Per Worker	–0.2135	FBMC
111	Tax Burden	0.2523	GIS
112	Deposit Interest Rate	–0.3446	GIS
113	Traffic Congestion	–0.3548	QLID
114	Population	–0.4509	QLID
115	Labour Force	–0.5405	FBMC
116	External Debt	–0.5655	GIS
117	Budget Balance	–0.6524	GIS
118	Freedom of Speech	–0.6547	QLID
119	Freedom of Religion	–0.7454	QLID
120	Daily Organic Water Pollutant Emissions	–1.0348	QLID
121	International Monetary Fund Credit	–1.1841	GIS

Source: Asia Competitiveness Institute.

playlist to galvanise credibility for "Malaysia Boleh" (Malaysia Can). It is more than its iconic infrastructure like the multimedia super-corridor comprising Kuala Lumpur city centre, Kuala Lumpur International Airport and Port Klang in the vicinity, with Putrajaya as its new government hub. With its controversial capital controls proved effective during the AFC and acceptable to some belatedly even by IMF, Malaysia still needs IMF credit (#121) and FDI (#101) for its gross domestic capital formation (#102) and external foreign debt (#116) and budget balance (#117), among its other weaknesses.

Myanmar seems to be lagging, taking the 10th position in many instances simply as a latecomer to competitiveness, but Table 2.17 shows its strengths in water quality, air quality and traffic (#3, #7, #14 and #22), which is quite atypical of other highly urbanised and crowded ASEAN environs. Both population and labour indicators seem favourable in Table 2.17 (#6, #11, #17, #19 and #23), implying that it takes the right leaders to put them into action with real GDP growth (#12).

On the flipside, Myanmar's weaknesses in ICT (#105 and #121) are evident in Table 2.18. Similar to Thailand or Indonesia, much awaits the political scene to be resolved for Myanmar to move forward. However, Myanmar is competitive in agriculture (#20, #23) with the potential of becoming a food basket in the tradition of Burmese rice.

Reinforcing high quality management staff (#3) and labour force (#24), as seen from Table 2.19, is required for the Philippines to tap into its overseas talent pool, particularly in professionally skilled categories. Returnees need job creation that is amiss at home; job creation can translate into a transfusion of capital, skills, experience and contacts from all around the world. As an English-speaking country, its people are more globally proficient than most ASEAN nationals.

The Philippines's list of weakest indicators in Table 2.20 shows the usual suspects in power supply (#98) and other infrastructure (#99, #103, #109 and #111). Weaknesses as cronyism (#116) combined with transparency issues for investors (#100) and government (#101) are as

Table 2.17. Top 20% Strongest Indicators List for Myanmar, 2011

Rank	20% Strongest Indicator	Score	Environment
1	Tax Burden	2.1291	GIS
2	Deposit Interest Rate	1.5183	GIS
3	Daily Organic Water Pollutant Emissions	1.3594	QLID
4	Cost of Management Staff	0.7136	FBMC
5	External Debt	0.7069	GIS
6	Cost of Production Labour	0.6146	FBMC
7	Traffic Congestion	0.5918	QLID
8	International Monetary Fund Credit	0.5229	GIS
9	Claims on Private Sector	0.4044	FBMC
10	Interest Rate Spread	0.3196	GIS
11	Literacy Rate	0.2675	QLID
12	Real GDP Growth	0.2468	MS
13	Inflation	0.2447	MS
14	Air Quality	0.1168	QLID
15	Exchange Rate Appreciation	0.1121	GIS
16	Access to Sanitation	0.0217	QLID
17	Labour Force	0.0004	FBMC
18	Urban Population Growth	–0.0963	QLID
19	Population	–0.1116	QLID
20	Output Agriculture (Value Added)	–0.2348	MS
21	Unemployment Rate	–0.3957	FBMC
22	Access to Water	–0.4039	QLID
23	Agriculture, Value Added Per Worker	–0.4747	FBMC
24	Current Account Balance	–0.5032	MS

Source: Asia Competitiveness Institute.

Table 2.18. Top 20% Weakest Indicators List for Myanmar, 2011

Rank	20% Weakest Indicator	Score	Environment
98	Gross Domestic Savings	–1.0735	MS
99	Local Road System	–1.1000	QLID
100	Sovereign Debt Risk	–1.1043	FBMC
101	University and Post-Graduate Education	–1.1122	QLID
102	Money Supply (M2)	–1.1813	GIS
103	Regional Competitiveness	–1.1969	GIS
104	Legislature/Parliament (Functioning of Government System)	–1.2066	GIS
105	Internet Subscribers	–1.2101	QLID
106	Domestic Credit to Private Sector	–1.2199	FBMC
107	Openness to Trade	–1.2612	MS
108	Lack of Corruption	–1.2710	GIS
109	Human Development Index	–1.3392	QLID
110	Health Expenditure	–1.4089	QLID
111	Government Effectiveness	–1.6233	GIS
112	Quality of Government Policies	–1.6340	GIS
113	Gross Fixed Capital Formation	–1.6503	MS
114	Government Consumption Expenditure	–1.7004	GIS
115	Freedom of Press	–1.8147	QLID
116	Money Supply Growth (M2)	–1.8309	MS
117	Primary Schooling	–1.8794	QLID
118	Corporate Income Tax	–1.8823	MS
119	Quality of Regulatory Environment	–1.9111	GIS
120	Tax Revenue/Government Revenue	–1.9402	GIS
121	Cellular Mobile Telephone Subscribers	–2.5810	QLID

Source: Asia Competitiveness Institute.

Table 2.19. Top 20% Strongest Indicators List for Philippines, 2011

Rank	20% Strongest Indicator	Score	Environment
1	Air Quality	1.6167	QLID
2	Freedom of Speech	1.5275	QLID
3	High Quality Management Staff	1.4883	FBMC
4	Money Supply Growth (M2)	1.3219	MS
5	Labour Activism	1.2255	QLID
6	Tax Revenue/Government Revenue	1.1023	GIS
7	Daily Organic Water Pollutant Emissions	0.9721	QLID
8	Lending Rate	0.7827	GIS
9	Literacy Rate	0.7666	QLID
10	Freedom of Religion	0.7454	QLID
11	Interest Rate Spread	0.6483	GIS
12	Lack of Market Distortion due to State-Ownership	0.6030	GIS
13	Traffic Congestion	0.5394	QLID
14	Cost of Production Labour	0.5318	FBMC
15	Population	0.5026	QLID
16	Extent of Staff Training	0.4362	FBMC
17	Freedom of Press	0.4265	QLID
18	Health Expenditure	0.3884	QLID
19	Tax Burden	0.3525	GIS
20	Social Unrest	0.3333	QLID
21	Inflation	0.3293	MS
22	Telecommunications System	0.3136	QLID
23	Access to Water	0.3041	QLID
24	Labour Force	0.2925	FBMC

Source: Asia Competitiveness Institute.

Table 2.20. Top 20% Weakest Indicators List for Philippines, 2011

Rank	20% Weakest Indicator	Score	Environment
98	Electric Power	–0.7503	QLID
99	Telephone Main Lines	–0.7735	QLID
100	Transparency of Processes for Investors	–0.7819	MS
101	Transparency of Government	–0.7819	GIS
102	Business Impact of Rules on FDI	–0.7899	MS
103	Rail Facilities	–0.8386	QLID
104	Gross Domestic Savings	–0.8619	MS
105	Public Security and Safety	–0.8755	QLID
106	Levelness of Playing Field	–0.9177	MS
107	Quality of Police	–0.9183	GIS
108	Government Environmental Protection Policies	–0.9263	GIS
109	Port Facilities	–0.9497	QLID
110	Quality of Judiciary	–0.9960	GIS
111	Airport Facilities	–0.9970	QLID
112	Religious Unrest	–1.0029	QLID
113	Bureaucracy/Red Tape	–1.0071	GIS
114	Monopolies and Cartel	–1.0456	GIS
115	Effectiveness of Legal System	–1.0583	GIS
116	Lack of Cronyism	–1.0668	GIS
117	Corporate Income Tax	–1.0678	MS
118	Legislature/Parliament (Functioning of Government System)	–1.2066	GIS
119	Political Change	–1.3621	GIS
120	Unemployment Rate	–1.8300	FBMC
121	Primary Schooling	–1.8794	QLID

Source: Asia Competitiveness Institute.

absolute as they are relative to others in ASEAN for attracting FDI and MNCs, as well as ensuring a backflow of overseas Filipino talents and capital as remedies for Philippines's sluggish competitiveness.

Singapore, as seen in Table 2.21 and 2.22, is *sui generis* as a city-state evolving from a port city in *entrepôt* trade. Its globalised way is reflected in its strength in attracting FDI (#1) and services value added per worker as productivity (#2), all reinforced by quality of political leadership (#3). Nothing in Table 2.21 is a happenstance; they are instead birthed by crafted policies and strategies to ensure economic survival.

Its smallness in country size is a paranoia that also contributes to many of its weakest indicators seen in Table 2.22, from traffic congestion (#121) and rising manpower costs (#120 and #119) to high quality management staff (#98). Less government and more private sector activities is not achieved merely by privatising government-linked companies (GLCs) alone. Entrepreneurship and promotion of small- and medium-sized enterprises (SMEs) seem as elusive despite its policy for strengthening private enterprises (#16).

Thailand, a "free land" that was never colonised, is not a widely English-speaking country compared to other ASEAN economies. Yet its strongest indicator in Table 2.23 is international tourism receipts (#1). It also takes care of ease of starting business (#17) and other infrastructure including airport facilities (#15) and electric power (#20).

As evident from Table 2.24, Thailand is right to be concerned about its weakest indicator, real GDP growth (#119). Given weak social stability (#115) and political change (#116), both domestic in origin, it has to be as resolute to restore investors' confidence as it fought the AFC contagion.

Vietnam (Tables 2.25 and 2.26) has broad-based strengths including HRD (#2 and #4) and labour (#11, #14, #15 and #18). Its financial indicators (#1, #7, #9, #12 and #18) are strong in contrast to its weaknesses in inflation (#121) and exchange rate appreciation (#120).

Table 2.21. Top 20% Strongest Indicators List for Singapore, 2011

Rank	20% Strongest Indicator	Score	Environment
1	Foreign Direct Investment Inflows	2.8005	MS
2	Services, Value Added Per Worker	2.7600	FBMC
3	Quality of Political Leadership	2.7574	GIS
4	GDP Per Capita	2.6330	MS
5	Transparency of Processes for Investors	2.5932	MS
6	Transparency of Government	2.5932	GIS
7	Openness to Trade	2.5563	MS
8	Social Unrest	2.5556	QLID
9	Barriers to Trade	2.5452	GIS
10	Quality of Central Bank/Monetary Authority	2.5236	GIS
11	Business Impact of Rules on FDI	2.4840	MS
12	Foreign Owned Companies	2.4705	MS
13	Lack of Discrimination Against Investors	2.4690	MS
14	Telephone Main Lines	2.4609	QLID
15	Integrity of Legal System	2.4121	GIS
16	Policy Towards Private Enterprise Rating	2.3814	GIS
17	Exports of Goods and Services	2.3738	MS
18	Networked Readiness Index	2.3690	QLID
19	Institutional Sophistication	2.3571	GIS
20	Labour Unrest	2.3247	QLID
21	Imports of Goods and Services	2.3221	MS
22	Lack of Corruption	2.3085	GIS
23	Effectiveness of Legal System	2.2842	GIS
24	Intellectual Property Rights Protection	2.2775	GIS

Source: Asia Competitiveness Institute.

Table 2.22. Top 20% Weakest Indicators List for Singapore, 2011

Rank	20% Weakest Indicator	Score	Environment
98	High Quality Management Staff	0.4891	FBMC
99	Domestic Credit Provided by the Financial Sector	0.4539	FBMC
100	Interest Rate Spread	0.2792	GIS
101	Output Industry (Value Added)	0.2461	MS
102	Health Expenditure	0.2252	QLID
103	Unemployment Rate	0.1978	FBMC
104	Inflation	0.1923	MS
105	Tax Burden	0.1288	GIS
106	Religious Unrest	0.1237	QLID
107	Government Consumption Expenditure	–0.0499	GIS
108	Telecommunications System	–0.2452	QLID
109	Agriculture, Value Added Per Worker	–0.3353	FBMC
110	Tax Revenue/Government Revenue	–0.4719	GIS
111	Urban Population Growth	0.5877	QLID
112	Freedom of Speech	–0.6547	QLID
113	Population	–0.7900	QLID
114	Labour Force	–0.8235	FBMC
115	Daily Organic Water Pollutant Emissions	–0.8613	QLID
116	Output Agriculture (Value Added)	–0.9169	MS
117	Deposit Interest Rate	–0.9747	GIS
118	Government Environmental Protection Policies	–1.1243	GIS
119	Cost of Management Staff	–1.8974	FBMC
120	Cost of Production Labour	–1.9687	FBMC
121	Traffic Congestion	–2.8338	QLID

Source: Asia Competitiveness Institute.

Table 2.23. Top 20% Strongest Indicators List for Thailand, 2011

Rank	20% Strongest Indicator	Score	Environment
1	International Tourism Receipts	2.2018	MS
2	Domestic Credit Provided by the Financial Sector	1.8923	FBMC
3	University and Post-Graduate Education	1.7642	QLID
4	Tax Revenue	1.6591	GIS
5	Total Value of Stocks Traded	1.3794	FBMC
6	Net Foreign Assets	1.3072	GIS
7	Unemployment Rate	1.2859	FBMC
8	Domestic Credit to Private Sector	1.2458	FBMC
9	Money Supply (M2)	1.2250	GIS
10	International Reserves	1.1988	GIS
11	Gross Domestic Product	1.1971	MS
12	Government Revenue (Including Grants)	1.1438	GIS
13	Tax Revenue/Government Revenue	1.1372	GIS
14	Regional Competitiveness	1.0236	GIS
15	Airport Facilities	0.9334	QLID
16	Government Consumption Expenditure	0.9292	GIS
17	Ease of Starting Business	0.9092	GIS
18	Secondary Schooling	0.8736	QLID
19	Listed Domestic Companies	0.8415	FBMC
20	Electric Power	0.8400	QLID
21	Output Industry (Value Added)	0.8304	MS
22	Access to Sanitation	0.8096	QLID
23	Imports of Goods and Services	0.7774	MS
24	Freedom of Religion	0.7454	QLID

Source: Asia Competitiveness Institute.

Table 2.24. Top 20% Weakest Indicators List for Thailand, 2011

Rank	20% Weakest Indicator	Score	Environment
98	Intellectual Property Rights Protection	–0.3570	GIS
99	Industry, Value Added Per Worker	–0.3813	FBMC
100	Religious Unrest	–0.3815	QLID
101	Agriculture, Value Added Per Worker	–0.3865	FBMC
102	Telecommunications System	–0.4122	QLID
103	Monopolies and Cartel	–0.4670	GIS
104	Lack of Cronyism	–0.4671	GIS
105	Government Responsiveness	–0.4946	GIS
106	Quality of Police	–0.5017	GIS
107	Deposit Interest Rate	–0.5035	GIS
108	International Monetary Fund Credit	–0.5998	GIS
109	Integrity of Legal System	–0.6030	GIS
110	Tax Burden	–0.6372	GIS
111	Government Stability	–0.6529	GIS
112	Freedom of Speech	–0.6547	QLID
113	Urban Population	–0.6635	QLID
114	External Debt	–0.7584	GIS
115	Social Unrest	–0.7778	QLID
116	Political System Risk	–0.9056	GIS
117	Air Quality	–0.9288	QLID
118	Political Change	–1.0577	GIS
119	Real GDP Growth	–1.1395	MS
120	Daily Organic Water Pollutant Emissions	–1.2846	QLID
121	Urban Population Growth	–1.3099	QLID

Source: Asia Competitiveness Institute.

Table 2.25. Top 20% Strongest Indicators List for Vietnam, 2011

Rank	20% Strongest Indicator	Score	Environment
1	Deposit Interest Rate	2.1115	GIS
2	Health Expenditure	2.0274	QLID
3	Domestic Credit to Private Sector	1.0745	FBMC
4	Primary Schooling	1.0228	QLID
5	Cellular Mobile Telephone Subscribers	1.0018	QLID
6	Tax Revenue/Government Revenue	0.9683	GIS
7	Domestic Credit Provided by the Financial Sector	0.8926	FBMC
8	Quality of Police	0.8726	GIS
9	Money Supply (M2)	0.8369	GIS
10	Gross Fixed Capital Formation	0.7747	MS
11	Cost of Management Staff	0.7136	FBMC
12	Interest Rate Spread	0.7072	GIS
13	Information and Communication Technology (ICT) Expenditure	0.6712	QLID
14	Unemployment Rate	0.6430	FBMC
15	Labour Force	0.6381	FBMC
16	Claims on Private Sector	0.6307	FBMC
17	Traffic Congestion	0.6246	QLID
18	Cost of Production Labour	0.6146	FBMC
19	Money Supply Growth (M2)	0.5886	MS
20	Access to Water	0.5776	QLID
21	Regional Competitiveness	0.5642	GIS
22	Urban Population Growth	0.4864	QLID
23	Political Change	0.4615	GIS
24	Government Stability	0.4204	GIS

Source: Asia Competitiveness Institute.

Table 2.26. Top 20% Weakest Indicators List for Vietnam, 2011

Rank	20% Weakest Indicator	Score	Environment
98	Bureaucracy/Red Tape	–0.8586	GIS
99	Quality of Stock Market Regulatory Authority	–0.8706	FBMC
100	Electric Power	–0.8773	QLID
101	Lack of Market Distortion due to State-Ownership	–0.9045	GIS
102	Intellectual Property Rights Protection	–0.9062	GIS
103	High Quality Management Staff	–0.9440	FBMC
104	Government Environmental Protection Policies	–0.9674	GIS
105	Barriers to Trade	–0.9764	GIS
106	Lending Rate	–0.9890	GIS
107	Corporate Governance	–0.9898	GIS
108	Extent of Staff Training	–0.9938	FBMC
109	Foreign Owned Companies	–1.0335	MS
110	Strength of Auditing and Reporting Standards	–1.0478	GIS
111	Labour Activism	–1.0558	QLID
112	Air Quality	–1.0730	QLID
113	Local Road System	–1.1000	QLID
114	Sovereign Debt Risk	–1.1043	FBMC
115	Government Consumption Expenditure	–1.1135	GIS
116	Secondary Schooling	–1.3058	QLID
117	Tax Burden	–1.4836	GIS
118	Freedom of Press	–1.8147	QLID
119	Real GDP Growth	–2.3965	MS
120	Exchange Rate Appreciation	–2.7440	GIS
121	Inflation	–2.8427	MS

Source: Asia Competitiveness Institute.

2.3.7.2 Median Competitiveness Web Analysis

Starting with Brunei's median competitiveness web (Figure 2.32), its high Standard of Living, Education and Social Stability and Productivity Performance exceeds the ASEAN-10 median, but also very off in terms of Labour Market Flexibility as well as Financial Deepening and Business Efficiency. For the rest of the sub-environments in Figure 2.32, Brunei is only a tad above the median in Economic Vibrancy, Openness to Trade and Services and Attractiveness to Foreign Investors. Rethinking to widen its competitiveness *vis-à-vis* ASEAN in Government Policies and Fiscal Sustainability and Competition, Regulatory Standards and Rule of Law is advisable, given its strong Institutions, Governance and Leadership.

As seen from Figure 2.33, Cambodia is below the ASEAN-10 median, except for its coincidence in Productivity Performance, Attractiveness to Foreign Investors as well as Standard of Living,

Figure 2.32. Median Competitiveness Web Analysis for Brunei, 2011

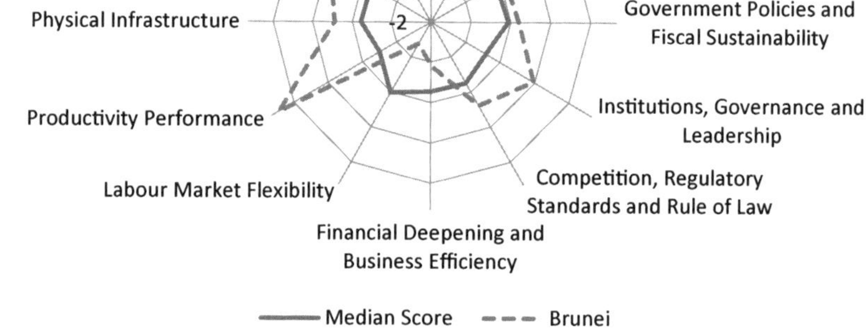

Source: Asia Competitiveness Institute.

Figure 2.33. Median Competitiveness Web Analysis for Cambodia, 2011

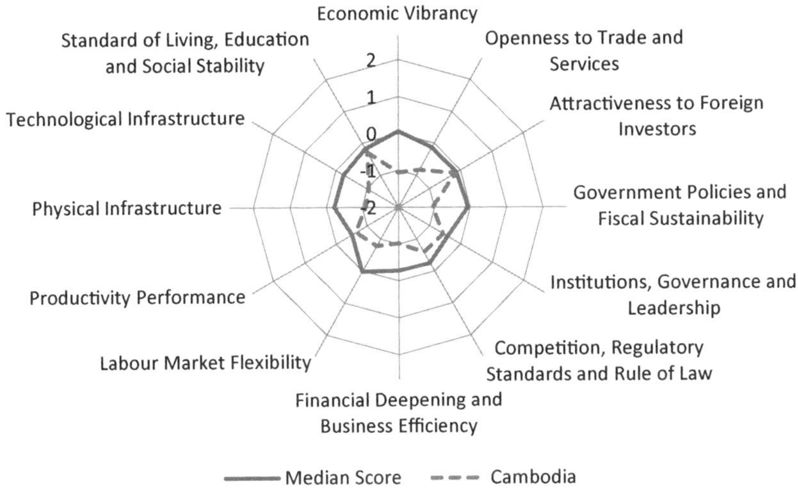

Source: Asia Competitiveness Institute.

Education and Social Stability. Improvement on Economic Vibrancy, Government Policies and Fiscal Sustainability, Physical as well as Technological Infrastructure, which are far off from the regional median, is imperative for Cambodia to catch up with the more mature ASEAN members. Cambodia needs to make its mark to foreign investors in order to attract their resources away from those countries with rising costs and other bottlenecks, including neighbouring China.

As evident from Figure 2.34, Indonesia has performed exceptionally above the ASEAN-10 median for Economic Vibrancy, and slightly above the median for Physical Infrastructure, Financial Deepening and Business Efficiency, and Labour Market Flexibility. However, it is performing below the ASEAN median in Government Policies and Fiscal Sustainability, Standard of Living, Education and Social Stability, and Technological Infrastructure. If both central and provincial governments work hand-in-hand, especially on regional clusters, to find

Figure 2.34. Median Competitiveness Web Analysis for Indonesia, 2011

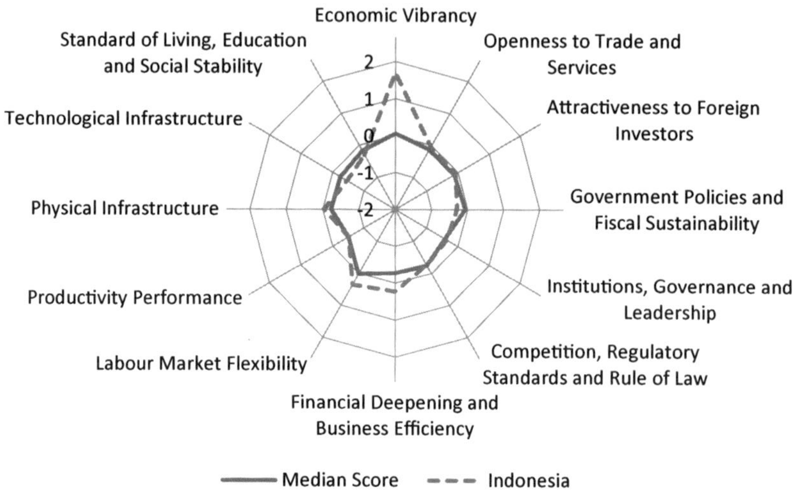

Source: Asia Competitiveness Institute.

regional solutions for regional issues as recommended by the ACI, such gaps can be improved more satisfactorily.

Laos (Figure 2.35) is in a good stead only for Technological Infrastructure and Productivity Performance as they coincide with ASEAN-10 median. The rest are below par, implying that there is plenty of room to catch up even among the CLMV grouping.

It is of no surprise to see Malaysia to always be second to Singapore in competitiveness, as all of its sub-environments are above the ASEAN-10 median (Figure 2.36). Its performance for Financial Deepening and Business Efficiency is gratifying, as it demonstrated recovery from the AFC, somewhat proving its capital control was more effective in practice than wrong in conventional wisdom. Without over-generalising, this is a small example that what is suitable for each ASEAN-10 nation has to be appreciated in its own terms and conditions while heeding general theories and practices to define ASEAN cooperation.

Figure 2.35. Median Competitiveness Web Analysis for Laos, 2011

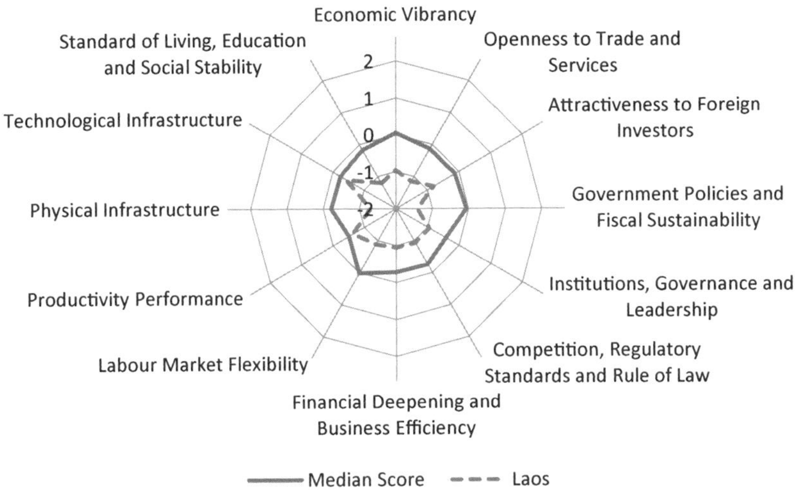

Source: Asia Competitiveness Institute.

Figure 2.36. Median Competitiveness Web Analysis for Malaysia, 2011

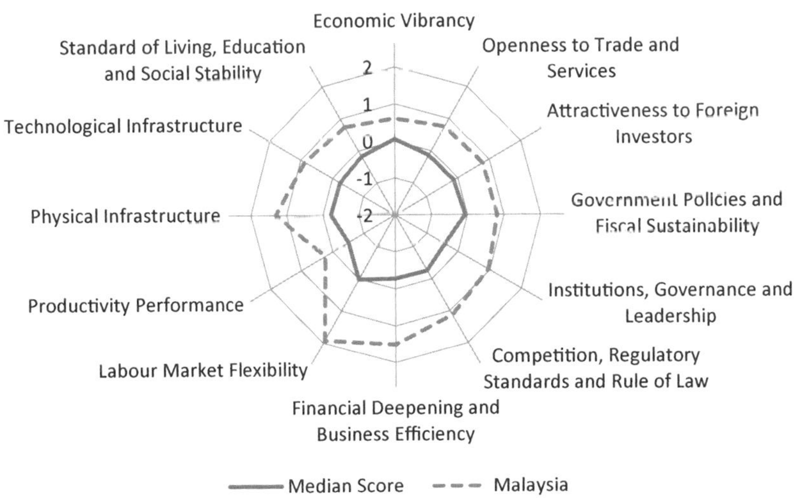

Source: Asia Competitiveness Institute.

Figure 2.37. Median Competitiveness Web Analysis for Myanmar, 2011

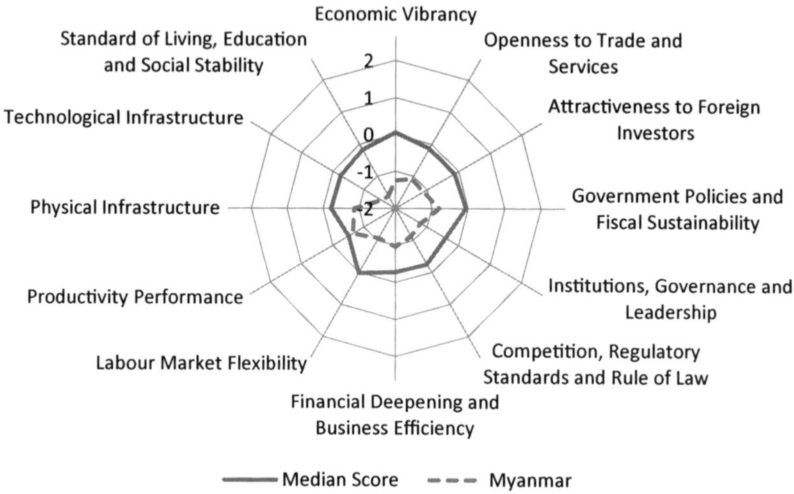

Source: Asia Competitiveness Institute.

It is unsurprising that for Myanmar, all of its sub-environments are below the ASEAN-10 median as it is ranked 10th in most instances of competitiveness (Figure 2.37). However, it is hopeful for Productivity Performance as it coincides with the median. Focusing on one of the largest gaps, namely Technological Infrastructure, would modernise production methods to the 21st century, with English language as a British legacy.[15]

As seen in Figure 2.38, the Philippines is below the ASEAN-10 median for Physical Infrastructure, but above it for Standard of Living, Education and Social Stability and Government Policies and Fiscal

[15] Interestingly, the common British legacy has encouraged Singapore entrepreneurs to set up schools in Myanmar as they did in Hong Kong, which follows Singapore's curriculum enabling students to further their secondary and even tertiary education in Singapore, both for its ambition to be an international education hub as well as to tap foreign talents and manpower.

Figure 2.38. Median Competitiveness Web Analysis for Philippines, 2011

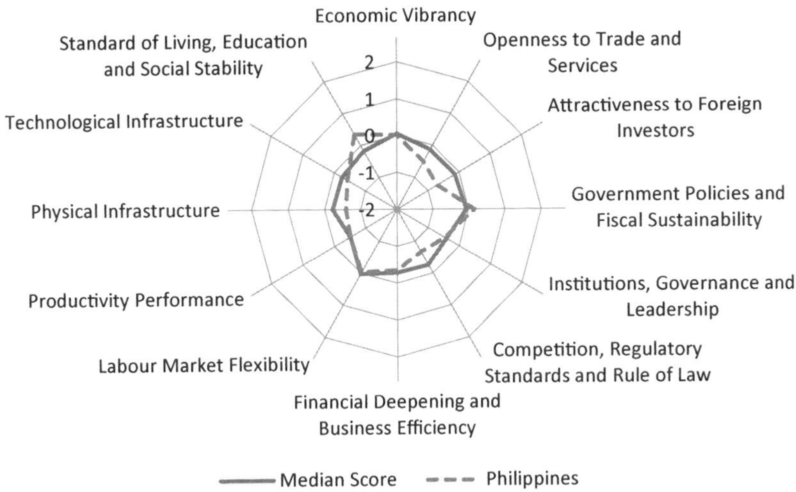

Source: Asia Competitiveness Institute.

Sustainability. As noted earlier, more dynamic growth and job creation would entice a backflow of Filipinos working abroad, a competitive advantage intrinsic for the Philippines that will not only raise capital flows, but also Productivity Performance and Labour Market Flexibility as a start.

Singapore (Figure 2.39) is *fait accompli*. However, it has to watch its Labour Market Flexibility, to not be too restrictive in practice given other socio-political considerations.

As seen in Figure 2.40, Thailand is generally above ASEAN median in all aspects. Nonetheless, it has to work more on its Standard of Living, Education and Social Stability, Technological Infrastructure, Competition, Regulatory Standards and Rule of Law, Productivity Performance, and Attractiveness to Foreign Investors to mirror Openness to Trade and Services that is already above the median. As in most ASEAN cases, the apparent discrepancy, anomaly or contradiction may be due to interests in nationalism in protecting ownership by the nationals.

Figure 2.39. Median Competitiveness Web Analysis for Singapore, 2011

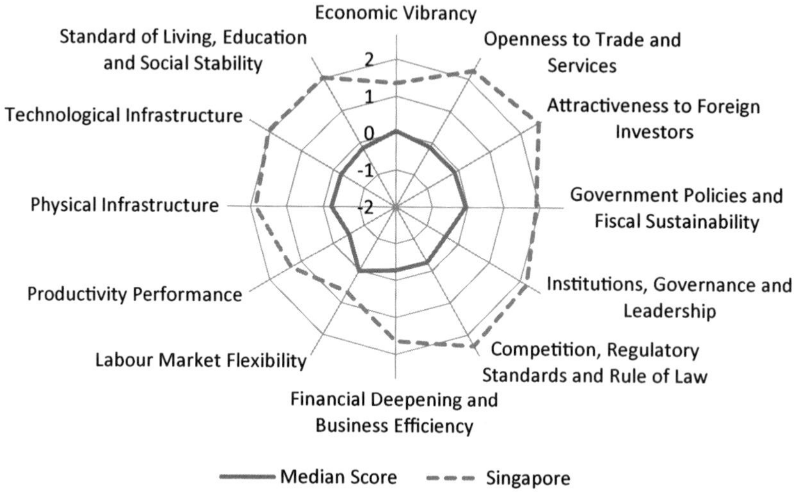

Source: Asia Competitiveness Institute.

Figure 2.40. Median Competitiveness Web Analysis for Thailand, 2011

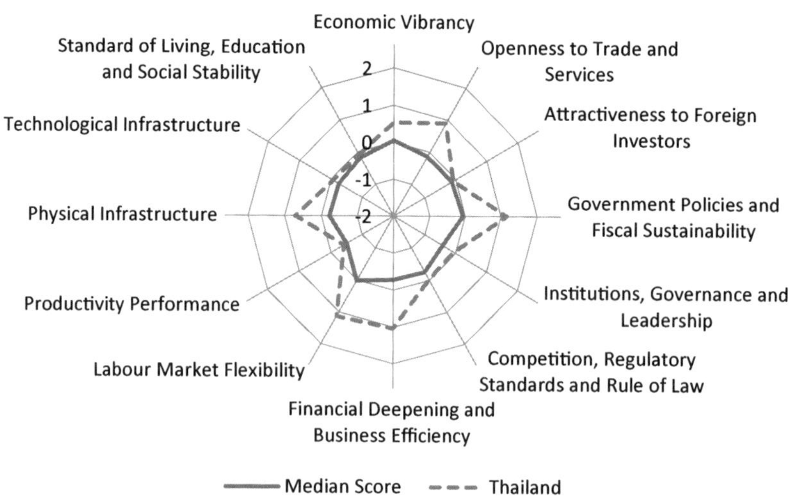

Source: Asia Competitiveness Institute.

Figure 2.41. Median Competitiveness Web Analysis for Vietnam, 2011

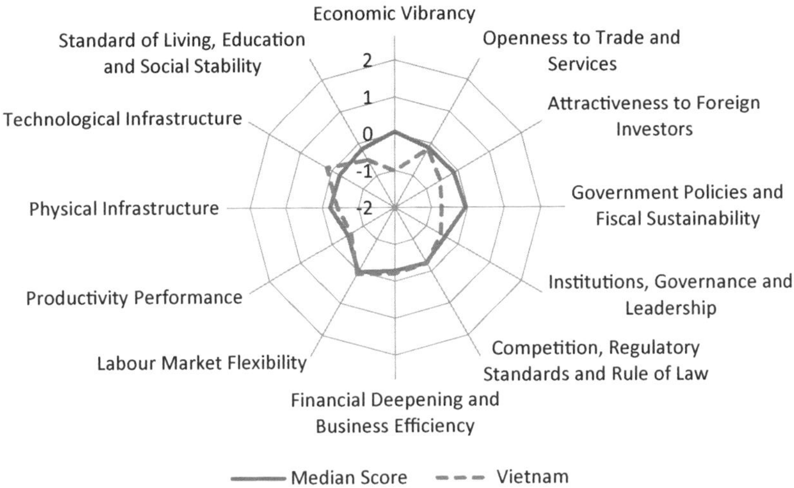

Source: Asia Competitiveness Institute.

Similar to Malaysia's own way of capital control, it is also heartening for Thailand to recover well from the AFC, which was triggered by Thailand before contagion spread, through the IMF bailout. Financial Deepening and Business Efficiency and Government Policies and Fiscal Sustainability, which are above the median, are positively appreciated.

Vietnam (Figure 2.41) is above the ASEAN median in Technological Infrastructure but has to improve on Economic Vibrancy, Attractiveness to Foreign Investors and Government Policies and Fiscal Sustainability. Perhaps Vietnam needs another *Doi Moi*; it has been done successfully once, but more maintenance work is required to take advantage of the many attributes of the sub-environments that coincide with the ASEAN median, including Labour Market Flexibility, for a sustainable pathway, while fending off some friendly rivalry from the rest in the CLMV grouping.

2.3.7.3 *Maximum Competitiveness Web Analysis*

As seen in Figure 2.42, Brunei is below the ASEAN-10 maximum despite it being in the high-income band with Singapore. These two ASEAN economies' different routes to wealth and prosperity also lead to different appetites for competitiveness. It bears serious rumination on whether Brunei can channel its oil-based wealth into a more sustainable future as what the United Arab Emirates (UAE)[16] and Qatar are doing. Brunei at the maximum performance for Productivity Performance is a very encouraging start for action.

Cambodia (Figure 2.43) is well below the ASEAN-10 maximum, especially for all sub-environments. Whether tackling the biggest gap first or dealing with the smaller ones for confidence-building is a matter that Cambodia would know best given its resources, time and appetite for structural reform.

Figure 2.42. Maximum Competitiveness Web Analysis for Brunei, 2011

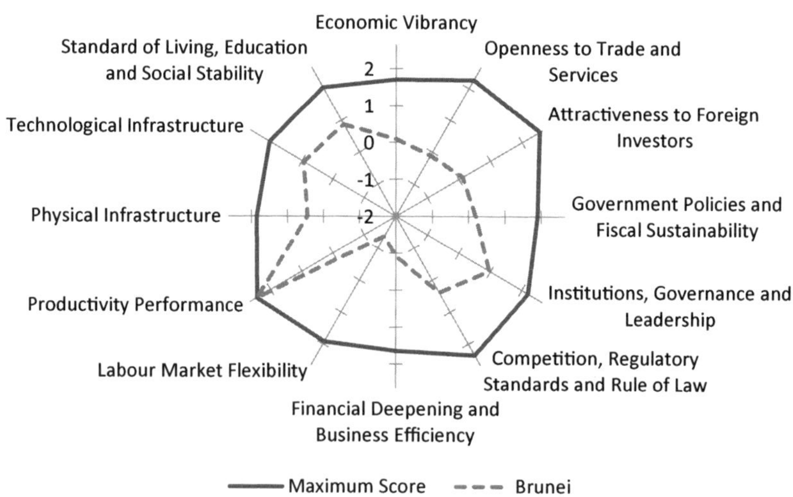

Source: Asia Competitiveness Institute.

[16] See Low (2012).

Figure 2.43. Maximum Competitiveness Web Analysis for Cambodia, 2011

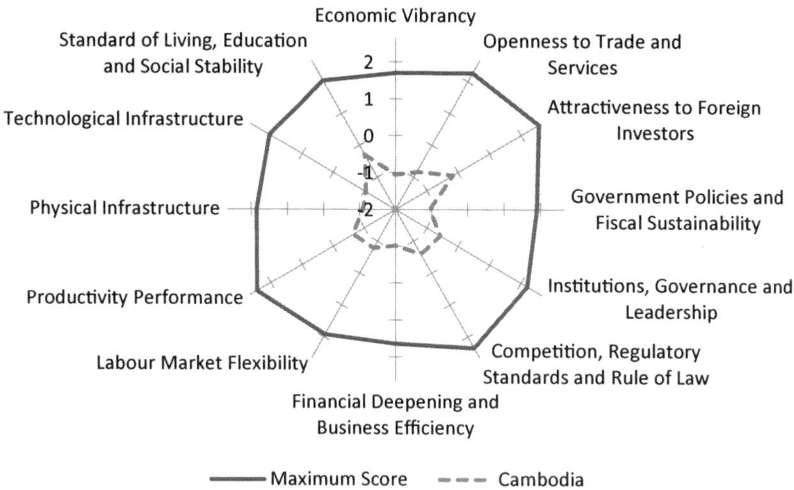

Source: Asia Competitiveness Institute.

For Indoncsia (Figure 2.44), Economic Vibrancy sets the pace for the rest of ASEAN-10. Unlike Malaysia and Thailand, Indonesia does not seem to have fully recovered from the AFC based on its Financial Deepening and Business Efficiency that is still below the ASEAN-10 maximum.

Laos (Figure 2.45) is still well below the ASEAN-10 maximum in all sub-environments. Laos, like the rest of CLMV, has both labour force and land in abundance that allow it to choose both paths as dualistic food baskets-cum-industrialisation while taking over some labour-intensive and low-skilled industries from China, for instance. By that logic, Laos can choose what suits it best and gradually move into a class of its own, as well as emulating first the CLMV grouping then the rest of ASEAN-10.

Malaysia (Figure 2.46) has done exceptionally well for Labour Market Flexibility and Financial Deepening and Business Efficiency,

Figure 2.44. Maximum Competitiveness Web Analysis for Indonesia, 2011

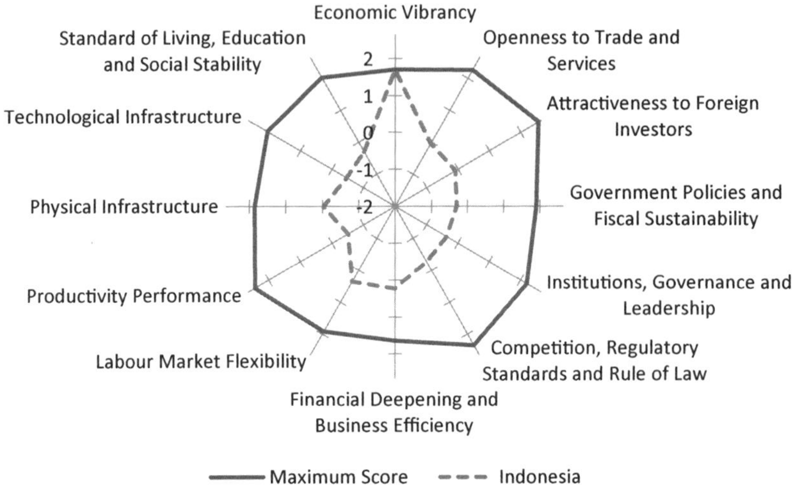

Source: Asia Competitiveness Institute.

Figure 2.45. Maximum Competitiveness Web Analysis for Laos, 2011

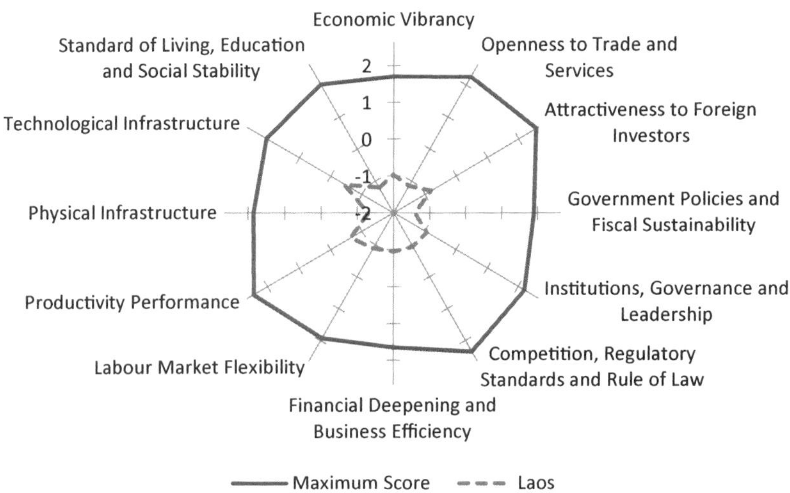

Source: Asia Competitiveness Institute.

Figure 2.46. Maximum Competitiveness Web Analysis for Malaysia, 2011

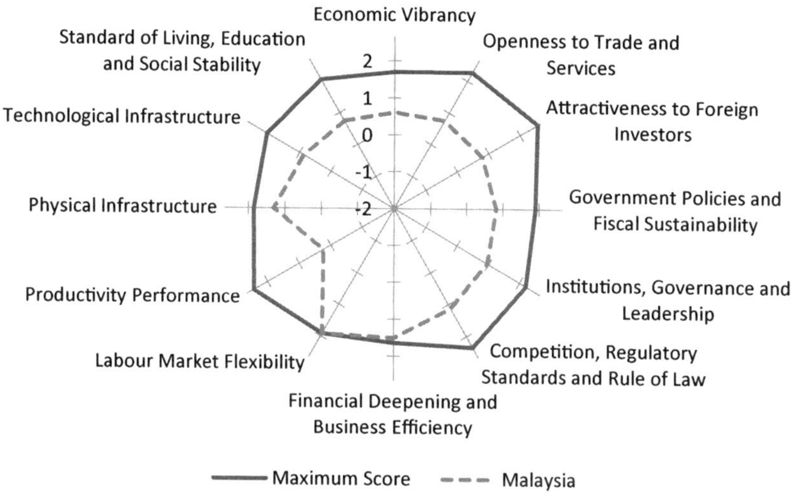

Source: Asia Competitiveness Institute.

the latter being a saving grace as it has recovered from the AFC. However, given its *bumiputera* policy, some trade-off has to be ruminated for Openness to Trade and Services and Attractiveness to Foreign Investors. On the whole, Competition, Regulatory Standards and Rule of Law seems to be well secured, with Government Policies and Fiscal Sustainability and Institutions, Governance and Leadership not too distant from the ASEAN-10 maximum. The widest gap is seen with Productivity Performance.

Myanmar (Figure 2.47) is well below the ASEAN-10 maximum for all sub-environments. It is an ongoing catch-up to improve its scores in order to move away from its 10th position in the ACI's competitiveness ranking, especially for Standard of Living, Education and Social Stability. While still in the early days, more Openness to Trade and Services and Attractiveness to Foreign Investors are expected to follow with a mindset change. Myanmar, formerly Burma, had close

Figure 2.47. Maximum Competitiveness Web Analysis for Myanmar, 2011

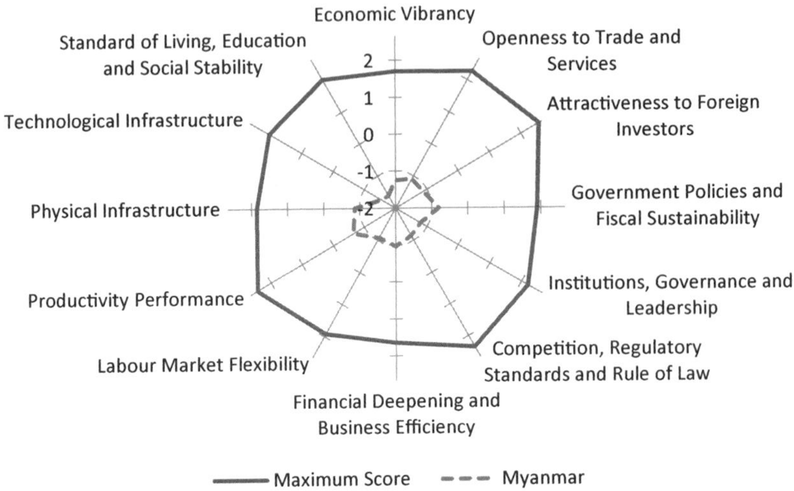

Source: Asia Competitiveness Institute.

economic ties with its neighbour, India's states on the northeast, and restoring such old trade and relationships may be part of ASEAN-10's effort with India as a whole.

The Philippines (Figure 2.48) seems to tell a tale of two archipelagos with much larger Indonesia, with ups-and-downs in competitiveness features. It is unfortunate that so many Filipinos are abroad instead of being the catalyst at home. Job creation may begin with Competition, Regulatory Standards and Rule of Law, Openness to Trade and Services and Attractiveness to Foreign Investors for long-term sustainable progress.

Singapore (Figure 2.49) may be setting the maximum for ASEAN-10 in most of the sub-environments, except for Indonesia that leads in Economic Vibrancy (Figure 2.44) given the latter's much larger size and resource abundance. While Singapore has cause for concern, especially in Productivity Performance and Labour Market Flexibility, its

Figure 2.48. Maximum Competitiveness Web Analysis for Philippines, 2011

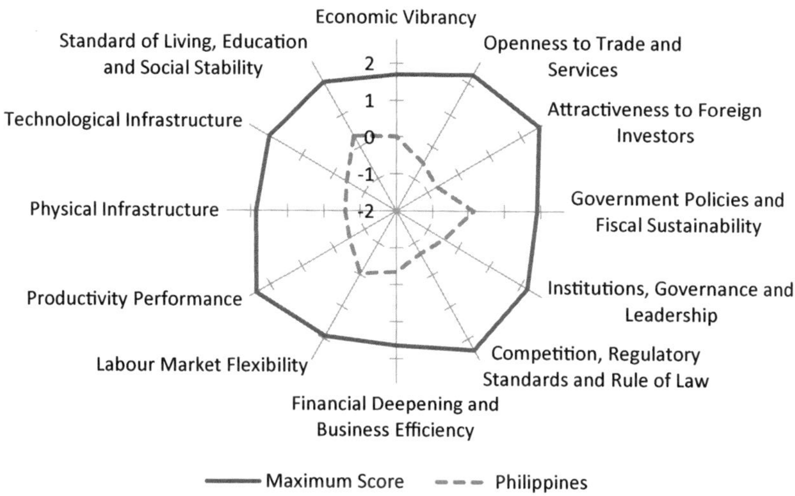

Source: Asia Competitiveness Institute.

Figure 2.49. Maximum Competitiveness Web Analysis for Singapore, 2011

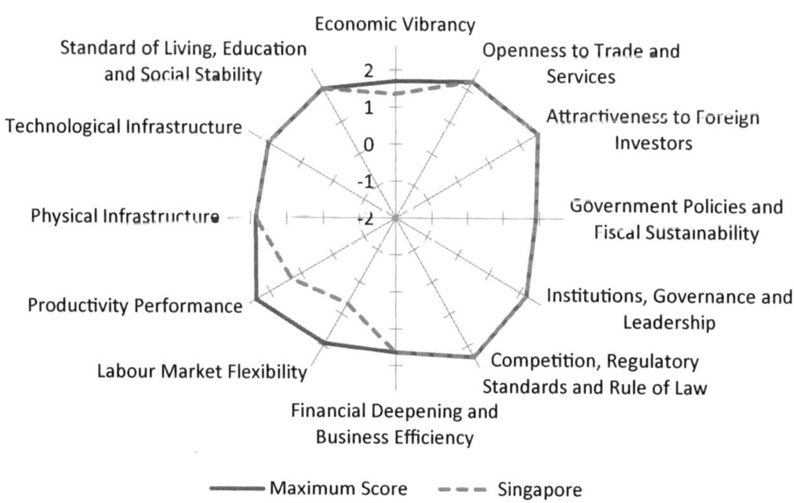

Source: Asia Competitiveness Institute.

small size in affording nimble competitive policies is a blessing in disguise. Yet, too many fast changes may cause confusion and affect its credibility for longer-term investors and business. Their bottom-line rests on stability and predictability with risk assessment finessed by transparency and accountability which visionary leaders have.

Thailand (Figure 2.50) is near the ASEAN-10 maximum for Labour Market Flexibility and Financial Deepening and Business Efficiency, with the latter reflecting a resounding recovery from the AFC. It is not doing too badly in Economic Vibrancy either. However, with much socio-political instability from internal sources, a rethinking of the resultant loss of competitiveness seems pertinent as well. Thailand has a proven track record as a successful dualistic agri-industrial structure with Thai hospitality for tourism to continue its growth and competitiveness trajectory.

Figure 2.50. Maximum Competitiveness Web Analysis for Thailand, 2011

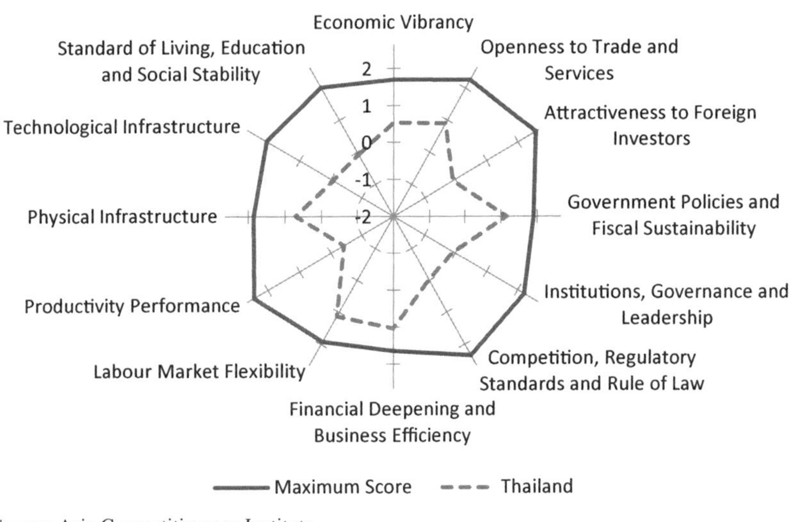

Source: Asia Competitiveness Institute.

Figure 2.51. Maximum Competitiveness Web Analysis for Vietnam, 2011

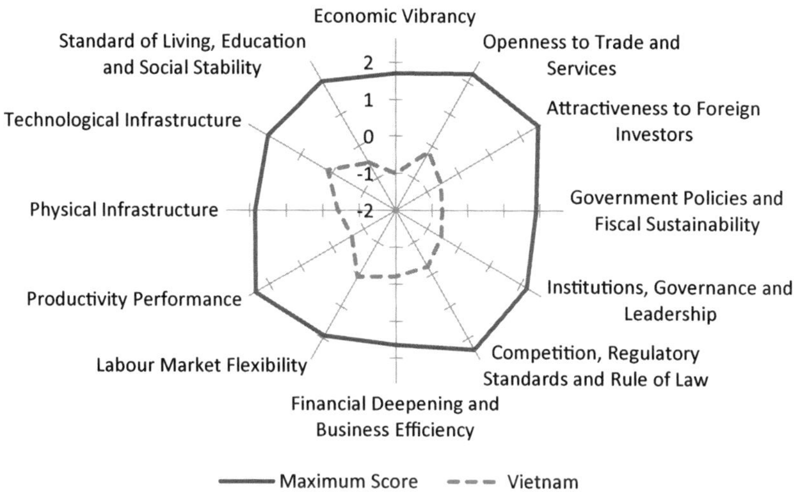

Source: Asia Competitiveness Institute.

Vietnam (Figure 2.51) remains distant in all sub-environments from the ASEAN-10 maximum. Another round of *Doi Moi* is more than a maintenance of competitiveness as there is growing competition from the rest of CLMV as well. Foreign investors can be spoilt for choice.

2.3.8 Upgrading Competitiveness through Policy Simulation Analysis

In this section, a *what-if* simulation analysis was conducted according to the methodology explained in Section 2.2.5. It is then followed by further elaboration from two generalised observations with policy implications for greater competitiveness. One is economic restructuring and diversification and the other is dealing with production bottlenecks and trade liberalisation and globalisation.

Table 2.27. *What-if* Competitiveness Simulation Analysis on Overall Competitiveness, 2011

	Rank		Score	
Economy	**Before**	**After**	**Before**	**After**
Brunei	4	3	0.3683	0.8407
Cambodia	8	8	–0.8869	–0.5063
Indonesia	5	5	0.0013	0.3426
Laos	9	8	–1.1085	–0.7833
Malaysia	2	2	1.1388	1.2218
Myanmar	10	8	–1.2699	–0.8918
Philippines	6	6	–0.3593	–0.0765
Singapore	1	1	2.0944	2.2470
Thailand	3	3	0.4710	0.6362
Vietnam	7	6	–0.4492	–0.0808

Source: Asia Competitiveness Institute.

Table 2.27 shows that the Overall Competitiveness for ASEAN economies in the first, second, third, fifth and eight ranking remained unchanged, but with improved scores after policy simulation. The most impressive outcome from the simulation is seen with Myanmar, moving from the 10th to eighth position, together with Laos from the ninth to eighth position. Brunei moved from the fourth to third place and Vietnam, from the seventh to sixth position.

As seen in Table 2.28, Macroeconomic Stability rankings for six ASEAN economies, namely Singapore, Malaysia, Indonesia, Thailand and Philippines, remained unchanged, but with improved scores after policy simulation. At the bottom, Myanmar and Laos ratcheted to the eighth position in ranking, followed by Cambodia moving up one place to the seventh place, while Vietnam moved to the sixth position.

Table 2.29 shows that for Government and Institutional Setting, those ASEAN economies in the first, second, third and fifth ranking

Table 2.28. *What-if* Competitiveness Simulation Analysis on Macroeconomic Stability, 2011

	Rank		Score	
Economy	**Before**	**After**	**Before**	**After**
Brunei	5	5	0.0409	0.3931
Cambodia	8	7	–0.7457	–0.5284
Indonesia	3	3	0.5680	0.6680
Laos	9	8	–1.0551	–0.7123
Malaysia	2	2	0.7825	0.7901
Myanmar	10	8	–1.2514	–0.8422
Philippines	6	6	–0.4335	–0.1982
Singapore	1	1	2.2375	2.2617
Thailand	4	4	0.4867	0.5434
Vietnam	7	6	–0.6299	–0.3340

Source: Asia Competitiveness Institute.

Table 2.29. *What-if* Competitiveness Simulation Analysis on Government and Institutional Setting, 2011

	Rank		Score	
Economy	**Before**	**After**	**Before**	**After**
Brunei	3	3	0.5430	0.8723
Cambodia	8	7	–0.7659	–0.5430
Indonesia	5	5	–0.3216	0.0617
Laos	10	8	–1.1339	–0.6415
Malaysia	2	2	1.0061	1.1361
Myanmar	9	8	–1.0832	–0.6382
Philippines	6	5	–0.3356	–0.0776
Singapore	1	1	2.2404	2.2871
Thailand	4	3	0.3730	0.6137
Vietnam	7	5	–0.5225	–0.0572

Source: Asia Competitiveness Institute.

remained unchanged, but with improved scores after policy simulation. Notably, Thailand joined Brunei at the third place. Cambodia at seventh was ahead of Laos and Myanmar, both at the eight position in the ranking. Vietnam improved by two places to the fifth position, putting it on par with Indonesia and the Philippines.

In Table 2.30 for Financial, Businesses and Manpower Conditions, Cambodia, Laos and Myanmar were on par at the eighth place, while Vietnam stepped up from the sixth to fifth place after policy simulation.

Table 2.31 for Quality of Life and Infrastructure Development shows that the ASEAN economies in first, second, third and fourth ranking were unchanged after policy simulation, but with improved scores. Cambodia leapt from the eight to fifth position, on par with Indonesia that improved from the seventh place. Myanmar moved from the bottom 10th to eight place, similar to the improvement seen with Laos.

Table 2.30. *What-if* Competitiveness Simulation Analysis on Financial, Businesses and Manpower Conditions, 2011

	Rank		Score	
Economy	**Before**	**After**	**Before**	**After**
Brunei	4	3	0.0608	1.1075
Cambodia	8	8	−1.0941	−0.6489
Indonesia	5	4	0.0347	0.5145
Laos	9	8	−1.1028	−1.0448
Malaysia	1	1	1.6294	1.7020
Myanmar	10	8	−1.2002	−1.0790
Philippines	7	6	−0.4007	−0.1438
Singapore	2	1	1.6175	2.0669
Thailand	3	3	0.7782	0.8875
Vietnam	6	5	−0.3231	0.0590

Source: Asia Competitiveness Institute.

Table 2.31. *What-if* Competitiveness Simulation Analysis on Quality of Life and Infrastructure Development, 2011

	Rank		Score	
Economy	**Before**	**After**	**Before**	**After**
Brunei	3	3	0.7913	0.8988
Cambodia	8	5	–0.8524	–0.2492
Indonesia	7	5	–0.2763	0.0970
Laos	9	8	–1.0304	–0.6480
Malaysia	2	2	1.0225	1.1349
Myanmar	10	8	–1.4165	–0.9078
Philippines	5	5	–0.2313	0.1214
Singapore	1	1	2.0707	2.2067
Thailand	4	4	0.1986	0.4396
Vietnam	6	5	–0.2762	0.0167

Source: Asia Competitiveness Institute.

The ACI's simulation results on the top 20% weakest indicators as well as its findings on the top 20% strongest indicators are suggestive of potential policy prescriptions for improved competitiveness as well as fitter and more sustainable economies, which will be elaborated in Section 2.3.8.1, 2.3.8.2 and 2.3.8.3.

2.3.8.1 *Economic Restructuring and Diversification*

The primary (agricultural, forestry, fishery, mining and activities derived from land), secondary (manufacturing, construction and utility) and tertiary sectors (services), in this sequence, are typical of most ASEAN-10 economies, except Singapore that has almost negligible primary sector and thrived historically on *entrepôt* trade to the Knowledge-Based Economy (KBE) it aspires now. Singapore's industrialisation follows the conventional resource-based comparative advantage of firstly abundant labour for labour-intensive industries to higher value-added and capital- and technology-intensive ones cum servicisation especially in financial and ICT services.

Economic structures of other ASEAN-10 morph in the same way from comparative advantage (natural, resource-based) to competitive advantage induced by policies (artificial comparative advantage). Some directions are demonstrated by the ACI's *what-if* policy simulation as a further guidance to policymakers.

Some indicators relating to economic structure include output (value-added) and value-added per worker (productivity) for agriculture, manufacturing and services. As strongest or weakest indicators in Section 2.3.7, they show broad restructuring and diversification (for instance, Brunei [Table 2.7] and Malaysia [Table 2.15]) or lack thereof. More specialisations in specific services sector development are in finance, tourism (Thailand [Table 2.23]) and ICT (Laos [Table 2.13]), among others.

Tracking such ACI indicators over time points to the right direction for economic restructuring and diversification, as they reshape ASEAN-10 economies in accordance with dynamic responses to regionalisation and globalisation. Oil-based Brunei and Indonesia need to monetise their wealth into a sustainable economic structure with diversification and not putting all eggs in one basket for greater resilience.

Doing that right and well leads to changing not only shares of GDP but also the needed types of jobs creation and levels of technology in commensurate. This takes time with policy guidance from the government in the first instance, creating incentives for a further role for the private sector with accompanying entrepreneurship to blossom. This is not a one-off strategy, but is constantly changing as both domestic and international factors are always evolving and interacting with each other. More than hard physical infrastructure and soft skill sets including technological infrastructure, a mindset change towards a culture of industrialisation or servicisation is necessary.

2.3.8.2 *Unblocking Production Bottlenecks, Liberalising Trade and Embracing Globalisation*

Indicators on strengths and weaknesses in Section 2.3.7 show more than physical infrastructure and technological infrastructure as an impediment that causes bottlenecks in production to unlock. The same goes for financial development to unlock savings to go into investment for both capacity and capability development. The median and maximum web charts in Section 2.3.7.2 and 2.3.7.3 are useful for gap analyses to distil the right policies.

Singapore and Malaysia are exemplary or prime ASEAN cases of facilitating investment and production, more than merely unblocking infrastructural bottlenecks. The CLMV countries have much to do until a certain momentum is attained to maintain smooth operations. Bottlenecks, other than those shown in various indicators such as rail, air and sea port facilities, range from HRD (education and health) to ICT for connectivity in a globalised setting.

Two more generic approaches to unblocking bottlenecks come from Openness to Trade and Services and Attractiveness to Foreign Investors. Openness to Trade and Services harnesses output from freeing production to become export-oriented in tandem with the Attractiveness to Foreign Investors for FDI. In turn, globalisation has to be embraced. All come with pros and con; the good, bad and ugly of globalisation underscore the importance of learning to maximise the benefits while minimising the costs. Globalisation is not an option; it has arrived. The more critical issue is to be globalisation-ready, as firewalls are needed to ward off the contagion effects of financial globalisation. This can be in financial development for instance, as much as working smartly and competitively.

Myanmar, as the last in ASEAN-10 to rise to the occasion, has a potential in agriculture for it to be a food basket for others.[17] It is also the expressed wish of Aung San Suu Kyi to take the road less travelled in agriculture as the engine of growth, unlike China which turned from a food exporter to food importer in its aggressive industrialisation.

There is a logic and competitiveness in Myanmar's agricultural aspiration with the growing middle-income class and the rise in prosperity to demand more and higher quality food, as much for food security across-the-board. Thailand is, and Malaysia can be, as dualistic in having agriculture as food basket as well as raw materials for downstream manufacturing and other agribusiness pursuits. The two archipelagos, Indonesia and the Philippines, can be as agricultural as they are also into industrialisation.

2.3.8.3 *Strengthening Leadership, Improving Governance and Transiting to Market Economy*

Insofar as the role of government in ASEAN-10 is not necessarily bad for competitiveness, in view of the successful developmental state of Singapore as discussed, strengthening leadership and improving governance are the usual prescriptions. It takes both time and incentives to grow and develop the role of private sector as two hands clapping in

[17]The Agri-Food and Veterinary Authority (AVA) and the Institute of Molecular and Cell Biology (IMCB) are among some institutions in Singapore for science and technology (S&T), the latter established in 1987 at the National University of Singapore, which also hosts several R&D facilities of the Agency for Science, Technology and Applied Research (A*STAR) to reflect Singapore's *forte* and interest in ASEAN food baskets among other related development. See also The Economist, 10 May 2014, on the new green revolution with prospects of a bigger rice bowl, another green revolution is stirring in the world's paddy fields in ASEAN economies.

unison, specifically the PPPs. Singapore and Malaysia are proven cases where leadership and governance matter.

While both top-ranking Singapore and Malaysia have their government-linked companies (GLCs) or state-owned enterprises (SOEs) as champions in industrialisation and competitiveness, their private sectors are maturing. More pertinently, the resultant stability engendered by good leadership and governance are prerequisites for credibility to sporting high levels of Openness to Trade and Services and Attractiveness to Foreign Investors as conduits to further competitiveness.

If the CLMV countries adopt these strategies, their transition to market economies like the rest of ASEAN-10 is not so hard to attain. In the final analysis of ASEAN-10, leadership as a whole, especially in economic integration and realising the AEC in 2015 or later, is as vital.

2.4 Problems and Issues at Stake

2.4.1 Conclusions on the ACI Competitiveness Ranking

Before reviewing two other areas that remain problematic as structural and divisive, which are neither unique in the theory of development economics nor in the practice of ASEAN-10 in strategic policy-making, a graphic summary of the ACI competitiveness ranking by geographic distribution is germane. Figures 2.52 to 2.56 for the Overall Compatitiveness and the other four environments are presented as a snapshot.

The geographic distribution of the rankings of Overall Competitiveness, Macroeconomic Stability and Government and Institutional Setting, as shown in Figure 2.52, 2.53 and 2.54 respectively, are mirror images of each other, with Singapore followed by Malaysia in the green zone, while the CLMV are generally in the red zone and the rest, including Brunei, in the yellow zone.

Figure 2.52. Geographical Distribution — Overall Competitiveness Ranking, 2011

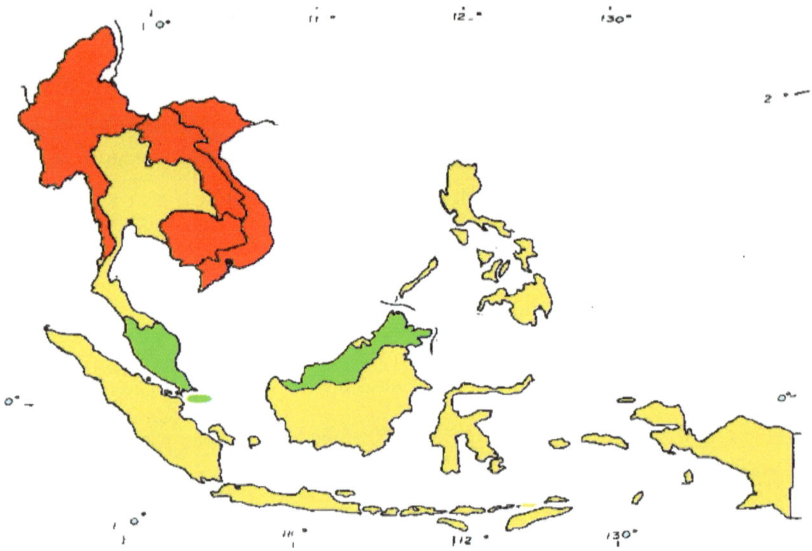

Notes: Green: Top 20% economies; Yellow: Middle 40% economies; Red: Bottom 40% economies.
Source: Asia Competitiveness Institute.

Clearly, liberalisation and globalisation are hard taskmasters, but Singapore and Malaysia heed them well in their respective first and second ranking. Notably, Brunei is not at the top in competiveness although it is in the high-income category, implying that high income does not automatically guarantee competitiveness. Brunei's wealth is oil-based, while Singapore took the harder routes of liberalisation and globalisation to earn its high-income status by being competitive.

Those less open and competitive take different routes dictated by other socio-political agenda or priorities. It may also be a matter of stages of economic growth and development that takes time for the

Figure 2.53. Geographical Distribution — Macroeconomics Stability Ranking, 2011

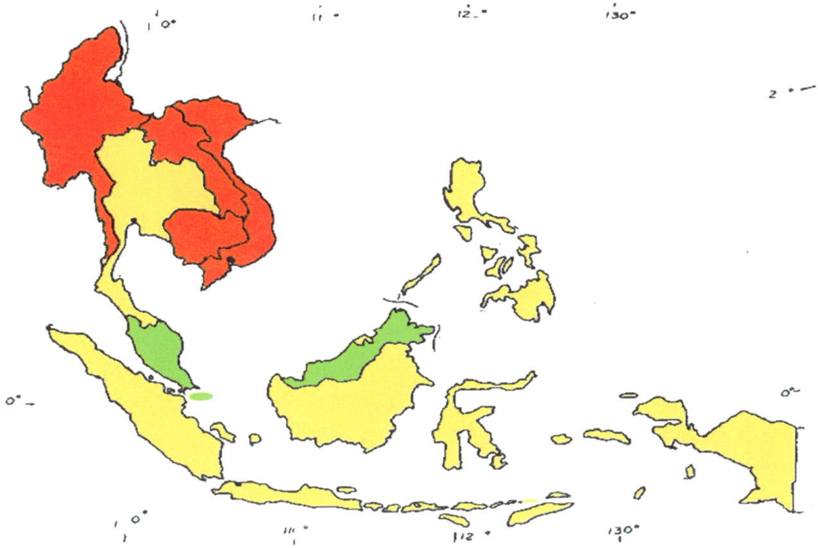

Notes: Green: Top 20% economies; Yellow: Middle 40% economies; Red: Bottom 40% economies.
Source: Asia Competitiveness Institute.

CLMV in particular. What is undoubtedly imperative is economic growth as the first and the last. Without growth, only stagnation pervades, be it a young economy as stillborn or a mature state regressing back to poverty.

Figure 2.55 for Financial, Businesses and Manpower Conditions shows that the Philippines plus CLMV without Vietnam are in the red zone, while Figure 2.56 for Quality of Life and Infrastructure Development has Indonesia and the CLMV without Vietnam in the red zone; all others in the green and yellow zones remain unchanged. As more mature ASEAN economies that are supposed to be in the upper tier, the interchange of Indonesia and the Philippines in joining the CLMV is of concern and worrisome. Are they regressing or it is just a

Figure 2.54. Geographical Distribution — Government and Institutional Setting Ranking, 2011

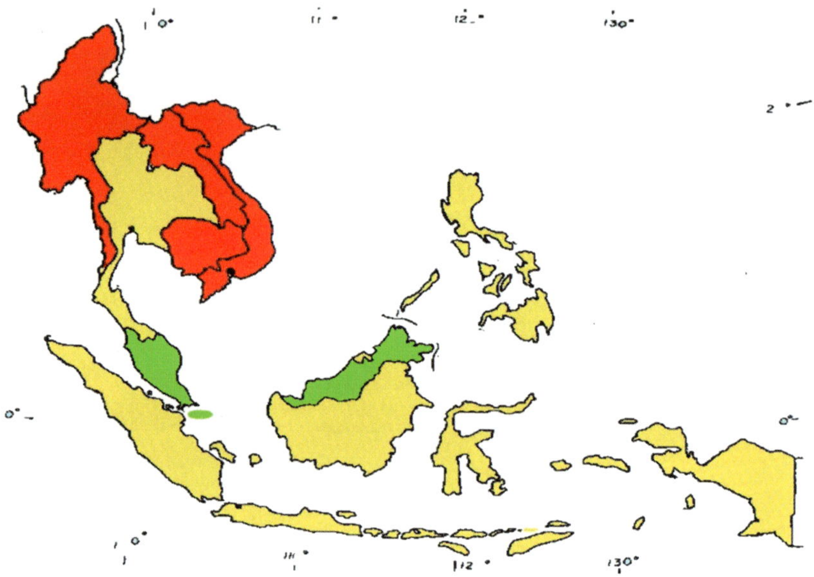

Notes: Green: Top 20% economies; Yellow: Middle 40% economies; Red: Bottom 40% economies.
Source: Asia Competitiveness Institute.

temporary downside with both having chequered pathways not commensurate with their size and status in ASEAN-10? On the other hand, CLMV as a group is young, but not as credible yet.

The ACI's Overall Competitiveness index with its environments and sub-environments provides a valuable policy framework for assessing the current competitiveness of each of the ASEAN-10 economies. It also offers useful insights for each country to enhance its competitiveness through *what-if* policy simulations focusing on each economy's

Figure 2.55. Geographical Distribution — Financial, Businesses and Manpower Conditions Ranking, 2011

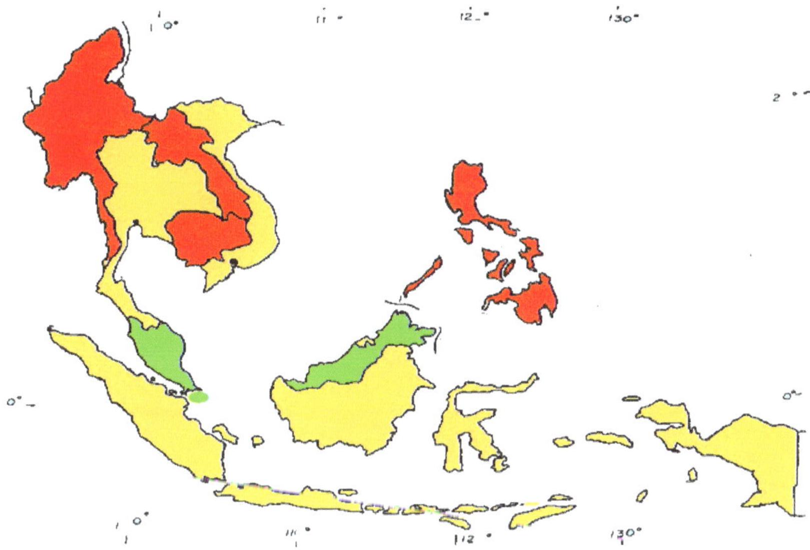

Notes: Green: Top 20% economies; Yellow: Middle 40% economies; Red: Bottom 40% economies.
Source: Asia Competitiveness Institute.

top 20% weakest indicators that were adjusted to the ASEAN-10 average. While the thrust of this study on ASEAN-10 has focused more on relative performance in competitiveness of these economies, such policy simulations and a broad array of indicators reviewed enable some development strategies or policies to be tendered.

Apart from the four areas discussed in Section 2.4.1 that are directly from the competitiveness dimensions, two more follow as policy recommendations.

Figure 2.56. Geographical Distribution — Quality of Life and Infrastructure Development Ranking, 2011

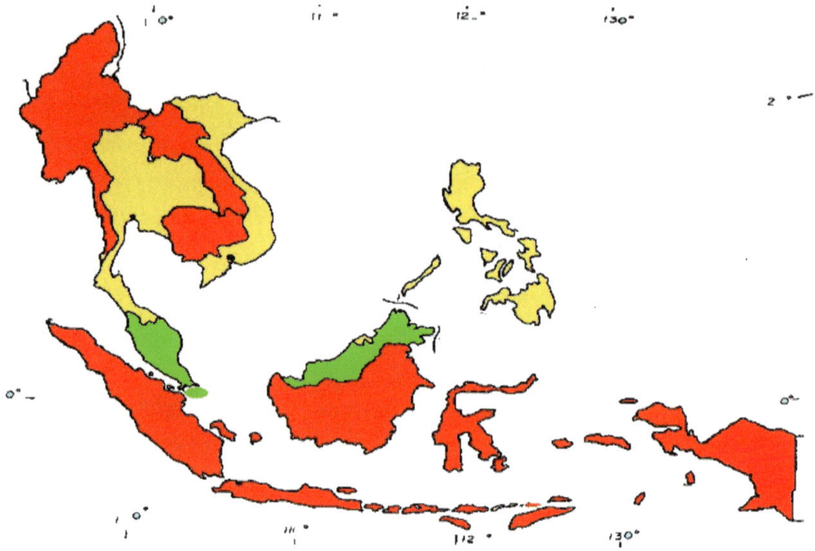

Notes: Green: Top 20% economies; Yellow: Middle 40% economies; Red: Bottom 40% economies.
Source: Asia Competitiveness Institute.

2.4.2 Upgrading Agriculture and Managing Rural Migration and Sustainable Urbanisation

The role of agriculture and related issues of rural-urban migration are affecting sustainable urbanisation and the potential growth and development of some ASEAN economies as food baskets. Rising food prices, which happened in the 2008 agflation (due to inclement weather and other natural factors) and rice shortage are crises to avert. Rice remains the staple food in ASEAN and Asia. Ensuring an adequate supply of food for more than 600 million in ASEAN-10 is one complex and complicated problem that is tied up with issues ranging from poverty and income inequality to sustainable environment and the ecosystem.[18]

At stake is an equally perplexing issue of the disappearing rural community as agricultural share in GDP loses *vis-à-vis* manufacturing and services. Competitiveness in agricultural pursuits with potential for raw materials as downstream value-adding for manufacturing, which in turn jumpstarts services from financial and telecommunications to socio-economic services in health and education, forms a virtuous circle in economic development and competitiveness. It is not a stark choice of agriculture or manufacturing, but they complement and supplement each other as a duo engine of growth.

There are many rich and well-served rural farm sectors, such as those seen in Australasia, Europe, the US, and other developed economies in the league of the Organisation for Economic Cooperation and Development (OECD). Agriculture needs as much infusion of foreign investment, technology and skill transfer, organisation and management to be as prosperous and competitive as manufacturing. It is more of a mindset change with the right incentives and motivation for equally satisfactory jobs and human resource development in agriculture.

That ASEAN-10, except Brunei and Singapore, is not pure agriculture in competitiveness is clear. It is clear too that even these two non-agricultural economies have the competitiveness as finessing development in agriculture for the requisite acquisition of capital, manpower, science and technology and other dynamics as in industrialisation.

[18] As noted, more S&T and R&D in ASEAN-based institutions to tap the second green revolution among others is a vital aspect of cooperation and integration.

2.4.3 Development Divide and Catching-Up for Transitional Economies

An inevitably two-tiered ASEAN-10 is neither necessarily bad nor implying eventual balanced economic growth and development. As natural as resource endowment, diversity is as inherent to different economic structures, models and no less the respective roles of government and private sector. While catching-up seems politically correct, gaps are as intuitive as they lend themselves to competition in areas that suit each ASEAN economy best. Indeed, diversity and variety in both quantitative and qualitative terms of competitiveness make ASEAN-10 as attractive as they are complementing and supplementing each other for overall competitiveness of the region.

If a two-tiered ASEAN-10 means a dualistic ASEAN structure with agriculture and agro-based industrialisation-cum-servicisation, it is a virtuous circle in and of itself. East Asian miracle economies such as Taiwan and South Korea, even Japan to a lesser extent, are food baskets in feeding themselves if not also agricultural exporters. Thailand is one successful dualistic economy from rice to fishery products, no less Indonesia with its forestry, oil and mineral production added in. China has realised the cost of industrialisation as the factory of the world, turning from a food exporter to food importer with ambitious yet unpleasant land grabs from ASEAN and South Asia to Africa.

The older and more developed ASEAN-6, in contrast to the CLMV, forms a pair like two hands clapping together in terms of agricultural resource endowments and potential dualism. Once competitiveness rankings are reckoned with serious policy rumination, whether it is the ASEAN Free Trade Area (AFTA), ASEAN Trade in Goods Agreement (ATIGA) or the AEC as projects of mutual benefits to all in various ways, ASEAN-10 has many areas to unlock and opportunities to be seized.

Apart from the transitional CLMV, food baskets from Indonesia to the Philippines are potentially engines of economic growth, development and competitiveness. It is however right to stress that catching-up is not a static game, which means that there will always be some order of ranking by any set of indicators. There is no idealistic scenario of catching-up to mean almost equal or near equal, be it GDP per capita or quality of life across ASEAN-10. Political culture and relative roles of government and private sector, however defined, do and must vary in ASEAN-10. Certain key performance indicators to emulate are as necessary as they need to be suitable to each economy's stage and appetite for what is each respective pathway.

Going forward, ASEAN integration, however defined and conceptualised, is *sui generis*. Given that the ASEAN-10 countries have a distinct geographic advantage in terms of their proximity to other Asian fast-growing emerging markets, such as China and India, they can benefit immensely from the potential benefits of greater integration like the AEC that is due to come into existence by the end of 2015. However, furthering such regional integration is likely to be beneficial for the ASEAN-10 bloc only if they systematically pay attention to addressing their weaknesses in areas they lag behind in terms of relative competitiveness, in addition to leveraging on their strengths.

More specifically, some countries in the region would benefit immensely from investing in building good governance and institutional capacity, which remain a fundamental prerequisite to ensure sustainable growth, as evident from the experience of Singapore. In addition, investing in human capital and promoting entrepreneurship, improving the business environment and pushing for a fundamental structural change in the economies would also enable the ASEAN-10 economies to reap the benefits of greater regional integration. To that end, the ACI competitiveness index offers a valuable policy tool for the policymakers in the region.

Globalisation has a steep price unless economies are globalisation-ready rather than try to remain sheltered and protected to counter the tides of FDI, which has its advantages of infusion of science and technology, management and other skills for industrialisation and growth of agriculture and services. Equally imperative is ASEAN integration through the ASEAN Community's three pillars of economic, political security and socio-cultural. By whichever ASEAN platform, be it AFTA, ATIGA or AEC, it is not merely for catching-up. It is also to achieve one's aspirations and visions through self-defined and targeted approaches based on strategic pragmatism.

References

ASEAN Secretariat. 2008. *ASEAN Economic Community Blueprint*. Jakarta: The ASEAN Secretariat. http://www.asean.org/archive/5187-10.pdf (accessed September 5, 2013).

Basu Das, Sanchita. 2012. "A critical look at the ASEAN Economic Community Scorecard". *East Asia Forum*, 1 June. http://www.eastasiaforum.org/2012/06/01/a-critical-look-at-the-asean-economic-community-scorecard/ (accessed September 5, 2014).

Basu Das, Sanchita, Jayant Menon, Rodolfo Severino and Omkar Lal Shrestha, eds. 2013. *The ASEAN Economic Community: A Work in Progress*. Singapore: Asian Development Bank and Institute of Southeast Asian Studies.

Bristow, Gillian. 2010. *Critical Reflections on Regional Competitiveness: Theory, Policy, Practice (Routledge Studies in Human Geography)*. Oxon: Routledge.

Camagni, Roberto. 2002. "On the Concept of Territorial Competitiveness: Sound or Misleading?" *Urban Studies* 39 (13): 2395–2411.

Eurochambres. 2007. *Regional Competitiveness Atlas*. Brussels: Eurochambres.

European Union. 2011. *EU Regional Competitiveness Index*. European Union.

Geiger, Thierry. 2013. "Charting ASEAN's competitiveness landscape". *World Economic Forum Blog*, 6 June. http://forumblog.org/2013/06/charting-aseans-competitiveness-landscape/ (accessed September 5, 2013).

Hansakul, Syetarn. 2013. *ASEAN Economic Community (AEC): A Potential Game Changer for ASEAN Countries*. Frankfurt: Deutsche Bank Research.

IMD World Competitiveness Center. 2014. *IMD World Competitiveness Yearbook*. Lausanne: International Institute for Management Development.

Kitson, Michael, Ronald Martin, and Peter Tyler. 2004. "Regional Competitiveness: An Elusive yet Key Concept?" *Regional Studies* 38 (9): 991–999.

Krugman, Paul. 1994. "Competitiveness: A Dangerous Obsession." *Foreign Affairs* 73 (2): 28–44.

Low, Linda. 2001. "The Singapore Developmental State in the New Economy and Polity". *The Pacific Review* 14 (3): 411–441.

Low, Linda. 2004a. "Association of Southeast Asian Nations economic cooperation and challenges". In *Southeast Asia Background Series, No. 3* edited by Saw Swee Hock. Singapore: Institute of Southeast Asian Studies.

Low, Linda, ed. 2004b. *Developmental States: Relevancy, Redundancy or Reconfiguration?* New York: Nova Science.

Low, Linda. 2008. "The Oil Developmental States: Brunei and the Middle East". Paper for the Brunei Forum 2008 organized by the Institute of Southeast Asian Studies, Singapore, February 19–20.

Low, Linda. 2012. *Abu Dhabi's Vision 2030: An Ongoing Journey of Economic Development*. Singapore: World Scientific.

Porter, Michael E. 1980. *Competitive Strategy: Techniques for Analyzing Industries and Competitors*. New York: Free Press.

Pushpanathan, Sundram. 2010. "*ASEAN Connectivity and the ASEAN Economic Community*". Paper presented at the 24th Asia-Pacific Roundtable, Kuala Lumpur, June 7–9. http://www.asean.org/ resources/item/asean-connectivity-and-the-asean-economic-community-by-s-pushpanathan-deputy-secretary-general-of-asean-for-asean-economic-community-2 (accessed September 5, 2014).

Tan, Khee Giap, Mulya Amri, Linda Low and Kong Yam Tan. 2013a. *Competitiveness Analysis and Development Strategies for 33 Indonesian Provinces*. Singapore: World Scientific.

Tan, Khee Giap, Linda Low, Kong Yam Tan and Amanda Lijuan Lim. 2013b. *Annual Analysis of Competitiveness, Development Strategies and Public Policies on ASEAN-10: 2000–2010.* Singapore: World Scientific.

Tan, Khee Giap, Linda Low, Kong Yam Tan and Kartik Rao. 2013c. *Annual Analysis of Competitiveness, Simulation Studies and Development Perspective for 35 States and Federal Territories of India: 2000–2010.* Singapore: World Scientific.

Tan, Khee Giap, Randong Yuan, Sangiita Wei Cher Yoong, and Mu Yang. 2013d. *Annual Analysis of Competitiveness, Simulation Studies and Development Perspective for 34 Greater China Economies.* Singapore: World Scientific.

Tan, Khee Giap and Kong Yam Tan. 2014. "Assessing competitiveness of ASEAN-10 economies". *International Journal of Economics and Business Research* 8 (4): 377–398.

The Economist. 2014. "A bigger rice bowl". May 10. http://www.economist.com/news/briefing/ 21601815-another-green-revolution-stirring-worlds-paddy-fields-bigger-rice-bowl (accessed September 5, 2013).

Verbiest, Jean-Pierre A. 2011. *"Opportunities and challenges for the ASEAN economic community in a global perspective." Presentation at the Workshop on "Managing Regional and Global Governance in Asia", Indonesia, October 3–14.* http://www.bi.go.id/en/publikasi/artikel-kertas-kerja/artikel/Documents/ed2257dd82014071a3cfbd331f9cde19131011_DrJPVerbiest Opportunitiesandchallenges.pdf (accessed September 5, 2013).

World Economic Forum. 2014. *Global Competitiveness Report 2013–2014.* Geneva: World Economic Forum.

Discussant Notes 2.1

Mr Steven Wong
Deputy Chief Executive, Institute of Strategic and International Studies, Malaysia

I have gone through the ASEAN-10 competitiveness ranking and found it well worth the investment of time. Overall, the results seem intuitively plausible to me. As you would expect actions for a region that is growing, the scores show that shifts are happening, especially in the middle order. You would be disappointed if nothing moved very much and scores were not being improved upon. As a matter of fact, we also see scores decline as well. If the same exercise were done in Europe today, many of the scores would have declined.

The addition of the Competitiveness Over Time analysis, in particular, is very interesting. Certainly, the improvements in the scores of Indonesia and the Philippines appear to also be reflected by current investor sentiments and rating agency assessments. Also, the *what-if* analytics is very useful and the policy implications generated quite sound. My concerns are more about the implications of the findings rather than the findings themselves.

Country improvements are represented in two ways: rankings and scores. Rankings are fine but if a country really wants to move ahead, it has to look at its scores. While any improvements are to be welcomed, however, those that we observe are far from anything that we can call transformational. The declines or only slight improvements in sub-pillars can be a bit worrying. Singapore, while on top, seems to have maxed out, while Malaysia, firmly in the number two spot, has bounced around a bit.

Singapore is, of course, the benchmark. However, should the benchmark really be Singapore or other fast emerging economies? Quite often, when you look at some competitiveness indices, there have been remarkable score improvements in an unexpected part of the world and countries which have overtaken you. Last year in the World Competitiveness Yearbook, the United Arab Emirates (UAE) leaped from 16th place to overtake eight economies, including Malaysia.

The scores captured by the ACI are worrying in the sense that they do not seem to be reflecting changes that are needed to stay on top of the game. Let me give you an example. In 2001, South Korea basically had the living standard of Malaysia today (around US$17,000 in purchasing power parity terms). In the space of short 12 years, Korea went from Malaysian standard of living to just behind Japan (US$33,000). Now that is truly transformational. If the ACI were to track South Korea over the 12 years, what kinds of changes would have been seen? ASEAN countries need to make those kinds of dramatic, unprecedented movements.

In closing, I have three suggestions for the ACI. First, these days, people want to see scores, rankings and so on, but they also want you to tell them a story. Other index compilers are beginning to tell the story of not only macro-trends but context more effectively. I think perhaps the ACI could also do the same. What is happening within the ASEAN-10? What are the local constraining issues? As has been pointed out, some countries are falling behind in the governance pillar. These things can be fleshed out and magnified.

Second, the implicit weakness of the *what-if* methodology is that it only basically raises weak countries to the group average and the group average may well be sub-optimal. We should be using benchmarks that can challenge and push us further and faster. It may be better to look at other countries, including China, to get an accurate perspective of the changes required to stay ahead of the game.

The last point I want to make is this: When I look at indices, and this is not a criticism of the ACI, I often wonder whether or not it is possible to go beyond the contemporaneous. Basically, the data used is with one- or two-year lag. It is like looking at the rear view mirror of a car to see what is behind. I wonder whether a methodology can be established that can help us look ahead and tell us what the prospects are in the next one or two years. In other words, we need leading indicators in addition to coincident ones. These kinds of things are interesting and different from what have been done so far. From this, we can begin to tell a story not only of the past and present but a peek into the future. I think that it is well worth trying and can be done.

Discussant Notes 2.2

Dr Bustanul Arifin
Professor, University of Lampung and Board of Founder/ Senior Economist, Institute for Development of Economics and Finance, Indonesia

First of all, there have been many indices. I am focusing on the rationale and the indicators you have mentioned. Normally, in global competitiveness indices, there are stages that have been defined, from resource-driven economies to investment-driven economies then to innovation-driven economies. That is very clear in terms of stages of development of competitiveness of a country. It has been widely used. My point is, apart from the four environments which include hundreds of indicators from macroeconomic stability, government and institutional setting, financial, businesses and manpower conditions to quality of life, you could also consider the indicators of sustainability, as everybody is talking about sustainability for the future. I know the indicators are not easy to find, but I would like to add quality of environment which is also very challenging for businesses. Businesses are talking about green economy as a simplified concept of sustainability development — how green your business is, how green your long-term vision to stay in the business is, and so on.

Why am I mentioning this? The competitiveness index, at least, has to be a vision of universality. If people spend time to go through your index like Mr Wong did, you could be sure that people will kind of replicate your index at the sub-regional level. Indonesia has 34 provinces and over 500 districts, and the ACI have also established a competitiveness index at the sub-national level for Indonesia. If you could provoke people to replicate your index, you would be successful. World

Economic Forum has been successful in this kind of thing. Michael Porter has been successful in creating a competitiveness index according to his term. In terms of micro-business, Mark Kramer and Michael Porter have been promoting another index called 'Creating Shared Value'. So, if people are willing to adopt and replicate that, I think people will look for the ACI and will be waiting for the ACI.

Regarding updating the competitiveness index and ranking, if you could include the 2012 and 2013 indicators, I think people will look forward to the 2014 book, because the 2012 was not updated. Is it possible to do the 2013 as well?

With regard to Korea, I read an article saying that President Park has paid serious attention to a creativity index as they have been trying to establish their own model. President Park believes creative industry indicators are the most important. I read that, she read the book *Start-up Nation: The Story of Israel's Economic Miracle* ten times in order to have an idea of how to establish a nation that has a truly competitive creative industry. My point is that the future of competitiveness is in sustainability, innovation and creative industry which the ACI may want to incorporate in your competitiveness framework.

Chapter 3

EXAMINING THE CAUSAL RELATIONSHIP BETWEEN FINANCIAL DEPTH AND ECONOMIC GROWTH IN CAMBODIA, LAOS AND VIETNAM

3.1 Introductory Notes

Cambodia, Laos and Vietnam (CLV) have come to be recognised as the new growth frontiers in the Association of Southeast Asian Nations (ASEAN) bloc, especially since the 2000s. These countries have individually registered an average growth rate of about 7% between 2001 and 2014 (see Figure 3.1), along with a relatively stable macroeconomic environment characterised by robust growth in exports and relatively subdued inflation on average during this period.

In fact as highlighted in Figure 3.1, with the notable exception of the year 2008 that coincided with the Global Financial Crisis (GFC), one can find that growth in these three economies far outstripped their respective domestic inflation rates, indicating the sustained high growth momentum that these economies maintained throughout the last decade along with a stable domestic macroeconomic environment.

Among the CLV countries, although the World Bank has classified Cambodia as a low-income country, the country has remained to be one of the ASEAN's most consistent performers in terms of economic growth. With the exception of the GFC phase during 2007–2009, as seen in Figure 3.1, Cambodia's growth rates averaged around 10% in

Figure 3.1. Annual Real GDP Growth and Inflation in CLV Countries, 2001–2014[a]

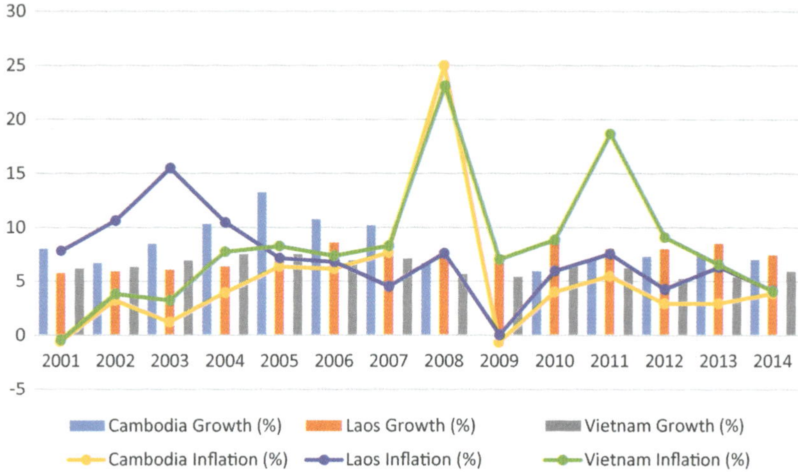

[a] Inflation is measured by the Consumer Price Index (%).

Source: The World Bank.

the run up to the crisis. Cambodia started with its entry into the ASEAN bloc in 1999 and subsequently entered the World Trade Organisation (WTO) in 2004. These moves were not only complementary, but also provided a boost to the country's efforts to benefit from the increased regional cooperation as well as global integration, which is believed to have placed it on track to graduating to a middle-income country status. The GFC shock significantly slowed down the speed of the Cambodian economy, mainly owing to the country's high dependence on exports.

Laos, with a middle-income status, has registered an average growth rate of over 7% over the last decade, starting from 2001 with a largely favourable macroeconomic environment that was supported by its vast natural resource base. In addition to its growth record, which has been nothing short of impressive, the economy experienced a substantial drop in its inflation rates since the early 2000s (specifically in 2003), which played a crucial part in the country's sustained economic growth since then. Similar to Cambodia, Laos's growth slowdown occurred during the GFC but the country continued to maintain its robust 7% growth rate on average after the GFC, which was supported by a low inflationary environment. It is useful to reiterate that the inflation rate, which climbed up to around 8% in 2011, was largely driven by domestic agricultural supply shocks. However, inflationary pressures have been easing since then, especially since the entry of Laos into the WTO in 2012. There are also immense potentials for the country in terms of opportunities to boost its growth potential, with Laos joining the upcoming ASEAN Economic Community (AEC) that is likely to be launched by December 31st 2015. The AEC will not only provide a fillip to the growth prospects, but also allow the economy to achieve and maintain an overall macroeconomic discipline.

Vietnam, classified as a middle-income country, has been recognised to closely follow the pattern of Cambodia in terms of its achievements and challenges in the ASEAN region. Hailed as one of the success stories of Asia, Vietnam maintained a high and consistent average growth rate of over 7.5% from the beginning of the millennium. Though Vietnam emerged from the GFC relatively unaffected and experienced only a mild growth slowdown during the crisis, it is crucial to underline that an average of less than 6% growth since the GFC clearly is the lowest spell of growth experienced by Vietnam following the Asian Financial Crisis. Furthermore, the country has faced two sharp inflationary episodes. The first event in 2007, when inflation rates soared to about 23%, was attributed to the country's entry into the WTO that resulted in massive capital inflows causing an appreciation of prices. The second episode in 2011 was primarily driven by the massive fiscal stimulus that Vietnam allowed to recover from the GFC. However, it is clear that both of these events were isolated episodes, as by and large, the inflationary tendencies in the economy quickly petered out and gradually brought back the economy to its growth path.

Although all the CLV countries were hit by the GFC (with Cambodia affected more relative to the rest), there has been a sharp recovery in all the economies from around 2010. This growth has been partly aided by the rapid development of the financial sector in these countries, which has formed the basis for optimism about the future growth potential of these countries.

One specific element of financial sector development pertains to financial deepening, which refers broadly to the increased provision as well as choices of financial services. Financial sector development is a rather broad term capturing "the factors, policies, and institutions that lead to effective financial intermediation and markets, and deep and broad access to capital and financial services" (World Economic Forum, 2012, 3).

Financial deepening has been an integral part of the policy discourse in the CLV countries in the years following the GFC, specifically in terms of its potential to generate economic growth. However, there have also been concerns that transitional countries, such as Cambodia and Vietnam, have experienced a period of excessive credit growth — an offshoot of rapid financial deepening — in recent years, which in turn has generated fears about hampering growth and aggravating financial instability in these economies.[1]

Despite such concerns, it is pertinent to emphasise one important aspect of financial deepening in the context of the Asia Economic Connectivity Vision 2030 (AECV2030) elaborated in Chapter 1 of this book. It is being increasingly recognised that in order to build the requisite infrastructure to achieve region-wide connectivity, developing financial markets is paramount. In fact, several regional initiatives that

---

[1] See for instance the series of discussions in IMF Article IV staff consultation reports on Cambodia or Vietnam since 2011 to 2015.

are being taken in Asia to promote stronger connectivity within the ASEAN context suffer from huge financing needs. One plausible way of addressing such financial shortcomings is to facilitate the development of region-wide bond and equity markets that results in greater financial sector development, which could then spur the overall economic growth.

In this light, this chapter focuses its interest in re-examining the nexus between financial deepening and economic growth in a causality framework. The chapter makes a contribution to the existing literature by employing a novel empirical methodology — the Geweke causality analysis — to understand the causal relationship that governs financial deepening and economic growth in the CLV countries. The empirical results will try and ascertain the importance of the most common indicators capturing financial depth in these economies in explaining economic growth.

The Geweke causality analysis helps us understand and measure the linear dependence and feedback between multiple time series variables. To that effect, we performed both a bi-variate as well as multi-variate causality analysis. The uni-directional causality analysis that is popularly employed in the literature does not investigate the degree of dependence or the extent of various kinds of feedback between different time series variables. However, the method suggested by Geweke (1982) overcomes this problem and helps measure the linear dependence and feedback between multiple time series variables. In essence, the linear dependence is defined as "the sum of the measure of linear feedback from the first series to the second, linear feedback from the second to the first, and instantaneous linear feedback" (Geweke, 1982). The direction of causality and the interplay of the variables can be examined in a more detailed manner with a reduced form quantitative framework under the Geweke causality analysis.

The remainder of the chapter is organised as follows. Section 3.2 begins by providing some broad trends capturing the experiences of the

CLV countries with respect to financial deepening and also highlights the policy concerns associated with excessive financial deepening in these economies. Section 3.3 discusses the relevant theoretical and empirical literature concerning financial deepening and growth and highlights the pertinence of the issue to the CLV countries. This discussion will thus form the basis for the hypotheses to be tested in the chapter outlined in Section 3.4. Following this, Section 3.5 outlines a detailed exposition of the empirical methodology and the data used for the analysis. The empirical results are discussed in Section 3.6. Finally, Section 3.7 concludes the chapter with a discussion of the policy implications emanating from our analysis and the key lessons for the CLV countries.

3.2 Background: Trends in Financial Deepening in Cambodia, Laos and Vietnam

In this section, we will provide some background context to our analysis by discussing the trends and patterns in financial sector deepening in the CLV countries. How does one measure financial sector deepening? What are the proxies that the literature uses in explaining the various dimensions of financial sector depth? There are four indicators that can be drawn from the literature, providing some useful insights on the dynamics of financial sector depth that can be broadly used in capturing financial sector deepening.

The first is a measure relating to banking sector depth that captures the domestic credit-to-GDP ratio, defined by the World Bank as the financial resources provided to the private sector, expressed as a share of the country's output. As seen from Figure 3.2, there has been a significant rise in credit-to-GDP ratio in the run up to the GFC in all three countries. Interestingly, even though Vietnam consistently has had higher credit growth than Cambodia or Laos, Vietnam's excessive credit growth concerns have driven the country to rein in the excess

Figure 3.2. Credit to Private Sector (% of GDP) in CLV Countries, 1996–2014

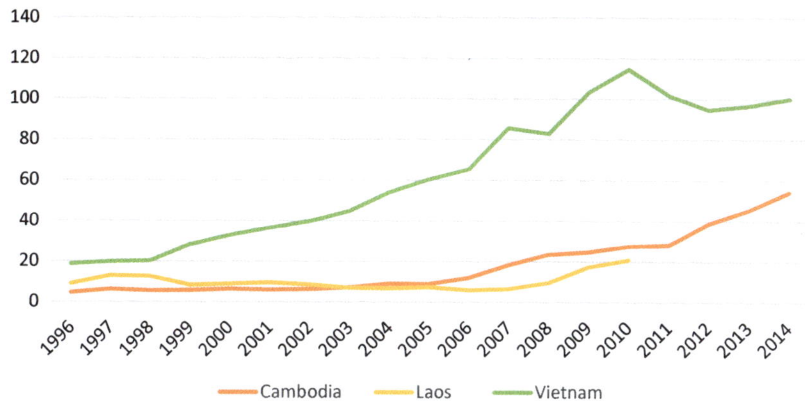

Source: The World Bank.

leverage as reflected by the downward trend since 2010. While there appears to be a slight upward tick once again in credit growth in 2014, it is difficult to say if this is a one-off instance or indicative of a repeat of old trends. This appears to be the opposite for Cambodia (analysis for Laos could not be done due to unavailability of data). It can be clearly seen that the credit-to-GDP ratio is on an upward trajectory and aptly reflects the concerns of the policymakers in Cambodia, of whether this upward trend is symptomatic of potential financial instability that will hamper future growth prospects.

The second measure of financial sector depth is given by the growth in monetary aggregates such as broad money (M2). M2 typically comprises the sum of currency outside banks, demand deposits other than those of the central government, and the time, savings, and foreign currency deposits of resident sectors other than the central government. This is the standard definition of broad money supply and is expressed as a proportion of GDP. The M2-to-GDP ratio closely follows the patterns of the credit-to-GDP ratio, as shown in Figure 3.3.

Figure 3.3. M2 to GDP (%) in CLV Countries, 1996–2014

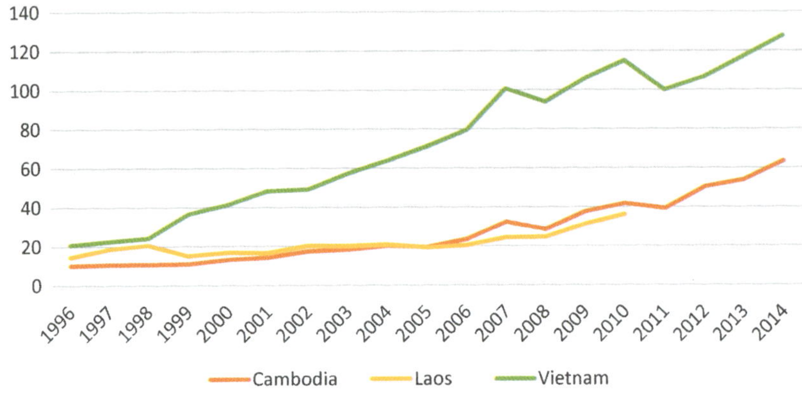

Source: The World Bank.

Figure 3.4. Deposit Money Bank Assets to GDP (%) in CLV Countries, 1996–2013

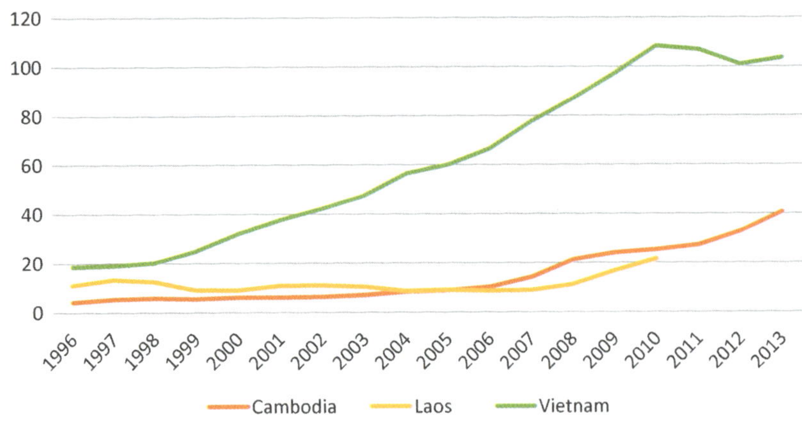

Source: The World Bank.

However, one distinctive trend that is clear when compared to the credit growth figures is that Vietnam appears to be facing another explosion of broad money growth after a phase of consolidation since 2010. This is also very obvious for Cambodia, where signs of rapidly expanding broad money growth are suggestive of the rapid pace of financial deepening in these economies.

The third indicator relates to the assets held by deposit money banks, expressed as a share of GDP. The variable is defined as the total assets held by deposit money banks and assets are taken here to include 'claims on domestic real nonfinancial sector which includes central, state and local governments, nonfinancial public enterprises and private sector'. Deposit money banks in general refer to those commercial banks and other financial institutions that accept transferable deposits, such as demand deposits. We find that the assets share of the deposit money banks also synchronise with the trends we observed for the three countries with respect to the other standard indicators, reflecting the pace of financing deepening.

The fourth indicator captures the financial system deposits, which include demand, time and savings deposits in deposit money banks as well as other financial institutions, as a share of GDP. It is interesting to note that there is a slight deviation from the previous set of results that we have analysed so far, in that Laos appears to have a fairly high

Figure 3.5. Financial System Deposits to GDP (%) in CLV Countries, 1996–2013

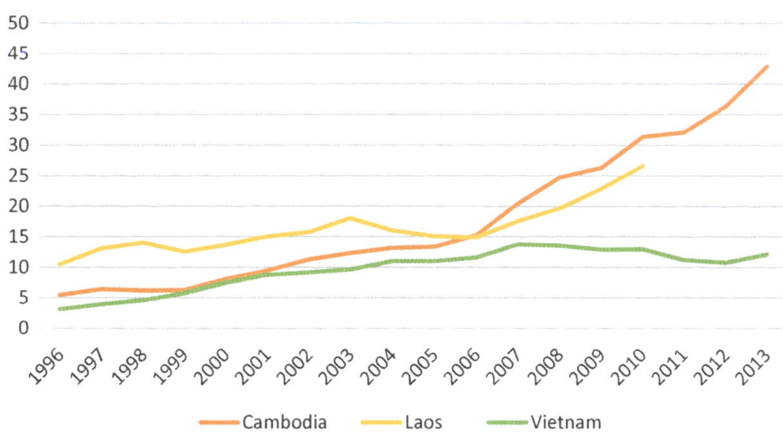

Source: The World Bank.

financial system deposits. Furthermore, Vietnam's overall trajectory seems to be fairly flat and there are no visible signs of overheating.

Overall, it is important to take note of the fact that countries like Cambodia and Vietnam stand out in terms of the significance of credit growth. Various other measures and proxies used in the literature were also employed to understand the trends in financial deepening in the CLV countries. The clear trend that emerges from a cursory look at all the figures is that the CLV countries have seen their financial sectors deepened in a significant manner and the pace of such development has also been striking. This has paved the way for some alarm bells as there is a growing literature pointing out to the dangers of "too much finance" that could lead to diminishing returns, which will affect the economic growth negatively.

Understandably, these developments have rightly been treated with cautious optimism and have generated some concerns among the CLV policymakers, whether this is a harbinger for another credit bust in the near future. Such trends may have implications on financial stability of these countries and therefore, economic growth is a matter of continuing policy debate. This is quite obvious in the case of Cambodia, and as Senghor (2014, 3) noted strikingly:

> "... the strong credit growth has occurred rapidly from a relatively small base... Based on cross-country experiences, there are some concerns that credit growth seems to be excessive. Cambodia's credit-to-GDP ratio is already well above the median for a low-income country having reached middle-income country level. Moreover, there have been concerns about the use and destination of credit and the financial sector's effectiveness in managing credit risks.... Experience in many countries suggests that interactions between financial system elements can amplify quickly beyond certain thresholds thus creating systemic instabilities."

Given the importance of financial sector deepening, the magnitude and pace at which it is expanding in the CLV countries and the potential concerns they have given rise to, it is imperative to delve further into the subject to understand the role of financial sector deepening in propelling future economic growth. The next section will focus on surveying the related theoretical and empirical literature on the issue of financial depth and economic growth, and highlighting the key predicaments along the way prior to developing our hypotheses and discussing our empirical strategy and results of our chapter.

3.3 Related Literature

A vast literature emphasises that there is a strong and positive nexus between different dimensions of financial development and economic growth, particularly in emerging and developing economies. While there is a long body of established theoretical literature that associates financial development with economic growth, the empirical literature is less conclusive owing to several challenges in disentangling the plausible two-way relationship that financial development and economic growth could possess.

Some early works in the last few decades pertaining to this field of literature include Goldsmith (1969), McKinnon (1973) and Shaw (1973). For instance, Goldsmith (1969) found that the size of the financial system and long-run economic growth were positively correlated, largely driven by effective financial intermediation that in turn improves the efficiency of investments. Studies done by McKinnon (1973) and Shaw (1973) outlined how constraining financial sector development by financial repression policies would impede economic growth, as the magnitude of savings available for investments are limited, which prevents financial intermediation from funnelling the resources to productive activities in the economy. In the same spirit, as already noted, there is an established theoretical literature that outlines various other channels through which financial development (and financial deepening) affects economic growth. As noted by Levine

(2004), some of the other instrumental channels that are expected to influence growth (at least in theory) include: capital allocation to productive sectors and activities, facilitating risk diversification and management as well as mobilising and pooling savings.

The related literature also leaves us with an important insight. While it is reasonable to expect financial development and economic growth or the levels of per capita income of a country to have a strong association with each other, the relationship between the two concerned variables could be bi-directional, meaning that the direction of causality could run both ways. Intuitively, expansion of real economic activity facilitates the growth of finance, which occurs owing to the increased demand for financial services from the economy. At the same time, greater financial development can contribute to higher economic growth as well. Thus it becomes empirically challenging to disentangle the direction of causality (see Sahay *et al.*, 2015 for a succinct review and discussion of this literature).

In a cross-country regression setup, King and Levine (1993) for instance found that initial levels of financial depth proxied by the size of the banking system in the economy relative to its output could be a good predictor of subsequent growth rates. Other commonly used proxies in the literature to measure financial sector deepening involves stock market depth, which was used by Levine and Zervos (1998) who attributed a causal relationship between greater stock market development and economic growth. Other important contributions, primarily on the methodological front by using instrumental variable estimation and dynamic panel data models were studied by Beck and Levine (2004), Beck *et al.* (2000) and Sahay *et al.* (2015). These papers attempt to move beyond examining correlations between financial development and growth, and instead tease out the casual relationships driving economic growth and whether financial development plays an important role in fostering it. While this body of literature continues to grow, it is important to emphasise the following caveat: despite the various attempts in the literature to use sophisticated empirical techniques to circumvent this problem of reverse causality, the findings still remain relatively unsatisfactory, although financial depth is a key determinant of economic growth.

Leaving aside the methodological issues, the literature acknowledges that financial sector development can occur through greater banking sector depth or development of bond or stock markets, which in turn is likely to increase a country's resilience and boost economic growth. However, this positive nexus can be negated when a country undergoes "excessive" financial development that could result in serious policy trade-offs between economic growth and financial stability.

More importantly, a related strand of literature has identified the presence of non-linearities in the way financial development and economic growth is related. Easterly *et al.* (2000) for instance empirically showed that there is a "convex and non-monotonic" relationship between financial depth and the volatility of output growth. Their results suggested that output volatility starts increasing when credit to the private sector (the most commonly used proxy for financial development) reaches 100% of the GDP. More recently, Arcand *et al.* (2012) empirically established that financial development beyond a particular threshold exerts a negative effect on output growth. They specifically found that when credit to the private sector reaches 100% of a country's GDP, then there appears to be a "vanishing effect" of financial development that essentially overturns the conventional positive finance-growth nexus. They argued that at "intermediate levels" of financial depth, one can identify a strong positive relationship between financial sector development and economic growth, but also add that once financial depth passes a specific threshold, it results in less growth. Evidence of a "non-monotonic" relationship is an important finding that arises from this literature.

Several explanations have been offered in the literature as to why this positive relationship between financial development and growth is non-monotonic and can actually disappear at higher levels of financial depth. For instance, Cecchetti and Kharroubi (2015) posited that it occurs largely due to the negative effects arising from allocative inefficiency and crowding out of human capital away from the real sector to the financial sector, which in turn is a by-product of the economy scaling up higher levels of income. In another interesting paper, Dabla-Norris *et al.* (2015) suggested that resources in high-income economies are being diverted away from productive sectors towards the financial sector, which results in the negative relationship. De Gregorio and Guidotti (1995) argued that high-income and advanced countries tend to reach a point where greater expansion of financial sector depth beyond what already exists is counter-productive, because such credit growth expansion is no longer contributing to enhancing the efficiency of investments in the economy.

In a similar vein, studies by Barajas *et al.* (2013), Khan *et al.* (2001), Nili and Rastad (2007) and Aizenmann *et al.* (2015) found that the contribution of financial development to growth is quite heterogeneous; the effects differ across geographies, income levels of the countries as well as sectors within countries. There is also a related strand of literature that focuses on understanding the factors that determine the differences in financial development, which in turn affects economic growth across countries. For instance, La Porta *et al.* (1998) emphasised the importance of the differences in legal systems to explain the differences in financial development across countries. The emphasis on legal traditions is largely driven by the observation that there are differences among countries in the degree to which they prioritise in protecting the property rights of private investors. These differences in turn determine the efficiency of contract enforcements that are fundamental to financial sector development. Related to protection of legal rights and contract enforcement is good governance (Kaufmann *et al.* 1999), which has been noted as another pre-requisite for financial development.

Focusing specifically on financial deepening, in a survey of cross-country determinants of financial depth for 129 countries, Djankov *et al.* (2007) found that a combination of macroeconomic and institutional variables such as GDP per capita, inflation, legal creditor rights, private and public credit registries turns out to be significantly associated with financial depth. They found that while both creditor protection through the legal system and information sharing institutions tend to be associated with higher financial depth, legal rights appear to be more relatively important in richer countries. They also reiterated the importance of GDP per capita and the role that economic development plays in fostering higher financial depth. In addition to the factors concerning the institutional environment, domestic political economy factors such as rent-seeking behaviour of incumbents also determine the extent of financial development (Rajan and Zingales, 2003).

Though most of the literature has looked at institutional and macroeconomic variables as determinants of financial depth, a small but growing literature identifies openness to international financial flows as another important determinant of financial depth in emerging markets and developing economies. One of the central conclusions from this literature is that higher international financial openness is positively associated with domestic financial sector depth, although it is conditional on countries achieving a certain threshold level of institutional development (for instance, see Baltagi *et al.*, 2009; Calderon and Kubota, 2009; Chinn and Ito, 2006 and Kose *et al.*, 2011). As Kose *et al.* (2011) suggested, financial sector development is one of the primary "collateral benefits" of international financial openness and that the development of domestic financial markets as well as enhanced corporate and public governance indirectly contribute to overall economic growth.

The foregoing discussion from this literature leaves us with some valuable takeaways, which are applicable to the CLV countries and will form the basis of our hypothesis outlined in the next section. First, it is clear that the causality between financial depth and economic growth could be bi-directional. Second, despite the acknowledgement of the importance of financial depth to economic growth, the relationship is non-monotonic, implying that there is a "bell-shaped" distribution capturing the dynamics between financial depth and economic growth. This clearly implies that countries in the intermediate stages of financial development or those transitioning to that phase are likely to be the greatest beneficiaries from financial sector deepening and this positive nexus disappears as countries experience rapid financial sector development. Third, considering the heterogeneity observed among countries and income levels in how financial depth affects economic growth, it is clear that income thresholds do play a role in how financial depth affects economic growth. To be clear, countries with very low or high levels of income may not necessarily benefit positively from financial sector deepening, although those in the middle-income category or transitioning to one are likely to reap relatively more benefits. With this background, this chapter is specifically interested in undertaking a Geweke causality analysis for the CLV countries, to ascertain the importance of financial deepening on their economic growth, factoring in their levels of development.

3.4 Hypotheses and Data

The CLV countries have witnessed fast-paced financial deepening in recent years. Vietnam especially has seen a massive increase in credit-to-GDP ratios (see Figure 3.2 and 3.3). Cambodia has also seen a significant increase in the proportion of expansion of credit. In addition, it has been noted that intensifying competition for market shares has increased the risk appetite of banks in these countries, leading to deterioration in the quality of loan portfolios. In light of the concerns that the CLV countries are facing with respect to financial deepening, we are increasingly interested in examining its relationship with economic growth.

Furthermore, based on the discussion in the above section, recognising the importance of financial depth in contributing to economic growth, we formulated that a concerted effort to promote greater financial depth in the CLV countries would contribute to sustaining their growth momentum. More specifically, through primarily the channel of credit creation and greater banking sector deepening, the CLV countries could reap substantial growth benefits. However, we also hypothesised, based on the earlier literature discussion about non-linearities and non-monotonicity governing the relationship between financial depth and growth, that there could be income thresholds involved in the process; the effects of financial deepening will fade out as countries become richer, although there is a certain minimum threshold of development that countries have to achieve in order to reap the benefits of greater financial depth. With that in mind, we would like to posit that financial deepening would affect economic growth positively and exert a causal influence in middle-income countries, although the effect may not be as pronounced in low-income countries. Since our sample consists of two middle-income countries (as classified by the World Bank), namely Laos and Vietnam (both classified as lower-middle income), we would like to perform a causal investigation between financial depth and economic growth, factoring in their levels of economic development, using quarterly data between 1996–2010 for the CLV countries.

While we would like to ideally use the same set of variables on financial deepening for all the countries for ease of comparison and analysis, data constraints for specific countries prevent us from doing so. Hence, although the variables broadly capture financial deepening in the respective country, the proxy used for each country differs from each other. Data for all the variables were obtained from World Bank's *World Development Indicators* database and transformed to meet the stationary requirement of the Geweke analysis. Furthermore, annual data was converted into quarterly data using quadratic-sum/average

Table 3.1. Variables used in Geweke Causality Analysis for Cambodia and Laos

Variable	Notation	Definition
X	GGPC	Growth Rate of Real GDP per Capita (in local currency)
Y1	ΔM2	Change in Money and Quasi Money (M2) as a Percentage of GDP
Y2	ΔDCPS	Change in Domestic Credit to Private Sector as a Percentage of GDP

Source: Asia Competitiveness Institute.

Table 3.2. Variables used in Geweke Causality Analysis for Vietnam

Variable	Notation	Definition
X	GGPC	Growth Rate of Real GDP per Capita (in local currency)
Y1	BDG	Bank Deposits to GDP (%)
Y2	ΔPCDM	Change in Private Credit by Deposit Money Banks and Other Financial Institutions to GDP (%)

Source: Asia Competitiveness Institute.

method. The list of variables, their notations and definitions used for each of the countries are presented in Table 3.1 and 3.2.

3.5 Research Methodology

The Geweke causality analysis is used as a tool to identify causal relationships in the field of economics and neuroscience. Some recent and prominent applications of Geweke causality to macroeconomic issues include Tan and Cheng (1995), Calderón and Liu (2003) and Aizenman and Noy (2006). While Tan and Cheng (1995) employed Geweke's approach to examine the causal nexus of money, output and prices in Malaysia, Calderón and Liu (2003) explored the direction of causality between financial development and economic growth. Aizenman and Noy (2006) investigated the two-way linkages between foreign direct investment (FDI) and trade.

Like Granger and Sims, Geweke's causality analysis focussed the attention on a wide-sense stationary, purely non-deterministic multiple time series $Z = \{z_t,\ t \text{ real}\}$. Therefore, the vector z_t can be expressed under the following autoregressive representation:

$$z_t = \sum_{s=1}^{\infty} B_s z_{t-s} + e_t$$

where e_t is white noise and z_t can be partitioned into $k \times 1$ and $l \times 1$ sub-vectors x_t and y_t.

Geweke also showed that a canonical form for the wide-sense stationary time series $z_t = (x_t, y_t)$ is of the form:

$$x_t = \sum_{s=1}^{\infty} E_{1s} x_{t-s} + u_{1t} \qquad var(u_{1t}) = \Sigma_1 \tag{1}$$

$$x_t = \sum_{s=1}^{\infty} E_{2s} x_{t-s} + \sum_{s=1}^{\infty} F_{2s} y_{t-s} + u_{2t} \qquad var(u_{2t}) = \Sigma_2 \tag{2}$$

$$x_t = \sum_{s=1}^{\infty} E_{3s} x_{t-s} + \sum_{s=0}^{\infty} F_{3s} y_{t-s} + u_{3t} \qquad var(u_{3t}) = \Sigma_3 \tag{3}$$

$$x_t = \sum_{s=1}^{\infty} E_{4s} x_{t-s} + \sum_{s=-\infty}^{\infty} F_{4s} y_{t-s} + u_{4t} \qquad var(u_{4t}) = \Sigma_4 \tag{4}$$

$$y_t = \sum_{s=1}^{\infty} G_{1s} y_{t-s} + v_{1t} \qquad var(v_{1t}) = T_1 \tag{5}$$

$$y_t = \sum_{s=1}^{\infty} G_{2s} y_{t-s} + \sum_{s=1}^{\infty} H_{2s} x_{t-s} + v_{2t} \qquad var(v_{2t}) = T_2 \tag{6}$$

$$y_t = \sum_{s=1}^{\infty} G_{3s} y_{t-s} + \sum_{s=0}^{\infty} H_{3s} x_{t-s} + v_{3t} \qquad var(v_{3t}) = T_3 \tag{7}$$

$$y_t = \sum_{s=1}^{\infty} G_{4s} y_{t-s} + \sum_{s=-\infty}^{\infty} H_{4s} x_{t-s} + v_{4t} \qquad var(v_{4t}) = T_4 \tag{8}$$

3.5.1 Definition: Measure of Linear Dependence and Feedback

The measure of linear feedback from *Y* to *X* is defined as:

$$F_{Y \to X} = \ln\left(|\Sigma_1| / |\Sigma_2|\right) \tag{9}$$

The measure $F_{Y \to X}$ is always non-negative and takes the value of zero only if the linear feedback running from *Y* to *X* is absent. Symmetrically, the measure of linear feedback from *X* to *Y* is defined as:

$$F_{X \to Y} = \ln\left(|\mathrm{T}_1| / |\mathrm{T}_2|\right) \tag{10}$$

The instantaneous feedback is defined as

$$F_{X \cdot Y} = \ln\left(|\mathrm{T}_2| \times |\Sigma_2| / |\gamma|\right) \tag{11}$$

where $\gamma = \mathrm{var}\begin{pmatrix} u_{2t} \\ v_{2t} \end{pmatrix} = \begin{bmatrix} \Sigma_2 & C \\ C' & \mathrm{T}_2 \end{bmatrix}$.

Thus, the measure of linear dependence between two vectors *X* and *Y* can be decomposed into the sum of measure of linear feedback from *X* to *Y*, the measure of linear feedback from *Y* to *X*, and the instantaneous linear feedback between the two vectors. That is,

$$F_{X,Y} = F_{X \to Y} + F_{Y \to X} + F_{X \cdot Y} \tag{12}$$

Geweke also proved that the equations in the following set are equivalent:

$$F_{X,Y} = \ln\left(|\Sigma_1| \times |\mathrm{T}_1| / |\gamma|\right) = \ln\left(|\Sigma_1| / |\Sigma_4|\right) = \ln\left(|\mathrm{T}_1| / |\mathrm{T}_4|\right) \tag{13}$$

$$F_{X \to Y} = \ln\left(|\mathrm{T}_1| / |\mathrm{T}_2|\right) = \ln\left(|\Sigma_3| / |\Sigma_4|\right) \tag{14}$$

$$F_{Y \to X} = \ln\left(|\Sigma_1| / |\Sigma_2|\right) = \ln\left(|\mathrm{T}_3| / |\mathrm{T}_4|\right) \tag{15}$$

$$F_{X \cdot Y} = \ln\left(|\mathrm{T}_2| \times |\Sigma_2| / |\gamma|\right) = \ln\left(|\Sigma_2| / |\Sigma_3|\right) = \ln\left(|\mathrm{T}_2| / |\mathrm{T}_3|\right) \tag{16}$$

3.5.2 Distribution of Statistics

Under the null hypothesis that there is no uni-directional causality running from Y to X, i.e. if $\hat{F}_{Y\to X} = 0$, then

$$n\hat{F}_{Y\to X} \sim \chi^2(klp), \tag{17}$$

Similarly, it follows that if $\hat{F}_{X\to Y} = 0$,

$$n\hat{F}_{X\to Y} \sim \chi^2(klp), \tag{18}$$

and if $\hat{F}_{X\cdot Y} = 0$,

$$n\hat{F}_{X\cdot Y} \sim \chi^2(kl), \tag{19}$$

As these are nested hypotheses, all three restrictions could be tested simultaneously since if $\hat{F}_{X,Y} = 0$, then

$$n\hat{F}_{X,Y} \sim \chi^2\left[kl(2p+1)\right] \tag{20}$$

3.5.3 Confidence Interval

The 95% confidence interval (CI) could be calculated approximately as follows:

For $\hat{F}_{Y\to X} = 0$,

$$\left\{\left[\left(\hat{F}_{Y\to X} - \frac{klp-1}{3n}\right)^{1/2} \pm \frac{1.96}{\sqrt{n}}\right]^2 - \frac{2klp+1}{3n}\right\} \tag{21}$$

For $\hat{F}_{X\to Y} = 0$,

$$\left\{\left[\left(\hat{F}_{X\to Y} - \frac{klp-1}{3n}\right)^{1/2} \pm \frac{1.96}{\sqrt{n}}\right]^2 - \frac{2klp+1}{3n}\right\} \tag{22}$$

For $\hat{F}_{X \cdot Y} = 0$,

$$\left\{\left[\left(\hat{F}_{X \cdot Y} - \frac{klp-1}{3n}\right)^{1/2} \pm \frac{1.96}{\sqrt{n}}\right]^2 - \frac{2kl+1}{3n}\right\} \tag{23}$$

For $\hat{F}_{X,Y} = 0$,

$$\left\{\left[\left(\hat{F}_{X \cdot Y} - \frac{kl(2p+1)-1}{3n}\right)^{1/2} \pm \frac{1.96}{\sqrt{n}}\right]^2 - \frac{2kl(2p+1)+1}{3n}\right\} \tag{24}$$

3.6 Empirical Results

3.6.1 Geweke Causality Results for Cambodia

Table 3.3 presents the estimated bi-directional feedback between Growth Rate of Real GDP per Capita (GGPC) and our set of financial deepening variables that include Change in Money and Quasi Money (M2) as a Percentage of GDP (ΔM2) as well as Change in Domestic Credit to Private Sector as a Percentage of GDP (ΔDCPS).

Our empirical results reveal some important findings. Starting with the results for the bi-variate causality analysis for GGPC and ΔM2, interestingly, there was no evidence of bi-directional association between GGPC and ΔM2. Instead, in both cases, the measures of linear dependence between GGPC and ΔM2 ($F_{x,y}$) were highly statistically significant at the 1% level and so was the instantaneous feedback between GGPC and ΔM2 ($F_{x \cdot y}$). Given that the instantaneous feedback accounted for most of the total linear dependence between GGPC and ΔM2, it could plausibly indicate that the current as well as the past values of ΔM2 possess significant explanatory power to predict GGPC, which also appears to be consistent with the broader macroeconomic literature emphasising the importance of financial depth for economic growth. However, it is worth noting that no evidence of explicit bi-directional causation can be found for Cambodia.

Table 3.3. Estimated Measures of Bi-Directional Feedback between Growth Rate of Real GDP per Capita (GGPC), Change in Money and Quasi Money (M2) as a Percentage of GDP (ΔM2) and Change in Domestic Credit to Private Sector as a Percentage of GDP (ΔDCPS) for Cambodia, 1996–2010[a,b]

Economic Aggregates		$H_0(F_{x,y} = F_{x\to y} + F_{y\to x} + F_{x\cdot y})$			
x	y	$F_{x,y}$	$F_{x\to y}$	$F_{y\to x}$	$F_{x\cdot y}$
GGPC	ΔM2	0.2226*** (0.0054)	0.0000 (0.9721)	0.0354 (0.1555)	0.1872*** (0.0011)
ΔM2	GGPC	0.2005*** (0.0096)	0.0123 (0.4023)	0.0010 (0.8106)	0.1872*** (0.0011)
GGPC	ΔDCPS	0.2498*** (0.0026)	0.0000 (0.9764)	0.0385 (0.1387)	0.2113*** (0.0005)
ΔDCPS	GGPC	0.2128*** (0.0069)	0.0004 (0.875)	0.0010 (0.8121)	0.2113*** (0.0005)

[a] *, ** and *** denote 10%, 5% and 1% level of significance, respectively.
[b] confidence interval would be provided upon request.
Source: Asia Competitiveness Institute.

Similar findings can be found when considering the bi-variate analysis for Growth Rate of Real GDP per Capita (GGPC) and Change in Domestic Credit to Private Sector as a Percentage of GDP (ΔDCPS). The third and fourth rows of Table 3.3 show the relevant results; the aggregate measure of linear dependence between GGPC and ΔDCPS ($F_{x,y}$) was highly significant. While this could be suggestive of the aggregate association between the two variables, as found in the case of instantaneous feedback ($F_{x\cdot y}$) between the two variables as well, decomposing the linear feedback between GGPC and ΔDCPS resulted in an insignificant relationship in both directions.

So for Cambodia, it is important to highlight that only the aggregate measure of linear dependence and the instantaneous feedback between financial depth and economic growth were highly significant (at the 1% level). Decomposing the linear feedback between the two variables resulted in insignificant results for causality in both directions.

We extended this bilateral framework to estimate the multi-directional causality between GGDP and the vector of variables. Empirical results capturing a multi-variate approach to understanding the causal relationship between financial deepening and growth is shown in Table 3.4.

The multivariate results are fairly consistent with the bilateral results, with the linear feedback between y to x exhibiting some weak uni-directional causality. On the whole, however, the aggregate linear dependence and instantaneous feedback between financial depth and economic growth were highly significant although no evidence for linear feedback between the variables of interest can be found.

As shown in Table 3.4, the measure of linear dependence between x and y ($F_{x,y}$) and the instantaneous feedback between x and y ($F_{x \cdot y}$) were all highly significant at the 1% level, while the linear feedback from y to x ($F_{y \to x}$) was marginally significant at the 10% level. The multivariate analysis results further indicated that the linear feedback from y to x ($F_{y \to x}$) accounted for around 20% of total linear dependence between the two vectors, and the instantaneous feedback between x and y ($F_{x \cdot y}$) accounted for the remaining 80% of total linear dependence.

Table 3.4. Estimated Measures of Multi-Directional Feedback between Growth Rate of Real GDP per Capita (GGPC), Change in Money and Quasi Money (M2) as a Percentage of GDP (ΔM2) and Change in Domestic Credit to Private Sector as a Percentage of GDP (ΔDCPS) for Cambodia, 1996–2010[a,b]

Economic Aggregates		$H_0(F_{x,y} = F_{x \to y} + F_{y \to x} + F_{x \cdot y})$			
x	y	$F_{x,y}$	$F_{x \to y}$	$F_{y \to x}$	$F_{x \cdot y}$
GGPC	ΔM2 ΔDCPS	0.4824*** (0.0001)	0.0013 (0.9624)	0.0924* (0.0719)	0.3886*** (0.0000)

[a] *, ** and *** denote 10%, 5% and 1% level of significance, respectively.
[b] confidence interval would be provided upon request.
Source: Asia Competitiveness Institute.

3.6.2 Geweke Causality Results for Laos

The empirical results for Laos are summarised in Tables 3.5 and 3.6. Similar to Cambodia, we performed two different kinds of estimation, with the first one focussing on bi-variate causality analysis (see Table 3.5) and the other one throwing light on the causal relationship between financial depth and Laos' economic growth using a multi-variate approach (see Table 3.6).

Since a similar set of data is available for Laos, based on the hypothesis set out earlier, we probed the importance of Change in Money and Quasi Money as a Percentage of GDP (ΔM2) and Change and in Domestic Credit to Private Sector as a Percentage of GDP (ΔDCPS), in causally driving growth rates of real GDP per capita in Laos over 1996–2010.

The results for the bi-variate causality analysis are presented in Table 3.5. While the significance of the measure of linear dependence between GGPC and ΔM2 ($F_{x,y}$) can be clearly observed, it was largely

Table 3.5. Estimated Measures of Bi-Directional Feedback between Growth Rate of Real GDP per Capita (GGPC), Change in Money and Quasi Money (M2) as a Percentage of GDP (ΔM2) and Change in Domestic Credit to Private Sector as a Percentage of GDP (ΔDCPS) for Laos, 1996–2010[a,b]

Economic Aggregates		$H_0(F_{x,y} = F_{x\to y} + F_{y\to x} + F_{x\cdot y})$			
x	y	$F_{x,y}$	$F_{x\to y}$	$F_{y\to x}$	$F_{x\cdot y}$
GGPC	ΔM2	0.3554*** (0.0002)	0.0048 (0.5992)	0.0127 (0.3945)	0.3378*** (0.0000)
ΔM2	GGPC	0.4247*** (0.0000)	0.0116 (0.4152)	0.0752** (0.0384)	0.3378*** (0.0000)
GGPC	ΔDCPS	0.2681*** (0.0016)	0.0181 (0.3094)	0.0073 (0.5177)	0.2427*** (0.0002)
ΔDCPS	GGPC	0.3490*** (0.0002)	0.0087 (0.4819)	0.0977** (0.0183)	0.2427*** (0.0002)

[a] *, ** and *** denote 10%, 5% and 1% level of significance, respectively.
[b] confidence interval would be provided upon request.
Source: Asia Competitiveness Institute.

driven by the instantaneous feedback between GGDC and ΔM2 ($F_{x \cdot y}$), which was highly significant at the 1% level. However, the decomposition of causality between the two variables pointed to the fact that there was a significant uni-directional causal feedback from ΔM2 to GGPC that cannot be ignored. As seen from the second row of Table 3.5, about 20% of the total linear dependence between ΔM2 and GGPC was accounted for by the linear feedback from y to x ($F_{y \rightarrow x}$). This is a stronger and different result than what we observed with Cambodia.

Next, we considered the bi-variate analysis for GGPC and Change in Domestic Credit to Private Sector as a Percentage of GDP (ΔDCPS). The aggregate measure of linear dependence between GGPC and ΔDCPS ($F_{x,y}$) was highly significant at the 1% level. So was the instantaneous feedback ($F_{x \cdot y}$) between the two variables. Interestingly, in contrast to the results observed for Cambodia, domestic credit appeared to have a significant uni-directional causal impact on Laos' GGPC at the 5% level. Over a quarter of the aggregate linear dependence between the two variables was accounted for by linear feedback from y to x ($F_{y \rightarrow x}$).

Extending this bilateral setting to a multi-directional setting, we tested the causal importance of the vector of all the above variables in explaining economic growth in Laos. The results are shown in Table 3.6.

Table 3.6. Estimated Measures of Multi-Directional Feedback between Growth Rate of Real GDP per Capita (GGPC), Change in Money and Quasi Money (M2) as a Percentage of GDP (ΔM2) and Change in Domestic Credit to Private Sector as a Percentage of GDP (ΔDCPS) for Laos, 1996–2010[a,b]

Economic Aggregates		$H_0(F_{x,y} = F_{x \rightarrow y} + F_{y \rightarrow x} + F_{x \cdot y})$			
x	y	$F_{x,y}$	$F_{x \rightarrow y}$	$F_{y \rightarrow x}$	$F_{x \cdot y}$
GGPC	ΔM2 ΔDCPS	0.4265*** (0.0005)	0.0081 (0.7935)	0.0128 (0.6941)	0.4056*** (0.0000)

[a] *, ** and *** denote 10%, 5% and 1% level of significance, respectively.
[b] confidence interval would be provided upon request.
Source: Asia Competitiveness Institute.

There was a strong association between the x variable, GGPC, and the y vector consisting of the two financial deepening variables we discussed above. The results are strongly consistent with the earlier bilateral causality framework, with the measure of linear dependence between x and y ($F_{x,y}$) and the instantaneous feedback between x and y ($F_{x\cdot y}$) being highly significant at the 1% level.

3.6.3 Geweke Causality Results for Vietnam

Tables 3.7 and 3.8 show the results for Vietnam. Prior to discussing the results, it is important to note that for Vietnam, a different set of proxies for measuring financial deepening was used due to data unavailability of the other measures that were used for Cambodia and Laos. To that end, we tested for the bi-directional causal feedback between Growth Rate of GDP per Capita (GGPC) on Bank Deposits to GDP (BDG) and

Table 3.7. Estimated Measures of Multi-Directional Feedback between Growth Rate of GDP per Capita (GGPC), Bank Deposits to GDP (%) (BDG) and Change in Private Credit by Deposit Money Banks and Other Financial Institutions to GDP (%) (ΔPCDM) for Vietnam, 1996–2010[a,b]

Economic Aggregates		$H_0(F_{x,y} = F_{x\to y} + F_{y\to x} + F_{x\cdot y})$			
x	y	$F_{x,y}$	$F_{x\to y}$	$F_{y\to x}$	$F_{x\cdot y}$
GGPC	BDG	0.4081*** (0.0004)	0.0096 (0.7681)	0.0205 (0.5691)	0.3780*** (0.0000)
BDG	GGPC	0.3823*** (0.0008)	0.0037 (0.9026)	0.0006 (0.9839)	0.3780*** (0.0000)
GGPC	ΔPCDM	0.2540*** (0.0023)	0.0013 (0.7873)	0.0030 (0.6793)	0.2497*** (0.0002)
ΔPCDM	GGPC	0.2923*** (0.0008)	0.0004 (0.8777)	0.0421 (0.1212)	0.2497*** (0.0002)

[a] *, ** and *** denote 10%, 5% and 1% level of significance, respectively.
[b] confidence interval would be provided upon request.
Source: Asia Competitiveness Institute.

Table 3.8. Estimated Measures of Multi-Directional Feedback between Growth Rate of GDP per Capita (GGPC), Bank Deposits to GDP (%) (BDG) and Change in Private Credit by Deposit Money Banks and Other Financial Institutions to GDP (%) (ΔPCDM) for Vietnam, 1996–2010[a,b]

Economic Aggregates		$H_0(F_{x,y} = F_{x\to y} + F_{y\to x} + F_{x\cdot y})$			
x	y	$F_{x,y}$	$F_{x\to y}$	$F_{y\to x}$	$F_{x\cdot y}$
GGPC	BDG ΔPCDM	0.4544*** (0.0054)	0.0414 (0.6854)	0.0218 (0.8786)	0.3913*** (0.0000)

[a] *, ** and *** denote 10%, 5% and 1% level of significance, respectively.
[b] confidence interval would be provided upon request.
Source: Asia Competitiveness Institute.

Change in Private Credit by Deposit Money Banks and Other Financial Institutions to GDP (ΔPCDM) for 1996–2010.

Contrary to our previous findings, despite being a middle-income country, we found that the results seem to be more aligned with that of Cambodia than Laos; none of the linear feedbacks, either between x and y ($F_{x\to y}$) or between y and x ($F_{y\to x}$), appeared to be significant in any of the combinations.

The results for the bi-variate causality analysis are presented in Table 3.7. Similar to Cambodia, with regard to the measure of linear dependence between GGPC and BDG ($F_{x,y}$), almost all of it was driven by the instantaneous feedback between the two variables ($F_{x\cdot y}$), which was highly significant at the 1% level, accounting for over 90% of the total linear dependence between the two variables. However, the decomposition of causality between x and y did not reveal any significant linear causal feedback between the two variables.

We then considered the bi-variate analysis for GGPC and ΔPCDM. Likewise, the aggregate measure of linear dependence between GGPC and ΔPCDM ($F_{x,y}$) was highly significant at the 1% level, with the instantaneous feedback ($F_{x\cdot y}$) between the two variables also highly significant at the 1% level as before. However, aggregate linear dependence was not accounted for by linear feedback from y to x ($F_{y \to x}$) or vice versa.

Extending this bilateral setting to a multi-directional setting, we tested the causal importance of the vector of all the above variables in explaining economic growth in Vietnam. The results are shown in Table 3.8.

There was a strong association between the x variable, GGPC, and the y vector consisting of the two financial deepening variables as discussed above. The results are strongly consistent with earlier findings in the bilateral causality framework, with the measure of linear dependence between x and y ($F_{x,y}$) and the instantaneous feedback between x and y ($F_{x \cdot y}$) being highly significant at the 1% level. None of the linear feedbacks, either between x and y ($F_{x \to y}$) or y and x ($F_{y \to x}$), appeared to be significant.

3.7 Concluding Remarks and Policy Implications

The transitional economies of Cambodia, Laos and Vietnam have been identified as potential growth centres in the ASEAN region since the turn of the millennium. Despite the growth slowdown that these economies experienced during the GFC, all the economies have recovered significantly, partly aided by the rapid development of their financial sector. Although this has formed the basis for optimism about the future growth potential of these countries, policymakers have been concerned about excessive financial deepening in these countries that not only has the potential to hamper future economic growth but also aggravates financial instability. In light of this discussion, this chapter examined the nexus between financial deepening and economic growth using a Geweke causality framework and quarterly data for the CLV countries from 1996 to 2010.

Overall, the empirical results appeared to reiterate the importance of financial deepening in spurring economic growth only in Laos. This result is much stronger than Cambodia's, which may have issues with too much leverage and credit growth contributing to potential instabilities in the system. In fact, this could also plausibly suggest that the impact of financial deepening on economic growth in middle-income countries, such as Laos, is much stronger than in low-income countries like Cambodia.

Our results do not show any significant causal relationship governing financial depth and growth in Vietnam despite being a middle-income country. This could plausibly be driven by the fact that Vietnam has had an explosive credit growth for several years and lies far above the acceptable thresholds defined in the literature. This appears to be consistent with the broader literature that finds a non-monotonic relationship between financial depth and economic growth.

In the final remarks, it is useful to stress the importance of financial market development in the region to spur intra-ASEAN connectivity. In fact, one of the key objectives must be to specifically lead the countries to develop a framework to achieve holistic financial sector development by developing financial markets and institutions in the region. The scope of financial sector development and regional integration of the financial sector includes development of bond markets, equity markets as well as the banking systems in the region. A greater impetus to the initiatives that will foster regional financial integration would enhance the depth, quality and efficiency of the financial sector in the region. This is likely to provide the much-needed base for plugging the infrastructure finance gap that would in turn facilitate regional connectivity.

Some notable progress has been made in terms of development of bond markets through the Asian Bond Market Initiative (ABMI) and the Asian Bond Market Forum and Credit Guarantee Investment Facility that was set up to provide credit guarantees for local currency denominated bonds issued by the companies in ASEAN+3. While significant improvements at the country level can be observed in terms of bond market development, it is unclear how much the ABMI has contributed to it. In line with the blueprint of the AEC, which has a goal of strengthening regional capital market integration, with specific measures to harmonise standards, promote mutual recognition, set up infrastructure to facilitate trading exchanges, promote ASEAN as an asset class etc., there have been positive developments through the ASEAN Capital Markets Forum in terms of equity market integration. Countries, such as Malaysia, Singapore and Thailand, have implemented the ASEAN Disclosure Standards scheme for multi-jurisdiction offerings of equity and plain debt securities in the region. Finally, in terms of bank flows, the ASEAN Banking Integration Framework aims to harmonise prudential regulations, promote financial stability infrastructure, developing capacity building by enhancing competitiveness of domestic banking institutions. The efforts have largely focused on five areas for harmonisation of regulations that include bank accounting standards and disclosure requirements; minimum capital requirements; Prompt Corrective Action rules for resolution of failed banks; restrictions on large exposure; anti-money-laundering and consumer protection regulations.

While progress appears to have been made in terms of initiatives taken to develop financial markets and an effective implementation of the pending initiatives that will be the first step to move the region in the right direction, there is clearly a need to deepen them and expand the policy initiatives to the broader ASEAN region.

References

Aizenman, Joshua, Yothin Jinjarak, and Donghyun Park. 2015. "Financial Development and Output Growth in Developing Asia and Latin America: A Comparative Sectoral Analysis." NBER Working Paper 20917, National Bureau of Economic Research, Cambridge.

Aizenman, Joshua, and Ilan Noy. 2006. "FDI and trade — Two-Way Linkages?" *The Quarterly Review of Economics and Finance* 46 (3): 317–337.

Ayhan Kose, M., Eswar S. Prasad, and Ashley D. Taylor. 2011. "Thresholds in the Process of International Financial Integration." *Journal of International Money and Finance* 30 (1): 147–179.

Baltagi, Badi H. Panicos O Demetriades, and Siong Hook Law. 2009. "Financial Development and Openness: Evidence from Panel Data." *Journal of Development Economics* 89 (2): 285–296.

Barajas, Adolfo, Ralph Chami, and Seyed Reza Yousefi. 2013. "The Finance and Growth Nexus Re-Examined: Do All Countries Benefit Equally?" IMF Working Paper 13/130, International Monetary Fund, Washington DC.

Beck, Thorsten and Ross Levine. 2004. "Stock Markets, Banks, and Growth: Panel Evidence." *Journal of Banking and Finance* 28 (3): 423–442.

Beck, Thorsten, Berrak Büyükkarabacak, Felix K. Rioja, and Neven T. Valev. 2012. "Who Gets the Credit? And Does It Matter? Household vs. Firm Lending Across Countries." *The B.E. Journal of Macroeconomics* 12 (1) (Contributions), Article 2.

Beck, Thorsten, Ross Levine, and Norman Loayza. 2000. "Finance and the Sources of Growth." *Journal of Financial Economics* 58 (1–2): 261–300.

Boyd, John H., Ross Levine, and Bruce D. Smith. 2001. "The Impact of Inflation on Financial Sector Performance." *Journal of Monetary Economics* 47: 221–248.

Calderón, César and Megumi Kubota. 2009. "Does Financial Openness Lead to Deeper Domestic Markets?" World Bank Policy Research Working Paper 4973, World Bank, Washington DC.

Calderón, César, and Lin Liu. 2003. "The Direction of Causality between Financial Development and Economic Growth." *Journal of Development Economics* 72 (1): 321–334.

Cecchetti, Stephen G, and Enisse Kharroubi. 2015. "Why Does Financial Sector Growth Crowd Out Real Economic Growth?" BIS Working Paper No. 490, Bank for International Settlements, Basel.

Chinn, Menzie D. and Hiro Ito. 2006. "What Matters for Financial Development? Capital Controls, Institutions, and Interactions." *Journal of Development Economics* 81 (1): 163–192.

Cihak, Martin, and A. Demirgüç-Kunt. 2012. "Benchmarking Financial Systems around the World." World Bank Policy Research Working Paper 6175, World Bank, Washington.

Dabla-Norris, Era, and Narapong Srivisal. 2013. "Revisiting the Link Between Finance and Macroeconomic Volatility." IMF Working Paper 13/29, International Monetary Fund, Washington DC.

De Gregorio, Jose, and Pablo E. Guidotti. 1995. "Financial Development and Economic Growth." *World Development* 23 (3): 433–448.

Djankov, Simeon, Caralee McLiesh, and Andrei Shleifer. 2007. "Private Credit in 129 Countries." *Journal of Financial Economics* 84 (2): 299–329.

Easterly, William, Roumeen Islam and Joseph E. Stiglitz. 2000. "Shaken and Stirred: Explaining Growth Volatility." In *Annual World Bank Conference on Development Economics,* eds. Boris Pleskovic and Nicholas Stern. Washington DC: World Bank.

Eichengreen, Barry. 2001. "Capital Account Liberalization: What Do Cross-Country Studies Tell Us?" *The World Bank Economic Review* 15 (3): 341–365.

Geweke, John. 1982. "Measurement of Linear Dependence and Feedback between Multiple Time Series." *Journal of the American Statistical Association* 77 (378): 304–313.

Goldsmith, Raymon W. 1969. *Financial Structure and Development.* New Haven: Yale University Press.

Granger, Clive W. J. 1969. "Investigating Causal Relations by Econometric Models and Cross-Spectral Methods." *Econometrica* 37 (3): 424–438.

Jean-Louis Arcand, Enrico Berkes and Ugo Panizza. 2012. "Too Much Finance?" IMF Working Paper 12/161, International Monetary Fund, Washington DC.

Khan, Mohsin S., Abdelhak S. Senhadji, and Bruce D. Smith. 2001. "Inflation and Financial Depth." IMF Working Paper 01/44, International Monetary Fund, Washington DC.

King, Robert G. and Ross Levine. 1993. "Finance and Growth: Schumpeter Might Be Right." *The Quarterly Journal of Economics* 108 (3): 717–737.

Kose, M. Ayhan., Eswar S. Prasad, and Ashley D. Taylor. 2011. "Thresholds in the Process of International Financial Integration." *Journal of International Money and Finance* 30 (1): 147–179.

La Porta, Rafael, Florencio Lopez-de-Silanes, Andrei Shleifer, and Robert W. Vishny. 1998. "Law and Finance." *Journal of Political Economy* 106 (6): 1113–1155.

Levine, Ross. 2004. "Finance and Growth: Theory and Evidence." NBER Working Paper 10766, National Bureau of Economic Research, Cambridge.

Levine, Ross, and Sara Zervos. 1998. "Stock Markets, Banks, and Economic Growth." *American Economic Review* 88 (3): 537–558.

McKinnon, Ronald I. 1973. Money and Capital in Economic Development. Washington DC: Brooking Institution Press.

Nili, Masoud, and Mahdi Rastad. 2007. "Addressing the Growth Failure of the Oil Economies: The Role of Financial Development." *The Quarterly Review of Economics and Finance* 46 (5): 726–740.

Rajan, Raghuram G, and Luigi Zingales. 1998. "Financial Dependence and Growth." *American Economic Review* 88 (3): 559–586.

Sahay, R., M. Cihak, P. N'Diaye, A. Barajas, R. Bi, D. Ayala, Y. Gao, A. Kyobe, L. Nguyen, C. Saborowski, K. Svirydzenka and S.R. Yousefi. 2015. "Rethinking Financing Deepening: Stability and Growth in Emerging Markets," IMF Staff Discussion Note SDN/15/08, International Monetary Fund, Washington DC.

Senghor, Senh. 2014. *Financial Access and Stability in Cambodia: Opportunities and Challenges*. Development Research Forum Synthesis Report No. 5, Cambodia Development Resource Institute, Phnom Penh.

Shaw, Edward S. 1973. *Financial Deepening in Economic Development*. London: Oxford University Press.

Tan, Khee Giap and Chee-Seng Cheng. 1995. "The Causal Nexus of Money, Output and Prices in Malaysia." *Applied Economics* 27 (12): 1245–1251.

The World Bank. 2015. *World Development Indicators Online*.

World Economic Forum. 2012. The Financial Development Report 2012. New York: World Economic Forum.

Chapter 4

UNDERSTANDING THE CAUSAL FACTORS DRIVING ECONOMIC GROWTH IN SINGAPORE AND MALAYSIA

4.1 Introductory Notes

Both Malaysia and Singapore have been viewed as success stories in economic development and are widely hailed as role models for other developing countries to follow. While Singapore, with a Gross Domestic Product (GDP) per capita of US$55,182 in 2013 has moved to a high income status, Malaysia, with a GDP per capita of US$10,538 (in 2013) has become a *bone fide* upper middle-income country. Though both countries have come a long way in their respective economic growth paths since the mid-1960s, Singapore has visibly outpaced Malaysia in terms of economic growth as well as overall macroeconomic performance ever since it obtained independence from Malaysia in 1965 (see Figure 4.1). Despite a period of convergence between the growth rates of both economies between 1990 and 2000, broadly Singapore has experienced a much faster average growth rate than Malaysia for over three decades or so starting in 1970.

Though both countries have followed their own unique developmental models, there are some striking commonalities. One such common denominator that can be identified between the two countries in terms of their development strategies is the fact that both Singapore and Malaysia have focused on developing world-class infrastructure and

Figure 4.1. Real GDP Growth in Singapore and Malaysia, 1970–2014

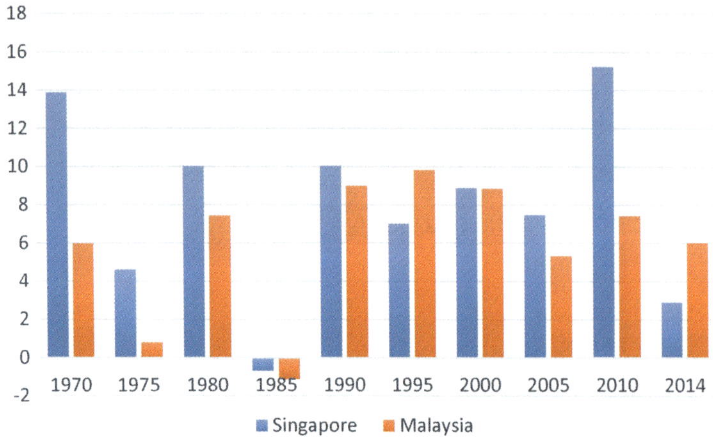

Source: The World Bank.

sound macroeconomic management, while being plugged into the regional production networks. In particular, the two countries have benefited from being part of the regional 'flying geese pattern' of comparative advantage, whereby countries developed industries consistent with their comparative advantage based on their endowment structure (Akamatsu, 1962).[1] The model, which can essentially be understood as an international division of labour based on dynamic comparative advantage, has in fact remained one of the notable features of the broader East Asian growth and economic transformation story. As the comparative advantages of the "lead goose" (Japan) cause the leader to shift away from labour-intensive production to more capital-intensive

[1] According to the flying geese model, developed countries or regions tend to relocate their manufacturing and labour-intensive industries to developing countries or regions through international trade and investment, resulting in industrial restructuring and technological upgrading (Akamatsu, 1962). For a specific discussion on the flying geese model and East Asian growth story, see Chapter 1 of this book and Tan *et al.* (2015).

activities, the leader passes its low-productivity production to other follower countries aligned behind in the hierarchy, resembling a pattern of flying geese.[2]

More generally, developed countries or regions move up the production value chain or industrial ladder towards high value-added activities. The East Asian fragmentation of manufacturing production and exports was characterised by China, Japan, and Korea being the source countries for production networks, and China increasingly serving as the prime 'assembly base'. Countries like Malaysia and Singapore absorbed new production technologies and became major exporters of parts and components. This was then passed on to countries like Indonesia, Cambodia, Laos, Myanmar and Vietnam, as they were able to absorb the relocation of labour-intensive segments.

Data highlights that the share of production network exports in parts and components for Singapore grew from about 30% in 1992–1993 to 50% in 2006–2007, with the corresponding figure for Malaysia rising from around 28% to 54% during the same period (Chia, 2013). As a phenomenon, the relocation of labour-intensive and low value-added manufacturing industries stems from Adam Smith's theory of international division of labour and specialisation, supplemented by foreign direct investment (FDI) (Tan *et al.*, 2015).

Nearly five decades after undergoing a structural transformation and navigating several external shocks like the Asian Financial Crisis (AFC) in 1997–1998 and the Global Financial Crisis (GFC) in 2008–2009, both Singapore and Malaysia are now grappling with some crucial policy challenges that necessitate a course-correction in order to sustain their growth momentum.

There is a growing recognition that Malaysia is now struggling to avoid falling into the much talked about "middle income trap" (Flaaen *et al.*, 2013), while Singapore is finding it somewhat difficult to ramp up

[2] See Tan *et al.* (2015) and Kumagai (2015) for more discussion on the relevance and application of the flying geese model to East Asian growth model.

its stagnating labour productivity especially among small- and medium-sized enterprises (SMEs) along with growing concerns of income inequality (Tan and Tan, 2014; Tan, 2014; Tan and Tan, 2012). In fact, the policy discourse in Singapore has been drifting towards the need for the city-state to adopt a holistic approach to economic growth and development. Such an approach must go beyond relying heavily on FDI as a key source of economic growth and instead focus on policies that aim at reviving internal demand. Enhancing investments in industrial, technological capabilities and human resource in the country would be the key to enact such policies (Tan, 2014). Similarly, in Malaysia, the policy discussions have been focused on how to help the country develop a robust and strong services sector alongside its manufacturing, which would facilitate the country's transition to a high-income status.

In light of the renewed interest in understanding the growth constraints faced by the two countries and the subsequent policy interest that the issue has generated, this chapter aims to revisit the issue of drivers of economic growth in both Singapore and Malaysia. Specifically, the chapter attempts to provide an empirical explanation for the sources of growth in Singapore and Malaysia by identifying the key causal variables that ought to be the focus of policymakers in order to sustain the growth momentum. To do this, the chapter employs a novel empirical approach — the Geweke causality analysis — to investigate the causal drivers of economic growth in both countries. Intuitively, Geweke causality analysis helps us understand and measure the linear dependence and feedback between multiple time series variables. To that effect, we perform both bi-variate as well as multi-variate causality analysis.

The remainder of the chapter is organised as follows. Section 4.2 offers some background literature concerning the growth experiences and structural transformation of both Singapore and Malaysia, as well as some of the contemporary policy challenges faced by each of them. This discussion will inform the hypotheses to be tested in the chapter as outlined in Section 4.3. Following this, Section 4.4 outlines a detailed exposition of the empirical methodology and the data used for the analysis. Section 4.5 discusses the empirical results. Section 4.6 concludes the chapter with a brief discussion on the policy implications emanating from our analysis.

4.2 Growth Transformation of Singapore and Malaysia

The "state capitalist" nature of the East Asian growth model has been a topic of extensive discussion in the literature.[3] Characterised by a fine balance between active state intervention and market dynamics, the region maintained consistent and prolonged period of robust growth for the most part of the last four decades. The major phases in the sustained high growth era of the East Asian economies were marked by the rise of Japan from the 1950s to the 1970s, with the next two decades witnessing the emergence of East Asia's four newly industrialised economies (NIEs), comprising Singapore, Hong Kong, South Korca and Taiwan, on the back of robust manufacturing base. These NIEs were followed later by the NIEs of Malaysia, Indonesia and Thailand as well as the Philippines.[4]

In what follows, we will specifically zoom in on the structural transformation that Singapore and Malaysia underwent since the mid-1960s to date, and also highlight some of the policy challenges that the countries' policymakers are confronting today.[5] This would lead us to

[3] See Naughton and Tsai (2015) for a recent assessment; also see Xing and Shaw (2013) and The Economist (2012).

[4] The more recent phase from the early 1980s has largely been a China story, with China leading the third wave of the economic growth in terms of regional trade and investment.

[5] See also chapter 5 of this book for a detailed discussion on Singapore's growth transformation since independence.

develop some testable hypotheses for our empirical analysis in the next section.

4.2.1 Singapore

Singapore grew at an annual growth rate of about 8% on average for a period of over three decades between 1970 and 2014, with three significant exceptions. The exceptions were during those years that dented the economy severely owing to external shocks, which are the oil shock in mid-1980s, the AFC in 1997–1998 and the GFC in 2008–2009.

Considering that Singapore is a small and open economy, the astounding economic growth that the country has registered over the last three decades has largely been driven by a concomitant growth in exports along with favourable inflation rates. As the snapshot view of growth and inflation rates captured in Figure 4.2 illustrates, Singapore has experienced an annual inflation rate of less than 3% during the

Figure 4.2. Read GDP Growth and Inflation in Singapore, 1970–2014

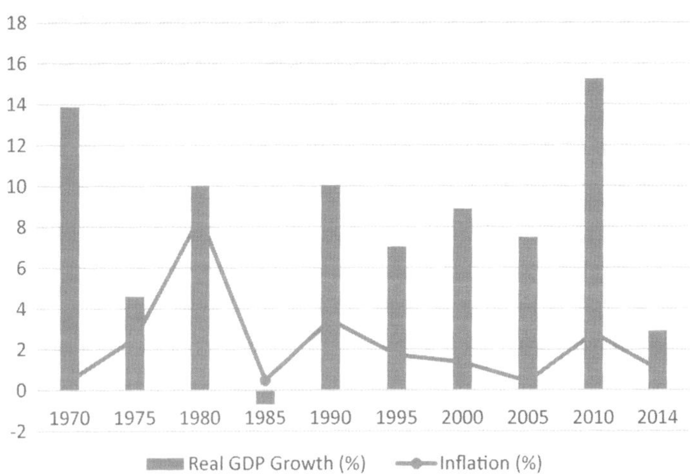

Source: The World Bank.

corresponding period between 1970 and 2014, with the period since the AFC witnessing an even lower average inflation rate of about 2%. Overall, the country has seen a favourable growth-inflation differential since its independence, thus reflecting its sound macroeconomic management that has in turn enabled the small city-state to undergo a sustained pace of economic growth, at least up until the GFC.

Given the outward-orientation of Singapore, it was only natural that the pace of growth slowed down when the GFC intensified. The economic growth not only slowed down, but the recovery post-GFC was also rather volatile. While it appeared as if the economy was rebounding strongly in 2010, with the average growth rate being close to 10% in 2010–2011, the subsequent three years (2012–2014) saw Singapore's economic growth stuttering at around 3.5% on average, which was also predictably correlated with the movements in the country's growth of exports of goods and services.

The initial two decades after independence was largely the time that Singapore channeled its efforts to employ export-led industrialisation and rapid capital accumulation as a primary economic strategy to foster its economic growth. The government's foremost policy objective was to promote growth by attracting FDI that was expected in turn to create employment as well as enhance the productive capacity of the economy (Vu, 2011; also see Figure 4.3).

As seen from Figure 4.3, the significance of FDI inflows as a proportion of Singapore's output has broadly exhibited an increasing trend, reflecting its importance in the country's transformation. The FDI inflows into Singapore have had three distinct phases. The first phase was during the first decade starting in 1970, when FDI inflows averaged about 6% of the GDP, with the share peaking at around 11% in 1980–1981. There was a brief period of slowdown coinciding with the oil shock in the mid-1980s, with FDI inflows hitting a relative low of 5% in 1985 before it picked up again. From around 1986 leading up to the GFC, the average FDI inflows as a share of the GDP was well

Figure 4.3. FDI Inflows as a Share of GDP in Singapore, 1970–2014

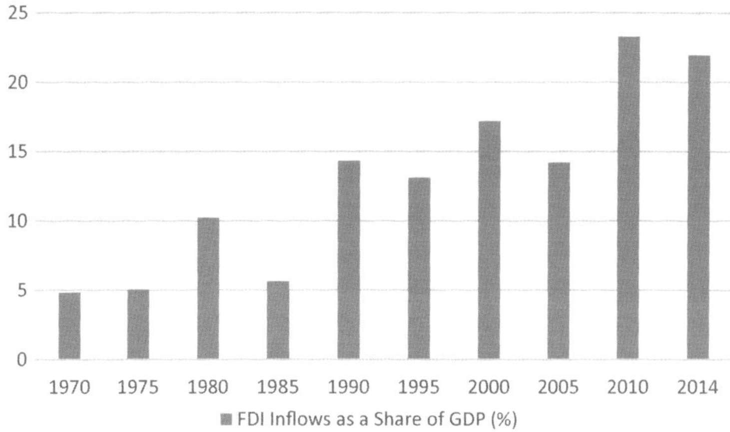

Source: The World Bank.

above 10%, with the peak touching over 25% of Singapore's output just before the GFC struck in 2007. Once again, after losing some momentum for about two years, FDI inflows picked up again since 2009. These trends just point out the important role FDI has played in supplementing domestic investments in the country, which also aided Singapore in scaling up the income ladder.

In effect, if one were to summarise Singapore's transformation experience, one can say that there were two key strategic decisions that were the hallmark of Singapore's growth strategy. The first was to shift away from import-substitution policies in favour of export-led industrialisation post-independence from Malaysia, and the second was to go after specific global multinational corporations (MNCs) to attract the much-needed FDI that would translate into the growth of its industrial sector.

The growth transformation of Singapore really began when the government started seeing the fruits of these two key strategies, which in many ways defined the country's development approach for a long time. The world witnessed the rise of Singapore through the development of industrial land, infrastructure facilities, reformed and conducive labour laws, as well as investments in basic technical education relevant to industrialisation (Menon, 2015).

It is important to highlight that by 1975, Singapore had established a substantial industrial base, with its manufacturing sector's share in the GDP climbing to about 22% from around 14% or so in 1965. Singapore was compelled to move up the value chain towards more capital-intensive and skill-intensive activities. The restructuring and structural transformation occurred in the early 1980s when the focus shifted towards high-tech manufacturing and higher value-added services. Economic restructuring through the "New Industrial Revolution" helped the country develop more capital- and skill-intensive industries (Saner *et al.* 2014). The structural transformation that occurred during this phase was considered a development success as it helped in the creation of higher value-added sectors and jobs.

The final turnaround in Singapore's growth transformation occurred in 1985 when the country was hit by a severe economic downturn, which then paved the way for a series of structural reforms in the 1990s. As Menon (2015) pointed out:

> "...In fact the 1985 recession was a significant milestone in Singapore's development history... The most important outcomes from that period of review which continued into the 1990s were the structural reforms to: enhance wage flexibility in the labour market; tap more decisively into regional markets for trade and outward investment; step up the pace of industrial upgrading; promote innovation, enterprise, and entrepreneurship in the economy; and liberalise various services sectors such as finance, telecommunications, and utilities... In fact, the key story post-1985 recession up till the Global Financial Crisis of 2008 was the rise of modern services as a twin engine of growth alongside manufacturing."

Indeed, one of the highlights of Singapore's growth performance since the 1990s has been the dynamism of its services sector, as also reflected in the growing importance of the share of modern services in Singapore's GDP. Modern services (financial, business, communications and entertainment services) have almost doubled from 16% in 1965 to just less than 30% in 2010 as a share of Singapore's output (Menon, 2015).[6]

As noted earlier, while Singapore rebounded from the GFC and posted impressive growth rates in 2010 and 2011, there appears to have been a dip in the average growth rates since then. Between 2012 and 2014, the average annual growth rate has been hovering around 3.5%, much less than the average 10% growth that it posted in 2010 and 2011. Among the various cyclical factors that one may associate with this slowdown, there are also structural concerns that need closer attention such as lagging productivity that Singapore is facing.

As Rajan *et al.* (2014) noted pertinently, Singapore has seen a sharp increase in wages, partly driven by the caps imposed on foreign workers, which again broadly reflects sluggish productivity growth (see Figure 4.4). Singapore has been witnessing some structural concerns such as the slowing down of labour productivity growth since the mid-2000s and the trend appeared to have accelerated since 2010. One of the key points to note from Figure 4.4 is the growing disconnect between wage growth and productivity, which seems to be on the rise. This in turn underscores the need for the country's policymakers to align both wages and productivity so that the long-term competitiveness of the country is secure.[7]

---

[6] Data has shown that well before 2010, when the integrated resorts took off, Singapore experienced a significant jump in its services sector FDI compared to manufacturing FDI. The share of financial and insurance services alone as a percentage of total stock of FDI into Singapore rose from 42% in 2007 to about 48% in 2013, while the corresponding share of manufacturing FDI dipped from around 25% to 17% during the same period (For more, see Department of Statistics, Singapore, accessible from: http://www.singstat.gov.sg/statistics/browse-by-theme/investment)

[7] See Rajan *et al.*, 2014 for a detailed discussion on competitiveness issues and policy concerns in Singapore

Figure 4.4. Growth, Productivity and Unit Labour Costs in Singapore, 1999–2012

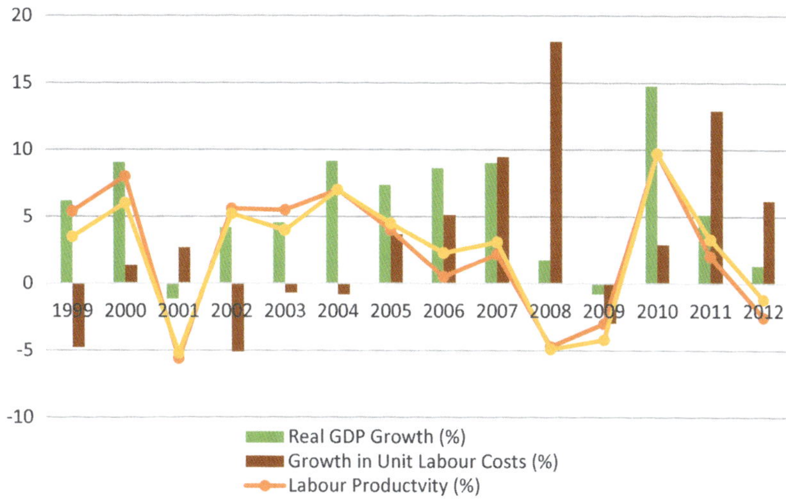

Source: The World Bank, Economist Intelligence Unit and Rajan *et al.* (2014, 153).

Furthermore, it is also imperative to recognise that as Singapore moves up the technological ladder, the skill sets possessed by the local population need upgrading to match with the demands of higher value-added jobs. This implies that those with secondary or lower education may be becoming increasingly trapped in an 'economic underclass', underlining the importance of investments in education to strengthen human capital required for a knowledge-intensive economy as well as to promote upward mobility and incomes (Tan and Tan, 2012).

4.2.2 Malaysia

Malaysia has also had a relatively successful growth story, with the country witnessing strong and sustained growth between 1970 and 2014, growing at an average annual rate of over 6% (see Figure 4.5).

Figure 4.5. Real GDP Growth, Exports Growth and Inflation in Malaysia, 1970–2014

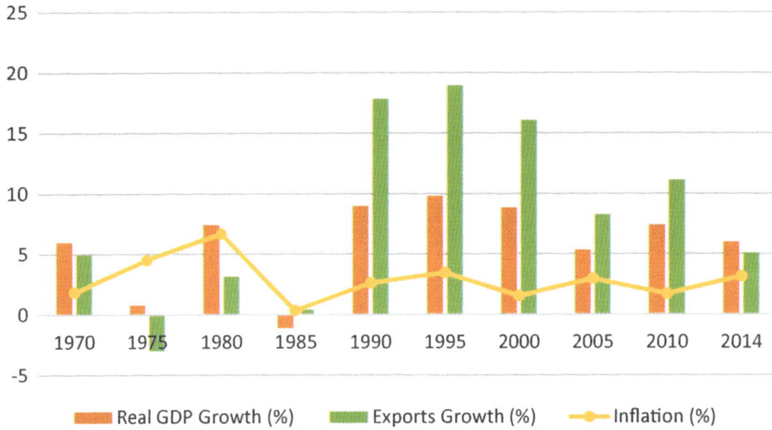

Source: The World Bank.

Although Malaysia's growth performance was lacklustre relative to that of Singapore, there are some notable similarities between the two experiences, in that Malaysia was also significantly affected by exogenous shocks. Most notably, the oil shock in the mid-1980s, the AFC in 1997–1998 and the GFC in 2008–2009 contributed to the slowdown of Malaysia's otherwise sustained growth rates since the 1970s.

It is also useful to note that Malaysia's sustained period of strong and robust growth has been backed by a strong expansion of exports and low inflation. Post-AFC, for instance, the country posted an average growth rate of around 6% or so until the GFC; after which, there was again a temporary cyclical slowdown. As far as inflation rates are concerned, Malaysia witnessed a spell of sustained low inflation of about 3% on average during the corresponding period, although the previous two decades between 1970 and 1990 saw a comparatively higher inflation rate of about 5% or so on average.

As noted, exports growth has been a significant contributor to Malaysia's overall economic growth and this is clearly visible since the 1990s, where one finds that the pace of growth in exports exceeded that of output growth. However, since the mid-2000s, one could trace a gradual but steady emergence of domestic demand as a significant driver of economic growth. Notwithstanding the rising importance of domestic demand, the broader point to keep in mind is that growth in exports and overall output have tended to move in tandem for most of the last three decades.

During the last three decades, the Malaysian economy also witnessed some notable structural shifts that allowed it to transition to a middle-income country from a low-income country (Flaaen *et al.* 2013). From a country that was known to be a producer of primary products, its transformation into an economy with a robust industrial base occurred in the 1970s, which happened to also be the tipping point in the economic history of Malaysia. It was at this juncture that the country started actively promoting export-oriented manufacturing and FDI inflows into export-oriented firms (Yusof and Bhattasali, 2008; also see Figure 4.6). Figure 4.6 shows this gradual transformation as captured by the falling share of agriculture value-added as a proportion of the GDP, paving the way for the rise of manufacturing and services value-added over the years.

In a nutshell, the Malaysian economic growth story can be understood as a classic case of structural transformation of a largely agricultural economy to a more industrialised economy, supported by export-orientation and FDI inflows, which is currently stuck in its attempt to migrate from its middle-income status. As Flaaen *et al.* (2013, p. 23) noted, "like many other middle income economies, it is squeezed by the competition from low-wage economies on the one hand, and more innovative advanced economies on the other… (there is a) need for broad structural transformation; that is, moving to higher productivity production in both goods and services".

Figure 4.6. Manufacturing, Services and Agriculture Value Added (% of GDP) in Malaysia, 1975–2014

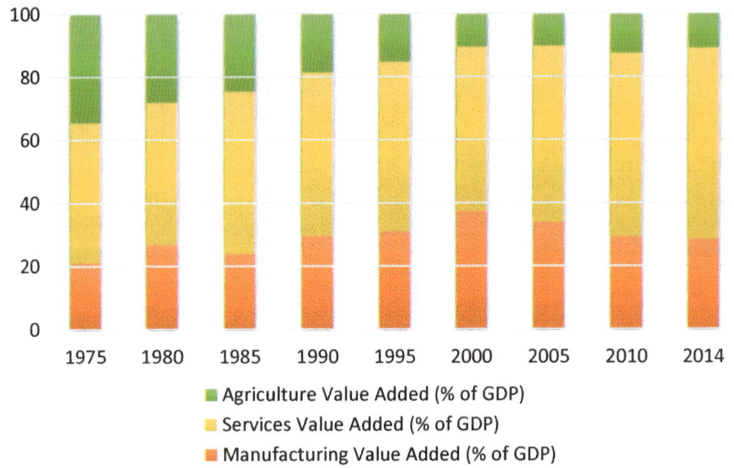

Source: The World Bank.

While Malaysia remains a highly-open economy dependent on external demand, it is pertinent to note that domestic demand has increasingly become an important driver of economic growth in recent years (Bank Negara Malaysia, 2012). This has in turn triggered structural changes within the economy, enhancing stronger economic growth and employment creation in the domestic-oriented industries. As emphasised by Bank Negara Malaysia (2012), strong private consumption and resilient total investments have been enabling the economy to expand despite the weak export performance after the GFC. Hence, policymakers must pay more attention towards harnessing internal demand by strengthening local manufacturing and services sectors.

It becomes imperative here to also recognise that although Malaysia has long relied on an outward-oriented model, with FDI inflows providing the necessary technology and skills for the country to effectively participate in the global value chains, scaling up those value chains require investments in strong local capacity building and investments in human capital. This underlines the need for the country to focus on enhancing high productivity and competitiveness.

Although Malaysia managed to expand its tradable sector over the last few decades, which allowed it to become a sophisticated manufacturing exporter, it has lagged in terms of the development of its services sector. An empirical analysis examining the productivity levels in manufacturing and services by Flaaen *et al.* (2013) confirmed the yawning gaps in productivity between manufacturing and services in Malaysia, which have especially accelerated in recent years. This highlights the urgency for Malaysia to engage in another round of structural transformation, but one that is much broader that will allow them to reap higher productivity in both goods and services sectors.

To this end, Malaysia has been undertaking a host of policy initiatives to overcome its middle-income trap and transition to a high-income status. As the IMF (2015, 14) noted in its most recent assessment of the macroeconomic health of Malaysia, these reforms have been viewed favourably as steps in the right direction that will facilitate the country's transition through effecting a structural transformation. To quote the IMF (2015, 14):

> "(...) for Malaysia to avoid a middle income trap and reach high income status by 2020...they are intent on pursuing reforms that would create the conditions for a knowledge-based economy. Their multi-year transformation programs place appropriate emphasis on synergies between the ingredients needed to deliver on this, including plans to improve infrastructure, upgrade the quality of education, and boost Malaysia's research and development spending and raise its effectiveness in generating home-grown innovation....Taken together, these reforms, reinforced by better services delivery, continued financial sector development and greater financial inclusion, and supported by a strong social safety net, can accelerate productivity growth and encourage higher value-added activities."

The foregoing discussion leaves us with some important points that can be the basis for developing some empirically testable hypothesis. While there are a number of factors that could have driven economic growth at different stages, it is pivotal to recognise the structural constraints currently faced by these economies. The policy priorities of the countries have to change accordingly, factoring in their respective growth constraints.

In this light, we attempt to identify empirically the key variables that Singapore and Malaysia should focus on that will help relieve their growth constraints in moving forward. We take into consideration the need for a balanced growth between manufacturing and services on the supply side as well as the need to focus on promoting domestic consumption on the demand side and outline our hypotheses accordingly for both countries in the next section.

4.3 Hypotheses and Data

Based on the discussion above with respect to the structural transformation of Malaysia and Singapore, we put forward the following set of hypotheses for both countries, underscoring the importance of a particular set of variables that will be crucial for both countries to pay attention to for sustaining their growth momentum.

4.3.1 Hypothesis, Variables and Data for Malaysia

For Malaysia to escape the middle-income trap, we propose the following hypothesis:

An expansion of household consumption and deepening of both manufacturing and services sector as reflected in increases in domestic value-added in both sectors would enhance the country's real GDP growth, thereby propelling it to the rank of high-income industrialised economies.

Table 4.1. Variables Used in Geweke Causality Analysis for Malaysia

Variable	Notation	Definition
X	GGDP	Growth Rate of Real GDP (2005 USD)
Y1	ΔHFC	Change in Household Final Consumption (current local currency)
Y2	ΔMVA	Change in Real Manufacturing Value Added (2005 USD)
Y3	ΔSVA	Change in Real Services Value Added (2005 USD)

Source: Asia Competitiveness Institute.

We will test the above hypothesis for Malaysia using annual data between 1975 and 2012. The data were obtained from World Bank's World Development Indicators database and transformed to meet the stationary requirement of the Geweke analysis. The list of variables, their notations and definitions are presented in Table 4.1.

4.3.2 Hypothesis, Variables and Data for Singapore

With regard to Singapore, we propose the following hypothesis:

Private consumption, net FDI inflows, enhancement in services value-added and investment in education are the key driving forces for Singapore's trajectory towards an advanced, knowledge-based economy.

We will test the above hypothesis for Singapore using annual data between 1975 and 2012. The FDI net inflows in current USD and services value-added in constant 2005 USD were obtained from World Bank's World Development Indicators database. Private consumption expenditure and government expenditure on education in local currency are from the Singapore Department of Statistics. All data were transformed to meet the stationary requirement of the Geweke analysis. The list of variables, their notations and definitions are presented in Table 4.2.

Table 4.2. Variables Used in Geweke Causality Analysis for Singapore

Variable	Notation	Definition
X	GGDP	Growth Rate of Real GDP (2005 USD)
Y1	ΔPCE	Change in Private Consumption Expenditure (local currency, 2010 market prices)
Y2	ΔFDI	Change in FDI Net Inflows (current USD)
Y3	ΔSVA	Change in Real Services Value Added (2005 USD)
Y4	ΔGEE	Change in Government Expenditure on Education (current local currency)

Source: Asia Competitiveness Institute.

4.4 Research Methodology

As discussed and elaborated in detail in Chapter 3 of this volume, the uni-directional causality analysis that is popularly employed in the literature does not investigate the degree of dependence or the extent of various kinds of feedback between different time series variables. However, the method suggested by Geweke (1982) overcomes this problem and helps measure the linear dependence and feedback between multiple time series variables. In essence, the linear dependence is defined as "the sum of the measure of linear feedback from the first series to the second, linear feedback from the second to the first, and instantaneous linear feedback" (Geweke, 1982). The direction of causality and the interplay of the variables can be examined in a more detailed manner with a reduced form quantitative framework under the Geweke causality analysis.[8]

It is useful to recollect from our discussion in Chapter 3 that Geweke causality analysis is used as a tool to identify causal relationships in the field of economics and neuroscience. Some recent and prominent applications of Geweke causality to macroeconomic issues include Tan

[8] For a more detailed treatment and discussion of causality analysis, see Geweke (1984) and Granger (1988).

and Cheng (1995), Calderón and Liu (2003), and Aizenman and Noy (2006). While Tan and Cheng (1995) employed Geweke's approach to examine the causal nexus of money, output and prices in Malaysia, Calderón and Liu (2003) explored the direction of causality between financial development and economic growth. Aizenman and Noy (2006) investigated the two-way linkages between FDI and trade.

Like Granger and Sims, Geweke's causality analysis focussed the attention on a wide-sense stationary, purely non-deterministic multiple time series $Z = \{z_t, t \text{ real}\}$. Therefore, the vector z_t can be expressed under the following autoregressive representation:

$$z_t = \sum_{s=1}^{\infty} B_s z_{t-s} + e_t$$

where e_t is white noise and z_t can be partitioned into $k \times 1$ and $l \times 1$ sub-vectors x_t and y_t.

Geweke also showed that a canonical form for the wide-sense stationary time series $z_t = (x_t, y_t)$ is of the form:

$$x_t = \sum_{s=1}^{\infty} E_{1s} x_{t-s} + u_{1t} \qquad var(u_{1t}) = \Sigma_1 \qquad (1)$$

$$x_t = \sum_{s=1}^{\infty} E_{2s} x_{t-s} + \sum_{s=1}^{\infty} F_{2s} y_{t-s} + u_{2t} \qquad var(u_{2t}) = \Sigma_2 \qquad (2)$$

$$x_t = \sum_{s=1}^{\infty} E_{3s} x_{t-s} + \sum_{s=0}^{\infty} F_{3s} y_{t-s} + u_{3t} \qquad var(u_{3t}) = \Sigma_3 \qquad (3)$$

$$x_t = \sum_{s=1}^{\infty} E_{4s} x_{t-s} + \sum_{s=-\infty}^{\infty} F_{4s} y_{t-s} + u_{4t} \qquad var(u_{4t}) = \Sigma_4 \qquad (4)$$

$$y_t = \sum_{s=1}^{\infty} G_{1s} y_{t-s} + v_{1t} \qquad var(v_{1t}) = \mathrm{T}_1 \qquad (5)$$

$$y_t = \sum_{s=1}^{\infty} G_{2s} y_{t-s} + \sum_{s=1}^{\infty} H_{2s} x_{t-s} + v_{2t} \qquad var(v_{2t}) = \mathrm{T}_2 \qquad (6)$$

$$y_t = \sum_{s=1}^{\infty} G_{3s} y_{t-s} + \sum_{s=0}^{\infty} H_{3s} x_{t-s} + v_{3t} \qquad var(v_{3t}) = \mathrm{T}_3 \tag{7}$$

$$y_t = \sum_{s=1}^{\infty} G_{4s} y_{t-s} + \sum_{s=-\infty}^{\infty} H_{4s} x_{t-s} + v_{4t} \qquad var(v_{4t}) = \mathrm{T}_4 \tag{8}$$

4.4.1 Definition: Measure of Linear Dependence and Feedback

The measure of linear feedback from *Y* to *X* is defined as:

$$F_{Y \to X} = \ln\left(|\Sigma_1| / |\Sigma_2|\right) \tag{9}$$

The measure $F_{Y \to X}$ is always non-negative and takes the value of zero only if the linear feedback running from *Y* to *X* is absent. Symmetrically, the measure of linear feedback from *X* to *Y* is defined as:

$$F_{X \to Y} = \ln\left(|\mathrm{T}_1| / |\mathrm{T}_2|\right) \tag{10}$$

The instantaneous feedback is defined as

$$F_{X \cdot Y} = \ln\left(|\mathrm{T}_2| \times |\Sigma_2| / |\gamma|\right) \tag{11}$$

where $\gamma = \mathrm{var}\begin{pmatrix} u_{2t} \\ v_{2t} \end{pmatrix} = \begin{bmatrix} \Sigma_2 & C \\ C' & \mathrm{T}_2 \end{bmatrix}$.

Thus, the measure of linear dependence between two vectors *X* and *Y* can be decomposed into the sum of measure of linear feedback from *X* to *Y*, the measure of linear feedback from *Y* to *X*, and the instantaneous linear feedback between the two vectors. That is,

$$F_{X,Y} = F_{X \to Y} + F_{Y \to X} + F_{X \cdot Y} \tag{12}$$

Geweke also proved that the equations in the following set are equivalent:

$$F_{X,Y} = \ln\left(|\Sigma_1| \times |\mathrm{T}_1| / |\gamma|\right) = \ln\left(|\Sigma_1| / |\Sigma_4|\right) = \ln((|\mathrm{T}_1| / |\mathrm{T}_4|) \tag{13}$$

$$F_{X \to Y} = \ln\left(|\mathrm{T}_1| / |\mathrm{T}_2|\right) = \ln\left(|\Sigma_3| / |\Sigma_4|\right) \quad (14)$$

$$F_{Y \to X} = \ln\left(|\Sigma_1| / |\Sigma_2|\right) = \ln\left(|\mathrm{T}_3| / |\mathrm{T}_4|\right) \quad (15)$$

$$F_{X \cdot Y} = \ln\left(|\mathrm{T}_2| \times |\Sigma_2| / |\gamma|\right) = \ln\left(|\Sigma_2| / |\Sigma_3|\right) = \ln\left(|\mathrm{T}_2| / |\mathrm{T}_3|\right) \quad (16)$$

4.4.2 Distribution of Statistics

Under the null hypothesis that there is no uni-directional causality running from Y to X, i.e. if $\hat{F}_{Y \to X} = 0$, then

$$n\hat{F}_{Y \to X} \sim \chi^2(klp), \quad (17)$$

Similarly, it follows that if $\hat{F}_{X \to Y} = 0$,

$$n\hat{F}_{X \to Y} \sim \chi^2(klp), \quad (18)$$

and if $\hat{F}_{X \cdot Y} = 0$,

$$n\hat{F}_{X.Y} \sim \chi^2(kl), \quad (19)$$

As these are nested hypotheses, all three restrictions could be tested simultaneously since if $\hat{F}_{X,Y} = 0$, then

$$n\hat{F}_{X,Y} \sim \chi^2\left[kl(2p+1)\right] \quad (20)$$

4.4.3 Confidence Interval

The 95% confidence interval (CI) could be calculated approximately as follows:

For $\hat{F}_{Y \to X} = 0$,

$$\left\{\left[\left(\hat{F}_{Y \to X} - \frac{klp-1}{3n}\right)^{1/2} \pm \frac{1.96}{\sqrt{n}}\right]^2 - \frac{2klp+1}{3n}\right\} \quad (21)$$

For $\hat{F}_{X\to Y}=0$,

$$\left\{\left[\left(\hat{F}_{X\to Y}-\frac{klp-1}{3n}\right)^{1/2}\pm\frac{1.96}{\sqrt{n}}\right]^2-\frac{2klp+1}{3n}\right\} \tag{22}$$

For $\hat{F}_{X\cdot Y}=0$,

$$\left\{\left[\left(\hat{F}_{X\cdot Y}-\frac{klp-1}{3n}\right)^{1/2}\pm\frac{1.96}{\sqrt{n}}\right]^2-\frac{2kl+1}{3n}\right\} \tag{23}$$

For $\hat{F}_{X,Y}=0$,

$$\left\{\left[\left(\hat{F}_{X\cdot Y}-\frac{kl(2p+1)-1}{3n}\right)^{1/2}\pm\frac{1.96}{\sqrt{n}}\right]^2-\frac{2kl(2p+1)+1}{3n}\right\} \tag{24}$$

4.5 Empirical Results

4.5.1 Geweke Causality Results for Malaysia

Our empirical results reveal some important findings. As noted earlier, we performed two different kinds of analysis, with the first one focusing on bi-variate causality analysis (see Table 4.3) and the second one focusing on a multi-variate approach to causality analysis (see Table 4.4). Similar exercises were carried out for Singapore, which will be the subject of discussion in Section 4.5.2.

The results for the bi-variate causality analysis for Growth Rate of Real GDP (GGDP) and Change in Household Final Consumption (ΔHFC) are presented in the first two rows of Table 4.3. It can be clearly seen that there was a strong bi-directional association between GGDP and ΔHFC. In both cases, the measures of linear dependence between GGDP and ΔHFC ($F_{x,y}$) were highly statistically significant at

Table 4.3. Estimated Measures of Bi-Directional Feedback between Growth Rate of Real GDP (GGDP), Change in Household Final Consumption (ΔHFC), Change in Real Manufacturing Value Added (ΔMVA), and Change in Real Services Value Added (ΔSVA) for Malaysia, 1975–2012[a,b]

Economic Aggregates		$H_0(F_{x,y} = F_{x\to y} + F_{y\to x} + F_{x\cdot y})$			
x	y	$F_{x,y}$	$F_{x\to y}$	$F_{y\to x}$	$F_{x\cdot y}$
GGDP	ΔHFC	0.8485*** (0.0000)	0.1357 (0.1065)	0.2467** (0.0171)	0.4661*** (0.0001)
ΔHFC	GGDP	0.9828*** (0.0000)	0.1648* (0.0659)	0.3519*** (0.0030)	0.4661*** (0.0001)
GGDP	ΔMVA	1.1181*** (0.0000)	0.0001 (0.9618)	0.0873* (0.0805)	1.0307*** (0.0000)
ΔMVA	GGDP	1.1507*** (0.0000)	0.0991* (0.0625)	0.0208 (0.3935)	1.0307*** (0.0000)
GGDP	ΔSVA	0.8591*** (0.0000)	0.0033 (0.7322)	0.0873* (0.0804)	0.7684*** (0.0000)
ΔSVA	GGDP	0.9586*** (0.0000)	0.1237** (0.0375)	0.0665 (0.1270)	0.7684*** (0.0000)

[a] *, **, and *** denote 10%, 5%, and 1% level of significance, respectively.
[b] Confidence interval would be provided upon request.
Source: Asia Competitiveness Institute.

the 1% level. Similarly, in both cases, the instantaneous feedback between GGDP and ΔHFC ($F_{x.y}$) was also highly significant at the 1% level. Furthermore, it is notable that the instantaneous feedback accounted for almost half of the total linear dependence between GGDP and ΔHFC, which implies that the current as well as the past values of ΔHFC possess significant explanatory power to predict GGDP.

Next, we consider the bi-variate analysis for Growth Rate of Real GDP (GGDP) and Change in Real Manufacturing Value Added (ΔMVA). The third and fourth rows of Table 4.3 show the relevant results; we find yet again that the aggregate measure of linear dependence between GGDP

Table 4.4. Estimated Measures of Multi-Directional Feedback between Growth Rate of Real GDP (GGDP), Change in Household Final Consumption (ΔHFC), Change in Real Manufacturing Value Added (ΔMVA), and Change in Real Services Value Added (ΔSVA) for Malaysia, 1975–2012[a,b]

Economic Aggregates		$H_0(F_{x,y} = F_{x\to y} + F_{y\to x} + F_{x\cdot y})$			
x	y	$F_{x,y}$	$F_{x\to y}$	$F_{y\to x}$	$F_{x\cdot y}$
GGDP	ΔHFC ΔMVA ΔSVA	1.4196*** (0.0000)	0.0862 (0.3890)	0.1940* (0.0789)	1.1394*** (0.0000)

[a] *, **, and *** denote 10%, 5% and 1% level of significance, respectively.
[b] confidence interval would be provided upon request.
Source: Asia Competitiveness Institute.

and ΔMVA ($F_{x,y}$) was highly significant, indicating the strong bi-directional association between the two variables. While similar result can be observed for the instantaneous feedback ($F_{x\cdot y}$) between the two variables, which was also significant at the 1% level, interestingly, the results from the bi-variate analysis were different. When we decomposed the linear feedback between GGDP and ΔMVA, there was only a weak uni-directional relationship that could be observed from ΔMVA to GGDP, in line with economic intuition whereby changes in manufacturing value-added exert a notable influence on enhancing economic growth. Very similar results can be observed for the relationship between GGDP and Change in Real Services Value Added (ΔSVA). The aggregate measure of linear dependence as well as the instantaneous feedback between the two variables were highly significant (at the 1% level); decomposing the linear feedback between the two variables, the causality was uni-directional, running from ΔSVA to GGDP. On the whole, the bi-variate analysis empirical results for Malaysia imply that an enhancement in manufacturing and services value-added would help the country reap considerable growth benefits.

We extended this bilateral framework to estimate the multi-directional causality between GGDP and the vector of variables including Change in Household Final Consumption (ΔHFC), Change in Real Manufacturing Value Added (ΔMVA), and Change in Real Services Value Added (ΔSVA). The results are shown in Table 4.4.

As shown in Table 4.4, there was a strong association between the x variable, GGDP, and the y vector. The story appears to be consistent with the results of bilateral causality that we observed earlier. To be certain, the results showed that the measures of linear dependence between x and y ($F_{x,y}$) and the instantaneous feedback between x and y ($F_{x \cdot y}$) were all highly significant at the 1% level, while the linear feedback from y to x ($F_{y \to x}$) was marginally significant at the 10% level. The multi-variate analysis results further indicated that the linear feedback from y to x ($F_{y \to x}$) accounted for around 14% of total linear dependence between the two vectors, and the instantaneous feedback between x and y ($F_{y \cdot x}$) accounted for over 80% of total linear dependence. These two measures put together contributed to roughly 95% of the total linear dependence.

These results conform to our stated conjectures of the chapter, whereby changes in household final consumption, changes in real manufacturing value-added as well as services value-added are important causal factors that have significantly contributed to Malaysia's economic growth over the last four decades or so from the mid-1970s. Furthermore, these results imply that these variables are likely to drive growth in the future as well (based on its predictive ability of the past relationships), suggesting that there is a need for policymakers to re-orient their focus towards internal demand.

4.5.2 Geweke Causality Results for Singapore

The empirical results for Singapore are summarised in Tables 4.5 and 4.6. Similar to the analysis of Malaysia, we performed two different kinds of

Table 4.5. Estimated Measures of Bi-Directional Feedback between Growth Rate of Real GDP (GGDP), Change in Private Consumption Expenditure (ΔPCE), Change in FDI Net Inflows (ΔFDI), Change in Real Services Value Added (ΔSVA), and Change in Government Expenditure on Education (ΔGEE) for Singapore, 1975–2012[a,b]

Economic Aggregates		$H_0(F_{x,y} = F_{x\to y} + F_{y\to x} + F_{x\cdot y})$			
x	y	$F_{x,y}$	$F_{x\to y}$	$F_{y\to x}$	$F_{x\cdot y}$
GGDP	ΔPCE	0.9325*** (0.0000)	0.0537 (0.1702)	0.2459*** (0.0033)	0.6329*** (0.0000)
ΔPCE	GGDP	0.9967*** (0.0000)	0.3070*** (0.0010)	0.0569 (0.1584)	0.6329*** (0.0000)
GGDP	ΔFDI	0.4290** (0.0147)	0.0024 (0.9611)	0.3339*** (0.0040)	0.0927* (0.0804)
ΔFDI	GGDP	0.5074*** (0.0050)	0.4108*** (0.0011)	0.0040 (0.9367)	0.0927* (0.0804)
GGDP	ΔSVA	1.1500*** (0.0000)	0.0004 (0.9098)	0.1355** (0.0294)	1.0142*** (0.0000)
ΔSVA	GGDP	1.2859*** (0.0000)	0.1836** (0.0112)	0.0881* (0.0790)	1.0142*** (0.0000)
GGDP	ΔGEE	0.3947*** (0.0032)	0.0396 (0.2391)	0.2604*** (0.0025)	0.0948* (0.0686)
ΔGEE	GGDP	0.3324*** (0.0087)	0.2317*** (0.0044)	0.0060 (0.6467)	0.0948* (0.0686)

[a] *,**, and *** denote 10%, 5%, and 1% level of significance, respectively.
[b] Confidence interval would be provided upon request.
Source: Asia Competitiveness Institute.

estimation, with the first one focusing on bi-variate causality analysis (see Table 4.5) and the other one throwing light on causal factors affecting Singapore's growth story using a multi-variate approach (see Table 4.6).

Based on the hypothesis set out earlier for Singapore, we were interested in probing the importance of the following set of variables, namely Change in Private Consumption Expenditure (ΔPCE), Change in FDI Net Inflows (ΔFDI), Change in Real Services Value Added (ΔSVA)

Table 4.6. Estimated Measures of Multi-Directional Feedback between Growth Rate of Real GDP (GGDP), Change in Private Consumption Expenditure (ΔPCE), Change in FDI Net Inflows (ΔFDI), Change in Real Services Value Added (ΔSVA), and Change in Government Expenditure on Education (ΔGEE) for Singapore, 1975–2012[a,b]

Economic Aggregates		$H_0(F_{x,y} = F_{x\to y} + F_{y\to x} + F_{x\cdot y})$			
x	y	$F_{x,y}$	$F_{x\to y}$	$F_{y\to x}$	$F_{x\cdot y}$
GGDP	ΔPCE	1.9012*** (0.0000)	0.2593 (0.3811)	0.8736*** (0.0003)	0.7683*** (0.0000)
	ΔFDI				
	ΔSVA				
	ΔGEE				

[a] *,**, and *** denote 10%, 5%, and 1% level of significance, respectively.
[b] Confidence interval would be provided upon request.
Source: Asia Competitiveness Institute.

and Change in Government Expenditure on Education (ΔGEE) in causally driving growth rates of real GDP in Singapore over 1975–2012.

The results for the bi-variate causality analysis for Growth Rate of Real GDP (GGDP) and Change in Private Consumption Expenditure (ΔPCE) are presented in the first two rows of Table 4.5. It can be clearly observed that the causality ran from ΔPCE to GGDP and the results were visibly symmetric. To elaborate, as seen through the measure of linear dependence between GGDP and ΔPCE ($F_{x,y}$), the causality ran from ΔPCE to GGDP, implying that changes in private consumption expenditure has strongly driven growth in real GDP in Singapore over the years, as captured by its high statistical significance. This is also evident from the second row when we interchanged the x and y variables; the causality was strictly uni-directional, with ΔPCE causally influencing GGDP. It is also notable that in both cases, the instantaneous feedback between GGDP and ΔPCE ($F_{x\cdot y}$) was not just highly significant at the 1% level but also accounted for over 60% of the total linear dependence between GGDP and ΔPCE.

Next, we considered the bi-variate analysis for GGDP and Change in FDI Net Inflows (ΔFDI). The third and fourth rows from Table 4.5 again are consistent with our hypothesis. The third row suggests that FDI flows appeared to have a significant uni-directional causal impact on Singapore's GGDP, although it was relatively weaker compared to private consumption expenditure. The aggregate measure of linear dependence between GGDP and ΔFDI ($F_{x,y}$) was significant only at the 5% level. Interestingly, the instantaneous feedback ($F_{x \cdot y}$) between the two variables was also only weakly significant at the 10% level, which implies that over 80% of the aggregate linear dependence was accounted for by linear feedback from y to x ($F_{y \rightarrow x}$). On a similar note, as pointed out in the fourth row of Table 4.5, the causal direction from ΔFDI to GGDP was consistent with what was mentioned earlier, that is the linear dependence between ΔFDI and GGDP was driven by linear feedback from x to y ($F_{x \rightarrow y}$).

When we examined the importance of services value-added (captured in the fifth and sixth rows of Table 4.5), consistent results can be observed; services value-added exerted a strong causal influence on Singapore's economic growth. By decomposing the aggregate linear dependence between GGDP and ΔSVA, it was found that about 90% of that dependence was accounted for by the instantaneous feedback ($F_{x \cdot y}$) between the two variables, although there was a relatively strong uni-directional relationship that can be observed from ΔSVA to GGDP ($F_{y \rightarrow x}$). The results are also consistent in the next row; when the x and y variables were interchanged, the direction of causality running from ΔSVA to GGDP remained to be seen, which is in line with economic intuition whereby greater orientation towards services value-added would enhance economic growth.

Comparable results can be observed for the relationship between GGDP and Change in Government Expenditure on Education (ΔGEE). The aggregate measure of linear dependence between the two variables was not only highly significant (at the 1% level), but a decomposition of the linear dependence between the two variables also revealed that about 70% of it was driven by the linear feedback from ΔGEE to GGDP.

Extending this bilateral setting to a multi-directional setting, we then tested the causal importance of the vector of all the above variables in explaining economic growth in Singapore. The results are shown in Table 4.6.

It can be observed that there was a strong association between the *x* variable, GGDP, and the *y* vector consisting of the four variables we discussed above. The results are strongly consistent with what we have found earlier in the bilateral causality framework, with the measures of linear dependence between *x* and *y* ($F_{x,y}$) and the instantaneous feedback between *x* and *y* ($F_{x \cdot y}$) being highly significant at the 1% level. Furthermore, the linear feedback from *y* to *x* ($F_{y \to x}$) continued to be highly significant at the 1% level and also accounted for about 45% of the linear dependence between *x* and *y*.

These results reiterate the strong causal importance of variables such as private consumption expenditure, services value-added as well as government expenditure on education in driving Singapore's economic growth. They have not only contributed to Singapore's impressive growth transformation since 1975, but are also crucial variables to pay attention to from a policy point of view, to sustain the growth momentum in going forward. It is also pertinent to underline that despite the significance of FDI inflows in generating a significant and causal impact on Singapore's economic growth, in relative terms, other variables exert a more decisive influence than FDI inflows, underscoring the need to look beyond FDI as a source of growth.

4.6 Concluding Remarks and Policy Implications

Both Malaysia and Singapore have been considered in the growth literature as successful examples of countries that have managed to deliver impressive, sustained and robust economic growth over the last three decades or so. The development models adopted by these two economies, while unique in their own way, also have notable commonalities such as their outward orientation and emphasis on FDI and infrastructure-driven growth. Such policy strategies have been recognised as role models for other emerging and developing economies in the Asian region to emulate. While Singapore has already moved to a high-income status, fuelled in part by the rapid development and upgrading of its services sector, Malaysia has become an upper middle-income country, currently undertaking a lot of structural reforms to transition into the high-income category.

Decades after undergoing a structural transformation and navigating several external shocks, both countries are now grappling with some serious policy challenges that constrain their growth momentum in moving forward. Using this as the context, this chapter has empirically attempted to explore the causal drivers of economic growth in both Singapore and Malaysia, using data from 1975 to 2012 under the framework of Geweke causality. The idea of carrying out such exercise was not only to throw some light on the variables that have contributed to past growth, but also for policymakers to understand where the focus should be in the future for these economies to revitalise their growth momentum and continue to move on a sustainable growth trajectory.

The empirical results of the chapter suggest that Malaysia's new development trajectory should lie in rebalancing the economy towards a greater domestic demand and Singapore should embrace a growth model that goes beyond relying heavily on FDI as a source of economic growth.

The results also leave us with some important policy implications that warrant a mention. For Malaysia, firstly, it is important to recognise that while the country has been reliant on exports and FDI as the primary engines of growth since its independence, the transition from a middle-income to high-income status requires a substantial boost in domestic consumption. The shift from external demand to internal demand as a driver of economic growth has been observed in practically all high-income industrialised economies. Therefore, the thrust of Malaysia's new development trajectory should lie in rebalancing the economy towards greater domestic demand. Measures to stimulate private consumption may include:

(i) Reduction of consumption taxes, import tariffs and non-tariff barriers,
(ii) Maintaining low interest rates,
(iii) Provision of social services including health care and education to facilitate upward mobility and thus incomes,
(iv) Fiscal transfers to poor and lower middle-class households.

Secondly, strengthening local manufacturing and services sectors is paramount for Malaysia to sustain the growth momentum. While FDI provides the necessary technology and skills for the country to effectively participate in the global value chains, climbing up the value chains necessitates strong local capability. Furthermore, as competition for FDI has intensified with the emergence of numerous low-cost, labour-abundant countries, Malaysia has to compete on the basis of high productivity and more value add. Policies for boosting local industries may comprise:

(i) Improving the quality of education with an emphasis on technology and innovation,
(ii) Implementing programmes for skill development in collaboration with the private sector, particularly foreign firms,
(iii) Facilitating technological transfer from multinational corporations to local firms,
(iv) Providing incentives for firms to innovate and capitalise on new inventions.

For Singapore, as illustrated through the Geweke causality analysis, there is a need for the city-state to adopt a holistic approach to economic growth and development, a model that goes beyond relying heavily on FDI as a source of growth. As indicated earlier, the linear dependence between FDI and real GDP growth appears to be weaker than the linear dependence between the remaining variables and real GDP growth. To make a conscious effort in promoting a holistic approach to economic growth and development, Singapore's policy-makers must shift their policy attention towards:

(i) Strong internal demand,
(ii) Competitive local industries as indicated by an increase in domestic value added in the services sector, the leading sector in the Singapore's economy,
(iii) Investment in education both to strengthen human capital required for a knowledge-intensive economy and to promote upward mobility and incomes.

The Geweke causality results for Singapore also shed important light on the dynamics between FDI, local sector and economic development. While FDI remains vital in today's increasingly globalised world, it must be complemented by an equal, if not higher, amount of investment in industrial and technological capabilities, as well as human resource in the host country.

References

Aizenman, Joshua, and Ilan Noy. 2006. "FDI and trade — Two-Way Linkages?" *The Quarterly Review of Economics and Finance* 46 (3): 317–337.

Akamatsu, Kaname. 1962. "A Historical Pattern of Economic Growth in Developing Countries." *Journal of Developing Economies* 1: 3–25.

Bank Negara Malaysia. 2012. "Changing Drivers of Economic Growth in Malaysia," *Economic Developments in 2012*, Annual Report, 34–39.

Calderón, César, and Lin Liu. 2003. "The Direction of Causality between Financial Development and Economic Growth." *Journal of Development Economics* 72 (1): 321–334.

Chia, Siow Yue. 2013. "The ASEAN Economic Community: Progress, Challenges and Prospects." ADBI Working Paper No. 440, Asian Development Bank Institute, Tokyo.

Flaaen, Aaron, Ejaz Ghani and Saurabh Mishra. 2013. "How to Avoid Middle Income Traps? Evidence from Malaysia," Policy Research Working Paper 6427, World Bank, Washington DC.

Geweke, John. 1982. "Measurement of Linear Dependence and Feedback between Multiple Time Series." *Journal of the American Statistical Association* 77 (378): 304–313.

Geweke, John. 1984. "Measures of Conditional Linear Dependence and Feedback Between Time Series." *Journal of the American Statistical Association* 79: 907–915.

Granger, Clive W.J. 1988. "Some Recent Developments in a Concept of Causality." *Journal of Econometrics* 21: 161–194.

IMF. 2015. *2014 Article IV Consultation Staff Report on Malaysia.* IMF Country Report No. 15/58, International Monetary Fund, Washington DC.

Kumagai, Satoru. 2015. "The Middle-Income Trap from the Viewpoint of Trade Structures: Are the Geese Trapped or Still Flying?" *Journal of International Commerce Economics and Policy* 6 (3): 1–23.

Menon, Ravi. 2015. "An Economic History of Singapore: 1965–2065." Keynote Address at *the Singapore Economic Review Conference 2015*, Singapore, 5 August 2015. http://www.mas.gov.sg/News-and-Publications/Speeches-and-Monetary-Policy-Statements/Speeches/2015/An-Economic-History-of-Singapore.aspx.

Naughton, Barry and Kellee S. Tsai, eds. 2015. *State Capitalism, Institutional Adaptation and the Chinese Miracle.* New York: Cambridge University Press.

Rajan, Ramkishen S., Khee Giap Tan and Kong Yam Tan. 2014. *Fiscal Sustainability and Competitiveness in Europe and Asia.* London: Palgrave Macmillan.

Saner, Raymond, Lichia Yiu, and S. Gopinathan. 2014. "Policy Debate: Learning to Grow Beyond the Middle-Income Trap — Singapore as a Export Model?" *International Development Policy* 5 (3) (Online). https://poldev.revues.org/1803.

Tan, Khee Giap. 2014. "Hard Questions to Answer for Singapore's Development." *The Business Times*, March 6.

Tan, Khee Giap and Chee-Seng Cheng. 1995. "The Causal Nexus of Money, Output and Prices in Malaysia." *Applied Economics* 27 (12): 1245–1251.

Tan, Khee Giap and Kong Yam Tan. 2012. "More Productive Economy Still Needed." *The Straits Times*, June 13.

Tan, Khee Giap, Kong Yam Tan and Quek Xuan Yu. 2012. "Growing Pains in Growing Fairly." *The Straits Times*, January 4.

Tan, Khee Giap and Yan Yi Tan. 2014. "Promoting SMEs and Enhancing Labor Productivity in Singapore: A Policy Analysis." *Journal of International Commerce, Economics and Policy* 5 (3): 1–12.

Tan, Khee Giap, Randong Yuan and Sangiita Wei Cher Yoong. 2015. "Assessing Competitiveness and Development Strategies in 34 Greater China Economies." *International Journal of Chinese Culture and Business Management* 3 (4): 323–350.

The Economist. 2012. "The Rise of State Capitalism." January 21. http://www.economist.com/node/21543160.

The World Bank. 2015. *World Development Indicators Online.*

Vu, Khuong M. 2011. "Sources of Singapore's Economic Growth, 1965–2008: Trends, Patterns and Policy Implications." *ASEAN Economic Bulletin* 28: 315–336.

Xing, Li and Timothy M. Shaw. 2013. "The Political Economy of Chinese State Capitalism." *Journal of China and International Relations* 1 (1): 88–113.

Yusof, Zainal Aznam, and Deepak Bhattasali. 2008. "Economic Development and Growth in Malaysia: Policy Making and Leadership." Working Paper No. 27, Commission on Growth and Development, World Bank, Washington DC.

Discussant Notes 4.1

Mr Steven Wong
Deputy Chief Executive, Institute of Strategic and International Studies, Malaysia

The findings of the Geweke analysis of Malaysia appear intuitive to me, with a few of them actually giving pause for thought. I will start with comments on the structural features of the Malaysian economy to complement the findings from reduced form equations.

The Malaysian economy is a small and open economy. Trade is about 160% of GDP. It is often thought that the country has unlimited degrees of policy freedom but in reality the freedom is restricted to particular windows of opportunities and/or times. One common mistake is to always expect fiscal spending to cause trade imbalances (positive correlation). In Malaysia, fiscal and trade balances are quite often in opposition. Times of lowest economic activity can be associated with high trade balances and vice versa. For much of the 2000s, it took fiscal stimulus to keep the economy ticking over. During this time, high current account surpluses were also experienced and excess savings were invested abroad.

After 2009, fiscal spending went into overdrive. This may not be immediately obvious from federal government accounts but can be seen when the entire public sector is pieced together. In 2012, public sector debt actually exceeded 100% of GDP. In response to the fiscal impulses, we began to see reducing (but still positive) trade balances. This needs to be understood because the strength and directionality of causality can be muted.

It is to the discredit of Malaysia that we do not have good investment numbers. In order to track foreign direct investment movements, we have to rely primarily on corporate investment figures in the balance of payments. The problem is that this includes retained profits of multinational companies, including those of big oil companies. If the latter do not decide to repatriate (via dividends or loan repayments), the money is treated as going out of the country and coming back in again. Investment trends therefore can, to some degree, be dictated by decisions that are unrelated to economic development.

The Malaysian economy today is of course not the economy of the mid-1980s. As the paper on Malaysia has found, there has been massive structural change in the post-1998 period. The composition of GDP and exports are very different today. When it comes to present-day policy implications, it is important that we do not get trapped in the idea of the Malaysian economy in the past.

Going forward, between 2010 and 2020, Malaysia will need investment of RM1.3 trillion or US$334 billion if it is to meet its target of US$15,000 per capita Gross National Income (GNI). It is a simple model: you prime the economy with foreign and domestic investment and get the growth. This is economic transformation by PowerPoint not by economic theory — you only need a calculator. Little account has been taken as to what happens to factor markets, prices, balance of payments and everything else in the interim.

The approaches also gloss over the qualitative differences that have been happening. There has been little hand-wringing that the share of manufacturing output has shrunk to about 25% of GDP at present from 30% two decades ago. This decline is not necessarily of concern because new and higher value-added products are replacing the inventory of existing ones. In contrast to semi-conductors, for example, Malaysia is now receiving investments in such things as energy storage devices such as electrical batteries for cars. Previously, there were investments in solar panels, something that we did not have before.

On policy implications, industrial parks are less important now than they were in the past. Today, the focus is on corridors and hubs, especially oil and gas. Inclusive growth and sustainable development are good recommendations at any time but it must be understood that for Malaysia to move out of the middle-income trap, it will have to grow at a faster rate than it has been. Certain sectors of the economy, labour market and regions will invariably lag, while others sprint ahead. At the end of the day, technology, innovation and investment increase the degrees of freedom that a country has. Like Singapore, Malaysia depends on remaining keen and sensitive to the exogenous change variables rather than believing in the total efficacy of domestic policy levers and controls.

One thing that comes out from the paper is that success breeds success. It is when you have growth that you find people, companies and countries start to get very interested in you. This is something that we do not make enough of: how economic growth sets a country apart and attracts investment. These are some structural perspectives and observations to complement the findings from the reduced form equations. I think a bit more work is required on the policy section but overall a very interesting paper.

Discussant Notes 4.2

Dr Basant Kumar Kapur
Professor, Department of Economics,
National University of Singapore

This is a thought-provoking study. I will first start with some general comments before going into the specifics. I will take a bit of liberty to not only be confined to the model but also offer some general reflections on the Singapore economy. In addition, I will focus more on the conceptual framework of the study and not so much on the detailed results for the various periods.

This study essentially adopts a reduced form approach which has its merits. However, sometimes we may wish to take a step back and look at some underlying structural considerations so as to have a deeper understanding of the dynamics of the economy and of factors which drive the economy. Such structural considerations can help to guide the reduced form modelling in future works.

One of the most important determinants of a country's competitiveness is its productivity, which has to be understood in a broad sense. It is not simply productivity in manufacturing but rather the overall productivity of the economy — the quality of the infrastructure, the educational system and so on. Furthermore, we should look not only at the level of productivity at a point in time, but also the rate of productivity growth over time. With high productivity, a country can afford to pay higher wages to its workers and still maintain competitiveness. In other words, high wages do not necessarily imply low competitiveness if productivity is sufficiently high.

Another important determinant of a country's competitiveness is its exchange rate *vis-à-vis* other countries'. A useful summary measure of the foregoing considerations is the concept of relative unit labour cost (RULC). This is the labour cost per unit of output, measured in a common currency, relative to that of our competitors in ASEAN, China, India and elsewhere in the world. RULC takes into account labour wages, productivity (since we are looking at unit labour costs), and exchange rate (since we are measuring the various countries' unit labour costs in a common currency). Furthermore, aside from affecting GDP directly, RULC also works through foreign direct investment (FDI) and export. It is an important determinant variable for a number of key variables for our economies. Thus, I think it would be nice if the authors can incorporate the RULC measure into their econometric analysis.

One problem with the study is that the data used seem to be very country-specific. To analyse a particular country, it only uses the dataset of that country. However, given the inter-connectedness of economies, it is advisable to incorporate other countries' variables into the analysis. Even though the causality could be uni-directional, incorporating other countries' variables can help us understand better what drives key economic variables in Singapore.

Next, for Singapore, and other countries as well, another important factor is R&D. It is a major driver of Singapore's competitiveness, increasingly so as the years go by and especially as we move up the value chain. Both domestic and foreign R&D are important influences on our productivity growth over time and also on our competitiveness through the creation of new products, new services and so on. In addition, foreign R&D can help Singapore through various technology transfer mechanisms — through FDI, imports of sophisticated capital goods and other channels. In short, the entire R&D sector is an important driver of the Singapore economy.

In general, some key variables such as RULC, productivity, and R&D which impact upon and which are also influenced by the variables investigated in the study could have been incorporated into the econometric analysis.

Let me now turn to more specific comments on particular variables in the study. The study rightly points out that human capital is an important factor for Singapore's GDP growth but there seems to be no variable in the model which represents human capital explicitly. Next, the study downplays the importance of external demand, finding it not significant in the econometric analysis. However, this is rather puzzling since Singapore is an export-oriented economy. The authors should explore other measures of external demand besides external balances. For example, they can directly investigate exports to see if they can obtain better results on the role of external demand.

On the attraction of FDI, it is mentioned that one of the attractions is the well-functioning financial market in Singapore. However, much FDI into Singapore tends to be externally financed, in particular from the source countries. So it is not clear how important the Singapore financial market is in terms of attracting FDI. The issue here, in my opinion, is one about data: if we confine ourselves to Singapore data alone, we cannot capture the effects of other determinants. It is quite puzzling as to why net income of Singapore from abroad, and Singapore's net foreign assets held abroad, should be major explanatory factors for FDI inflows. It is intuitive to think that FDI inflows are strongly linked to economic conditions in source countries. For example, if the US is doing well, companies there may have more funds to finance investments abroad. This highlights the need to bring other countries' variables into the analysis.

In addition, some scaling of the variables would also be helpful. For example, instead of only studying GDP growth, the authors may also look at studying the growth of GDP per capita. Additionally, the authors might want to consider using the ratio of FDI to GDP, instead of just FDI by itself.

Finally, I would like to share some general reflections on the Singapore economy. The Singapore economy is facing some degree of 'hollowing out' whereby many manufacturers are moving out of Singapore in recent years due to our curbs on foreign worker inflows and rising labour costs. From my point of view, this is to some extent a healthy development. We seek to move up the value chain so having lower value-added industries moving out of Singapore is in line with this objective. However, too rapid a pace of hollowing out may also be problematic, and so the nature and speed of economic restructuring need to be carefully studied.

Our future lies in us moving up the value chain. This should be one of our primary concern. Singapore should look to diversify into service activities, have more high value-added products in our manufacturing sector and place a stronger emphasis on headquarter functions. Though firms have relocated their factories to elsewhere in the region, we should strive to retain their finance, sales and marketing, corporate strategy, and R&D activities in Singapore. This is one way in which we can continue to provide valuable services to the region and to the world economy, thereby maintaining our competitiveness.

Chapter 5

SINGAPORE'S ECONOMIC DEVELOPMENT, 1965–2020: REVIEW, REFLECTION AND PERSPECTIVE

5.1 Introductory Notes

To review the past is not just to retain our harsh memory, but more importantly, it is to better understand how far Singapore has travelled and transformed in the process of nation-building from the long and uncertain road of fear and anxiety into a cosmopolitan city-state today. Only through a better appreciation of the past efforts of Singapore's founding leaders and contributions by the pioneer generation of Singaporeans can we continue to move forward with resilience and optimism.

To provide a broad background for contrast, it is useful to compare the growth of the economic pie or Gross Domestic Product (GDP) and the level of GDP per capita achieved over time amongst Singapore, Hong Kong and Malaysia. It is interesting to compare the achievements of Singapore to Malaysia given how these two countries went their separate ways five decades ago, while benchmarking Singapore against Hong Kong is always relevant as both city-states are approximately of the same population size although very different in terms of socio-political economy.

As exhibited in Figure 5.1, the GDP of Hong Kong began to surge ahead of Singapore and Malaysia after the mid-1970s with aggressive expansion of the economic pie occurring through the 1980s and beyond 2000 — this was mainly fueled by the robust growing of China

Figure 5.1. Nominal GDP for Singapore, Malaysia and Hong Kong, 1961–2013

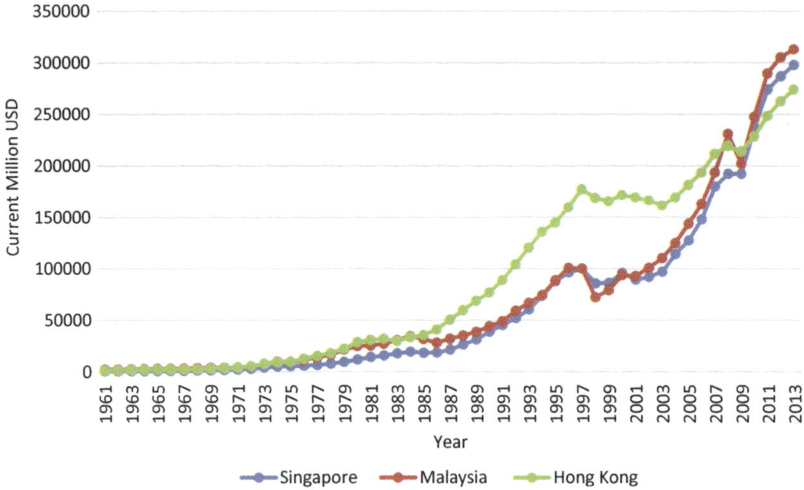

Source: The World Bank.

economy, especially after her motherland's accession to the World Trade Organisation in 2002. The size of the Hong Kong economy slowed down in 2008 and was sharply overtaken by Singapore and Malaysia from 2009 onwards, while the latter was not much affected by the global financial tsunami that broke out around this time.

Notwithstanding Malaysia's well-endowed natural resources including plantation crops, commodities for exports, natural gas, as well as a relatively bigger domestic market and a much larger population base, Singapore has been able to closely track the size of the Malaysian economy throughout the last five decades of economic expansion even with great handicaps in terms of poor natural endowment, a smaller population and domestic market size. However, the GDP gap between the two economies began to marginally widen since 2011. Singapore's infrastructure bottleneck, manpower capacity constraint and domestic political pressure for a slower pace of economic growth may further restrict business and economic activities.

Figure 5.2. Nominal GDP Per Capita for Singapore, Malaysia and Hong Kong, 1961–2013

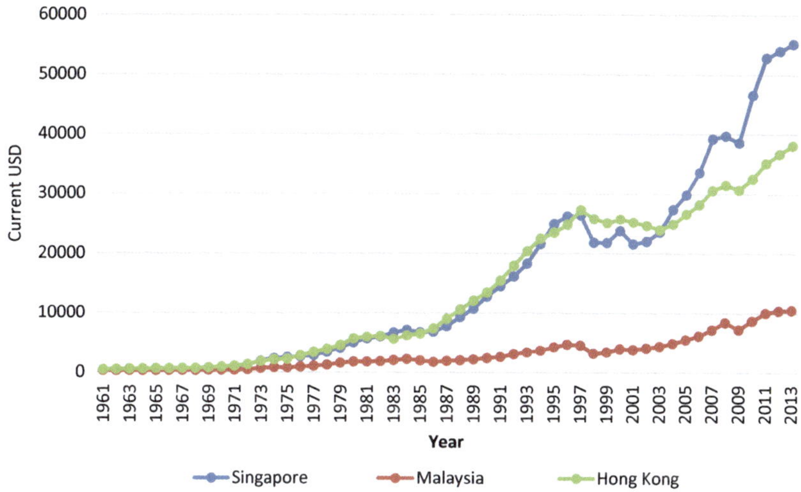

Source: The World Bank.

As summarised in Figure 5.2, in terms of GDP per capita, Singapore was tracking closely with Hong Kong throughout the 1970s and 1980s, before it dipped marginally below Hong Kong after the Asian Financial Crisis (AFC) that broke out in 1997. Singapore then recovered robustly to overtake Hong Kong with a widening margin since 2004, partly propelled by a stronger and appreciating Singapore dollar while the Hong Kong dollar remains pegged to the greenback since 1984.

By 2013, the nominal GDP per capita for Singapore with a population of 5.6 million stood at US$55,182, while Hong Kong registered at US$38,123 with a population of 7.8 million, substantially 30% lower. Rather worrisome for Malaysia, a nation of 28 million people, is that her GDP per capita dipped slightly in 1997 and has remained trapped at around the US$10,000 level since 2010, which warrants a closer study.

In comparing and contrasting the economic performances of Malaysia and Hong Kong, for the ensuing part of the chapter, we would dwell in greater detail into pinning down the essence of Singapore's economic growth strategies, in particular, the role of the government as to how it differs from others. We would address some of the problems Singapore encountered, identify issues pertaining to the challenging economic restructuring and implications related to the potential GDP path ahead.

5.2 Reviewing Singapore's Economic Development after the Exit from Malaysia

Exactly five decades ago, Singapore abruptly became a country overnight, literally and rather unexpectedly, on 9 August 1965, with no outpouring of triumph or jubilation accompanying the birth of the new nation. It was with shock and reluctance that Singapore took on the uphill task of nationhood building, as a resource-poor island-state with no economic hinterland, exacerbated by hostile relations with neighbouring economies, including Malaysia and Indonesia, as well as domestic political and social unrest.

A serious racial riot exploded in July 1964, which led to the declaration of curfew and a further severe racial rioting was repeated in July 1965. The social fabric of this island-state characterised as being multi-ethnic, multi-religious and multi-lingual was torn apart. Confrontation broke out with neighbouring Indonesia and only ended after a peace agreement was signed in August 1966, which disrupted economic development somewhat. Street rioting by leftwing activists throughout the 1960s caused tremendous tension amongst the multi-racial community. Singapore's long-term stability was seriously threatened.

As for many citizens then, including the political leadership from both sides of the Causeway, Singapore had neither the necessary attributes nor sufficient conditions to become a viable nation. In fact, there was a time when many people doubted Singapore could ever make it, but we did and the rest is now history. The Republic of Singapore today is a highly liveable and economically viable cosmopolitan city-state, enjoying the highest degree of racial harmony, sound industrial relations and social stability as measurable by any international yardstick, which should not therefore be taken for granted.

The cornerstone of Singapore's pioneering success lies in the facilitative role of the government exemplified by pragmatic public policy formulation through a proactive and lean civil service system with zero tolerance for corruption. In a relatively short period of time, an impressive 85% ownership of public housing by the populace was achieved under the innovative co-payment Central Provident Fund (CPF) scheme with contributions from both employers and employees, sparing the government from the need for an encumbering state welfare system.

Given the lack of natural resources, Singapore had to undertake long-term investment in its people through education by establishing high quality schools, tertiary institutions and universities. As Singapore aggressively solicited, grew and retained foreign direct investment from multinational corporations (MNCs) through the work of the Economic Development Board (EDB), skills of indigenous workers were fast becoming obsolete and could no longer match the modern skill contents required by the newly created jobs.

Over the decades, the Republic has gradually and consistently built up a comprehensive island-wide physical infrastructure network with roads, expressways and the mass rapid transit (MRT) system, integrating them with sustainable and environmentally conscious practices. In retrospect, infrastructure development and investment should have been ramped up by several notches to cope with greater demands from a rapid growth in population, but prudent consideration must be given in the light of the uncertain nature of economic performance. The balance needs to be struck between ensuring sustainable and efficient use of government revenues versus increasingly onerous government expenditures incurred. Preparation for a rapidly ageing population with longer life spans, owing to years of proper healthcare services, will also need further consideration.

Given its limited land mass, Singapore became one of the most densely populated cities globally in 2013, with the total population reaching 5.6 million. To grow and achieve the critical mass effect, Singapore embarked upon the external wing policy in the early 1990s with International Enterprise (IE), which was created by Singapore to help promote Singaporean companies to expand abroad to overcome her limited domestic market size. Singapore has thus successfully plugged herself into the global trading networks with international trade and services now amounting to three times the size of her GDP by running highly efficient regional hubs for financial, aviation, maritime, logistics and telecommunication activities.

After decades of prudent government budgeting and the establishment of professional investment vehicles such as the Government Investment Corporation (GIC) and Temasek Holdings to manage government surpluses, Singapore has accumulated ample financial resources that could be called upon to cope and deal with future challenges and potential long-drawn-out external shocks, so long as we think rationally as a group and behave with responsibility as one united people within a pluralistic society.

When Singapore left Malaysia in 1965, her nominal GDP was at US$0.97 billion as compared to Malaysia's US$3.2 billion, which was less than a third of Malaysia's economy. Singapore's economy quickly expanded to half of Malaysia's GDP size in 1977, reached nearly 69% by 1987 and continued to expand to reach the size of Malaysia's GDP by 1997, as both economies were propelled forward at around 9% per annum between 1987 and 1997. As a highly open export-oriented economy, Singapore was more vulnerable to external shocks, and the size of its economy has hovered around 95% of Malaysia between 2007 and 2013 as shown in Table 5.1.

Table 5.1. Major Macroeconomic Indicators for Singapore and Malaysia, 1987–2013

Singapore and Malaysia: GDP Growth*, Unemployment Rate, Inflation & Gini Coefficient

	Real GDP Growth/ Gini Coefficient		Unemployment Rate		Composite CPI Growth	
Fiscal Year	**Malaysia**	**Singapore**	**Malaysia**	**Singapore**	**Malaysia**	**Singapore**
1998	–7.4%	–2.2%	3.2%	2.5%	5.3%	–0.3%
1999	6.1%	6.1%	3.4%	2.8%	2.7%	0%
2000	8.9%	8.9%	3.0%	2.7%	1.5%	1.4%
2001	0.5% (0.46)	–0.9% (0.45)	3.5%	2.7%	1.4%	1.0%
2002	5.4%	4.2%	3.5%	3.6%	1.8%	–0.4%
2003	5.8%	4.4%	3.6%	4.0%	1.0%	0.5%
2004	6.8%	9.5%	3.5%	3.4%	1.5%	1.7%
2005	5.3%	7.5%	3.5%	3.1%	3.0%	0.4%
2006	5.6% (0.46)	8.7% (0.47)	3.3%	2.7%	3.6%	1.0%
2007	6.3%	9.1%	3.2%	2.1%	2.0%	2.1%
2008	4.8%	1.8%	3.3%	2.2%	5.4%	6.5%
2009	–1.5%	–0.6%	3.7%	3.0%	0.6%	0.6%
2010	7.4% (0.44)	15.2% (0.47)	3.4%	2.2%	1.7%	2.8%

GDP Growth	**1987–1997**	**1998–2008**	**GDP Size**	**1977/1987**	**1997**	**2007**	**2013**
Malaysia	8.9% p.a.	4.4% p.a.	Malaysia	US$14/32 billion	US$100 billion	US$194 billion	US$313 billion
Singapore	9.2% p.a.	5.2% p.a.	Singapore	US$7/ 22 billion	US$100 billion	US$180 billion	US$298 billion
			Singapore/ Malaysia	50%/69%	100%	93%	95%

Source: The World Bank, Department of Statistics Singapore, Department of Statistics Malaysia.

Note: *2000–2020 Potential GDP Growth Rate: Malaysia: 5.5%; Singapore: 4.5% (projected by the ACI at LKYSPP, NUS); 2013 Per Capita GDP: Singapore US$55,182; Malaysia US$10,538.

Singapore started as a society of immigrants with multiple ethnicities, religions and languages. Being a poor and new nation, improving standards of living through job creation and public housing provision within a harmonious social setting was the immediate task of the government, which was still undergoing intense struggles with the left-wing political movement then. Given that ethnic Chinese-Singaporeans formed the big majority of the population, the collaboration of the Chinese merchants and their leadership role in the community, working in support of the government's development strategy, underpinned the strong economic foundation and social environment vital for Singapore's subsequent economic takeoff since the 1980s.

President Tony Tan Keng Yam, in his speech at the Singapore Chinese Chamber of Commerce & Industry SG50 Outstanding Chinese Business Pioneer Awards on 6 February 2015 at Ritz Carlton Hotel, Singapore, said, "The pioneer generation of Chinese entrepreneurs demonstrated great fortitude in the face of many difficulties in the early year of Singapore's growth journey. As the Singapore economy evolved and progressed, these business pioneers seized opportunities and adapted to the environment. Our pioneers believed in Singapore's future and remained rooted here. Apart from succeeding in their respective fields, many of these pioneers also made it a point to give back to society".

In fact, we should also pay tribute to the broader business communities, especially the small- and medium-sized enterprises (SMEs) that have provided crucial social stability to the society in terms of employment, exemplary work ethic and entrepreneurship. During the transition of economic restructuring, the government tried very hard to attract MNCs to create jobs and acquire global corporate management skills for Singaporeans. The Singapore business community, including big and small companies, has contributed to Singapore's national defence plan and in preservation of promoting education, which helps to ensure a competitive economy, strong security in defence, the values of traditional culture and harmonious racial relations.

According to estimations by the Asia Competitiveness Institute (ACI) at the Lee Kuan Yew School of Public Policy (LKYSPP), National University of Singapore (NUS), the potential GDP growth for Singapore and Malaysia was projected to be at 4.5% and 5.5%, respectively, for the period of 2000 to 2020; the former appears to have grown above its potential level whereas the latter grew considerably below its potential output over the period of 1998 to 2008. Price stability prevailed in both countries from 1998 to 2010, as inflation was registered at 1.3% for Singapore and higher for Malaysia at 2.4%. Correspondingly over the same period, Singapore managed to achieve fairly low unemployment rate averaging at 2.9% as compared to a higher rate of 3.4% for Malaysia. As for income disparity measured by the Gini coefficient, it was around 0.46 for Singapore and Malaysia from 2000 onwards, and both countries could have done better on this count.

Based on the annual economic competitiveness ranking conducted by the ACI at LKYSPP that tracks ASEAN-10 economies from 2000 onwards, Singapore consistently ranks in the top position, followed by Malaysia. As revealed by the standardised score, the former (1.4463) is almost twice as competitive as the latter (0.5766; see Tan *et al.*, 2013; Tan and Tan, 2014).

We thus conjectured that such superior relative economic competitive advantage enjoyed by Singapore over Malaysia can be traced to differences in policy formulation and implementation. There exist relative government inefficiencies, a lack of adequate governance and discriminatory policies in favour of "sons of soil" or *bumiputra* as it is referred to in the Malay language, which have been broadly implemented in various fields including businesses, education, housing and land policies. Furthermore, as Malaysia moved into a two-party system since more than a decade ago, precious effort and time have been diverted to long-drawn public policy debates, political conflicts and social confrontations at the expense of formulating longer-term economic growth strategies and realising policy objectives.

5.3 Singapore's Economic Takeoff and Transformation into a Cosmopolitan City

To fully appreciate Singapore's economic growth model, we have to look at the growth strategies at different phases of transformation over the past five decades. Between 1965 and 1986, Singapore experienced an average GDP growth of 8.6% per annum under the labour-intensive production-driven phase where the primary objective was employment creation. Between 1987 and 1997, the Republic registered an average GDP growth of 9.3% per annum under the capital-intensive investment-driven phase where the objective was to upgrade the quality of economic growth through labour-saving strategy.

Between 1998 and 2008, Singapore went through a much lower average GDP growth of 5.2% per annum under the innovation-based technology-driven phase as the city-state attempted to move up the technological ladder. By 2009 and beyond, as regional competition intensified and business costs started to hike, Singapore entered into the productivity enhancement value-added-driven phase where the economy is currently facing some adjustment difficulties, especially in the business services and construction sectors, which have become used to an abundant supply of relatively cheaper foreign labour.

Currently, the densely populated cosmopolitan island-state is facing twin policy dilemma with some difficult choices to make. On one hand, it is about the desirable magnitude of economic growth, which would have a direct bearing on the levels of wage growth and labour productivity growth. On the other hand, the public must also decide on a socially tolerable and politically acceptable foreign workforce pool, which would impact on business costs and economic activities. Thus, this section intends to sharpen the focus pertaining to the discourse on public policies related to Singapore's growth strategies as all growth options will necessarily involve policy trade-offs.

Firstly, has Singapore's economy expanded too fast with too high GDP growth? Would problems such as income disparity, rising housing prices, public transportation and traffic congestion be avoided if growth were moderated? Secondly, how can the government significantly mitigate these problems through fundamental changes in public policies even as Singapore strives to be more inclusive? Thirdly, as public discontent escalates between the haves and the have-nots, can income disparity be significantly mitigated to prevent the emergence of an economic underclass without resorting to a comprehensive social welfare system that will not only be a financial burden on the state but a disincentive to taxpayers? This is especially pertinent as Singapore's population ages and lifespan increases.

As illustrated in Figure 5.3, Singapore went into an era of discontinued economic growth interspersed with recoveries and recessions, yet still managed to achieve an average GDP growth of 5.2% per annum over the period of 1998 to 2008, notwithstanding the three externally driven crises the nation encountered. These are the 1998 recession

Figure 5.3. Singapore's GDP Growth Cycles and Trends, 1965–2013

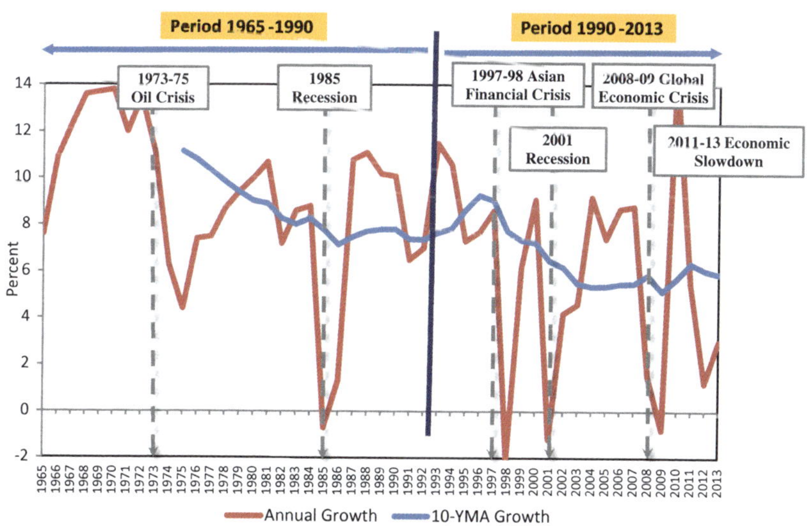

Source: The World Bank.

caused by the 1997 AFC, the bursting of the American 'dotcom' bubbles in 2001 and the outbreak of the Severe Acute Respiratory Syndrome (SARS) in 2003. Singapore's economy contracted again in 2009 due to the US subprime-led global financial tsunami.

Note that between 1987 and 1997, when the external environment was still favourable, Singapore went through robust annual GDP growth of 9.2%. As with all maturing economies, it is an enviable growth rate that is unlikely to be repeated. Interestingly in those years, not many in Singapore complained that growth was too high or too fast, as the economic gains were more evenly distributed and the public at large was less outspoken.

5.4 Did the Singapore Economy Grow Too High and Too Fast between 2000 and 2010?

According to the 2013 data from the International Monetary Fund (IMF), Singaporeans are the third wealthiest in the world in terms of per capita GDP, ranked after Qatar and Luxembourg. However, such rankings are not meaningful if we also recognise Singapore as perhaps the world's most vulnerable open economy with trade being three times the size of her GDP. When the 2009 US subprime-led crisis kicked in, Singapore was amongst the first to tailspin into a recession, forcing the government to dip into its coffers significantly to help ease the costs of the economic downturn for companies and minimise pains of unemployment by deploying the untargeted Jobs Credit Scheme.

Given the slow recovery of the US economy, notwithstanding quantitative easing by the European Central Bank starting in March 2015, the external debt-driven fiscal weakness will continue to ferment within the European Union (EU). The economic crisis plaguing European economies are unlikely to be quickly resolved as they reflect deep-seated structural problems of eroding competitiveness and heavy burdens of the welfare system. The US and the EU, being two major export markets, present unique challenges of external shocks for Singapore's highly open economy.

In our recent research on Asia's drivers of growth (see Tan *et al.*, 2014), we concluded that given existing trade linkages, the US and the EU are still amongst the major engines of growth for all Asian economies, except Taiwan and Hong Kong. As Western economies get chilled, economies in Asia, especially Singapore, will be the first to catch a severe cold even though we exercise regularly, with antibiotics on standby. We therefore cannot be immune from troubles from these developed Western regions.

Singapore went through a drastic economic slowdown in 2012 soon after the US subprime-led recession in 2009. It will become more expensive to finance the European sovereign debts with deteriorating international confidence as the required painful austerity measures continue to be resisted by the European public at large. In the face of such headwinds, no amount of jobs credit scheme could have averted the rapid economic slowdown in 2012 for Singapore because as a small and highly open economy, we can only strive to be better prepared and effectively deal with exogenous shocks over which we have very limited control.

Amongst the most misunderstood grievance the public often raise is that the Singapore economy has been growing too fast and was growing at all costs. Such arguments inappropriately assume that the government could easily control and decide the speed and magnitude of GDP growth, accelerating or decelerating the economy as desired.

Even if it were to be true, it does not make logical sense that when the external environment is highly favourable, the government should curtail employment growth by tightening the labour market and driving up business costs in a bid to slow economic growth. Such a direct intervention approach would lead to serious repercussions on businesses and potential investors. Should multinationals conclude such government measures are the official mode of economic management and make a decision to shift their investment plans elsewhere, it would be most unlikely to see them relocate back to Singapore.

5.5 Strategies and Policy Trade-Off Going Forward: Can We Have the Cake and Eat It?

It is thus unwise for the government to impede robust economic growth in good times through curtailing employment growth in response to public resistance to the presence of a large foreign workforce or being pressured by other social-political considerations. Such populist approaches could spell trouble for the government *du jour.* It is unrealistic to expect the government to dip into its funds regularly for special transfers or to be able to sustain balanced budgets for the full term of the elected government, should the future be riddled by a higher frequency of recessions that are propelled by circumstances outside of one's control.

During the period between 1998 and 2008, the average economic growth was 5.2% and this masked the volatility brought on by recessions that were followed by near double-digit growth rates. Over this period, Singapore actually achieved annual employment growth of 2.9% and annual average productivity growth of 2.5%. This performance nearly halved the annual growth rate of 9.3% for the period 1987 to 1997.

The question at hand, then, is not whether Singapore's GDP has expanded too fast or if the authorities have pursued growth at all costs. Regardless of growth quantum, it falls upon those in the government to muster better plans and coordinate government agencies to better manage anticipated infrastructure demand; identify and understand the types of jobs being generated, including the suitability of skill sets required from the local workforce; forecast public housing needed, make provision for affordable and accessible healthcare and maintain a sustainable living environment in support of a bigger population. In fact, we would venture to argue that even if the average GDP growth were to be slower by half for the period of 1998 to 2008, many of these aforementioned problems might continue to prevail with their severity, amidst growing pressure of budgetary difficulties.

It would be a misdirection of criticism to blame the government for seizing robust economic growth when the external environment permits. It is precisely the adoption of such pro-growth strategy that ensures prudent and sustainable budgets over the business cycles. It is now most timely for us to re-examine the fundamental philosophy underpinning our public policies, by re-assessing the new role of the government in the pursuit of an even more inclusive society even as we attempt to capture the available opportunities in favourable external environments.

Rephrasing again the issue and question at hand, which deserves serious consideration and rational thinking: Should the government cave in to populist political demands by artificially and abruptly choking off the essential foreign labour supply required for business expansion and hence, slowing down economic and wage growth, or should we rather deploy greater efforts and accumulate government surpluses to better coordinate public policies to help sharpen the ability to compete through transformational productivity and upskill enhancement programmes for those who fall behind?

5.6 Rapid Globalisation: Economic Restructuring and Issues Encountered

Singapore had taken full advantage of the globalisation process by plugging herself into a global trading network through the pioneering of free trade agreements (FTAs), facilitated by a rising stature as an international financial centre as well as an efficient international aviation and maritime hub. As much as Singapore has reaped the benefits of globalisation through trade and finance, with it were unwelcomed side effects such as widening income disparity, rising housing prices and overcrowded public transportation.

However, as Singapore moves up the technological ladder with intensified regional competition coming from neighbouring Asian countries such as China and India, skill sets possessed by Singaporeans born in the 1950s and 1960s are fast becoming irrelevant to higher value-added jobs generated. Attempts to boost productivity have not yielded the results needed to match the demand of a rapidly restructuring economy. Singaporeans from low-income households that received only secondary level or lower education are increasingly trapped in an economic underclass, and are further disadvantaged by factors such as larger family sizes, social capital and information network disadvantages. Singapore's income disparity as measured by the Gini coefficient has rapidly worsened since the late 1990s, registering its worst reading of 0.48 in 2012.

With the quickening pace of globalisation, heavy subsidies for education, healthcare, public utilities and CPF top-ups were made available through special transfers from the annual budget, which came to $2.6 billion per year from 2000 to 2009. According to computation by the Department of Statistics in 2013, such special transfers were able to contain the Gini coefficient at around 0.44, similar to the level achieved in 2000.

Over the same period, we have observed a widening gap in the growth of income for the highest 20 percentile households versus the lowest 20 percentile households. It behooves economists to examine why the income gap is widening; the thesis that globalisation and technology advances are rendering lowly-trained skills obsolete may not offer a comprehensive account of the widening gap.

5.7 Benchmarking Economic Performances of Two City-States: Hong Kong versus Singapore

Singapore is not as fortunate as Hong Kong, which was able to and is still benefitting from the Mainland and Hong Kong Closer Economic Partnership Arrangement (CEPA) as well as the World Trade Organisation (WTO) Plus concessions, with China rapidly expanding as an economic powerhouse. While Hong Kong's defence is entirely taken care of by the People's Liberation Army (PLA) of her motherland, Singapore reserves a substantial portion of her annual budget to maintain her defence capabilities. More than occasional frictions with neighbouring countries distract from what would have otherwise been even closer economic cooperation within ASEAN.

In comparison, Hong Kong's GDP grew at an annual rate of 6% in the 1987 to 1997 period and 3.8% in the 1998 to 2008 period, about 40% lower than what Singapore achieved over the same period. Interestingly, when we contrasted and observed the performances of the two city-states at times of recession, Hong Kong would sink deeper, and when the economy recovered, Singapore would rebound higher. In comparison, Singapore's GDP was only 43% of Hong Kong's between 1977 and 1987, before it quickly caught up to 56% and 85% in 1997 and 2007, respectively. It has since surpassed Hong Kong by 9% in 2013.

One may conclude that the positive interventionist approach enables the Singapore government to squeeze relatively more growth from the economy than the non-interventionist Hong Kong authorities. Furthermore, Hong Kong's economy is constrained by the rigid Hong Kong-US dollar pegged exchange rate regime that prevents the economy from making cost adjustments through exchange rate movements, which necessitates deep price corrections in the stock market and risks severe downturn in the real estate sector during recession.

The Hong Kong government's Long Term Fiscal Planning Working Group pointed out in 2014 that "if Hong Kong government still insists

Table 5.2. Major Macroeconomic Indicators for Singapore and Hong Kong, 1998–2013

Singapore and Hong Kong: GDP Growth*, Unemployment Rate, Inflation & Gini Coefficient

Fiscal Year	Real GDP Growth/ Gini Coefficient		Unemployment Rate		Composite CPI Growth	
	Hong Kong	Singapore	Hong Kong	Singapore	Hong Kong	Singapore
1998	–5.9%	–2.2%	2.2%	2.5%	2.9%	–0.3%
1999	2.5%	6.1%	4.6%	2.8%	–4.0%	0%
2000	7.7%	8.9%	6.2%	2.7%	–3.7%	1.4%
2001	0.5% (0.53)	–0.9% (0.45)	4.9%	2.7%	–1.7%	1.0%
2002	1.7%	4.2%	5.1%	3.6%	–3.1%	–0.4%
2003	3.1%	4.4%	7.3%	4.0%	–2.5%	0.5%
2004	8.7%	9.5%	7.9%	3.4%	–0.4%	1.7%
2005	7.4%	7.5%	6.7%	3.1%	0.9%	0.4%
2006	7.0% (0.53)	8.7% (0.47)	5.6%	2.7%	2.1%	1.0%
2007	6.5%	9.1%	4.8%	2.1%	2.0%	2.1%
2008	2.1%	1.8%	4.0%	2.2%	4.3%	6.5%
2009	–2.5%	–0.6%	3.6%	3.0%	0.6%	0.6%
2010	6.8% (0.53)	15.2% (0.47)	5.2%	2.2%	2.3%	2.8%

GDP Growth	1987–1997	1998–2008	GDP Size	1977/1987	1997	2007	2013
Hong Kong	6.0% p.a.	3.8% p.a.	Hong Kong	US$16/51 billion	US$177 billion	US$212 billion	US$274 billion
Singapore	9.2% p.a.	5.2% p.a.	Singapore	US$7/22 billion	US$100 billion	US$180 billion	US$298 billion
			Singapore/ Hong Kong	43%/43%	56%	85%	109%

Source: The World Bank, Department of Statistics Singapore, Hong Kong Census and Statistics Department.

Note: *2000–2020 Potential GDP Growth Rate: Hong Kong: 3.5%; Singapore: 4.5% (projected by the ACI at LKYSPP, NUS); 2013 Per Capita GDP: Singapore US$55,182; Hong Kong US$38,123.

on all kinds of public service expenditures and based on the present trend, structural government budget deficit is projected to prevail in seven years' time (2021), and all government surpluses will be used up by 2028, thereafter would have to resort to borrowing". This is the fiscal predicament of Hong Kong after having built up a comprehensive and expensive welfare system that Singapore must not be indulged in.

In contrast, the Singapore government has been under pressure on how to manage their surpluses from years of economic growth to cater for large demands for special transfers or subsidies in each annual government budget to mitigate income disparity and the effect of an ageing population. In fact, the special transfers from the annual budget have doubled since 2009, and are expected to remain at the same level or higher in the future.

5.8 Overcoming Demanding Public Expectations and External Challenges: Reflection and Perspective

After the robust GDP growth of 15% for 2010 from 1% contraction in 2009, Singapore has registered a GDP growth at an average rate of 3.3% per annum between 2011 and 2014, which is lower than the potential rate of 4.5% per annum estimated by the ACI. The lower growth performance was mainly due to labour supply adjustments by the government to improve productivity coupled with pressure from the widespread public demand to scale down on foreign workforce engagement. Companies with orders were therefore not able to expand their business activities with some considering relocation, which posed a bigger risk for Singapore. This is a policy area that Singapore needs to calibrate and tread very carefully on.

Singapore is being ranked by international agencies as among the world's top five positions in 2013 in terms of being the freest economy, least risky for investment, least corrupt and the most competitive economy overall, notwithstanding the fact that the nation is a highly open economy that has no natural resources, a small population base with geographical limitation with a total trade volume three times the size of her GDP, making her heavily dependent on external demand.

Over the business cycles, successive terms of pro-active governments were able to achieve above-potential GDP growth for nearly five decades and maintain healthy budgetary position due to political stability and racial harmony, coupled with its relentless effort to diversify the economy, contain costs, cultivate harmonious industrial relations while remaining competitive and innovative, notwithstanding the volatile external markets. Nevertheless, such a growth strategy, for various reasons and factors, began to be doubted by some in certain quarters and culminated in the watershed of dissatisfaction as expressed through the popular votes at the General Election (GE) of 2011.

5.8.1 An Inclusive Society: Public Housing Policy and Harmonious Industrial Relations

Improving income disparity and building an inclusive society is a national commitment, but how to go about achieving it requires consensus. Some of the pertinent questions include: what are the basic principles for growing the inclusivity, how costly and sustainable would it be, how is such an inclusive society funded and who will be paying for it?

Public housing is an important social equaliser, a unique facet of Singapore's way of life and an integral part of the asset enhancement programme within a land-scarce rapidly growing city-state. House ownership will be meaningless if its value does not appreciate or worse, stagnates or depreciates over time. Discounted prices and incentives are therefore necessary for first time would-be new house buyers. Discussion, as to how the government can ensure the fruits of land and property asset appreciation are to be fairly distributed to those citizens who aspire and are prepared to work for it, holds the key.

Effective tripartite relationships amongst workers, employers and the government will remain as the cornerstone of Singapore's harmonious industrial relations and productivity drive in exchange for employment stability and production efficiency. Such tripartite arrangements should not be taken lightly or for granted. It is indeed the bedrock of the economy, without which the erosion of competitiveness painstakingly built over decades would occur.

5.8.2 Subsidising Public Services and Tracking of Four Essential Affordability Indices

Provision of public services including education, healthcare, public housing and public transportation constitutes a significant portion of living cost for average citizens. Should such essential services be privatised or nationalised? Post-GE 2011, the Singapore government has quite rightly abandoned the break-even cost-recovery market pricing (BCMP) strategy for public services, moving away from the past ultra-prudent budgetary principle.

Such policy about-turn surely cannot come free-of-charge, as it would mean bigger government expenditures, which have to be funded from elsewhere, presumably from the taxpayers directly or indirectly. Are we prepared to do so knowing that the burden will likely to grow heavier over time with our rapidly ageing population, unless this weight is shared by a younger population through productive new immigrants?

The transparent tracking of affordability indices would assure and serve to allay public concerns. Periodically disclosed Transparent Affordability Indices (TAIs) may be computed, by working in conjunction with the government, to assess the affordability of essential public services for average Singaporean residents that can stand up to public scrutiny, further reinforcing public confidence and trust in the government.

Constructing annual international benchmarking indices to compare the world's major cities in terms of cost of living, wages and purchasing power, as per the study that the ACI has just completed, would be a useful complement to the TAIs (see Tan *et al.*, 2015 forthcoming).

5.8.3 Calibrated Steady-State National Manpower Policy: Allocating One-Third Foreign Workforce for the Economy

For continued development and growth, relying on a considerable foreign workforce is the reality for our city-state, but there is a trade-off involved. To what extent are we prepared to accommodate or tolerate their existence and how ready would the government be to meet their needs and requirements for hosting them in Singapore?

The government is committed to aiming towards a steady-state where not more than one-third of the total workforce will be foreigners, and ensuring that all Singaporeans who want to work will find jobs with decent pay through practical education curriculums, industrial internships, subsidised productivity training and workfare income supplement scheme. Singaporeans should feel confident in the workplace while competing against a foreign workforce.

It is therefore paramount for the public to understand and accept that, so long as the trend is moving towards the targeted one-third, fluctuation in the foreign workforce hovering above or below this quota would be tolerable over the business cycles. This is to say that whenever the external environment is favourable, we shall need to seize upon external demand to add revenues to the government budget that may have incurred deficits during global economic downturns.

Over the past decade, Singapore was able to create more jobs than the resident workforce can assume. It is therefore crucial for the public to understand and accept that highly skilled white-collar foreign professionals can help create more jobs and cheaper blue-collar foreign workers are also needed to work on infrastructure projects.

5.8.4 Quality Employment Creation: Ensuring Two-Third Indigenous Professionals, Managers, Executives and Technicians by 2030

As a policy objective, the government projected that indigenous Professionals, Managers, Executives and Technicians (PMETs) would increase from the current half of the occupation profile to two-thirds by 2030, so that we would require fewer Employment Pass and S-pass holders.

In the event of a protracted low growth economy, either due to companies relocating and/or worsening external demand, would Singapore still be able to create quality jobs for PMETs? Does it make logical sense that when the external environment is highly favourable, the government should curtail employment growth by tightening labour market condition so much that it raises business costs and removes 'unwanted' extra business growth, forcing the economy to slow down?

The steady-state projected population of 6.9 million by 2030 is critical in ensuring economic resilience and a consistent growth path for Singapore. The pertinent approach is therefore to monitor for quality immigrants who can contribute to tax income and who possess the ability to integrate locally, which depends on where they come from without disturbing the racial status quo or undermining social harmony.

5.9 Reflection: Stop Inward Looking, Avoid Blind Spots and Pursue Correct Public Policies

Given the ever-rising public expectations, the following are some pertinent questions that Singaporeans can attempt to think through. Are we prepared to see employment creation and business vibrancy in

Singapore slowing down as MNCs relocate? Would we accept continuing infrastructure bottlenecks and traffic congestions if we do not have enough foreign workers to build them? Would we accept delays in the timelines for building 200,000 units of public housing? Would we be prepared to pay higher taxes in the form of goods and services tax, personal income tax or corporate profit tax so as to fund higher social spending?

Meanwhile, the government may want to re-think some of the public policies that served well in the past but have since gone into autopilot that might need recalibration, fine-tuning or even a reverse of directions; in some cases, these reform efforts may have already been taking place.

The Housing & Development Board (HDB) may want to consider revamping the affordability index for public housing pricing and rentals in order to appropriately reflect weights assigned according to room types and income brackets.

The National Environmental Agency may want to look at the cost-of-living index in relation to the government-defined Monthly Living Wage when setting the rental and base-price bidding for hawker stalls.

The Public Transport Council may want to re-examine the formula for setting public transportation fares by indexing it to affordability according to per capita household income, age groups and inflation.

The Jurong Town Corporation may want to review land costs, factory rentals and selling prices for SMEs based on feasibility of business proposals judged by an independent private-sector led committee.

The Ministry of Manpower may want to require statutory declaration from human resource directors that they have actively sourced through the local workforce before approving the applications of foreign workforce for Employment Passes, S-passes and Work Permits.

New inclusive approaches would not only necessarily lead to lower revenues or bigger subsidies for statutory boards, ministries and government-linked companies, but they would also translate into higher income and employment for Singaporeans. It is certainly superior to implementing a more expensive, fiscally debilitating and comprehensive social safety nets proposed in some quarters.

These inclusive approaches are also more cost effective than the current Workfare Income Supplement (WIS) Scheme, which cannot significantly mitigate income disparity and would continue to be a funding burden with a very remote possibility of these individuals achieving income independence, unless we raise the level of income supplement and link it to upskilling programmes with a graduation timeline imposed.

Using benchmarks gathered over the past decade, the ACI simulated three medium-term GDP growth scenarios achievable under various levels of productivity growth targets required, by assuming a certain level of employment, labour share, total factor productivity, labour and capital quality growth.

Based on the actual economic performance of the economy over the period 1998 to 2008, we have simulated the associated GDP growth band and productivity target for pessimistic, optimistic and the base case scenarios that we perceived to be most likely to prevail for the period 2009 to 2020 as shown in Table 5.3.

In essence, our base case simulation results suggest that for a policy assumption of 1.5% employment growth coupled with other assumptions for capital and labour quality, Singapore economy would grow at an annual average rate of 4.2% with a required productivity target of 2.7% per year for the period 2009 to 2020. Such a GDP growth scenario would mean that Singapore's workforce must be prepared to deliver at the top end of the National Productivity Target (NPT) band of 2–3% as set by the 2009 Economic Strategies Committee (ESC).

For an optimistic scenario, if the authorities push for an annual average employment growth of 2%, then Singapore economy would be able to achieve an average annual GDP growth of 5.6% with a required productivity target growth of 3.6%. Such a situation would mean

Table 5.3. Simulation of GDP and Average Labour Productivity Growth, 2009–2020: Assumptions and Projections

	Actual 1998–2008	Pessimistic Scenario	Base Case	Optimistic Scenario	Remarks
Labour share	0.532	0.532^	0.532^	0.532^	^assumed
Labour quality growth (%)	1.24	1.00^	1.24^	1.50^	^assumed
Capital accumulation enhancement	0.08	0.08^	0.25^	0.50^	^assumed
Capital quality growth (%)	0.29	0.18^	0.29^	0.40^	^assumed
Total factor productivity growth (%)	0.51	0.30^	0.51^	0.70^	^assumed
Employment growth (%)	2.92	1.00	1.50	2.00	^assumed
Productivity growth (%)	2.52	1.79[+]	2.67[+]	3.61[+]	[+]projected
GDP growth (%)	5.45	2.79[+]	4.17[+]	5.61[+]	[+]projected

Source: The World Bank and Asia Competitiveness Institute.

achieving a productivity level well above the NPT — a tall order! Such an optimistic scenario implies continued public discontent against the government, as it requires a large foreign workforce especially during the good years to make up for the GDP lost during the bad years.

Even as we pursue the base case scenario, the biggest challenge remains to be how best and fair could the government judiciously utilise the budget surpluses generated to mitigate income disparity through careful calculations and allocation of resources to avoid the emergence of a potential economic underclass. Globalisation and inclusive growth are not mutually exclusive and positive interventionist policies for inclusivity have their places. The challenge for the government is to prove how income disparity can be addressed by enhancing inclusivity without retreating from globalisation in trade and finance. Singapore, being a small and highly open economy with no direct hinterland, probably does not have that many choices.

5.10 Why is Forging National Consensus under a Renewed Social Contract Imperative?

As Singaporeans become better educated, they are increasingly keen to participate in public policy formulation and often with vocal voices. Effective public policy presentations are thus essential if not paramount. However, there is an emerging danger, as seen happening in Taiwan, Hong Kong, Thailand and Malaysia just to name a few, when citizens are becoming so inward-looking, totally engrossed in domestic politics and social debates, such that the entire government and bureaucracy are embroiled in conflicts and deadlocks, thus draining away precious resources, time and effort.

While all political and cultural debates may ultimately be local, engagement on economic discourse for Singapore should always take the global perspective into consideration. Rational public policies must thus prevail over irrational public pressures. Most of all, public trust towards public institutions and civil servants must not be breached. Apart from the conventional media and press, public opinion shaping and public policy dissemination must be conducted closely in connection with the HDB heartlanders, in particular through the bi-directional policy feedback channeled from community-based grassroots workers.

Increased public participation in public policy consultation is a positive development. However, determining the type of citizen participatory model to adopt requires careful consideration — do we necessarily want a confrontational political process of the two-party system or do we prefer a strong check-and-balance approach by opposition parties on the incumbent government with proven track record, bearing in mind that the choice for the latter model could very well eventually lead back to the first option? Singaporeans will need to calibrate and contemplate deeply their choice of government and the political system that comes with it when casting their approvals.

5.11 Business as Usual for Singapore after the General Election 2015?

As the fervor of the General Election (GE) subsides and noises of post mortem settle, can we expect *business as usual* for the newly elected Singapore government? With such a strong mandate given to the ruling party, should we expect or can Singapore afford *business as usual*?

During the GE, among the People's Action Party (PAP) and opposition parties (OPs) including the Workers' Party (WP), Singapore Democratic Party (SDP), National Solidarity Party (NDP), Singapore Democratic Alliance (SDA), Singapore People's Party (SPP), Reform Party (RP), Singaporeans First Party (SFP) and People's Power Party (PPP), there were at least four broad common concerns pertaining to issues and plights to be addressed, but also stark differences in terms of how to deal with them.

5.11.1 Foreign Labour Dependence

Firstly, both the PAP and OPs (notably WP and SDP) wanted Singapore to be less dependent on cheap and abundant supply of blue-collar foreign workers and to ensure that the indigenous workforce continues to enjoy decent pay and good wage growth to cope well with rising cost of living. The OPs were in favour of a legislated minimum wage policy (MWP), swifter and significant reduction in foreign workers even if it means lower economic growth, whereas the PAP preferred to achieve decent pay and good wage growth through the painstaking effort in pushing for productivity gains, and through its progressive wage model policy. The PAP also believed in seizing the opportunities arising from good economic growth and a favourable external environment, arguing that this is the best way to cope with the rising cost of living.

5.11.2 Professionals, Managers, Executives and Technicians

Secondly, both the PAP and OPs wanted to see higher ratios of and better remunerated indigenous PMETs. While some OPs (notably SFP) advocated directly reserving jobs for Singaporeans and reducing foreign PMET numbers, the PAP argued for a hybrid PMET plan under SkillsFuture to ensure a Singaporean-core work team, augmented with foreign PMETs from diverse sources within a company and industry. A Fair Consideration Framework and a National Jobs Bank have also been put in place to ensure employers give opportunities to local workers.

5.11.3 Retirement Funding for Singaporeans

Thirdly, both the PAP and OPs wanted to ensure that Singaporeans have sufficient means for coping with retirement and old age, especially for lower income workers. The OPs (notably SDP) wanted to keep the withdrawal age for CPF unchanged at 55 years of age and objected to tampering with or raising the old minimum sum. The PAP argued for partial withdrawal at the age of 55, and a gradual rise in the minimum sum that people need to set for their old age. The PAP also introduced CPF Life, an annuity that pools CPF members' fund to give them a payout for life.

5.11.4 Social Safety Nets

Finally, both the PAP and OPs wanted to see significant improvement in social safety nets for the majority of Singaporeans. The OPs (notably SDP and WP) argued for the setting-up of the Western model of a welfare state with unemployment benefits and significant subsidy for basic public services including healthcare, housing, education and public transport. The PAP resisted the welfare state, preferring the option of tracking affordability indices for basic public services. It objected to unemployment benefits and opted instead for WIS, arguing that the best effort to mitigate income disparity was to get workers to stay in employment, not help them when they are unemployed.

5.12 Concluding Remarks

In the 2015 GE, nearly 70% of the voters must have accepted and been convinced by the PAP's party manifesto, as well as its policy stands in dealing with the four broad issues and plights discussed. Now that a strong mandate has been endorsed for the PAP to form a new government under the leadership of Prime Minister Lee Hsien Loong, are we going to be satisfied with *business as usual*, expecting the PAP government to continue as they have done over the past five decades, but now with the fourth generation of Singapore leaders?

Minister Mentor Lee Kuan Yew, our founding father, repeatedly reminded us that no one owes us a living, and the survival of Singapore hinges on how we collectively remake and ensure Singapore's relevance to the rest of the world by staying ahead of our competitors.

As we celebrate Singapore's 50 years of independence in 2015 or SG50, I think the next PAP government should be better prepared to deliver an even better future by planning for the longer-term survival of Singapore until SG80 and beyond! Now that we have entrusted the new PAP government with the responsibility of another five-year term, it is time to refrain from being inward looking. We should look at the bigger picture in which Singapore will always remain a little red dot.

Hence, we should come together to be better prepared in decades ahead by way of *evidence-based assessment* of Singapore's public policies and charting long-term growth strategies within a global context. We can think of three quantitative research clusters, which are quite different from the qualitative futuristic scenario planning exercises, to guide us in thinking through the challenges as follows:

(a) *Re-assess Singapore's public policies in the post-Lee Kuan Yew era: which were relevant in the past, continue to be relevant today and are likely to be so in the future within the globalised context?* A good example of this will be the external wing policy first mooted by then Senior Minister Lee in the early 1990s that led to the expansion of Singapore's external economy. Such global-driven growth for Singapore can be quantified and will no doubt continue to be the key engine of growth for Singapore's future.
(b) *Re-evaluate Singapore's public policies in the post-Lee Kuan Yew era that need fine-tuning due to changes in conditions and circumstances.* An appropriate public policy that comes to mind is the WIS; such policy, once introduced, is politically difficult to withdraw. Therefore, we ought to quantify how much it will cost future governments and whether we can design incentives for an exit mechanism for those who are benefiting from it.
(c) *Formulate public policies and future growth strategies for Singapore to stay relevant in the post-Lee Kuan Yew era, extrapolating from new emerging trends, with opportunities to be seized and challenges to be met and mastered.* This third research cluster is probably the most critical amongst the three clusters, as it deals with Singapore's longer-term survival as a nation.

A good example of cluster (c) would be the much discussed 100 km-long Isthmus of Kra Canal in Thailand, which was brought up again in 2015. It will allegedly cost US$28 billion to build and 10 years to complete. Assuming that this proposed project is realised, how would the top and bottom lines of the Port of Singapore be affected? Would Changi Airport, including Terminal 5 that is scheduled for completion by 2025, become more important in ensuring Singapore's economic connectivity to the rest of the world?

Another good example would be to identify shifts in global production networks within Asia and to seize opportunities for MNCs to engage in manufacturing migration, evaluate infrastructure investment and develop through opportunities such as the Belt & Road strategy advocated by China. Singapore could then be firmly placed as a leading international financial hub.

Conducting company-level studies on tracking productivity, monitoring efficiency and improving competitiveness would be paramount to spot potential synergies between Western and Asian companies, especially amongst SMEs. This would reinforce Singapore's reputation as a hub for regional headquarters.

We may even rethink over our National Service (NS) obligations, which could evolve to include female Singaporeans, and our education system, which could encompass both elitist and broad-based approaches. We can also afford to re-appraise the relevance of our transportation policy, which uses price to control private cars quantity, and the economic justifications of our public transportation system, which is a hybrid system of combining state subsidies with privatisation.

Re-examining the optimal mix of Singapore's manpower policy to enhance productivity in terms of foreign versus indigenous workforce is useful. Re-evaluating the longer-term feasible composition mix between manufacturing activities and services components could have important implications for employment creation for Singapore economy. Such analysis can lead to further study on longer-term optimal population targets for achieving economic critical mass, yet maintaining social harmony with environmental sustainability would still be in order.

Further evaluation of the economic costs versus benefits of defence spending for deterrent effect in order to ensure continued relevance of the city-state as a business, financial, logistics, communication, maritime and aviation hub would be paramount. Empirical analysis on economic rationales, social cost and externalities of maintaining a Singapore society that is multi-racial, multi-religious, multi-cultural and multi-lingual would be appropriate too.

We must be made aware or be reminded that decades of social and racial harmony, which did not come easy, are not to be taken for granted. While we are evolving towards a Singapore identity within a community of multi-culture, religion and ethnicity, different ways of life must be upheld and preserved.

Social divide exacerbated by income disparity, human capital deficiency, family disorientation and network disadvantages must be mitigated through constructive public policies, especially for ethnic minorities including Malay/Muslim Singaporeans, by ensuring a level playing field for all and by strengthening their ability to compete without being reliant on subsidies.

Potentially, there are many areas of longer-term public policy that can be identified to solicit active discussion and wider participation, especially amongst younger Singaporeans who would be in their prime adulthood by 2045 or the SG80. Fundamentally, this group of Singaporeans, who are in their early teens, may want to ask themselves what they want from and what they can offer to the city-state, and which sort of a future statehood they expect to live in and be accounted for. With imagination and creativity, be it SG50 or SG80, the best is yet to be for Singapore.

References

Tan, Khee Giap and Kong Yam Tan. 2014. "Assessing Competitiveness of ASEAN-10 Economies." *International Journal of Economics and Business Research* 8 (4): 377–398.

Tan, Khee Giap, Linda Low, Kong Yam Tan and Lijuan Lim. 2013. *Annual Analysis of Competitiveness, Development Strategies and Public policies on ASEAN-10: 2000–2010*. Singapore: Pearson Education South Asia Pte. Ltd.

Tan, Kong Yam, Tilak Abeysinghe and Khee Giap Tan. 2014. "Shifting Divers of Growth: Policy Implications for ASEAN-5." *Asian Economic Papers* 14 (1): 157–173.

Tan, Khee Giap, Kong Yam Tan, Randong Yuan and Le Phuong Anh Nguyen. 2015 (forthcoming). *2014 Indices on Cost of Living, Wages and Purchasing Power in World's 103 Major Cities.* Singapore: World Scientific.

Tan, Tony K.Y. 2015. Speech at the Singapore Chinese Chamber of Commerce & Industry SG50 Outstanding Chinese Business Pioneer Awards, Singapore, February 6.

Chapter 6

CONCLUDING REMARKS AND FUTURE RESEARCH AGENDA

6.1 Introductory Notes

This book started with the Asia Competitiveness Institute (ACI)'s proposal for the Asia Economic Connectivity Vision 2030 (AECV2030) in contrast to China's Belt & Road (B&R) strategy. The strategy combines the multi-tracked *One Belt* that spans across the former Soviet states to the Middle East and the European Union (EU) with the *One Road* that incorporates the 21st Century Maritime Silk Road (MSR); it does not only link to the Association of Southeast Asian Nations (ASEAN), but also spreads across and deep into the western, southern and eastern coastal region of China. The fundamental difference is that the ACI's version for the AECV2030 is ASEAN-centric while China's proposed B&R tends to be China-centric and quite naturally reflects China's needs and requirements.

Unlike the EU where member countries are bound by rules and regulations, ASEAN is both politically and economically a much looser entity and is consensus-driven. Thus, think tanks in ASEAN, especially those set up nationally, can play a crucial bridge role and serve as an extremely useful platform to articulate, formulate, disseminate and forge policy consensus, both domestically and regionally.

The AECV2030 aims to facilitate wider physical and information connectivity across Asia in a multi-modal way but focuses on maritime links that encompass ASEAN, India and part of the African continent, rendering ASEAN as the regional hub for maritime, aviation, logistics, business, financial, communication and e-commerce. The AECV2030 also twins with President Joko Widodo's ambition to transform Indonesia into a global maritime axis, welcoming foreign direct investment (FDI) from multinational corporations (MNCs) and state-owned enterprises (SOEs) from Greater China, the EU, the United States (US), Japan and Korea.

From the ASEAN's perspective, the AECV2030 also enables maritime ASEAN, which comprises archipelagic Indonesia (~14,000 islands) and the Philippines (~7,000 islands), to ratchet up and keep pace with mainland ASEAN. Interestingly, while ASEAN has a total land area of 4.4 million km^2, which is about 3% of the total land area on earth, its span in territorial waters is approximately triple that of its land area. All in all, mainland-cum-maritime ASEAN supports a population of about 617 million people (9% of the world's population), with a combined nominal GDP of US$2.3 trillion in 2012. Indeed, as noted by the ASEAN Secretariat, if ASEAN were a single entity, it would rank as the seventh largest economy in the world, preceded by the US, China, Japan, Germany, France and the United Kingdom.

6.2 Emerging Global and Regional Trends: Implications for ASEAN

There is an extensive body of literature on the economic growth and development of ASEAN, including its institutional milestones. For ASEAN as a whole, it continues to serve as a regional source of natural resources, supply of industrial capacity and market of consumers. The only difference is with the FDI and MNCs; traditionally, they are from the triad of the US, EU and Japan, and now from the quad with China's arrival. Whether the extent and quality of transfers of technology, management and skills accompanying the FDI and MNCs are as forthcoming and appropriate, it is for each ASEAN economy to make the right choice. The more significant development is the array of opportunities now made possible with the AECV2030.

Apart from a broader encompassing of China's B&R as demarcating a rising China in the midst of her faster-than-expected domestic economic rebalancing between domestic and external demand, the B&R track is concretised literally and figuratively, by another accompaniment, the Asian Infrastructure Investment Bank (AIIB). As noted in Chapter 1, the AIIB with over 40 founding members, especially non-Asian, from Europe to Australasia except the US, Canada and Japan as of the closing date in end of March 2015, is a mini United Nations if not serving as a complement or competition to the World Bank or Asian Development Bank (ADB). This 'Asianisation' of the new global financial architecture is deemed as key to fit the emergence of China as a global player to join the traditional triad of the US, EU and Japan in the old economic order.

Such a new China-initiated international mechanism presents ASEAN with remarkable opportunities to collectively assert itself on the global stage for the much needed infrastructure funding and investment in order to make ASEAN even more attractive as a top global investment destination. It is no coincidence that China's emphasis on ASEAN as a priority in its diplomatic initiatives concurs with the US's "pivot" toward Asia. While the specific details of the B&R Strategy and the AIIB initiative have not been unveiled yet, ASEAN has a major part to play in ensuring that these strategy and initiative are a harmonious symphony, where member states' interests are fully taken into account, and not a solo performance by China. After all, ASEAN is in itself a platform where newer developing member states get a chance to have their interests represented alongside relatively mature and more developed ones, to render ASEAN stronger and more credible.

Quintessentially, China's 21st MSR shares important similarities with the Master Plan on ASEAN Connectivity (MPAC)[1] in further opening the door to enhanced economic cooperation between China and ASEAN. Both the MSR and MPAC aim to enhance transport connectivity as a way to facilitate trade, investment, tourism and people-to-people exchanges.

---

[1] For references on MPAC, see ASEAN Secretariat (2010) and Basu Das (2013).

Like the MSR, the MPAC seeks to improve port connectivity to link insular Southeast Asian countries with one another as well as with hinterland areas.[2] While the MPAC for the most part had been laid out in 2010, it remains a work-in-progress; it is the same for China's 21st MSR and the AIIB that are packaged as a wider AECV2030 in Chapter 1 to offer scope for more consultative dialogues. Stakeholders from both sides have extensive experience in infrastructure construction, technical expertise and facilitating smoother documentation flows for cross-border transactions to allow for sharing and learning.

The devil is in the details; more serious and intensive examinations, clarifications and offers at high-level working groups to be convened by the ASEAN Secretariat with the Chinese government are surmised. The work of the second track in academic and policy think tanks[3] including the ACI is recognised as it incorporates business interests as well and other non-government organisations (NGOs) as stakeholders. For instance, the AIIB, which is currently in its infancy, provides a unique catalyst for ASEAN to assume some leadership role in infrastructure as the recipient of *in situ* projects within its borders. As the AIIB's governance structure has yet to be laid out, ASEAN countries as founding members need to rise to the occasion with their interests to help shape a new global institution in a profound way.

To some extent, such constructive interactions may help to allay and defuse certain concerns and scepticism as many still regard the AIIB as China-backed infrastructure project.[4] This needs more than mandatory

---

[2] See Pitlo (2015).

[3] The second track includes Pacific Economic Cooperation Council (PECC) and Asia Pacific Economic Cooperation (APEC), as well as many regional and country-based think tanks. Within the National University of Singapore, the East Asian Institute hosts both Singapore Network of East Asian Think-Tanks (NEAT) and Network of ASEAN-China Think-Tanks (NACT).

[4] For examples of controversial China-backed infrastructure projects, see Johnston and Bland (2011) and Tiezzi (2015).

environmental impact assessments, as corporate social responsibility for transparency and accountability, corruption-free procurement standards and best practices are as paramount. Across the board, ASEAN has important inputs to contribute to active engagement under the AECV2030, incorporating both the B&R and AIIB initiatives. By Partaking in the AECV2030 with China, ASEAN helps to make the 'Asianisation' of the global economic infrastructure more truly Asian than just China.

With ASEAN joining as the largest economy in the world after the United Kingdom, a few points come to mind. The first one is the over and above traditional ASEAN as supply bases for both natural resources, manufacturing activities as well as a growing market on the demand side; ASEAN-China connectivity in fruition makes ASEAN more invaluable than a buffer between China and the West and its economic partners. Secondly, the Western MNCs together with those from Japan and South Korea as part of the trio may be induced into some "friendly competition" with China, a situation that may well be healthy and beneficial to all. Thirdly, can this modality of inter-regional infrastructural development help attract even wider inter-regional interests, namely India and the rest of South Asia that obviously and urgently need infrastructure more than most? Finally, how would the relatively financially-strapped US and EU respond on the sidelines, whatever the political economy is with respect to containing or accommodating a rising China?

Prima facie, it is agreed that plugging gaps in connectivity and infrastructure is the key for all sorts of exchanges. However, tying up emerging global and regional trends, with much still being work-in-progress, is also important, and this concluding chapter at best can try to identify some projects in ASEAN's MPAC that fit in with China's 21st Century MSR. More ways to extend infrastructure projects on highways, such as the Singapore-Kunming link that would facilitate the 2014 China-Singapore Economic Corridor (CSEC) proposed by China and welcome by Singapore in Nanning, and maritime port activities that include containerisation, roll-on-roll-off, other facilitation and digitised documentation by advanced technology, may be included under the ACI's future agenda. In contrast to the old Silk Road, where the voyages of discovery were made, the AECV2030 will be thoroughly researched and canvassed by the ACI in consultative exchanges of all stakeholders.

Pragmatically, the ACI is cognisant of actionable and evidence-based policy-guiding recommendations that are vital for confidence-building and buy-in. Past successful models, ranging from the wild flying geese patterns to the East Asian economic development model forged by state capitalism rather than *laissez-faire* market forces, may be convincing. In the era of technology-accelerated globalisation and equally fast transmission of contagious financial and other crises,[5] tendencies for nationalism rather than calls for regional leadership are to be expected. Thus, the need for a bold AECV2030 is timely with projected outcomes to offer tangible deliverables well quantified by key performance indicators for tracking and monitoring project-based AECV2030.

With five broad proposals and many strategic thrusts identified for many projects under the AECV2030, more is needed from feasibility studies and cost-benefit analysis to prioritise funding and resource allocation for projects by both public and private sectors. The new AIIB may finance some of the projects when it is officially set up and running, and with competition, it may well speed up the project finance bureaucracy from the ADB and the World Bank. There is more that the ACI, along with the ASEAN Secretariat, can contribute to in further

[5] Some regional problems needing regional solutions include the seasonal haze from slash-and-burn practices, (see Varkkey, 2013) widening to acts of terrorism as, global problems needing global solutions; ASEAN's globalisation encompasses the good, bad and ugly.

research and in getting governments to be more committed. The same can be expected for the FDI from MNCs and other private sources of fund and capital. The modalities of partnerships, especially public-private partnerships (PPPs) that involve local and foreign stakeholders, would provide a greater voice from the communities with respect to the environment when sensitive land ownership issues need to be solved.

All stakeholders can rest assured that the AECV2030 with an economic mandate is in complete alignment with environmentally sustainable growth and development. It encompasses high quality human resource development in capability building as much as physical capacity building in infrastructure. Proposals are comprehensive in covering labour standards, intellectual property rights and trade facilitation, with many bilateral and regional free trade agreements focusing on customs procedures to lower transaction costs. It is paramount, both in theory and in practice, for policies to be holistic, integrated and systemic to join all the dots, within each ASEAN member state, across-the-board, as well as cognisant of the reality of different dreams of external partners, no less than the significance of the latest China dream.

The AECV2030 has set its sight on no less than a new regional master plan that takes stock of the prevailing willingness to explore closer Asian inter-sovereign cooperation. The window of opportunity is in grasping the new leadership in various countries. Dynamics are changing fast and furious, with respective state of affairs nurtured by the efforts of a pioneering generation of country planners and intelligentsia to be continued cohesively by the new generations. Every new regime wants and needs to make a difference without too much repudiation of the past and legacies while fusing with changing times and technology.

From what may begin historically for the old Silk Road as a regional project for better stability and national security, the AECV2030 is people-centric in market integration, envisioning an Asian mode of globalisation with confidence from the most dynamic region of growth coming out of the economic slump of 2008. People involved in the

AECV2030 have capabilities, foresight and wisdom to build upon a solid foundation with great promise to forge new relations and innovative institutions for the collective good. The ACI's boldly proposed AECV2030 ensures regional challenges are met with regional responses as workable solutions.

6.3 Summary of Key Findings

Chapter 1 sets the tone with rising China and her recent encounter of the so-called New Normal as the latest emerging economic phenomenon and trend. Explicitly, ASEAN-China relationship as alluded above is emphasised. There is nowhere to hide from China's arrival in ASEAN, with both Chinese and ASEAN aspirations to match or reconcile as appropriate. The best scenario is that deeper ASEAN-China relationship is not a zero-sum game, but a positive one along with ASEAN-EU, ASEAN-US and ASEAN-Asia Pacific relationships. Regional issues need regional solutions from financial to health-related crises, as much as global challenges need global cooperation and collaboration such as in climate change.

Chapter 1 has discussed at length the five tentative proposals from the ACI to drive the AECV2030 forward. The AECV2030 is ASEAN-centric as ASEAN is the most logical, legitimate and rightful partner in the China-initiated B&R with the AIIB and related infrastructure projects in connectivity. It bears repeating that both ASEAN Secretariat's resources and ongoing projects, particularly its MPAC, form the key to the AECV2030, which if successful economically, would lift more than 600 million of ASEAN people into a higher standard of living with gainful employment, enhanced human capital and a more inclusive society, as manifested by our projected target performance indicators for 2030.

As laid out in Chapter 2 in a comprehensive analysis of Overall Competitiveness and its four main components in terms of Macroeconomic Stability, Government and Institutional Setting,

Financial, Businesses and Manpower Conditions, Quality of Life and Infrastructure Development, ASEAN leadership is pivotal, with Singapore in the lead for most instances, except for its labour constraint. Malaysia ranks second and other older ASEAN member states are doing well despite the global financial tsunami (GFT) that is slowing down the Western counterparts. The bold yet realistic idea of an ASEAN-led era may not be too far-fetched if all the building blocks are assembled properly on firm foundations.

Resilient and able crisis management has been demonstrated as ASEAN grew from strength to strength since both financial contagions, from the Asian Financial Crisis (AFC) to GFT, and health-related crises, such as the Severe Acute Respiratory Syndrome (SARS) and bird flu. The understanding of various strengths and weaknesses of each ASEAN economy therefore becomes a necessary ingredient for ASEAN-centric leadership to flourish. The sufficiency condition lies in an effective implementation that takes political will and commitments of all parties into the AECV2030.

In Singapore, the implicit social contract between the government and its people has been struck with good balance between what was promised and what was being delivered. That being the case, Singapore still needs to deliver results that are aligned to expectations that come from being successful. In Chapter 2, Singapore's weakness in labour market flexibility should spark warning signs for its leaders to avoid complacency and remain competitive in all aspects. With its many foundations laid well in place, the next step should be one that is going to ensure seamless coordination amongst various government ministries and statutory boards. Such coordination is needed in terms of its ability in attracting FDI as vital for its high-technology growth, and to maintain and improve existing hard and soft infrastructure. In particular, human capital accumulation is critical for ensuring a more inclusive society, and it is a continual competitive developmental strategy without exception.

In Chapter 2, Malaysia has shown good progress and even surpassed Singapore to rank first in the categories of indicators that entail various aspects of financial, businesses and manpower conditions since 2011. Despite having natural resources in abundance and being open to trade with healthy FDI inflows, it is disappointing to note that Malaysia is seemingly in the middle-income trap. On a brighter note, what is crucial is that its leaders are committed and determined to render the economy truly competitive. Malaysia's growth model for the near future should be one that is inclusive, sustainable and directed at advancing upwards on the technological ladder in the manufacturing sector to push itself out of the middle-income trap. Further emphasis should also be placed on attracting FDI, an empirically proven key driver of its economy.

Infrastructure development, as the underpinning of the AECV2030, is as important in assessing ASEAN competitiveness in Chapter 2. It is a key aspect that will boost connectivity in the region, yet a bottleneck issue in Indonesia particularly. Despite being an archipelagic nation geographically, it can become the very nexus of growth for the region, notwithstanding President Widodo's 2014 vision of the country as a maritime axis.

Despite Indonesia's weakness in that respect, its post-crises performance since 2005 based on the ACI's competitiveness analysis in Chapter 2 has been remarkable. It is very promising that, given its diversity and growing importance as a source of food and natural resources, its potential in diversifying value-added activities can be attained with infrastructure overhaul. Drawing reference from another ACI's research on Indonesia,[6] initiation in the form of the Masterplan for Acceleration and Expansion of Indonesia's Economic Development (MP3EI) with its planned provision of infrastructure to facilitate economic activity serves as one of the many signs for progress.

---

[6] See Tan *et al.* (2015).

Globalisation is a double-edged sword that can bring immense benefits to an economy that embraces it, but could also make it vulnerable to external threats and shocks. A closely knitted ASEAN bloc should arguably bring about growth through the mobility of human, capital, goods and services in a more sustainable manner. However, on the flip side of the coin, the more open the economy, the more vulnerable it is to external influences as seen in the 1997 AFC and the 2008 GFT. Such recoveries and crisis management as the ability to absorb exogenous shocks are crucial aspects of ASEAN economic cooperation, which will be beneficial for newcomers such as Cambodia, Laos, Myanmar and Vietnam (CLMV).

Having recovered well from the various setbacks is a proof that ASEAN as a whole is resilient, however, earnest efforts must still be made to anticipate the impacts that the volatile global economy has on individual economies. There is no shortcut to ensuring that foundations on institutions, governance and infrastructure are as strong as it should be to withstand such external 'turbulences'. Only with ASEAN coordinated strategies forming the very bedrock of economies that the evolving ASEAN-centric AECV2030 will be able to lead the bloc to another level as a sustainable development model.

In Chapter 3, Geweke causality analysis was conducted on transitional economics of ASEAN, typifying Cambodia, Laos and Vietnam (CLV) with lessons and experiences to share; due to data constraints, we have left out Myanmar for the time being. The empirical evidence as revealed by our study appeared to reiterate the importance of financial deepening in spurring economic growth for Laos, which are much more stronger than in Cambodia, potentially due to excessive financial leverage and credit growth that introduced instability in the system. There appears to be no significant causal relation governing financial depth and economic growth in Vietnam, possibly driven by explosive credit growth for several years.

Notwithstanding the empirical evidence that examined the CLV over a specific time period between 1996 and 2010, the scope for financial sector development in terms of strengthening governance of financial markets and institutions should not and cannot be overlooked. In terms of regional financial integration, a greater impetus to ensure depth, quality, efficiency and connectivity of the financial sector in ASEAN must be forged, a necessary but not a sufficient condition for increasing the probability of achieving the ASEAN Economic Community (AEC).

Chapter 4 offers a contrasting view where Geweke causality analysis was conducted on more developed economies of ASEAN, namely Malaysia and Singapore. It is a matter of leadership and commitment for leading ASEAN economies, such as Singapore and Malaysia, as they forge ahead into the next couple of decades. Policymakers in these economies may be aware of what needs to be done but should be cautious that economic agenda may sometimes be fudged by political agenda.

The economic development strategies of Malaysia and Singapore, despite ruled by two very different governments with non-identical styles and philosophies, do have notable commonalities and have been widely hailed as role models. The empirical results verified that the external demand-driven export-oriented strategy through pro-active effort to attract FDI is common for both countries. However, both economies are confronting the rapid economic restructuring resulting from the volatile global export markets.

As the two countries move to a new and different economic trajectory, Malaysia with a bigger domestic market should consider rebalancing the economic structure with greater domestic demand by improving the quality of education and skill sets. Although having a smaller domestic market should make Singapore embrace a growth model that goes beyond heavily dependent on FDI, it should instead be innovation-driven through identifying niche technologies for economy upgrading, strengthening services-driven economy through productivity drive, and expanding the external economy by venturing abroad aggressively for those maturing indigenous local enterprises and well-equipped government-linked companies.

Fifty years on, as Singapore celebrates it golden jubilee year of the 1965 independence, it is appropriate in Chapter 5 to review, reflect and put in perspective how missions of the past 50 years or SG50 were accomplished and what lies ahead for the next 50 years. The essence of Singapore's survival as a nation lies in its ability to continue to stay relevant in the region and the globalisation process, to always seek new opportunities and be ahead of the competition curve.

Over the past five decades, three economies, namely Hong Kong, Malaysia and Singapore, have experienced different growth paths under dissimilar styles of governing philosophy, and hence the difference in development strategies. By 2013, Singapore was able to expand her economic pie to US$298 billion (with per capita income of US$55,182), nearly as big as Malaysia's US$313 billion (with per capita income of US$10,000) and bigger than that of Hong Kong at US$274 billion (with per capita income of US$38,123), notwithstanding its much smaller population of 5.6 million versus the 28 million and 7.8 million of Malaysia and Hong Kong population, respectively.

As Singapore looks towards the next 50 years of nation building, three categories of evidence-based assessment of public policies were stated as future research agenda. Firstly, to pin down Singapore's public policies in the post-Lee Kuan Yew era that were relevant in the past, continue to be relevant today and are likely to be so in the future within the globalised context. Secondly, to re-evaluate Singapore's public policies in the post-Lee Kuan Yew era that need fine-tuning due to changes in conditions and circumstances. Finally, to formulate public policies and future growth strategies for Singapore to stay relevant in the post-Lee Kuan Yew era by extrapolating from new emerging trends, for opportunities to be seized and challenges to be met and mastered.

The ACI is committed to conducting more research, including field-trips and road shows to communicate with and support all partners who are willing to join a shared AECV2030 blueprint that will offer an infinite array of opportunities from various combinations and permutations based on the flexible ASEAN-X formula. ASEAN will engage China, based on mutual benefits, and embrace India, whenever market forces prevail. Without any doubt, ASEAN has the track record to assume a leading role to continue to fuel the region's economic prosperity in a sustainable manner. Moving forward, the ACI aims to maintain relevance and strives to become the front-runner in the field of policy research on ASEAN economies.

6.4 Future Research Agenda

The ACI will continue to pursue and actualise the blueprint of the AECV2030, as well as a few other areas for future research that are part and parcel in continuation as consultative process unfolds.[7] Building on research done in this book and beyond, our research agenda in the next book may include at least three policy areas including a quantitative treatment on agricultural productivity for ASEAN-8, potential income traps at various levels and growth slowdown analysis for selected ASEAN economies and an assessment of challenges and opportunities for the realisation of the AEC.

6.4.1 Agricultural Productivity for ASEAN-8 Economies

With agriculture contributing to a large employment share in ASEAN, the region has the potential to not only become self-sufficient in food but is also capable of being a food basket for other Asian countries, and perhaps to a more ambitious extent, the world. ASEAN is a region consisting of many countries endowed with vast fertile land, rich natural resources, abundant and cheap labour supply; however, higher emphasis has been placed on manufacturing and services sectors due to

[7] With trade, FDI and MNCs, many related areas range from free trade agreements, whether bilateral, regional or multilateral (see Low, 2003), to labour issues such as differential wages and other working conditions (see for instance, Ramstetter, 2014).

urbanisation and industrialisation, hence leaving ASEAN with plenty of room for improvement in terms of agricultural productivity. The usual thesis of industrialisation as superior and the desired pathway leading to the neglect of agriculture activities is a false contention.

Human resource development, and applied science and technology with research and development are equally important ingredients for agriculture as well. Retention of talents is of critical consideration as rural-urban migration intensifies, lured by industrialisation, and needs to be rebalanced with downstream value-added industrialisation *in situ*. ASEAN leaders have increasingly come to realise the importance and influence of agriculture on economic growth and social stability.[8] As such, earnest effort has been made to forge cooperation in terms of food production and supply between nations. Economic diversification and restructuring including the strong emphasis on capacity building and providing extensive tertiary services are part and parcel of economic development and competitiveness.

With these challenges as identified, the ACI believes that fostering productivity growth in the agricultural sector will be an effective and strategic approach for some ASEAN economies to enhance their competitiveness, alleviate poverty and promote inclusive growth. By adopting various analytical methods, the future research agenda may focus on the contribution of Total Factor Productivity (TFP) change to agricultural output and its components across eight ASEAN countries (Brunei and Singapore[9] excluded). Based on the empirical results,

---

[8] The effect of industrialisation that led to the overlook of agriculture was felt in China where it transformed itself from a food exporter to importer in order to meet the demand of its billion-plus population.

[9] The Agri-food and Veterinary Authority (AVA), is a governing body in Singapore established to respond to the challenges faced by the nation's food and agriculture sector. Playing a similar role as the Palm Oil Research Institute of Malaysia (PORIM) and others alike in various ASEAN countries, the ACI hopes to be able to supplement and complement to their contributions in the respective countries.

policy implications can be drawn to help policymakers make informed policy decisions.

6.4.2 Potential Income Traps and Growth Slowdown Analysis for Selected ASEAN Economies

According to the World Bank, as of 2014, six of the ASEAN-10 economies are classified as middle-income countries. Malaysia, Philippines and Thailand are the three in Asia among 15 middle-income countries worldwide that have been trapped in the middle-income status for at least the last 50 years.[10] Unable to compete on two fronts, against countries that are able to export manufactured products more cheaply due to comparatively lower cost of labour and against more technologically advanced and innovative countries, these economies remain in a limbo. The success of the Republic of Korea in overcoming the middle-income trap[11] and propelling itself to finally become a high-income economy in 2000 should serve as an inspiration for the likes of Malaysia, Philippines and Thailand. The question at hand is what conditions enable the successful transition of a middle-income economy into a high-income economy.

For Vietnam, having leapfrogged out of the poverty trap and into the lower middle-income level since 2009,[12] how can they prepare themselves to avoid the middle-income trap? In order for economies to overcome the various income traps, carefully tailored policies need to be in place. Hence, robust research needs to be conducted on each selected economy to first identify areas that are susceptible to the trap before policy recommendations can be put forth. By adopting various methodologies, the ACI can investigate and identify the factors

---

[10] See Zhuang *et al.* (2012).

[11] See Tran (2013).

[12] See Berliner *et al.* (2013).

contributing to the middle-income trap and suggest possible remedies for ASEAN economies that are vulnerable to it.

6.4.3 The ASEAN Economic Community by 2016?

The ASEAN Community has three pillars, namely economic cooperation (ASEAN Economic Community or AEC), political stability and security (ASEAN Political-Security Community) and socio-cultural development (ASEAN Socio-Cultural Community). With a youthful population of less than 15% aged 55 and above, ASEAN demographic dividends from a dynamic workforce would help boost the AEC; if successful, it will enhance competitiveness with a more balanced economic development amongst member economies that is projected to grow by 2025 with an aggregate output of 7% per annum by creating 14 million new jobs, to be better plugged into the global economy, and to potentially become the fourth largest economy in the world by 2030, after the US, EU and China.

The AEC would see lower tariffs and higher trade flows within ASEAN by making it more attractive to foreign investors and stimulating business activities for small and medium enterprises as facilitated through the elimination of non-tariff barriers. Professional grouping including tour operators, engineers, dentists, architects, accountants, nurses and doctors are going be high in demand. More affluent middle class will emerge, well exceeding 100 million people by 2025, with rising household disposable income driving the consumption of goods and services as lifestyle is being tilted towards urban living with intensified migration from rural areas to bigger cities.

Can the AEC be completed by 2016? What is the progress status of the AEC so far and what remains to be done? With nearly 80% of the stipulated requirements for the AEC completed, what are the difficulties for the last final mile and what are the challenges ahead? In meeting the target of the AEC by 2016, could ASEAN members stay united or would we become disorganised with economic agenda being disrupted by disharmony in socio-cultural communities amongst ourselves and political insecurity resulted from tussles with foreign major powers? These are some of the frequently asked questions that we would like to answer through in-depth analysis in our next ASEAN book.

6.5 Concluding Remarks

This is not just another book on ASEAN. This is one of the twelve ACI flagship projects covering 34 Greater China economies, 33 provinces in Indonesia, 35 states and federal territories in India. They all knit together sub-national analyses of competitiveness, as defined by the ACI's framework and methodology, executed with its database through published sources, surveys and field trips. In-depth and insightful analyses into liveable cities and cost of living amongst expatriates and ordinary residents have also been conducted for world's major cities.

Under the Asia CompNet project, research on company-level competitiveness for 16 Asian economies, including ASEAN-10, China, Hong Kong, India, Japan, Korea and Taiwan, and business strategies for Asian family conglomerates are also being embarked upon. Such extensive efforts and comprehensive coverage are meant to make ASEAN and other sub-national economies of Asia more relevant to policymakers, industry captains and other policy researchers.

Finally, it is the mission of the ACI to see to ASEAN's further development and evolvement into an economically vibrant entity with a balanced, sustainable and inclusive growth. It is thus vital that ASEAN members must maintain a close and equitable relationship with major powers who are actively participating in the regional and ASEAN affairs. While free trade agreements such as the Trans-Pacific Partnership (TPP), Regional Comprehensive Economic Partnership (RCEP) and Free Trade Area of Asia-Pacific (FTAAP) shall take time to conclude, they are nevertheless important pathways to make ASEAN more globalised and better integrated as an internationalised economic community. However, investment agreements that involve mutual or tripartite benefits in specific industries or sectors agreeable by stakeholders ought to be encouraged as development waits for no man. With all the outstanding challenges and opportunities ahead for ASEAN, the best is yet to be!

References

ASEAN Secretariat. 2010. *Master Plan on ASEAN Connectivity*. Jakarta: The ASEAN Secretariat. http://www.asean.org/images/2012/publications/Master%20Plan%20on%20AS EAN%20 Connectivity.pdf (accessed April 13, 2015).

Basu Das, Sanchita. 2013. "Master Plan on ASEAN Connectivity: From Planning to Implementation". Institute of Southeast Asian Studies, Singapore, April 3. http://www.iseas.edu.sg/ISEAS/upload/files/Sanchita-Basu-Das%281%29.pdf (accessed April 14, 2015).

Berliner, Tom, Do Kim Thanh and Adam McCarty. 2013. *Inequality, Poverty Reduction and the Middle-Income Trap in Vietnam*. Hanoi: Mekong Economics. http://mekongeconomics.com/dev/images/stories/FILE%20 PUBLICATIONS/EU%20Blue%20Book.pdf (accessed October 30, 2014).

Johnston, Tim and Ben Bland. 2011. "Burma suspends $3.6bn China dam project". *Financial Times*, September 30. http://www.ft.com/intl/cms/s/0/520bcdb2-eb4f-11e0-9a41-00144feab49a.html#axzz3XFbCA4xY (accessed April 13, 2015).

Low, Linda. 2003. "Multilateralism, Regionalism, Bilateral and Cross regional Free Trade Arrangements: All Paved with Good Intentions for ASEAN?" *Asian Economic Journal* 17 (1): 65–86.

Pitlo, Lucio Blanco, III. 2015. "ASEAN Connectivity and China's 'One Belt, One Road'". *The Diplomat*, March 26. http://thediplomat.com/2015/03/asean-connectivity-and-chinas-one-belt-one-road/ (accessed April 13, 2015).

Ramsletter, Eric D. 2014. "Exporting, education, and wage differentials between foreign multinationals and local plants in Indonesian and Malaysian manufacturing". In *Trade, Development, and Political Economy in East Asia: Essays in Honour of Hal Hill*, edited by Prema-chandra Athukorala, Arianto A. Patunru and Budy P. Resosudarmo, 112–133. Singapore: Institute of Southeast Asian Studies.

Tan, Khee Giap, Nurina Merdikawati, Mulya Amri and Blake Harley Berger. 2015. *2014 Annual Competitiveness Analysis and Development Strategies for 33 Indonesian Provinces*. Singapore: World Scientific.

Tiezzi, Shannon. 2015. "What's It Like to Have China Build You a Port? Ask Cameroon". *The Diplomat*, February 27. http://thediplomat.com/2015/02/whats-it-like-to-have-china-build-you-a-port-ask-cameroon/ (accessed April 13, 2015).

Tran, Van Tho. 2013. "The Middle-Income Trap: Issues for Members of the Association of Southeast Asian Nations". ADBI Working Paper 421, Asian Development Bank Institute, Tokyo.

Varkkey, Helena. 2013. "Regional cooperation, patronage and the ASEAN Agreement on transboundary haze pollution". *International Environmental Agreements: Politics, Law and Economics* 14 (1): 65–81.

Zhuang, Juzhong, Paul Vanderberg and Yiping Huang. 2012. *Growing Beyond the Low-Cost Advantage: How the People's Republic of China can avoid the Middle-Income Trap*. Manila: Asian Development Bank.

Appendix 1

COMPETITIVENESS ANALYSIS OF ASEAN-10 ECONOMIES, 2000–2011 — LIST OF INDICATORS

No.	Indicator	Unit	Reversed Indicator
1	**MACROECONOMIC STABILITY**		
1.1	***Economic Vibrancy***		
1.1.01	Gross Domestic Product	US Dollars, Constant 2000 Prices	
1.1.02	Real GDP Growth	Percentage Change Per Annum	
1.1.03	GDP Per Capita	US Dollars, Constant 2000 Prices	
1.1.04	Output Agriculture (Value Added)	US Dollars, Constant 2005 Prices	
1.1.05	Output Industry (Value Added)	US Dollars, Constant 2005 Prices	
1.1.06	Output Services (Value Added)	US Dollars, Constant 2005 Prices	
1.1.07	Gross Domestic Savings	Percentage of GDP	
1.1.08	Gross Fixed Capital Formation	Percentage of GDP	
1.1.09	Inflation	Percentage Change Per Annum	R
1.1.10	Money Supply Growth (M2)	Percentage Change Per Annum	R

(Continued)

Appendix 1 (*Continued*)

No.	Indicator	Unit	Reversed Indicator
1.2	***Openness to Trade and Services***		
1.2.01	Current Account Balance	Percentage of GDP	
1.2.02	Exports of Goods and Services	US Dollars, Current Market Prices	
1.2.03	Imports of Goods and Services	US Dollars, Current Market Prices	
1.2.04	Openness to Trade	Ratio	
1.2.05	International Tourism Receipts	US Dollars, Current Market Prices	
1.3	***Attractiveness to Foreign Investors***		
1.3.01	Foreign Direct Investment Inflows	US Dollars, Current Market Prices	
1.3.02	Foreign Owned Companies	Survey Data	
1.3.03	Corporate Income Tax	Percentage of Profit	R
1.3.04	Lack of Discrimination Against Investors	Survey Data	
1.3.05	Levelness of Playing Field	Survey Data	
1.3.06	Transparency of Processes for Investors	Survey Data	
1.3.07	Business Impact of Rules on FDI	Survey Data	
2	**GOVERNMENT AND INSTITUTIONAL SETTING**		
2.1	***Government Policies and Fiscal Sustainability***		
2.1.01	Government Revenue (Including Grants)	US Dollars, Constant 2000 Prices	
2.1.02	Tax Revenue	US Dollars, Constant 2000 Prices	
2.1.03	Tax Revenue/Government Revenue	Percentage	

(*Continued*)

Appendix 1 *(Continued)*

No.	Indicator	Unit	Reversed Indicator
2.1.04	Government Consumption Expenditure	Percentage of GDP	
2.1.05	External Debt	US Dollars, Current Market Prices	R
2.1.06	International Reserves	US Dollars, Current Market Prices	
2.1.07	Net Foreign Assets	US Dollars, Current Market Prices	
2.1.08	International Monetary Fund Credit	US Dollars, Current Market Prices	R
2.1.09	Budget Balance	Percentage of GDP	
2.1.10	Tax Burden	Percentage of GDP	R
2.1.11	Money Supply (M2)	Percentage of GDP	
2.1.12	Deposit Interest Rate	Percentage	
2.1.13	Lending Rate	Percentage	R
2.1.14	Interest Rate Spread	Percentage	R
2.1.15	Exchange Rate Appreciation	Annual Average Percentage Change (Local Currency Unit per US Dollar)	R
2.2	***Institutions, Governance and Leadership***		
2.2.01	Quality of Government Policies	Survey Data	
2.2.02	Government Effectiveness	Survey Data	
2.2.03	Government Environmental Protection Policies	Percentage of Total Territorial Area	
2.2.04	Quality of Central Bank/ Monetary Authority	Survey Data	
2.2.05	Government Stability	Survey Data	
2.2.06	Government Responsiveness	Survey Data	

(Continued)

Appendix 1 (*Continued*)

No.	Indicator	Unit	Reversed Indicator
2.2.07	Quality of Political Leadership	Survey Data	R
2.2.08	Political System Risk	Survey Data	R
2.2.09	Legislature/Parliament (Functioning of Government System)	Survey Data	
2.2.10	Strength of Auditing and Reporting Standards	Survey Data	
2.2.11	Institutional Sophistication	Survey Data	
2.2.12	Bureaucracy/Red Tape	Survey Data	
2.2.13	Lack of Corruption	Survey Data	
2.2.14	Lack of Cronyism	Survey Data	
2.2.15	Lack of Market Distortion due to State-Ownership	Survey Data	
2.3	***Competition, Regulatory Standards and Rule of Law***		
2.3.01	Corporate Governance	Survey Data	
2.3.02	Quality of Regulatory Environment	Survey Data	
2.3.03	Transparency of Government	Survey Data	
2.3.04	Monopolies and Cartel	Survey Data	
2.3.05	Policy Towards Private Enterprise Rating	Survey Data	
2.3.06	Ease of Starting Business	Number	R
2.3.07	Barriers to Trade	Survey Data	
2.3.08	Intellectual Property Rights Protection	Survey Data	
2.3.09	Regional Competitiveness	Survey Data	
2.3.10	Quality of Judiciary	Survey Data	
2.3.11	Effectiveness of Legal System	Survey Data	

(*Continued*)

Appendix 1 (*Continued*)

No.	Indicator	Unit	Reversed Indicator
2.3.12	Integrity of Legal System	Survey Data	
2.3.13	Quality of Police	Survey Data	
2.3.14	Political Change	Survey Data	
3	**FINANCIAL, BUSINESSES AND MANPOWER CONDITIONS**		
3.1	***Financial Deepening and Business Efficiency***		
3.1.01	Claims on Private Sector	Annual Growth as Percentage of Broad Money	
3.1.02	Domestic Credit to Private Sector	Percentage of GDP	
3.1.03	Quality of Banking and Financial System	Survey Data	
3.1.04	Domestic Credit Provided by the Financial Sector	Percentage of GDP	
3.1.05	Listed Domestic Companies	Number	
3.1.06	Market Capitalisation	US Dollars, Current Market Prices	
3.1.07	Total Value of Stocks Traded	Percentage of GDP	
3.1.08	Sovereign Debt Risk	Number	R
3.1.09	Quality of Stock Market Regulatory Authority	Survey Data	
3.2	***Labour Market Flexibility***		
3.2.01	Labour Force	Number	
3.2.02	Unemployment Rate	Percentage	R
3.2.03	Cost of Production Labour	US Dollars, Current Market Prices	R
3.2.04	Availability of Scientists and Engineers	Survey Data	
3.2.05	Cost of Management Staff	US Dollars, Current Market Prices	R

(*Continued*)

Appendix 1 (*Continued*)

No.	Indicator	Unit	Reversed Indicator
3.2.06	High Quality Management Staff	Survey Data	
3.2.07	Extent of Staff Training	Survey Data	
3.2.08	Labour Market Rating	Survey Data	
3.3	***Productivity Performance***		
3.3.01	Agriculture, Value Added Per Worker	US Dollars, Constant 2005 Prices	
3.3.02	Industry, Value Added Per Worker	US Dollars, Constant 2005 Prices	
3.3.03	Services, Value Added Per Worker	US Dollars, Constant 2005 Prices	
4	**QUALITY OF LIFE AND INFRASTRUCTURE DEVELOPMENT**		
4.1	***Physical Infrastructure***		
4.1.01	Population	Number	
4.1.02	Local Road System	Survey Data	
4.1.03	Rail Facilities	Survey Data	
4.1.04	Airport Facilities	Survey Data	
4.1.05	Port Facilities	Survey Data	
4.1.06	Electric Power	Survey Data	
4.1.07	Access to Water	Percentage of Population	
4.1.08	Access to Sanitation	Percentage of Population	
4.2	***Technological Infrastructure***		
4.2.01	Telecommunications System	Percentage of GDP	
4.2.02	Telephone Main Lines	Number Per 100 Persons	
4.2.03	Internet Subscribers	Number Per 100 Persons	
4.2.04	Cellular Mobile Telephone Subscribers	Number Per 100 Persons	
4.2.05	Networked Readiness Index	Survey Data	

(*Continued*)

Appendix 1 (*Continued*)

No.	Indicator	Unit	Reversed Indicator
4.2.06	Personal Computers	Number Per 100 Persons	
4.2.07	Information and Communication Technology (ICT) Expenditure	Percentage of GDP	
4.3	***Standard of Living, Education and Social Stability***		
4.3.01	Literacy Rate	Percentage	
4.3.02	Primary Schooling	Percentage	
4.3.03	Secondary Schooling	Percentage	
4.3.04	University and Post-Graduate Education	Percentage	
4.3.05	Human Development Index	Composite Statistic	
4.3.06	Health Expenditure	Percentage of GDP	
4.3.07	Urban Population	Percentage of Total Population	
4.3.08	Urban Population Growth	Percentage Per Annum	
4.3.09	Public Security and Safety	Survey Data	
4.3.10	Freedom of Press	Survey Data	R
4.3.11	Freedom of Speech	Survey Data	
4.3.12	Access to Print Media	Number	
4.3.13	Freedom of Religion	Survey Data	
4.3.14	Religious Unrest	Survey Data	
4.3.15	Labour Unrest	Survey Data	
4.3.16	Social Unrest	Survey Data	
4.3.17	Labour Activism	Survey Data	R
4.3.18	Daily Organic Water Pollutant Emissions	Kilogram Per 100 Persons	R
4.3.19	Air Quality	Micrograms Per Cubic Meter	R
4.3.20	Traffic Congestion	Number of Vehicles Per Km of Road	R

Appendix 2

COMPETITIVENESS ANALYSIS — THE ALGORITHM

A step-by-step description of the ranking process is described below for N economies, M practical indicators and C environments, with each environment comprising S sub-environments.

(1) Compute the mean value of practical indicator j ($j = 1, \ldots, M$),

$$\overline{X}_j = \frac{1}{N}\sum_{i=1}^{N} X_{ij}$$

where X_{ij} represents the value that economy i ($i = 1, \ldots, N$) takes for practical indicator j.

(2) For each practical indicator j ($j = 1, \ldots, M$), calculate its standard deviation (SD),

$$\mathrm{SD}_j = \sqrt{\frac{1}{N}\sum_{i=1}^{N}\left(X_{ij} - \overline{X}_j\right)^2}$$

(3) Compute the standardised value of indicator (SVI) that each economy i ($i = 1, \ldots, N$) takes under each of the practical indicators j ($j = 1, \ldots, M$),

$$\mathrm{SVI}_{ij} = \frac{X_{ij} - \overline{X}_j}{\mathrm{SD}_j}$$

(4) Compute the 'ranked' standardised value of indicator (RSVI) that each economy i ($i = 1, \ldots, N$) takes under each of the practical indicators j ($j = 1, \ldots, M$):

$$\mathrm{RSVI}_{ij} = \begin{cases} \mathrm{SVI}_{ij}, & \text{if a higher value is better} \\ -\mathrm{SVI}_{ij}, & \text{if a lower value is better} \end{cases}$$

(5) For each of the practical indicators j ($j = 1, \ldots, M$), a ranking can be obtained for economies: economies with a higher value of RSVI for indicator j are ranked ahead of those with a lower value.

(6) For each economy i ($i = 1, \ldots, N$), calculate the RSVI for each sub-environment k ($k = 1, \ldots, S$) belonging to environment l ($l = 1, \ldots, C$),

$$\mathrm{Raw\_RSVI}_{i,lk} = \frac{1}{y_{lk}} \sum_{p=1}^{y_{lk}} \mathrm{RSVI}_{i,j_{lk,p}}$$

$$\mathrm{Mean\_RSVI}_{lk} = \frac{1}{N} \sum_{i=1}^{N} \mathrm{Raw\_RSVI}_{i,lk}$$

$$\mathrm{SD\_RSVI}_{lk} = \sqrt{\frac{1}{N} \sum_{i-1}^{N} \left(\mathrm{Raw\_RSVI}_{i,lk} - \mathrm{Mean\_RSVI}_{lk}\right)^2}$$

$$\mathrm{RSVI}_{i,lk} = \frac{\mathrm{Raw\_RSVI}_{i,lk} - \mathrm{Mean\_RSVI}_{lk}}{\mathrm{SD\_RSVI}_{lk}}$$

where y_{lk} is the total number of practical indicators under sub-environment k of environment l and (RSVI*i*,*jlk*,1, . . . , RSVI*i*,*jlk*,*ylk*) are the RSVIs for economy i that make up sub-environment k of environment l.

(7) For each economy i ($i = 1, \ldots, N$), calculate the RSVI for each environment l ($l = 1, \ldots, C$),

$$\text{Raw\_RSVI}_{i,l} = \frac{1}{S_l}\sum_{k=1}^{S_l} \text{RSVI}_{i,lk}$$

$$\text{Mean\_RSVI}_l = \frac{1}{N}\sum_{i=1}^{N} \text{Raw\_RSVI}_{i,l}$$

$$\text{SD\_RSVI}_l = \sqrt{\frac{1}{N}\sum_{i=1}^{N}\left(\text{Raw\_RSVI}_{i,l} - \text{Mean\_RSVI}_l\right)^2}$$

$$\text{RSVI}_{i,l} = \frac{\text{Raw\_RSVI}_{i,l} - \text{Mean\_RSVI}_l}{\text{SD\_RSVI}_l}$$

where (RSVIi,l1, . . . , RSVIi,lS) are the RSVIs for the S sub-environments under each environment l.

(8) Overall score of economy i ($i = 1, \ldots, N$),

$$\text{Raw\_}R_i = \frac{1}{C}\sum_{l=1}^{C} \text{RSVI}_{i,l}$$

$$\text{Mean\_}R = \frac{1}{N}\sum_{i=1}^{N} \text{Raw\_}R_i$$

$$\text{SD\_}R = \sqrt{\frac{1}{N}\sum_{i=1}^{N}\left(\text{Raw\_}R_i - \text{Mean\_}R\right)^2}$$

$$R_i = \frac{\text{Raw\_}R_i - \text{Mean\_}R}{\text{SD\_}R}$$

Economies with a higher *Ri* are ranked ahead of those with lower value of *Ri*, and the economy with the highest *Ri* is the most competitive economy.

Step (5) provides the ranking of each economy for each individual practical indicator. To achieve this ranking, Step (4) adjusts the value of the SVIs so that a higher value will lead to a better ranking in terms of 'competitiveness'. Depending on the nature of the indicator in question, a higher or lower value may reflect a more 'competitive' economy. For instance, the practical sub-indicators 'Gross Domestic Product (GDP)' and 'Unemployment Rate'. A higher GDP but a lower 'unemployment rate' suggest a better economic performance that makes an economy more 'competitive'. In most cases where a higher value is better (e.g., GDP), the SVIs of regions are considered, and those with a higher SVI value will have a better ranking. However, for indicators where the inverse is true (e.g., Unemployment Rate), the 'negative SVI' values are compared between economies and a lower SVI value will lead to a better ranking. Step (4) thus seeks to make all standardised values of all practical indicators consistent for ranking purposes.

Step (6) determines the sub-environment rankings of each economy. The average RSVI of all the indicators in the sub-environment are calculated, re-standardised across all the economies and compared to other economies. Economies with a higher average RSVI rank better in the sub-environment.

To arrive at the ranking for each environment, the RSVIs of the sub-environments are averaged and re-standardised across all economies as detailed in Step (7). Finally, Step (8) requires the RSVI values of each environment to be averaged and re-standardised across all economies to determine the overall ranking of the economy. Economies with a higher RSVI are ranked ahead of those with a lower RSVI.

Although the number of sub-environments and indicators may vary for each environment, the aggregate score for each environment is given an equal weight, which is 25% of the ASEAN-10 Overall

Competitiveness Index. This method is repeated and applied consistently across all economies to ensure precision of the ranking. Mathematically, this can be illustrated as follows:

ASEAN-10 Overall Competitiveness Index:

$$\begin{aligned} &= 25\% \times (\text{Macroeconomic Stability}) \\ &\quad +25\% \times (\text{Government and Institutional Setting}) \\ &\quad +25\% \times (\text{Financial, Businesses and Manpower Conditions}) \\ &\quad +25\% \times (\text{Quality of Life and Infrastructure Development}) \end{aligned}$$